I0605806

The Russian-Ukrainian War, 2023

To the men and women of the NATO Armed Forces:
the First and Last Bastion of Freedom

The Russian-Ukrainian War, 2023

A Second Year of Hell and the Dawn of Drone Warfare

John S Harrel

Pen & Sword
MILITARY

First published in Great Britain in 2024 by
Pen & Sword Military
An imprint of Pen & Sword Books Limited
Yorkshire – Philadelphia

ISBN 978 1 03610 163 3

A CIP catalogue record for this book is
available from the British Library

Typeset by Mac Style
Printed in the UK by CPI Group (UK) Ltd, Croydon, CR0 4YY.

Pen & Sword Books Limited incorporates the imprints of After
the Battle, Atlas, Archaeology, Aviation, Discovery, Family History,
Fiction, History, Maritime, Military, Military Classics, Politics,
Select, Transport, True Crime, Air World, Frontline Publishing, Leo
Cooper, Remember When, Seaforth Publishing, The Praetorian Press,
Wharncliffe Local History, Wharncliffe Transport, Wharncliffe True
Crime and White Owl.

For a complete list of Pen & Sword titles please contact

PEN & SWORD BOOKS LIMITED
47 Church Street, Barnsley, South Yorkshire, S70 2AS, England
E-mail: enquiries@pen-and-sword.co.uk
Website: www.pen-and-sword.co.uk
or
PEN AND SWORD BOOKS
1950 Lawrence Road, Havertown, PA 19083, USA
E-mail: uspen-and-sword@casematepublishers.com
Website: www.penandswordbooks.com

Contents

List of Abbreviations

AAA	Anti-Air Artillery
AD	Air Defence
ADA	Air Defence Artillery
AFR	Russian Armed Forces
APC	Armoured Personnel Carrier
ATGM	Anti-Tank Guided Missile
AWACS	Airborne Early Warning Command System
BMD	Air-Droppable IFV
BMP	IFV used by Ukraine and Russia
BOS	Battlefield Operating System
BTG	Battalion Tactical Group
BTR	APC used by Ukraine and Russia
C2	Command and Control
CAB	Combined Arms Battalion
DPR	Donetsk People's Republic
ENG	Engineer
EW	Electronic Warfare
HIMARS	High Mobility Artillery Rocket System
HQ	Headquarters
IFV	Infantry Fighting Vehicle
LPR	Luhansk People's Republic
MANPAD	Man-Portable Air Defence Weapon
MLRS	Multiple Rocket System
MOD	Ministry of Defence
MRB	Motorized Rifle Brigade
MRBAT	Motorized Rifle Battalion
MRC	Motorized Rifle Company
NGU	Ukrainian National Guard
NLAW	Next Generation Light Anti-Tank Weapon
OC	Ukrainian Operational Command
OK	Russian Operational Command
RU	Russia

TAC	Tactical Command Centre
TOC	Tactical Operation Centre
UA	Ukraine
UAF	Ukrainian Armed Forces
VDV	Russian Airborne Forces
VKS	Russian Air and Space Force

Map Symbols

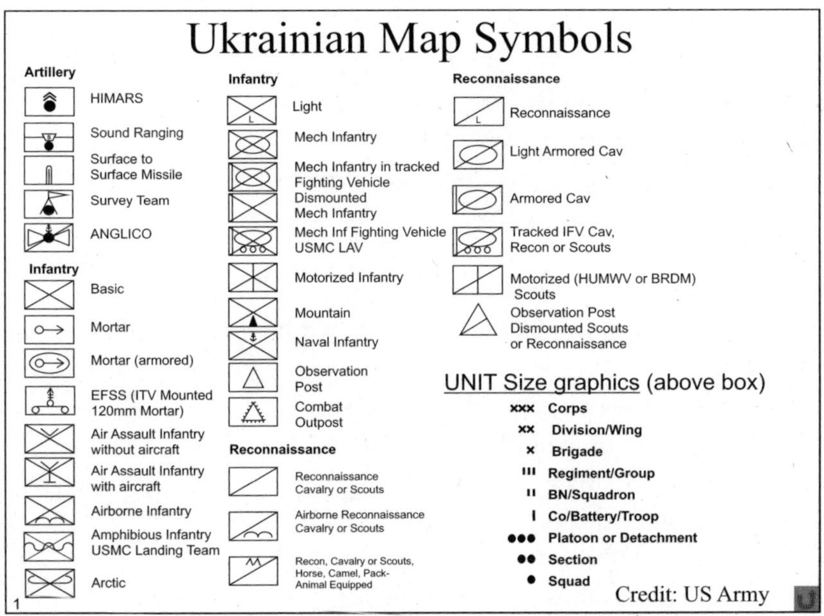

Russian Map Symbols

Infantry	Airborne Infantry	Armor	Artillery
Rangers	Air Assault Infantry with out aircraft	Mech Inf	Mortar
Light	Air Assault Infantry with aircraft	Light Armor/ Armored Cav	SP Artillery
Motorized Scouts	Air Cav	Mech or Armored (Wheeled)	MLRS
Motorized Inf	Attack Helo on the Ground	Anti-armor	Counter-battery Radar
Mountain	Attack Helo in Flight	AT Mech	Air Defense
Motorized	Marine Infantry	AT Motorized	Air Defense Radar
Recon/ Calvary	Naval Infantry	Mobile SSM (IRBM)	Mobile ASCM
Special Forces			

Credit: US Army

2

List of Maps

List of Charts

List of Photographs

14. US M1A1 Abrams tanks arrived too late to participate in Ukraine's summer/autumn 2023 counter-offensive. They were instrumental in the rearguard actions which enabled the Ukrainian defenders of Avdiivka to withdraw to the defensive line 10 km (6 miles) west of the city.
15. Ukrainian Marines, trained by UK and Norway, conducted raids along the Dnipro River and the west coast of the Crimean Peninsula.
16. Crowdfunded pick-up trucks from the 'Come Back Alive Foundation' were armed with HMGs for roving anti-drone patrols.

Acknowledgements

This volume is the second in a series of near-contemporary studies of the twenty-first century Russian-Ukrainian War. The first volume, entitled *The Russian Invasion of Ukraine, February–December 2022; Destroying the Myth of Russian Invincibility*, recorded the causes of the war and analysed the first year of fighting.

Credit for publication of this series of books on the Russian-Ukrainian War/ Russian invasion of Ukraine belongs to my friend and pen pal Philip Sidnell, Commissioning Editor for Pen & Sword. The production manager for this book was Matthew Jones. Matt had been the project manager for my previous books and has the skill to keep the project on track.The copy editor was George Chamier. He had the challenging job of standardizing the spelling of English translations of Cyrillic place names into consistent form. In addition, his attention to detail caught subtle errors, ensuring a better book. The eye-catching cover was the work of Dominic Allen. He was able to demonstrate the violence of war, while ensuring the cover was suitable for all audiences. Mat Blurton organized the plates, texts and photographs. I would like to thank Olivia Camozzi-Jones for guiding me though the marketing process.

The photographs were compiled from Ukrainian government sources, *Militarnyi* (defence industry of Ukraine), US and UK military and other open sources. Special mention should go to bloggers Preston Stewart (US), Paul Lewandowski (US), Deny Davydov (UA), Arthur Rehi (Estonia), Peron (Australia), Institute of the Study of War (US), Rochan Consulting (Poland), Colonel Markus Reisner (Austria), MG (Ret) Mick Ryan (Australia) and guest speaker on several YouTube channels, Lieutenant General (Ret) Ben Hodges (USA).

Major Austin Harrison (US) created several of the maps using *Open Street Map* service as the base document. As an amateur cartographer his work greatly improved the quality of maps in this volume. *Deep State* map service (UA) followed the day-to-day changes on the frontline, establishing a baseline Russian order of battle. *Deep State* used *Open Street Map* as the base map for their day-to-day reporting.

Only open-source materials were used in writing this book. Professionally, one of the author's three military occupational specialities (MOS) was Tactical

Intelligence (today 35A, All Source Intelligence). While the author has friends still serving in Washington DC, using leaks from 'friends in the Pentagon' as a source is disingenuous. The reader cannot fact-check the author's analysis when sources are undisclosed. When working with open-source materials the *Ground News* service compares sources on major events and evaluates them based on bias. This was an important service as all sides were flooding the internet and media with propaganda and biased reporting.

Final credit for translating this book from a War College Staff study to a near-contemporary study goes to Colonel (Ret) Linda Harrel, Staff Judge Advocate (US). Linda was a graduate of the US Army Command and General Staff College, participated in thirty years of division-level command post exercises and took part in the California Army National Guard's Partnership for Peace missions to Ukraine in the late twentieth and early twenty-first centuries. Her editing skills smoothed the edges of the book and manoeuvred it through differences in US and UK grammar.

Introduction: Ukraine Still Stands

We were living in dangerous times. NATO and Russia re-entered a Cold War, and the world was on the brink of a Third World War. Putin's ambition to dominate Europe and reinstate Russia as a world superpower ran into a roadblock on the steppes of Ukraine. By the end of 2023 the world's major powers had aligned in opposing camps; the UK, US,Ukraine's Western allies and most notably NATO, against an arrayed evil axis of Russia, Iran and North Korea, with China providing military support to Russia but otherwise sitting on the sidelines. The Third World War was being fought by proxy, while much of the world looked on, some interested and invested but many others not. In retrospect, with history guiding us, we were in a similar situation to that which the world was in during the late 1930s. Imperial Japan's invasion of Chinese Manchuria was the start of the worldwide conflict. That invasion began in 1931. History somewhat mistakenly records that the US had entered an isolationist period, but it would be incorrect to assume that it was a policy of total isolationism. Wary after the suffering and sacrifices of the First World War, the US sought isolation from events in Europe. However, the US was decisively engaged politically, economically and militarily throughout the Americas and Asia.

Just as Western appeasement of the demands of a dictator facilitated the Second World War, appeasement of a modern dictator facilitated the Russian-Ukrainian War.[1]

The Russian-Ukrainian War, started out as a near peer regional war, but by the end of 2023 Russia's worldwide cyber warfare distracted Ukrainian allies and the world at large, by clandestinely inciting conflict in the Middle East and Asia. Secretly supporting Hamas and Hezbollah through Iran and throughout the Middle East, Russia met with Hamas days before the attack on Israel on 7 October 2024. The resulting War in Gaza during the second year of Putin's Special Operation, just as Russia failed to achieve a quick victory, resulted in delayed aid to Ukraine as the West hurried to support Israel. Russia/Iran-backed terrorist groups in Syria attacked US bases, and Houthi terrorists from Yemen began attacking commercial shipping in the Red Sea. The US and allies provided naval protection to ensure uninterrupted international commerce. All of this came at a great cost.

With this backdrop, the war in Ukraine had changed. In 2022 the war was fought with weapons and systems dating back to the Cold War era of the 1980s, although there had been improvements in command and control (C2) with the employment of military-grade computers and other electronic systems. Russia and Ukraine initially relied on Soviet Cold War era equipment, some of which had received modern electronics, with upgraded software and targeting systems. In the second half of the second year of the war, Ukraine received modern twentieth century weapons, munitions, and systems from its allies and primarily from NATO. Some weapons, like the British 'Next Generation Light Anti-Tank Weapon' (NLAW) and the US man-portable anti-tank Javelin, used cutting edge technology. Command and control (C2) were greatly improved by Elon Musk's Starlink satellite system. Operationally, unmanned aerial vehicles (UAVs) or drones made a spectacular appearance on the battlefield with an historic 'life changing' impact. Tactical first-person view (FPV) drones cheaply and effectively conducted reconnaissance and directed artillery fire, while kamikaze drones attacked armoured vehicles. Strategically, long-range drones attacked cities and airfields. Surprisingly, drones were able to damage battleships in the Black Sea, destroy tanks and other heavily armoured vehicles on the front line and become effective 'hunter killer' machines.

The second year of the war, 2023, clearly became 'the year of the drone'. Civilian crowdfunding 'went to war' and provided tactical drones to the Ukrainian combat units. Ukrainian and Russian industries started mass producing drones of all types. Large military drones provided to Ukraine produced a tremendous advantage at the operational level, while small, adapted civilian hobby drones impacted tactics down to the lowest level. In many instances kamikaze drones became so plentiful that they were used to attack not just tanks but individual soldiers.

The genesis of this book on the second year of Putin's Special Operation was a series news letters to friends and family explaining the details and implications of Russia's unlawful invasion of Ukraine on 24 February 2022. Having trained with the Ukrainian Army and the US California Army National Guard under Partnership for Peace in the 1990s and 2006, I formed relationships with Ukrainian soldiers; soldiers whose sons and daughters now fight on the front line.[2] Having commanded Ukrainian soldiers in 2005 while peacekeeping in Kosovo, I have an obvious bias towards the Ukrainian cause, but nevertheless I have sought to provide unbiased coverage of the Russian-Ukrainian War. I have attempted to explain complicated aspects of twenty-first century warfare in basic terms. Military terminology such as 'line of contact', 'forward edge of the battlefield (FEBA)' and 'rear area' are terms of art, and I used them as required to efficiently describe military operations. For the layman, military terms have been limited in this work in order to enhance general understanding.

Details of weapon system capabilities have only been provided when required by the narrative. For example, the primary Russian tanks were the T-64, 72, 80 and 90 series of main battle tanks, fielded by both sides and equipped with the Soviet-era 125mm tank gun. The primary main battle tank for NATO members, such as Germany's Leopard II, the US Abrams M1A1 and the UK Challenger 2, were armed with a 120mm tank gun. The Russian and NATO guns generally had the same range and capabilities. Rounds from both tank guns were able to penetrate the frontal armour (where the armour is thickest) of all tanks on the Ukrainian battlefield, rendering model and upgrade comparisons moot. The Cold War NATO 105mm gun, mounted on the Leopard I, and the 115mm gun mounted on the Russian T-62s had generally the same capabilities. If either side scored a solid hit on the front armour of an opposing tank it was disabled or destroyed. The level of training and leadership of the crew was more important than the tank model and its capabilities. As an example, a US-provided M2 Bradley with its 25mm auto-cannon destroyed a Russian T-90 modern tank in a short-range encounter.

The ability to correctly identify deployed Russian combat units became easier in the second year of Putin's Special Operation. The Russian experiment with battalion tactical groups (BTG) failed during the first year of the Operation, and Russia reinstated traditional motorized rifle and tank battalions. Regimental, brigade, and division headquarters reappeared as intermediate C2 headquarters between battalion and army.

Generally, military ground forces are divided into three types of units: combat, combat support and combat service support. Combat units are tanks and infantry, direct action special forces and, arguably, attack helicopters, i.e., units that close with the enemy and seek to destroy them by fire, manoeuvre and close combat. Combat support units provide fire support and operational assistance to combat elements. They include artillery (tubed, rocket and missiles), air defence artillery, close air support, electronic warfare attack and defence, cyber-attack and defence, intelligence, military police, etc. Combat service support units include legal, administration, finance, ordinance, quartermaster and transportation units, providing logistical support from company to army level. At the basic level, a 120-person infantry company consists of 90 combat, 20 combat support (mortar platoon) and 10 combat service support troops, (a first sergeant or executive officer and ten soldiers).

A combined arms army will have more combat support and combat service support soldiers than combat soldiers. As an example, the Russian invasion force included nearly 200,000 soldiers, of whom only 65,000 were considered combat troops, with the remaining 135,000 providing combat support and combat service support.

Neither Ukraine nor Russia have published an official account of the second year of the Special Operation, and what has been published thus far was often fake news or propaganda designed to mislead the reader. Eyewitness reports provided colour, but accuracy suffered, depending on the witnesses' understanding of their observation. Often more accurate were the many unclassified reports from think tanks, military professionals and bloggers and civilian drone operators on YouTube, newspaper/internet articles, press releases and interviews of military personnel. 'Ground News' was helpful. This company analysed articles to aid the reader in determining bias. Particularly helpful were articles in the daily YouTube reports of Paul Lenwandowski (US Army Combat Veteran), Combat Veteran Reacts, Deny Davydov's (Ukrainian commercial pilot) daily reports, Artur Rehi's (former Lithuanian soldier) daily reports, Alex Robert (History Legends) Ukrainian Group's Daily Reports (probably Ukrainian MoD) 'War In Ukraine Explained', and the daily updated map of military operations and analysis, author identified only as 'Perun'. Four think tanks, the Institute for the Study of War, Five Coat Consulting, the Atlantic Council and Rochan Consulting, also provided valuable information.

This book covers the second year of Putin's Special Operation in general and focuses on the important battles, offensives and counter-offensives that made headlines. It covers the second year of the war at the operational level. Drone warfare was active in all domains, air, land and sea, at historic and unprecedented levels. Ukrainians depended on drones to make up for their lack of a fleet and to strike targets deep inside Mother Russia.

The Battles of Bakhmut and Avdiivka and the fight for the Black Sea are covered in detail because they were the only clear Russian and Ukrainian successes during the second year, even though Russia achieved primarily pyrrhic victories.

Unlike any previous war in history there was literally a constant and continuing flood of data from the battlefield. Using modern technology, civilians and soldiers from both sides posted details about battles and skirmishes. I encountered a problem with transliterating Cyrillic into Roman spelling, since names and geographic locations reported in the media were often spelled differently. I relied on the transliterations as reported by the 'Deep State' website's daily updated maps to identify geographic locations. Russian orders of battle heavily relied on Deep State's daily updates. These were incomplete, and the gaps were filled in by templating.

This book has adopted Ukrainian spelling, for example Kharkiv instead of Kharkov, Kyiv instead of Kiev, Dnipro River instead of Dnieper River, etc.

To prevent confusion where appropriate, Ukrainian mixed infantry and tank battalions are referred to herein as 'mechanized' and Russian as 'motorized rifle'.

Does Putin have an exit plan? His initial demands, based on the expectation of an easy victory, were that Ukraine should recognize Russia's 'annexation' of Crimea', sign a declaration stating it would not apply for NATO membership, demilitarize, and finally, recognize the Donetsk People's Republic (formerly Donetsk Oblast) and Luhansk People's Republic (formerly Luhansk Oblast) as sovereign states with their pre-2014 borders. Putin's desired goals were a Ukraine politically aligned with the Kremlin – militarily neutral and partnered with Russian armed forces (i.e. dependent upon Russia for defence) – and most importantly the establishment of transparent borders to facilitate cultural and economic integration of Ukraine into the Eurasian Economic Union (EAEU). In other words, the re-establishment of the former Soviet Empire under the economic dictatorship of the Russian Oligarchy, and the suppression of the developing liberal democracy in Ukraine.[3] Ukraine had repeatedly and loudly rejected all these demands.

Putin's demands did not change during the second year of the war. He was playing the long game. While his superior numbers in men and materiel on the battlefield did not achieve his political and military goals, his strategic cyber/disinformation campaign did achieve alarming success.

Chapter 1

Russia's Need for Security Drives Russian Need to Expand

In a time of relative peace and world-wide cooperation and commerce why did Putin invade Ukraine? The reason is clear when one reviews Russian history and geography. The need to defend against potential western aggression and a rapidly encroaching democratic economy threatened the very composition of the Russian Federation.

Putin's Russia was neither democratic in the Western sense nor as regulated as it was under the Soviet model. It was a hybrid regime with the illusion of a managed democracy. It followed the traditional model of Imperial Russia and Soviet autocratic rule, in which power was centralized in the Kremlin. Regional power centres were directed by Moscow. Compliance was ensured by the Federal Security Services (FSB) and internal security forces. Moscow kept tight control over the media. Putin had successfully reinstituted the long arm of control first implemented by Imperial Tsars and later by Stalin to stabilize the Russian empire. Putin's Russian Federation was not a nation state in the modern sense, but rather an empire with all roads leading to Moscow and the Russian heartland. Supported by the *siloviki* (behind the scenes power brokers who controlled Russian security and intelligence) and oligarchs, Putin ruled with an iron hand, casually disposing of all opponents. His invasion of Ukraine was in furtherance of his geopolitical goal to restore Russia's status as a world power, lost with the fall of the Soviet Union. He sought to roll back NATO's borders and bring Eastern Europe back within the Russian sphere of influence.

Historically, geography has not been conducive to ensuring the security of Moscow. The are no mountains, rivers, swamps or deserts to provide natural defences. The boreal forest stands alone, reinforced with severe winters to obstruct an invader. The resulting challenge to defenders of the Russian heartland resulted in the development of a strategy of attrition: delay the invaders, drag out their invasion and exploit the severity of the Russian winter to defeat them.

In the twenty-first century the Russian heartland stretched across the flatlands from St Petersburg in the north to Kazan in the south, and to the trade

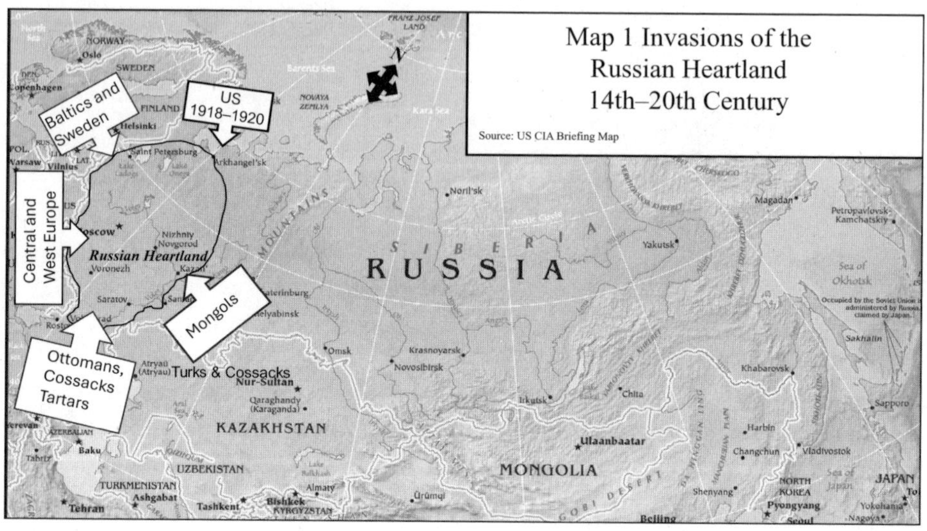

Map 1 Invasions of the Russian Heartland 14th–20th Century

Source: US CIA Briefing Map

centre of Volgograd in the east. This region held most of the ruling Russian population and was the centre of the Federation's power. Russia's 2,000 km (1,242 mile) flat western border (not including Finland but including Belarus) exposed its heartland to invasion.[1] When Finland joined NATO, that border grew by almost an additional 1,000 km (600 miles).

From the founding of Moscow in 1147, Russia has endured a history of surviving centuries of invasion from the south, east and west. These centuries of warfare impacted the development of Russian culture and psychology, the population becoming obsessed with security and survival.[2]

A pivotal moment in Russian history occurred in 1480 on the banks of the Agra River, when the Russian principalities defeated the Mongol Golden Horde, ending centuries of nomadic domination. With the threat of the Golden Horde from the east reduced, Russia faced attacks from the west by the Teutonic Knights, Poles and Swedes, while Cossacks, Persians and Ottomans threatened from the south. With these vulnerabilities in mind, the Russian principalities united into the Russian Empire. In the sixteenth century Tsar Ivan the Terrible (1530–1584) developed buffer zones around the heartland by employing a strategy of attrition to prolong wars, coupled with raids to attack invaders' supply lines. By 1552 Tsar Ivan had conquered the Tatar Kingdom of Kazan in the south. This campaign opened the Volga River as a supply route for further conquests east and south, and this series of campaigns expanded the empire's borders to modern Volgograd. The former Tatar kingdoms became buffers against any further incursions from the Eastern Steppes.

With the neutralization of the Tatar kingdoms, two centuries of war against the Poles, Swedes, Crimean Tatars, Ottomans and Ukrainian Cossacks followed. There were many setbacks, often threatening the very existence of the Russian Empire. In the absence of geographic barriers, strategic fortified cities were established in the eastern parts of the empire.

By the time of Tsar Peter the Great (1672–1725) Imperial Russia controlled large areas of land which gave the empire operational depth. If the Russians were losing a campaign, they could always take advantage of the option to withdraw into the interior to regroup. The Russian Empire continued its expansion into Siberia, stopping only when it reached the Altai and Syan Mountains and Lake Baikal in Central Asia, the Stanovoy mountain range north of Manchuria and the Sea of Okhotsk (north-western Pacific).[3]

At its height (1732–1867) the Russian Empire extended south along the coast of North America. In 1732 Russian Siberian fur traders followed the abundant fur seals and sea otters along the Aleutian Islands and Alaskan Peninsula down the Pacific Coast, and in 1799 the Imperial government claimed the land that is now Alaska. The challenge of supplying their newly acquired territory and fur trading centres like Sitka led to the establishment of Fort Ross in 1812, near the mouth of the Russian River on the northern California coast. Fort Ross was initially located at the edge of first Spanish and then Mexican territory. Neither government seriously attempted to expel the Russians. The outpost was never economically feasible, mostly because the settlers' crops were destroyed by gophers.[4] In 1841 the fort was sold to John Sutter, but he was never granted legal title by the Mexican Government.[5] Russia's North American holdings were not relevant to the Empire's defence.

Map 2 Russia European Defensible Borders

Based upon its history of invasion, Russian foreign and military policy was to expand to natural defensive borders on major terrain features. In Europe, the borders were the Baltic Sea, the Carpathian Mountains, and the Black Sea.

Imperial Russia and Soviet Russia established these borders by direct occupation or via client states (WARSAW Pact)

—— Soviet Russia's European Defensive Borders: Baltic Sea, Black Sea and Carpathian Mountains

Moscow Land Bridge This route, from Warsaw to Moscow lacked major river crossings was used by both Napoleon and Hitler to invade Russia

Source: US CIA Briefing Map

As the fur trade became less profitable, Russia eventually sold its Alaskan interests to the US in 1867 for $7.2million (2 cents per acre).[6]

Russia's expansion to the natural boundaries in the west incorporated Ukraine, the Caucasus, the Caspian Sea, Crimea, the Carpathian Mountains, Poland and the Baltic states into its defensive buffer zone. The gap in this defensive ring was the North European Plain, running from Berlin and Warsaw through the Russian heartland along the Moscow ridge. The ridge was an axis of advance lacking any major river crossings. Running along the northern edge of the Pyprit Marshes, the ridge was utilized by Napoleon and later by invading Germans in both world wars. One of the reasons the Soviet Union survived the initial onslaught in the Second World War was its geographical strategic depth, giving it the ability to move its industries east of the Ural Mountains.

The expanded Russian Empire had to be policed. The Empire historically incorporated many diverse ethnic and religious populations not particularly loyal to Moscow. Internal security forces enforced the Kremlin's iron rule. Mass deportations and large-scale genocides were common under both Imperial and Soviet rule. Internal intelligence services, such as the Tsar's secret police, the Soviet KGB and modern FSB, watched the population and exerted central control. New strategic cities were established throughout the empire. Control of the internal distribution of food and other necessities kept the diverse ethnic and religious populations in line. Control of the empire and defence of its borders required a large and costly standing military force.[7]

Corruption within autocratic Russia has been a constant problem. The high cost of funding internal security, exasperated by extreme corruption, has historically denied Russia available funding to exploit the natural resources east of the Urals. As an example, the Trans-Siberian Railway was the main lifeline to Siberian cities and the only link from Moscow to the Pacific Coast. In the twenty-first century this slender logistics corridor was still the major ground transportation system connecting European Russia with the Pacific.

Supporting the eastern cities serviced by the Trans-Siberian Railway was a drain on the Russian budget, but they provided strategic depth in the event that the heartland was captured. Over the nineteenth and twentieth centuries various Russian governments paid the high cost of maintaining them. The population of these mostly Siberian cities are not ethnic Russians and are not generally loyal to Moscow, but these cities (such as Grozny Chechnya) were strategically important to Russia's defence. It has strived to control nationalist movements on the part of ethnic minority populations by subjecting them to mass starvation and deportations.

At the end of the Second World War, the Soviet Union achieved its strategic geographic defensive goals; the buffer states of the Warsaw Pact provided the Soviets with control of the North European Plain.[8] With the dissolution of the Soviet Union and Warsaw Pact in 1991 the encroachment of democracy from Poland and Ukraine threatened Russia's system of autocratic government.[9] [10]

A democratic Ukraine was only 480 km (298 miles) from Moscow. Lacking any natural barriers, a potential invasion from Ukraine would only have to cross flat, forested steppe to reach Moscow. From the Ukrainian border 750 km (466 miles) south-east across the steppe was the Russian city of Astrakhan on the Caspian Sea. This wide corridor was known as the Volgorad Gap, a potential invasion route leading to the Russian strategic cities east of the Urals, the Caspian oil field, the Caucasus Mountains and the Black Sea. Capturing this gap would isolate the Russian heartland from Siberia and the cities east of the Urals. In 1917 Imperial Germany temporarily occupied Rostov-on-Don, the gateway to the gap. During the Second World War Nazi armies entered the gap but were halted at the Battle of Stalingrad.

In the twenty-first century maintaining the security of the Volgorad Gap was a cornerstone of the defence of the Russian Federation. The Southern Military District was the gatekeeper defending the Gap, and Russia viewed Ukraine as a critical buffer state to protect the Gap and the land route to Moscow. Given the geopolitical requirements, Russia needed to push the Ukrainian border to the Dnipro River or destroy Ukraine and push all the way to the Carpathian Mountains. Either way, Russia would re-establish the Soviet Union's border with the West, and reduce its exposed border from 2,000 km (1,242 miles) to 600 km (373 miles). Losing Ukraine to NATO would reset Russia's boundary to its sixteenth century parameters, and the coalition would sit right on the edge of the Russian heartland. Ukraine was in talks about becoming a member of NATO and had joined Partnership for Peace. Russian fears of a threat to the Volgorad Gap would materialize if Ukraine joined NATO. While Putin and the Russian leadership focused on a potential military threat, it was the seductive spread of liberal governments with their promise of a higher standard of living that might cause unrest in minority communities, undermining Moscow's authority. NATO's control of Crimea would also hinder Russia's ability to project political, economic and military power into and out of the Black Sea, which would turn into a NATO/Turkish lake.[11]

In response to the threat of an expanding NATO, Putin resorted to hybrid warfare to propel Russia back to becoming a dominating world power. Hybrid warfare entails the interplay of conventional and unconventional instruments of power and tools of subversion. The line between peace and war was obscured. As an example, in 2008 Putin planned, by using the Nord Stream pipeline, to

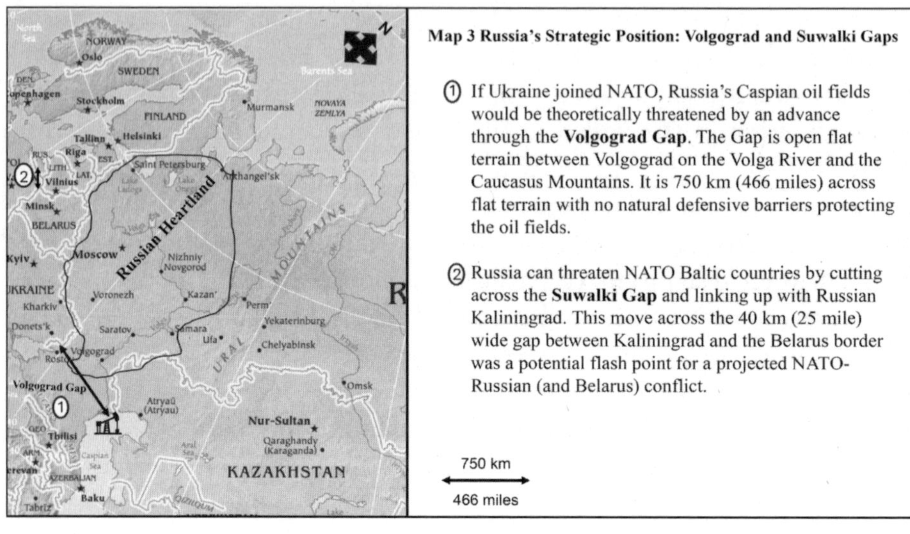

Map 3 Russia's Strategic Position: Volgograd and Suwalki Gaps

① If Ukraine joined NATO, Russia's Caspian oil fields would be theoretically threatened by an advance through the **Volgograd Gap**. The Gap is open flat terrain between Volgograd on the Volga River and the Caucasus Mountains. It is 750 km (466 miles) across flat terrain with no natural defensive barriers protecting the oil fields.

② Russia can threaten NATO Baltic countries by cutting across the **Suwalki Gap** and linking up with Russian Kaliningrad. This move across the 40 km (25 mile) wide gap between Kaliningrad and the Belarus border was a potential flash point for a projected NATO-Russian (and Belarus) conflict.

ensnare Western Europe in a petrochemical trap. In exchange for a continued supply of relatively cheap Russian oil to feed their never-ending need for fuel, Germany blocked NATO applications by both Ukraine and Georgia. As Sun Tzu advised, the supreme art of war is to subdue the enemy without fighting.[12]

Putin successfully engaged in hybrid war against NATO countries throughout the first two decades of the twenty-first century. Russian petrochemical surpluses were used as a bargaining chip to regain a position of power on the world stage. Feeble European and US reaction to Russia's invasions of Georgia in 2008 and Ukraine in 2014/15 inevitably led to bolder actions. Interference in worldwide elections, most notably in the US in 2016 and 2020, and other soft power engagements were employed freely. Putin understood that NATO would not attack Russia unless directly provoked. The expansion of NATO into the traditional Russian sphere of influence ostensibly justified Putin's actions in implementing his goal of re-establishing Soviet boundaries and influence.

By 2022 the hybrid war against NATO was well underway. Putin and Russian elites however miscalculated the time, expense and effort required to turn Ukraine into a vassal state. Putin's oil and gas trap failed to prevent the European countries from rallying to Ukraine's defence.[13] The invasion unexpectedly united NATO, the EU and the democratic world against a common enemy. Newly admitted Eastern European NATO members had warned the West of Putin's growing threat.[14] The West continued to discount Russian paranoia about invasion from the west, selfishly ignoring Putin's intent to re-establish Imperial Russia's defensive geographic borders.

NATO calculated that the Suwalki Gap or corridor would be the most likely invasion route for a Russian attack on Poland and the Baltic states, its northern members. The Gap spanned an accessible area where the borders of Russian Kaliningrad Oblast, Belarus, Poland and Lithuania met. The Russian exclave of Kaliningrad contained a Baltic Sea port and naval base and was sandwiched between Poland and Lithuania.

Kaliningrad's small ice-free port with anti-air and anti-ship missiles could hinder NATO sea and land operations in the eastern Baltic Sea. The Suwalki Gap was 65 km (40 miles) wide. If Putin closed the corridor, Russia could cut the only land route to NATO's Baltic Sea members. After the 2014 surprise attack and annexation of Crimea, a possible surprise ground attack by Russia to capture the gap shifted from an interesting NATO staff training exercise to a realistic hybrid war scenario. After Russia's 2022 attack on Ukraine, Lithuania and the EU imposed ground transit restrictions into Kaliningrad, across Poland from Belarus, along with other sanctions.[15] NATO quickly reinforced the Battle Groups defending the Gap in Poland and the Baltic States.

Chapter 2

Strategic Situation, February 2022–January 2023

Russia was unsuccessful in its initial attempt in 2022 to defeat Ukraine or usurp the Ukrainian government.[1] Amending its objective, Russia entered 2023 with the limited strategic goal of capturing the Donbas. Russia did not take an operational pause in January 2023 as expected, to reorganize, reconstruct or train its ground forces, but in the second half of 2022 mobilized approximately 300,000 reservists and sent them to the front.[2] The media referred to these soldiers as 'Mobiks'. Partially trained at best and severely under-equipped, the Mobiks were immediately sent forward. The best Mobiks supplemented Russia's elite Naval Infantry and airborne units. These individuals had probably completed their conscript service a few years before the invasion. The remaining Mobiks were formed into separate battalions and sent to the front lines.

When the invasion commenced in February 2022, Putin and the *siloviki* expected Ukraine to be decisively defeated within days if not weeks, and a puppet government to have been installed by mid-March. By the end of March 2022, the Kremlin realized it could not capture Kyiv by assault, nor could it effect a regime change. Russia's inability to gain air superiority in face of Ukrainian air defence in February and March ensured a long and drawn-out war. Defeated before the gates of Kyiv, Colonel General Sergei Rudskoy, Chief of Staff of the Russian General Staff's Main Operational Directive, announced that Russia would focus on seizing the Donbas. Russian forces retreated from Kyiv, Chernihiv and Sumy Oblasts and redeployed to the Kharkiv, Donbas and southern Ukraine.[3] The attempt to capture the Donbas would dominate Russian ground operations for the second half of 2022 and through 2023.

The reduction of Russia's strategic territorial objectives to the capture of the Donbas and maintaining the Crimean land bridge would not end the war. After ten months of fighting, and suffering hundreds of thousands of casualties, Russia failed to capture the Donbas by the close of 2022. Even if Russia had captured the Donbas and maintained the land bridge, there was no indication that Ukraine would have acceded to Russian demands. From

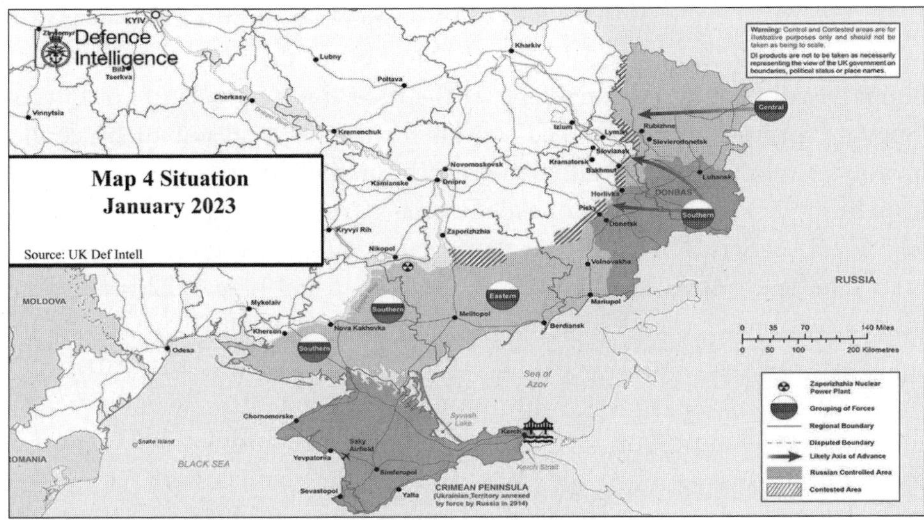

Map 4 Situation January 2023

Source: UK Def Intell

the beginning of the invasion Russia had demanded that Ukraine refrain from joining NATO, join the Russian Eurasian Economic Union, become politically aligned with Moscow and militarily neutral. Ukraine was never going to agree to such demands. Their resolve was strengthened over the course of the year by their unexpected success at defending themselves against the Bear and was hardened by discovery of the scale of war crimes committed against the Ukrainian people.[4]

The unexpectedly successful resistance of the Ukrainians took Putin by surprise. Russia had committed 80 per cent of its ready battalion tactical groups (BTGs), the army corps from the Lukansk and Donetsk People's Republics and the National Guard (Rosgvardia, paramilitary police) to Putin's 'Special Operation'. By comparison, during the 2003 Invasion of Iraq the US deployed only 40 per cent of its active manoeuvre battalions, excluding its eight combat divisions and fifteen manoeuvre brigades of the Army National Guard of the various states and territories.

To reinforce its operations, Russia sent additional BTGs from critical locations such as Kaliningrad, Abkhazia, South Ossetia and Tajikistan. The BTGs deployed from these regions arrived in theatre understrength and under-equipped, and they sustained heavy losses during the fighting between April–June 2022.[5] The heavy casualties suffered by Russia's professional soldiers and officers caused morale problems. Wounded soldiers refused to return to their units; soldiers retreating from northern Ukraine refused to re-enter the fight after discovering punishment was minimal. The problem of 'refuseniks' persisted throughout the attritional battles of late spring and summer 2022.[6]

By May 2022, the majority of the BTGs deployed into theatre were down to 50 per cent of their nominal strength. Most of the casualties were from the limited number of infantry soldiers. At the time, due to the nature of Putin's 'Special Operation', Russia lacked a viable force generation system. Since the invasion was a 'Special Operation' and not a war, the law prevented conscripts from being mobilized to fight outside Russia. Despite his inability to mobilize additional soldiers, Putin ordered the invaders to capture the Donbas at all costs. The heavy attritional fighting through May and June 2022 resulted in tactical successes in the Donbas but led to operational failure.[7]

Russia's 'Special Operation' had united the EU, NATO and the democratic world against the Kremlin. Arms, ammunition and other support began flowing into Ukraine days after the invasion, and by summer 2022 it was a flood. Putin had misjudged the West, and Russian soldiers were paying the price. Ukraine was outgunned in the Donbas between May and June 2022, but by July modern Western artillery started to balance the fight. While Russia enjoyed superiority in numbers of guns and rocket launchers, the Western weapons were more precise and had longer range.

The arrival of the truck-mounted US High Mobility Artillery Rocket System (HIMARS) and track-mounted Multiple Rocket System (MLRS) had an immediate impact on the battle for the Donbas and along the entire line of contact, often referred as the 'Zero-Line'. Firing percussion-guided rockets, Ukrainian targeted Russian ammunition depots and command posts. The destruction of the ammunition depots reduced the rounds the Russians could fire daily. The Western tubed artillery proved more effective at counter-battery fire. The precision-guided artillery rounds, directed by drones, negated Russia's biggest advantage in the Donbas, its massed artillery. Russia captured the town of Lysychanck in July 2022, but its summer offensive petered out due to lack of manpower to convert tactical success into operational victory.

Putin resisted the call from his Generals for a partial mobilization. Instead, Russia attempted half measures to solve its manpower problems. Russian regional volunteer battalions were formed and sent forward. Volunteers who had fought in the Donbas (2014/15) were recruited and generally signed three-to-six-month contracts. These volunteers either supported the war or were financially motivated.

Previously Ukrainian Oblasts, the Luhansk People's Republic (LPR) and Donetsk People's Republic (DPR) had succumbed to Russian-led separatists and had become independent (Russian puppet states) in 2014/15. Men from these Republics could be lawfully mobilized to fight outside Russia and outside their Oblasts.

By August 2022, as Ukraine launched its counter-offensives, the frontlines in the Kharkiv Oblast and Donbas were manned by recently mobilized and under-trained LPR and DPR troops, Rosgvardia police units, or under-strength battalions of newly contracted volunteers.[8]

Finally, Russia began to rely heavily on semi-private paramilitary organizations like the infamous Wagner Group. These mercenary organizations established a worldwide recruiting network to hire, train and equip mercenaries for various contracts. Wagner's contracts included operations in Africa and the Middle East as well as Ukraine.

Between July and August 2022, Ukraine telegraphed to the world that it would launch a counter-offensive to liberate Kherson. This city, occupied by the invaders during the initial phase of the war, is located at the only bridge across the southern Dnipro River and was the gateway to the major port of Odesa. The Russian staging area at this location threatened Ukrainian access to the Black Sea.

The influx of Western weapons and support allowed Ukraine to build a credible offensive capability in the Kherson region. Due to the observable build-up of weapons and munitions and other Ukrainian deception operations, the Kremlin shifted its elite Russian Airborne (VDV) and Naval Infantry brigades and regiments from the Eastern Military District into Kherson. The Ukrainians launched a supporting attack at Kherson in August, but met stiff resistance from the newly arrived elite Russian forces.

The Ukrainian main attack hit the weakened Russians at the Kharkiv and north Donbas sectors in September and immediately penetrated to operational depth. The Russian 1st Guards Tank Army positioned to defend Kharkiv Oblast was routed in a matter of days.

The counter-offensive was a well planned and executed combined arms operation. It exploited Russian weaknesses along the penetration and the inability of the 1st Guards Tank Army, which should have possessed sufficient force to contain the breakthrough, to react to the Ukrainians' high operational tempo. It took two months for the supporting attack in the south, using combined arms tactics, to liberate Kherson. The Russian paratroopers and Naval Infantry contested every metre with a well-organized defence, and a breakthrough was not achieved until mid-October 2022.

These battlefield reverses forced Putin to agree to a partial mobilization of 350,000 reservists in September 2022. This mobilization was in addition to the October/November bi-annual conscription of 125,000 18–20-year-olds. In addition, Moscow formally annexed the Oblasts of Luhansk, Donetsk, Kherson and Zaporizhzhia, the Russian media announcing that occupied Ukraine had been annexed into Mother Russia, eliminating the problem of how to employ conscripts in the 'Special Operation.' The democratic world denounced the annexation.

When the soldiers arrived at their mobilization stations, it was discovered that 1.5 million sets of uniforms and kit were missing. Many Mobiks were forced to buy their own equipment. Substandard body armour was often the only protection procurable on the black market. Some Mobiks were thrown into battle less than a week later to reinforce the units holding the city of Lyman and Luhansk Oblast. While the details were limited, these Mobiks had probably completed their conscript training within the past five to ten years and by Russian standards were fully trained. They slowed the Ukrainian advance, which stalled approximately 25 km (15 miles) east of Lyman, and prevented the capture of Kreminna in Luhansk Oblast.

After Russian reverses on the battlefield General Sergey Surovikin was given command of the Special Operation. Nicknamed 'General Armageddon' for his bombing campaign targeting civilians in Syria, this brutal commander was highly competent. In October 2022 he commenced a strategic bombing campaign to destroy the Ukrainian electric grid. The stated objective was to increase the suffering of the Ukrainian people during the winter in order to break their morale. In November 2022 Surovikin ordered a withdrawal from the Kherson bridgehead and redeployed the paratroopers and Naval Infantry to other sectors. Understanding the operational tactical realities of the situation, he ordered the combined arms armies (CAAs) to dig in and reorganized their battalions and battalion tactical groups (BTGs) during a short operational phase. The focus of Russian operations now became the capture of the town of Bakhmut.

The Battle for Bakhmut raged from August to December 2022, with the Wagner Group leading the operation. Yevgeny Prigozhin, Wagner Group CEO, was granted permission to recruit from Russian prisons. Convicts were promised a full pardon if they survived six months on the front lines. By 31 December 2022 it was reported that 40,000 inmates had volunteered to fight for Wagner Group. The Battle for Bakhmut became reminiscent of the trench warfare during the First World War. According to the US, Wagner suffered a total of 5,000 killed in action (KIA) and 10,000 wounded in action (WIA) by mid-December 2022.[9]

As the combatants entered 2023, Putin and the Kremlin faced the reality that the only political objective they had achieved was the establishment of a land bridge between Rostov-on-Don and Crimea. This secured the main supply land route from Mother Russia into the southern war zone. Meanwhile, Putin's war crimes had made him a pariah and Public Enemy Number One in the West. His continuing leadership of Russia made a negotiated peace in 2023 unlikely.

At the beginning of 2023, the war was in stalemate. The Kremlin's strategic and operational goal was the capture of the Donbas, and the general staff believed its 2023 winter offensive could tip the balance in its favour by capturing the town of Bakhmut at the crossroads to western Ukraine.

Capture of this politically significant but militarily irrelevant city became the focus of the Russian winter offensive. All other Russian operations, from Vuhledar in the south to Kreminna in the north, were diversionary or supporting attacks to force defenders to spread thin their forces and prematurely commit their operational reserves.

Russian strategic missile bombardment of civilian targets failed to break the Ukrainian population's will to resist. Despite a severe winter with only intermittent electricity to heat homes, the defenders fought on. Russia's only option to end the war in 2023 was a successful autumn and winter campaign in the hope of making significant territorial gains in the Donbas.

The top strategic priority for Putin was to apply external political pressure to isolate Ukraine from the West. Without support from the West Ukraine would quickly run out of resources. To diminish support from the US and EU Putin enthusiastically employed long-term hybrid warfare. Cyber operations, information warfare (fake news) and most importantly encouraging unrest throughout the world helped divert attention from and reduce support for Ukraine.

As battlefield failures mounted, Russia increased its use of psychological weapons against the West. Putin threatened to halt petrochemical supplies to the EU and rattled his nuclear sword to intimidate the world. He attempted to persuade the West that Ukrainian military victory was impossible, and a negotiated settlement was the only way forward. This information warfare promoted the narrative that Western aid would only prolong the war and the suffering of the Ukrainian people. A small number of Western experts blindly accepted the Russian narrative.[10] However, for the most part Western leaders held firm and instead of abandoning Ukraine, increased aid and support.

The Ukrainian people were overwhelmingly against concessions to Russia. Unprovoked invasion, illegal targeting of civilians and civilian infrastructure and horrendous war crimes have entrenched Ukrainian opinion against any settlement negotiations that do not include total withdrawal and reparations.

In 2023, Putin's main political objective was to undermine Western support. This campaign assumed that the US lacked the political will to maintain its support in a long, drawn-out conflict. Despite continuing support from the rest of the world, if US aid was curtailed, Ukraine would be forced to the negotiation table. Based upon the historical precedent of Vietnam, Somalia, Georgia and Afghanistan, it was believed that the US electorate could lose interest in Ukraine. Focusing on these US failures, however, overshadows US long-term commitments to Bosnia, Kosovo, Israel, Taiwan, and South Korea.

Most of the US Republican Party supported Ukraine in early 2023 and viewed Russia as a threat to the world order. In April 2023 62 per cent of registered Republicans polled agreed that 'Moscow represented a critical threat to US vital interests'. Another 29 per cent saw support of Ukraine as 'important but not critical'. Only 9 per cent indicated the Russia-Ukraine War was 'not an important threat to American interests'.[11] Despite these polls, Republican candidates Donald Trump, Ron DeSantis, Vivek Ramaswamy and Robert F. Kennedy Jr. advocated forcing Ukraine to the negotiating table and allowing Russia to retain occupied Ukraine.[12] Declining support for Ukraine at the polls encouraged Moscow. Putin placed his greatest hope in an isolationist Republican presidency for 2024.[13]

Moving into the sphere of cyber information warfare (fake news), Russia acted to undermine public confidence in the electoral process and exacerbate the socio-political divisions within the US. The Central Intelligence Agency (CIA) detected similar attempts to sway the US Presidential election in 2016 and took appropriate action, but failed, at least publicly, to report persistent Russian cyber efforts in 2020.[14]

In 2020 Russian intelligence agents infiltrated US policy-making organizations.The news media were co-opted with an alarming amount of false news.[15] One of the more interesting Russian undercover agents was Maria Butina. Between 2015 and 2017 she openly infiltrated the American National Rifle Association (NRA); worked with US political figures to influence American policy for the purpose of advancing the agenda of the Russian Federation; established lines of communication between American politicians and Russian officials; promoted a meeting of top NRA leaders in Russia to discuss common goals with Russian leaders who had been sanctioned by the US.[16] Butina pleaded guilty to the Federal charge of 'Conspiracy to Act as an Agent of a Foreign Government' and was sentenced to 18 months in prison. She was deported to Russia in October 2019.[17 18]

A more serious operation involved Russian Military Intelligence (GRU). On 13 July 2018, a federal grand jury indicted twelve Russian military intelligence officers for their alleged role in interfering with the 2016 US presidential elections. They were charged with computer hacking conspiracy involving gaining unauthorized access to computers, stealing documents and conspiracy to commit money laundering.[19] The information and cyber campaign to undermine Ukraine's external support will take years to uncover. Cyber operations are some of the most closely guarded secrets, and governments rarely acknowledge the success or failure of attacks and counter-measures.

From Russia's point of view, the strategic situation in Ukraine had transformed from one of manoeuvre warfare in order to gain territory to one of attrition and cyber and information warfare to undermine international support.

Chapter 3

Strategy, Operations and Tactics

The efforts of a society at war are divided into strategy, operations and tactics. At the strategic level, a country like Russia develops a war plan that focuses all aspects of national power (military, economic and political) to achieve a national objective. Putin's desired end state for his 2022 Special Operation was a new Ukraine. His goal was the re-establishment of a buffer state, politically aligned with the Kremlin, militarily neutral but partnered with Russian armed forces, with conditionally transparent borders to facilitate culture and economic integration into the Eurasian Economic Union. (EEU).[1] Putin's demands at the beginning of the Special Operation were nothing short of the end of Ukrainian democracy and incorporation into his new Russian Empire. These demands remained constant throughout 2023.

War is both an art and science. The principles of the 'Art of War' were developed thousands of years ago by the Chinese scholar General Sun Tzu. They have been reiterated by many theorists over the centuries. Together with Sun Tzu, the nineteenth century Prussian General Carl von Clausewitz's principles of war form the foundation for the study of war in most military academies and war colleges throughout the world.

Clausewitz viewed war as a 'continuation of foreign policy by other means'. The objective of war is linked to the foreign policy of the combatants. On the strategic level Clausewitz observed that victory required (1) the complete or partial defeat of the enemy's armed forces, (2) the occupation of all or part of the opponent's land, and (3) breaking the opponent's will to fight.

Applying these criteria to Putin's Special Operation, it may be concluded that Russia has not won the war. Russia captured some Ukrainian territory during the initial phase of the invasion; however, its army was defeated in several subsequent battles. Putin lost more than 50 per cent of the territory captured during the first few months of the war. Despite a terror bombing campaign of Ukrainian cities during the autumn of 2022 and winter of 2023, Putin failed to break the Ukrainians' will to fight.

In contrast, the Ukrainians failed to force a withdrawal of the invader, but they held the line and defeated the Russians in several significant battles. Their will to fight did not weaken into the second year of harsh wartime conditions.

Their objective remained to reoccupy the totality of their country, including the Crimean peninsula (occupied by Russia in 2014).

The execution of modern principles of war is more complex than in Clausewitz's day. Clausewitz wrote only about dominating two domains of war: land and sea, but these two domains have been supplemented in the twenty-first century. The execution of modern war can be divided into seven discernible domains: land, air, missile and drone defence, deep strike, naval (control of the Black Sea), information/cyber, and logistics (re-arming and reconstituting depleted formations).[2] Success or failure to achieve a goal within each domain can be analysed by examining its tactical, operational, strategic and political operation.[3]

There are three levels of war: tactical, operational and strategic. As Chart 1 demonstrates, linked tactical and operational actions achieve strategic goals.[4] The media often use these terms interchangeably, causing confusion.[5] Strategy combines national objectives with the military capacity to achieve its goals.[6]

Operations deal with the organization of campaigns, planning and the employment of tactical forces to achieve strategic objectives. Tactics employ direct action in battles and smaller engagements to achieve military objectives. As depicted in Chart 1, a tactical militia patrol destroyed supply trucks that potentially resulted in the disruption of the Russian supply line. Lack of supplies caused Russia to lose the Battle for Kyiv at the beginning of the war (2022). This tactical loss in the land domain thwarted the Kremlin's strategic political goal of replacing the Ukrainian leadership.

In the cyber world, the strategy may be to disrupt the government of an opponent and assume control of, or at least exert great influence on, the actions

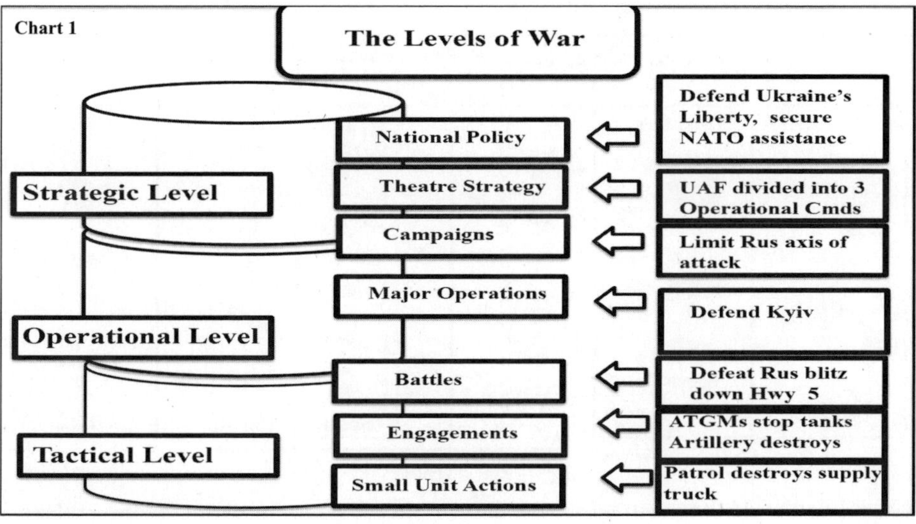

of that government. The operation's goal may be to influence an election, while the tactic would be publishing fake news or producing false messages on social media.

In the first example above, the 'operation' occurred in the context of actual combat (land domain), while the second 'operation' occurred and continued in the cyber and information domain. The campaign plan for both Ukraine and Russia required victory in a majority of these seven domains. Victory or defeat can be measured on a sliding scale between the two extremes.[7]

An operational campaign plan is divided into decisive and supporting operations linked to attainable objectives. Traditionally, decisive operations were on land; however, success in one of the other domains could become the decisive operation based upon the strategic goals of a country. As an example, the Kremlin failed to gain significant ground in its 2023 Winter Offensive. Its only success was the capture of the tactically insignificant city of Bakhmut. The city was destroyed during the eight-month-long battle, but the Ukrainian defensive line was not breached. Russian media spun the facts to equate the Battle for Bakhmut to the glorious Russian victory at the Battle for Stalingrad (1942–43). This one victory became the highlight of the Russian 2023 Winter Offensive, despite significant failures throughout the campaign. The Russian narrative highlighted the tactical victory at Bakhmut, ignoring the overall failure of the offensive.[8] The battle was hyped as a political victory in the face of a pyrrhic land victory.

From a combatant's perspective, a battlefield is divided into zones. The 'front lines'are called the 'forward edge of the battle area' (FEBA) or 'line of contact', and by the media, the 'zero line'. The main battle area of both sides

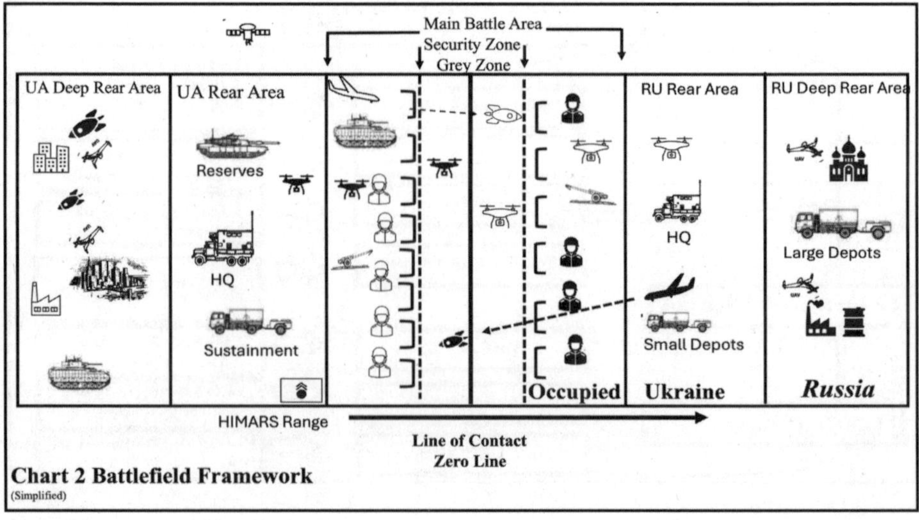

Chart 2 Battlefield Framework
(Simplified)

From January-June 2023 the 58 Combined Arms Army created a textbook multi-echeloned Soviet defence in depth. General Ivan Popov chose to fight an active defence in the security zone which was heavily fortified as this chart demonstrates. Popov had 6 months to train his troops in defensive tactics and dig in.

Sources: US Army FM 100-2-1 Soviet Operations and Tactics, Colonel Markus Riener Austrian Army

begins with a 'security zone', in front of the 'main battle area', 'rear area' and 'deep rear area'.

The zero line or line of contact separates the combatants' security zones. The two security zones can be as little as 100 metres or up to 10 km (6 miles) deep. Ukrainian and Russian reconnaissance patrols and drones mostly operated in their opponents' security zone during 2023. As the year progressed, reconnaissance and kamikaze drones replaced foot patrols to locate enemy positions and attack individual soldiers. Drone operators and light electronic warfare (EW) jammers from both sides would play a deadly game of cat and mouse within each other's security zone. Small quadcopters carrying hand or anti-tank grenades would fly a few feet off the ground and stalk enemy soldiers, following them into bunkers or strong points. Reconnaissance drones located enemy columns as they moved up to the security zone, then directed artillery and kamikaze drones to destroy vehicles and soldiers.

Defenders dug echelons of fox holes, trenches and strong points reinforced with minefields, anti-tank ditches and obstacles in the battle zone. Kill zones were established with turning obstacles designed to channel attackers into death traps. These defences were often dug in tree lines around the fields, making each open field a possible kill zone. The defensive battle zone, when fully developed, would begin with a minefield up to 200 metres deep, backed by an anti-tank ditch. These obstacles were covered by observation posts. As the second year of the war progressed, reconnaissance and loitering kamikaze drones (Lancets, etc.) performed this mission. The next 300–400 metres would include minefields and dragons' teeth obstacles, followed by a third mine field in front of a manned trench, bunker or strong point occupied by infantry anti-tank guided missiles (ATGMs) and mortars. This fortification would be a battalion's first echelon defence. Behind it would be a second and possibly third echelon defence protected by similar obstacles. The entire depth of the battalion's battle area would be from 1.5 to 2 km (0.7 to 1.2 miles). Behind these defensive lines were the battalion's reserves including tanks, mobile air defence (AD) weapons and small drone jammers. Behind this battalion would be the brigade's or regiment's second echelon battalion, organized like the first battalion's defensive area along with the regimental or brigade artillery. Crossing into the brigade rear boundary, the rear zone, extending up to 30 km (17 miles) from the line of contact, would be heavy drone jammers, reinforcing artillery groups, and firing areas for attack helicopters (Ka-52, Mi-24 and Mi-28s). Ground attack aircraft like the SU-25 would launch their gliding bombs from the rear zone. Logistically, small brigade supply depots and assembly areas for brigade, division or army reserves were in the rear zone.

In the attacker's battle zone the line of contact would be held by defending infantry and tanks, while the attacking company or battalion would move from an assembly area in the rear zone to an attack position in the battle zone. An attack position is the last covered and concealed location before the assaulting battalion or company crossed the line of departure/line of contact. Reconnaissance and loitering kamikaze drones would search the enemy security, battle and rear zones for targets. More skilled reconnaissance and special forces teams and squads, often equipped with small drones, would attempt to penetrate the enemy defence and enter their rear zone to locate command posts, logistics and communications. The locations of these headquarters and logistics depots were relayed to artillery or other fire support assets for destruction. Larger drone jammers and artillery would be in the rear zone 3–5 km (1.8–3.1 miles) from the line of contact.

Russian combat helicopters and ground attack aircraft would support their ground attack with ATGMs, rockets and gliding bombs. The Ukrainians had extremely limited air support which reduced their ability to provide cover for ground manoeuvres. Lacking sufficient air support, Ukrainians relied heavily upon operational artillery, such as the M142 High Mobility Artillery Rocket System (HIMARS) and M270 Multiple Rocket Launcher System (MRLS). These weapon systems could launch rockets deep into the Russian rear and deep rear zones.

The deep rear boundary was everything beyond 40–50 km (25–31 miles) from the line of contact or zero line. Large Russian railhead supply depots were located in cities and towns like Luhansk, Starobilsk and Melitopol within their deep rear zone, outside of HIMARS and MLRS range of 100 km (60 miles). Ukrainian operational supply depots were located along the numerous main supply routes leading to the front. While these Ukrainian depots were not in danger of Russian operational artillery strikes, they were within range of missiles and long-range drones. Both sides placed their sector operational reserve formations in their deep rear zone. Centrally located, these operational reserves could reinforce a sector of the main battle area in a few days.

In the Ukrainian theatre of operations, manned air operations were extremely difficult due to both sides air defence coverage. As both sides gained experience in 2023, air operations in support of ground operations increased, but did not become decisive. Russia developed effective 'over the shoulder' tactics. The modern Russian heavily armed Ka-52 Alligator (aka Hokim) attack helicopters were armed with a 35mm autocannon and had four hard points to attach ATGMs. The Ka-52 fired the LMUR ATGMs with a range of 14.5 km (9 miles). The Ka-52 could loiter beyond range of Ukrainian man-portable anti-air defence systems (MANPADS) and heavier air defence artillery (ADA) systems. The Ka-52s could fire over the Russian defenders and destroy Ukrainian tanks and armoured vehicles.

During the second year of the war the Russian Air Force (VVS) improved its ability to organize strike packages, combining EW, air superiority fighters and strike aircraft. In support of the 2023 winter offensive the VVS introduced guided gravity 'dumb bombs', which multi-role fighter bombers could employ outside Ukrainian ADA coverage. These cheap precision weapons modified 500 kg (1,102 lbs) dumb bombs into a guided bomb. The conversion kit is much cheaper ($24,000) than cruise and ballistic missiles. The aircraft can launch the bomb from up to 50 km (31 miles), well outside the average Ukrainian ADA system.[9] They were first employed on 24 March 2023 in Sumy Oblast, where

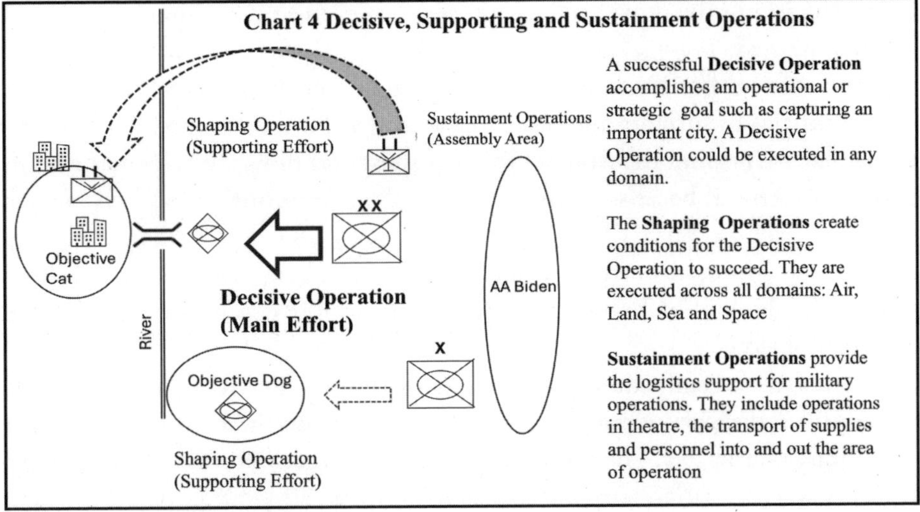

Russian aircraft launched eleven bombs. By the end of the year, hundreds of gliding bombs were dropped in the Kherson and Avdiivka battles.

Both sides conducted major offensive and defensive manoeuvres in 2023. These operations had many aspects, but they can be divided into three categories: decisive, shaping and sustaining. A decisive operation directly accomplishes an objective. The decisive operation is the focal point around which a commander designs the entire operation. It determines the outcome of a major battle or engagement. Multiple subordinate units may be engaged in the same decisive operation across multiple domains (space, air, land, cyber, sea and information) that lead directly to accomplishment of the overall mission.

Shaping or supporting operations are those at any echelon (platoon, company, brigade, division, and army) that create conditions for success of the decisive operation by affecting the enemy and the terrain. Synchronization of intelligence gathering, reconnaissance, air operations, artillery fire and obscurants to delay or disrupt the repositioning of enemy forces are shaping operations. In the middle of May 2023, the 3rd Assault Brigade attack that unhinged the Russian defence south of Bakhmut was a shaping operation in support of Ukraine's decisive operation in the south. The 3rd Assault Brigade's attack prevented Russia from shifting forces south.

A sustaining operation is one at any echelon that enables a decisive and shaping operation by generating and maintaining combat power. Sustaining operations focus internally on friendly forces, while decisive and shaping operations focus on the enemy. Sustaining operations include personnel and logistic support, medical, rear area security, movement control, terrain management and infrastructure development. Simply put, sustaining operations ensure supplies and ammunition reach the front. They ensure casualties are evacuated promptly, replacements are sent forward and equipment repaired and maintained.

Commanders designate main and shaping/supporting efforts to establish clear priorities of support and resources among subordinate units. Supporting efforts receive minimum resources to accomplish their mission. Often the main effort is successful because of the efforts of the supporting units.[10] Examples: a wild weasel aircraft (EW) jams air defences, allowing strike aircraft to blow up an ammunition depot; an infantry battalion captures Hill 124 to protect the flank of its brigade as it penetrates enemy defences to capture the division's objective.

There are normally multiple shaping operations executed over a period to support a decisive operation. They may begin months before the decisive operation materializes. The object is to create multiple dilemmas for the enemy. Deception is a critical supporting enabler in creating multiple dilemmas, achieving operational surprise and maintaining the initiative. Successful deception operations degrade the enemy's ability to decide and act on accurate information. Deception inhibits effective enemy action by disrupting his decision-making cycle, causing inaction, delay and misallocation of forces.[11] In 2022, Ukrainian shaping operations successfully convinced the Russians that the decisive operation in their counter-offensive was aimed at Kherson. Russia shifted its elite paratroopers and Naval Infantry from Donbas to Kherson. As the Ukrainian decisive attack materialized it struck the weakly held line to liberate part of Donbas, surprising the Russians.

The essential principles of warfare have not changed since Clausewitz. Russia's perceived need to conquer territory to create and maintain a buffer zone between its homeland and the West has not changed since Tsar Peter the Great (1682–1725). Russian military operations, command and control have not changed since the era of the Soviet Union. What has greatly changed are the technology and capabilities of modern weapons. Hybrid warfare is now a pervasive reality. These changes will alter the face of warfare forever.

Chapter 4

Russian Armed Forces, January 2023

The initial Russian invasion force abandoned traditional Soviet/Russian combat organization, instead deploying newly created battalion tactical groups (BTGs). Command and control was given to the BTGs, which answered directly to the combined arms army (CAA) commander instead of brigade and division headquarters co-located in the field.

By January 2023 it was estimated that the Russian invasion force had divided into four Operational Groups (OSK). OSK-South fielded twenty-one tank and infantry battalions along the Dnipro River guarding the gateway to the Crimean Peninsula. OSK-East fielded thirty-six battalions in the Zaporizhzhia-Vuhledar Sector. The sixty-seven battalions of OSK-Centre were stationed along the Donetsk Sector, including Bakhmut. In addition to the sixty-seven battalions in OSK-Centre there were a hundred detachments (battalions) from the 'Private Military Company Wagner' (PMC Wagner). OSK-West fielded fifty-four battalions in Luhansk. OSK-West maintained an operational reserve of four to six battalions near Smolensk and ten battalions in the vicinity of Kursk-Belgorod. In Bryansk Oblast, Russia positioned eight battalions, and another eight battalions were stationed in Belarus. Most of the battalions were grouped into regiments and brigades, a few of which were under the command and control of divisions and army corps. Behind these battalions, Russia was massing operational reserves and standing up new formations such as the 25th Command Arms Army (CAA).

Based upon combat operations in 2022, the media often presented an incorrect illusion that the Russians were systematically incompetent, irredeemably corrupt, armed with faulty weapons, had ineffective and unreliable C2 and were incapable of adapting.[1] Despite failures during the first year of the war and the destruction of the illusion of Russia's invincibility, they remained a dangerous adversary.

The first year of the invasion revealed that the Russian military, like its government, was fragmented.[2] This was a major inhibitor of Russian success, since the ground forces lacked cohesiveness. Russia's ground forces were divided between: the Army, paratroopers (VDV), Naval Infantry (NI), Private Military Companies (PMC), Luhansk People's Republic (LPR) and

Donets People's Republic (DPR) Armies,volunteer battalions, reserve (BAR) battalions and Chechen units under regional Governor Ramzan Kadyrov.[3] There was no unifying standard operating procedure within the force. The factions did not share intelligence gathered on the battlefield and lacked the ability to quickly disseminate intelligence and targeting information between formations at the tactical level. To make matters worse, the Russian ground forces were hampered by a culture of deceptive and dishonest reporting and unhealthy competition. Units being replaced on the front did not provide the incoming units with tactical intelligence. No standard operating procedure, such as the US Army and US Marine Corps have in place, linked the factions to work seamlessly together or support each other. Replacement battalions often attacked on the same routes and rolled into the same kill zones as the previous units.

The competition led to fratricide. Lack of communication between battalions led to intramural firefights. This was exacerbated by both sides being equipped with the same or similar tanks, infantry fighting vehicles (IFVs), armoured personnel carriers (APCs) and other weapons. Electronic Warfare and other systems were rarely deconflicted, while processes for 'Identifying Friend from Foe' transponder signals and the establishment of control measures were inadequate. At the operational level there was no joint doctrine or operating procedures between ground, air and naval forces.

Politically, in peace time there were good reasons for Putin to encourage this fragmentation, so that no one military leader could exercise sufficient power to overthrow his government.[4] During the Special Operation this policy of fragmentation was a significant factor in the defeats before Kyiv and Kharkiv. Recognizing these issues, entering the second year of war, Putin and the Ministry of Defence started adapting their operational and tactical procedures to the realities of twenty-first century warfare.

The first step was to re-establish traditional command and control (C2) with the appropriate strategic, operational and tactical headquarters. At the start of the Special Operation the military districts surrounding Ukraine were converted into operational commands (OSKs). Russia was divided into sixteen military districts, of which only the West, Central, East and South were involved in the Special Operation. During the Second World War, this level of command was referred to as a 'front' and each was given a geographical title such as the '1st Ukrainian Front'. Historical fronts and modern OSKs were also referred to as 'army groups'.

The intermediate command echelons between OSK and manoeuvre units (divisions, brigades or battalion tactical groups) were the combined arms army (CAA) or tanks army (TA). These armies were not uniformly organized.

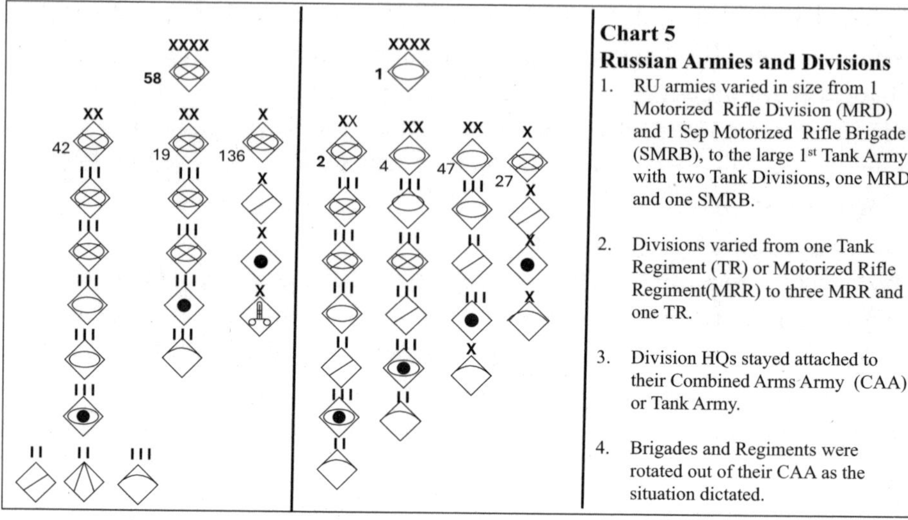

Generally, they controlled and provided combat support (artillery, combat engineers, etc.) and combat service support (logistics) to two tank divisions (TD) or motorized rifle divisions (MRD), six or more separate tanks (STB) or motorized rifle brigades (SMRB), or a combination of divisions and brigades.

During February 2022 the Russians invaded on the Northern Front, controlled by OSK-East, with the 29th, 35th and 36th CAA. The invaders from the north-eastern front were controlled by OSK-Central, with the 4th CAA and 2nd Guards CAA. The invasion from the east pushing toward Kharkiv and into the Donbas was OSK-West with the 1st Guards TA, 6th CAA and 20th CAA. Invaders approaching from Crimea, who pushed toward Kherson, Zaporizhzhia and Mariupol, were controlled by OSK-South and included the 8th, 49th and 58th CAAs, 22nd (Naval Infantry) Corps, VDV 7th Air Assault Division and 11th Air Assault Brigade. Before massing for the invasion, these armies were stationed along the Russian borders from the Baltic to the Caspian Sea and spread across the southern edge of Siberia to the Pacific Ocean.[5]

The new 25th CAA was formed in spring 2023 in the Eastern Military District. The cadre for the formation was pulled from the 2nd CAA. It was initially projected that the 25th CAA would not be combat-ready until 2024. The 25th CAA consisted of the 67th Motorized Rifle Division (MRD), 164th Motorized Rifle Brigade (MRB) and 11th Tank Battalion (TB), along with combat support and combat service support brigades, and mustered 30,000 new contract or mobilized troops.[6] The heavy fighting during the Ukrainian summer counter-offensive forced the 25th CAA to be committed to combat in autumn 2023.[7]

Russia also fielded a limited number of army corps that fulfilled a similar function to armies but were smaller. The pre-invasion corps were orientated for coastal defence and were assigned to and co-located with naval fleet headquarters. The 22nd Corps was based in Crimea and supported the Black Sea Fleet; the 11th Corps defended the isolated Kaliningrad while supporting the Baltic Fleet; the 14th Corps supported the Northern Fleet at Severomorsk.[8]

The Army of the DPR was designated the 1st Army Corps, and the LPR Army was designated the 2nd Army Corps. They were independent armies in name only and fell under the 8th CAA. After annexations of both republics into the Russian Federation in February 2023, the 1st and 2nd Army Corps were incorporated into the Russian Army, while the ill-trained 3rd Army Corps was organized from volunteer battalions raised in individual oblasts.[9]

Based upon a major reorganization of the Russian Army between 2005 and 2010, the ground forces became brigade-centric, disbanding most of their divisions and organizing separate motorized rifle and tank brigades to replace them. Some divisions remained and were assigned primarily to positions near the Ukrainian border.

The new separate motorized rifle brigades (SMRB) mustered between 3,000 and 4,500 officers and soldiers, while a fully manned motorized rifle division (MRD) contained 8,500 and was divided into motorized rifle (MRR) or tank regiments (TR). Tank divisions (TD) mustered 6,500 officers and soldiers, and tank brigades (TB) had 3,000 personnel. The MRR of the divisions contained one artillery battalion, while brigade artillery groups contained two self-propelled (SP) howitzer battalions and a multiple rocket launcher system (MRLS) battalion. The Air Assault and Airborne Divisions (VDV) contained

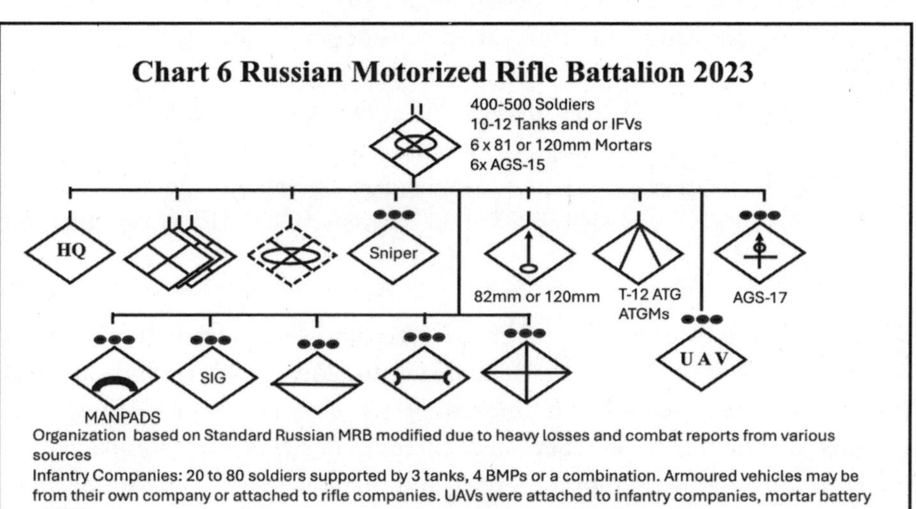

Chart 7 Separate Motorized Rifle Brigade (SMRB) 2023

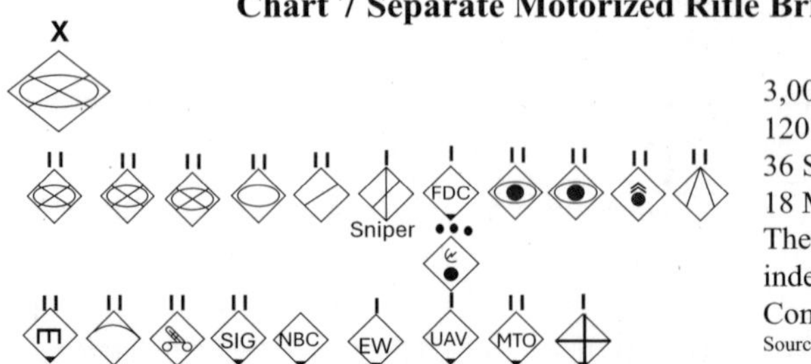

3,000 to 5,000 Troops
120 IFV and/or APCs
36 SP Howitzers
18 MRLS
The SMRB was organized to fight independently under the C2 of a Combined Arms or Tank Army
Source: *Russian War of War*, US Army

The **Motorized Rifle Regiment (MRR)** was organized similar to the Separate Motorized Rifle Brigade however, it was not organized to operate separately from its Motorized Rifle or Tank Division. It was organized with three motorized rifle and one tank battalions but contained only one self-propelled or towed artillery battalion and smaller combat support units and mustered 2,000 troops.

BARS, Volunteer, Storm-Z, DPR and LPR or Mobik battalions (300-500 soldiers) and regiments (2,000 soldiers) could be attached to MRRs or SMRBs.
In 2023, all SMRBs and MRRs were understrength and underequipped.

approximately 5,500 personnel. Naval Infantry (NI) and VDV brigades numbered approximately 2,500. The separate brigades had larger combat support and combat service support units than divisional regiments and could operate independently under an army's command and control. Half the size of a division, separate brigades could deploy quickly by rail to urgent areas.

The remaining tank and motorized rifle divisions varied in size and capabilities. Unlike their Soviet predecessor divisions, the number of subordinate regiments varied from two to four. Only the 150th Motorized Rifle (8th CAA) and 90th Guards Tank (41st CAA) retained four regiments. Most of the remaining divisions contained only two or three regiments, with a few containing one.[10] By the beginning of 2023, all Russian regiments, brigades and battalions had suffered heavy casualties and thus varied considerably in strength.

At full strength the Army, NI and to some extent the VDV battalions contained approximately 500 officers and men. All infantry battalions were fully motorized, except for some VDV parachute battalions that were partially motorized. In news releases and battle damage assessments published by the media, VDV units were easily identified by their BMD IFVs, a smaller and airdroppable version of the Army's BMP IFV.

In NATO terminology 'motorized' denotes battalions and brigades armed with wheeled IFVs or APCs, and 'mechanized' indicates a formation mounted on tracked IFVs or APCs. In Russian terminology 'motorized' includes all infantry whether mounted in tracked or wheeled IFVs and APCs. Each motorized rifle battalion contained three motorized rifle companies, an attached tank company, mortar battery and platoon-size combat support and combat service support units. In January 2023, many motorized rifle battalions lacked their full complement of armoured vehicles.

The Russian Ministry of Defence encountered administrative and legal issues which impacted its order of battle for the invasion. The ground forces were divided between the yearly conscripts, serving one year, and contract or regular soldiers serving on multi-year enlistment contracts. Russian law prohibited conscripts from serving outside of Russia unless they volunteered. This legal obstacle forced Russian planners to rely for the initial invasion on undermanned battalion tactical groups (BTGs) lacking a full complement of dismounted infantry.

The VDV and NI were composed almost exclusively of contract soldiers, and their BTGs entered combat at full strength, fully equipped and trained. The Army's BTGs were understaffed, underequipped and lacked combined arms training. The contract soldiers filled the vehicle crews and technical positions, while the conscripts filled the less technical positions such as dismounted infantry. Without the conscript soldiers, most of the Army BTGs committed to combat on 24 February 2022 lacked sufficient infantry to accomplish their assigned mission.

Historic corruption in the procurement process was widespread. Funding and materials were siphoned off at every level from 'Private Ivan' to the highest ranks. Equipment intended for the military was all too often found for sale on the black market. Uniforms, weapons and kit often never arrived at intended destinations but could be found for sale elsewhere. Copper wire was stripped from military vehicles and sold. Re-treads from China were procured with funding intended for military-grade tyres. Communication equipment such as secure radios were ordered but never delivered. False inventory and performance accounting and reporting known at *varanyo* was the acceptable norm.[11] The rampant corruption resulted in the lack of secure communications equipment, modern body armour, fully operational tanks, IFVs, APCs and howitzers. Ignoring the facts on the ground, BTG commanders falsely reported their units were fully mission-capable. The result was that although individual BTGs had reduced and varying combat capabilities, their higher headquarters assumed they were fully mission-capable as reported up the chain of command and assigned missions as if readiness reports were accurate.

To compound the impact of corruption and false reporting, war planners generally failed to deploy intermediate brigade and division headquarters to provide C2 and coordinate the tactical activities of two or more BTGs. These shortcomings were exacerbated by logistics planning erroneously based on the belief that the campaign would be over in two weeks.

President Putin, the FSB, Ministry of Defence General Shoigu and Chief of the General Staff General Gerasimov and their staffs secretly wargamed the Special Operation based on the flawed assumptions the Ukrainians would offer little resistance – their government would be toppled in a few days, and

NATO would not respond quickly enough to prevent a swift Russian victory. Without a proper 'Red Team' as an opponent, or a Napoleonic corporal to notify Putin he was walking around without his pants, the Special Operation commenced on 24 February 2022, resulting in disaster.

According to the Ukrainian Ministry of Defence, between the start of the Special Operation on 24 February 2022, and 31 December 2022, the Russian Armed Forces suffered 120,000 killed in action (KIA), while other sources reported the KIA number significantly lower but total casualties as over 200,000.[12] During Russia's winter offensive, January–April 2023, the Kremlin suffered 700 casualties per day, 250–300 of which were KIA. It was estimated that 1,576 company and field grade officers were KIA during the first fifteen months of the war.[13] Twenty-nine major generals and command colonels (the Russians do not have brigadier generals) were confirmed KIA, with another 114 reported as KIA.[14]

The loss of generals makes headlines, but they are easily replaced. The US Army promotes ninety colonels to brigadier (Regular, Reserve and Army National Guard) each year. As pointed out to the new generals at 'Charm School' (General Officer Basic Education), the entire cohort could be replaced nine times before standards are lowered.[15] The Russian ground forces would have had a similar depth of talent at the top.[16] The loss of company and field grade officers, however, could not be made good so easily.

In the first year of the war Russia had 2,300 company commanders participating in the invasion. An additional 500 combat arms captains and senior lieutenants in other assignments provided the invaders with a manpower pool of 2,800 fully trained company commanders. By the end of the first year 840 captains and senior lieutenants were confirmed killed. At the accepted ratio of 1:3 KIA/WIA Russian company grade officers suffered 2,520 casualties. Half of the WIA would return to duty, leaving 1,680 company grade combat arms officers permanently out of the war.[17]

The high loss of company grade officers (lieutenants and captains) significantly impacted the combat capabilities of platoons, companies, and battalion tactical groups. These junior officers led from the front, and at the beginning of the war were well trained. On average there was one junior officer per twenty Russian soldiers.[18] Lacking an NCO corps, these officers trained conscripts and created the combat teams and crews critical to modern combat. Officers from other branches could in theory fill the vacant officer slots, but they lacked infantry and tank commander skills. To be fully staffed a company required three platoon leaders and a company commander and deputy commander. By January 2023 the lack of officers probably forced the Russians to assign one officer per company, with senior surviving soldiers becoming platoon leaders. Soldiers promoted to replace officers killed were poorly trained and inexperienced in leadership. Their sole qualification may have been to have survived when their platoons and companies were nearly destroyed.

The loss of skilled company officers explains the inability of Russian manoeuvre companies in 2023 to execute the simplest combined arms tactics. Company officers were the highest-level officers on the front lines, daily interacting with and motivating troops. In the Russian top-down decision-making style, the company commander was the only person in the unit briefed on the battalion and brigade battle plan.

The influx of 300,000 Mobiks during the autumn of 2022 compounded the problem. Company grade officers should have been the primary trainers for the newly mobilized 300,000 soldiers. These officers had been deployed from the mobilization centres and garrisons to make good losses in the deployed BTGs. The lack of training officers resulted in inexperienced and untrained soldiers being sent to the front as replacements, even in elite VDV and NI Brigades.

During the first year of the invasion BTGs were rebuilt and their attached ad hoc artillery battalions were stripped and formed into independent artillery groups. Due to the high number of casualities as the year progressed there were insufficient experienced and fully trained junior officers to give the BTGs success on the battlefield. With each reconstitution more BTGs lost their artillery and were re-formed as traditional motorized rifle and tank battalions. As the first year of the war went on fewer BTGs remained on the battlefield, and the battalions got smaller.[19] Combat losses left motorized rifle battalions of 300 soldiers without a full complement of armoured vehicles. The sole benefit of such losses was that these smaller battalions were easier to command and control for inexperienced staffs and commanders.

The realization that the lack of efficient C2 structure (CAA to BTG) had resulted in major defeats led to the reintroduction of brigade and division C2 headquarters. By the second year of the war, brigade and division headquarters were fully reinstated, and the battalion tactical groups (BTGs) all but disappeared. As the war progressed with mounting casualities, surviving captains replaced majors and lieutenant colonels as battalion commanders. Trained for tactical direct combat, they lacked the expertise and skills to effectively coordinate a battalion's efforts in a brigade or regimental operation. The fix was to further centralize C2 at brigade and regimental level.

Suffering a series of defeats on the battlefield and failing to gain territory, the invaders changed tactics during the autumn of 2022. As Russian motorized forces attempted to capture fortified towns and cities in the Donbas, they reverted to First World War-style infantry and artillery tactics.

Re-equipping the battalions became a major issue for Russian logisticians. During the first year of the war Russia lost (destroyed or captured) 3,064 tanks, 6,124 IFVs and APCs, 2,059 artillery systems, 431 multiple launcher rocket systems, 215 air defence systems and 4,797 trucks.[20] The corruption in the Russian military storage faculties hindered newly created or rebuilt battalions from being fully equipped with modern or modernized T-64, 72, 80 or 90 series tanks (125mm main gun). The same problem occurred with IFV and APCs. In the autumn of 2022 the Russians pulled 800 T-62 (115mm main gun) tanks out of storage, and in late March 2023 T-54/55 (100mm main gun) tanks were spotted on trains moving from storage faculties. By May 2023 T-54/55 tanks were spotted in the Zaporizhzhia region.[21]

Making good battlefield losses in equipment required the Kremlin to pull post-Second World War T-54/55 tanks from storage. While incapable of going toe-to-toe with later Soviet and NATO Cold War and post-Cold War tanks, the T-54/55s provided increased firepower to motorized rifle battalions. They were armed with a 100mm D10-T rifled tank gun and coaxial and hull-mounted 7.62mm machine guns. Their heaviest armour of 120mm on the nose of the hull, while inferior to modern NATO and Russian tanks, was superior to all IFVs and APCs. Overall, the T-54/55's armour made it more resistant than IFVs and APCs, while the main gun provided direct immediate firepower.

At the time commentators compared these old tanks with modern ones and noted their deficiencies in armour and main guns. Their armour was easily penetrated by modern anti-armour weapons.[22] In a massed tank battle they would be death traps. However, except for the first few weeks in the autumn and winter of 2023, there had not been any massed tank battles. Rather than occurring at battalion level, tank battles were smaller section, platoon or company affairs.

By January 2023 Russian ground forces were divided between elite assault units (VDV, Naval Infantry, selected Army, Volunteer and PMC brigades and battalions) and ordinary forces. The elite units conducted offensive operations, and the ordinary forces with T-54/55 and 62 tanks were relegated to the defence of occupied territories.[23] The large number of reserve modern tanks were committed to combat during the Russian 2023 autumn offensive.

By the beginning of the second year of war Russian ground forces had failed to such an extent that the Kremlin reorganized the brigades and reverted from the newly implemented BTG organization to traditional Soviet-style organization and tactics. Intermediate command headquarters were re-introduced, and once again battalions came under direct command and control of brigades and divisions in the field.

Chapter 5

Russian Sea and Air Operations

At the start of the Special Operation Russia fielded approximately 900 tactical jet aircraft.During the first year, between 84 and 130 aircraft were lost. Several were shot down by Ukrainian air defence (ADA), while others fell in air combat. Many were the victims of drone strikes, friendly fire and crashes caused by pilot error and/or mechanical failure.[1] As the second year of the war commenced, the Russian Air Force (VKS) retained a large stockpile of munitions and an extensive aircraft fleet. The losses of aircraft in 2023 were minimal, and the VKS had the capability to cause severe damage to Ukrainian ground forces if the Kremlin was willing to accept the losses. As Ukraine acquired man-portable air defence (MANPADs) and surface to air missiles (SAMs), Russian aircraft became more vulnerable.

Despite deployment of MANPADs and SAMs, the VKS became more active in 2023, providing tactical air support to invading ground forces. Countering the threat of Ukrainian ADA, the VKS employed FAB-500 bombs with glide kits dropped from SU-34 jet fighters. The potential range of these modified dumb bombs was 70 km (43 miles) but their accuracy was poor.[2] By mid-year FAB-1500M-54-UGUM, a 1,500lb glide bomb entered service with a theoretical range of 40 km (25 miles).

At the beginning of the Special Operation the VKS fielded a total of eleven attack helicopter brigades and regiments.The invader's fleet contained 100 Ka-52s, 80 Mi-28s and 150 Mi-24 helicopter gunships. By February 2023 the VKS had lost thirty Ka-52s, eleven Mi-28s and eleven Mi-24s. During the first year of the war, the gunships operated behind Ukrainian lines and were exposed to layers of ADA. Their air bases were vulnerable to Ukrainian high mobility artillery rocket systems (HIMARS) and drone strikes. Despite defensive measures, the helicopter gunships were forced to relocate deeper into Russia. The further the helicopters had to fly to the front, the shorter time they had to support ground units.[3]

In 2023 the Ka-52 Alligator (NATO identification Hokum B) was Russia's newest highly manoeuvrable gunship with an operational range of 1,108 km (689 miles). It could be armed with autocannon, rockets, bombs and Vikhr 9K121 beam-riding ATGMs with a range of 10–12 km

(6–8 miles). Despite modern avionics and counter-measures, the Ka-52 Alligator was just as vulnerable to MANPADS as the older Hind Mi-24. The Russians adjusted their attack helicopter tactics in 2023 to reflect battlefield conditions. During the Russian winter offensive and Ukrainian summer counter-offensive the Ka-52 took advantage of the stand-off range of the Vikhr 9K121 and fired 'over the shoulder' of ground manoeuvre battalions. This enabled Ka-52s to target Ukrainian armour without entering the MANPAD engagement envelope.

The Royal Air Force estimated that at the beginning of the Special Operation the VKS operated approximately 900 helicopters of all types. In 2022 and 2023, the Ukrainian Ministry of Defence claimed Moscow had lost 350 helicopters from a combination of causes. Oryx, an independent report based on verified data, visually confirmed 115 Russian helicopters destroyed. As of October 2023, Oryx confirmed the destruction of forty-nine Ka-52 gunships.[4] The number of destroyed helicopters confirmed that the Russians used helicopter gunships to provide close air support. The gunships were based at airfields near the front and were able to respond quickly in support of ground forces. Due to 'stand-off over the shoulder' tactics employed by the gunships, most were destroyed on the ground by HIMARS using standard and army tactical missile system (ATACMS) rockets rather than MANPADS.

The VKS increased their sortie rate with glide bombs and long-range ATGMs in support of the Russian autumn and winter offensives and in response to the Ukrainian summer counter-offensive. The change in tactics reduced the VKS loss rate from ADA systems. The primary threat became long-range ATACMS, drone and missile attacks on Russian airfields.

The performance of Russian Air Defence systems (ADA) improved in 2023. A more robust coverage challenged Ukrainian aircraft supporting ground operations. A battle between Ukrainian high speed anti-radiation missiles (HARMs) and HIMARS and Russian air defence network (missiles, guns, radars and anti-missile missiles) played out over the ground forces. Long-range surface-to-air missiles (SAMS) remained a significant threat to the Ukrainian air force. These ground-based ADA missiles were integrated with combat air patrols. The Russian aircraft armed with long range air-to-air R-37 missiles threatened the Ukrainian Air Force out to 177 km (109 miles).[5]

At the beginning of the Special Operation the Black Sea Fleet was the most successful of the three main branches of the Russian military. It was involved in the initial bombardment of Ukrainian cities, turned the Sea of Azov into a Russian lake and blockaded the Ukrainian Black Sea ports.

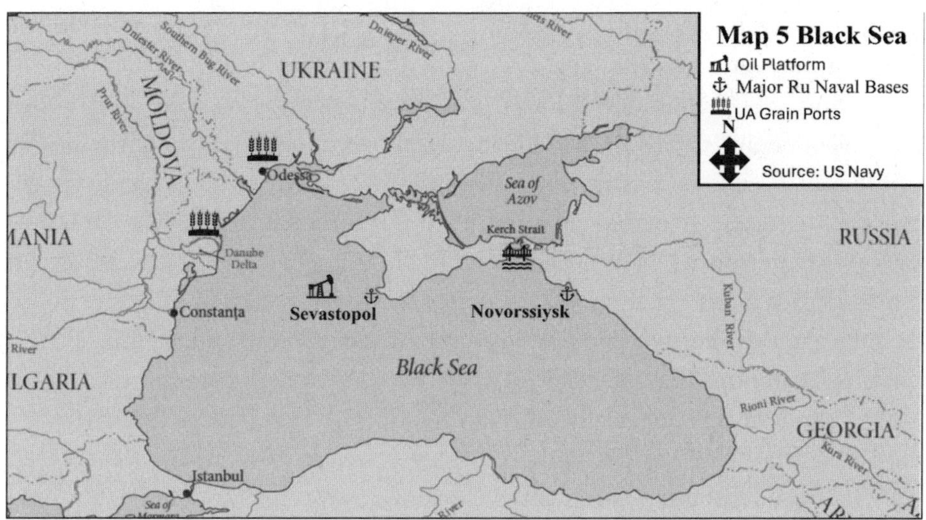

Sevastopol, on the Crimean Peninsula, was the home port of the Black Sea Fleet. During January/February 2022, the fleet contained a combined total of forty-nine ships of various classes and seven kilo-class submarines.[6] The surface fleet consisted of twenty-four missile corvettes, frigates and amphibious ships, led by the flagship cruiser *Moskva*.[7] Seven amphibious landing ships provided the lift for two naval infantry battalion tactical groups.[8] Russia had sufficient ships but lacked a solid doctrine for conducting littoral warfare.

Naval manoeuvres in the Black Sea were not blue water operations. The semi-enclosed sea has access to the Mediterranean only via a narrow strait, with NATO members controlling the southern and western coasts. It was the perfect test arena for littoral warfare theories. Prior to Russia's invasion, the US, China and other countries had been examining what modern littoral warfare would look like, what it would require and how their naval doctrine would need to be adapted. Russia apparently failed to modernize its naval doctrine, and Russian admirals were unprepared for Ukraine's viable littoral defence, developed hastily and out of necessity.

Modern littoral warfare requires close cooperation between all services. In contrast to open ocean combat focused on fleet and task force coordination, littoral engagements are comparatively small tactical operations. Modern littoral operations require highly decentralized command and control to be successful. In this environment naval forces face far more diverse threats than historic naval battles at sea. The weaker defending naval force does not need to rely on ships. The primary anti-access/area-denial capabilities in littoral warfare are land-based aircraft, diesel-electric attack submarines, multipurpose corvettes, fast attack small craft, coastal missile batteries, UAVs/drones, mines, and medium and short-range ballistic missiles.[9]

Lacking a clear understanding of littoral operations and employing traditional tactics, the Black Sea Fleet gained operational control of the nearly landlocked Black Sea by the end of March 2022. In total the Russian Navy had approximately 346 ships and patrol craft manned by 150,000 to 160,000 active-duty personnel. It was, however, unable to use any of these to reinforce the Black Sea Fleet because on 1 March 2022 Turkey blocked military transit through the Bosphorus Strait (between the Mediterranean and the Black Sea), isolating the entire Black Sea Fleet.[10]

As a result of this politically motivated action by Turkey, a NATO member, the Black Sea Fleet was left in a precarious situation. Nevertheless, the Fleet, with its Naval Infantry complement, either destroyed Ukrainian's tiny pre-war navy or forced its ships to scuttle to prevent capture. The Black Sea Fleet successfully established a blockade and conducted Naval Infantry amphibious operations along the eastern Ukrainian coast. However, it was unprepared for Ukrainian counter-measures.

Maintaining the blockade became costly and embarrassing as the 'curse of Snake Island' soon took its toll. Snake Island was a small Ukrainian outpost in the western Black Sea, home to a temple dedicated to the Greek hero Achilles and rumoured to be haunted by his spirit. At the beginning of the invasion the island's 50-man garrison defied the invader's call to surrender with a much-publicized verbal flip of a finger. Despite the heroics of the Ukrainian garrison they were captured, and the island fell under Russian control.[11]

On 13 April 2022, Achilles' ghost appeared and cursed the Fleet. The Flagship Cruiser *Moskva*, pride of the Black Sea Fleet, was patrolling off Snake Island while providing anti-aircraft missile support to the ground attack toward Kherson, when two Neptune anti-ship missiles slammed into her. The loss of the *Moskva* opened a gap in the Russian anti-air missile coverage along the western Ukrainian coast and was extremely embarrassing to the Kremlin.

Once the Bosphorus Strait was closed to military ships, the Russians could have deployed naval assets to the Black Sea via three alternate routes. The Rhine-Main-Danube Canal and river system links the North Sea with the Black Sea, but this route was controlled by NATO. The Volga-Don-Caspian Sea Canal and river system would have allowed the Russian Caspian Flotilla to enter the Sea of Azov.[12] In 2021 this flotilla contained two guided missile frigates, eight corvettes, four patrol boats, seven minesweepers, six landing craft and one gunboat.[13] The flotilla lacked a cruiser to replace the *Moskva*.

The final route linked the Baltic and Black Seas through a series of rivers and canals, but was only viable for corvettes and smaller-class ships.[14]

On 2 March 2022, two Russian Raptor Assault boats were damaged or destroyed near Snake Island by Ukrainian-operated, Turkish-supplied TB2 armed drones. Ukraine was able to deploy drones over Snake Island only because the *Moskva* had been sunk.

Russia suffered other embarrassing naval losses. On 22 March 2022, Ukrainian commandos heavily damaged a Raptor Assault ship off Mariupol, firing an anti-tank missile to set off ammunition on the ship's deck. On 3 March 2022, a landing ship at a pier in Berdyask was spotted by Ukrainian intelligence. It was destroyed by a Ukrainian OTR-21 Tochka ballistic missile. On 24 March 2022, the tank-landing ship *Saratov*, in a still unexplained incident, unexpectedly blew up.[15] On 27 June 2022, Ukraine conducted more than ten high-precision missile strikes on Snake Island.[16] The small, haunted island had become a death trap, and Russia abandoned it on 30 June. In 2022 and 2023 the Black Sea Fleet lost seventeen warships, including the *Moskva*, the submarine *Rostov-on-Don*, and a total of four Ropucha and Saratov Tapir-class landing ships.[17]

Initially, Ukraine tackled the Russian Navy with coastal defence anti-ship cruise missile batteries.[18] Rather than fixed defences, like old coast defence artillery, the missile launchers were mobile and tied into a series of targeting radars and various manned and unmanned intelligence collection systems. These weapon systems prevented the Russian Navy and its naval infantry from closely blockading Ukraine's western coastline.[19]

Toward the end of the first year of the war, the Black Sea Fleet suffered serious losses from Ukrainian asymmetrical operations by air and sea drones. By 2023 small drone 'mosquito' attacks morphed into deadly swarms, sinking warships and destroying land-based AD missile batteries, radars and headquarters. Unable to make good its losses, the Black Sea Fleet was forced onto the defensive. Towards the second half of 2023 the mosquito swarm became a torrent as increasing cruise missiles, air and sea drone attacks and commando raids forced Russia to lift the blockade of Ukraine's western coastline, forcing the Fleet from its home base on the Crimean Peninsula to the eastern Black Sea.

Chapter 6

PMC Wagner and The Spetsnaz

During the first half of 2023 most of the Russian ground force battalions fought in the traditional reinforced motorized rifle battalion configuration, while the Ministry of Defence (MoD) became over reliant on private military companies such as (PMC) Wagner. Over the past decade the Kremlin had created thirty-seven PMCs, to provide deniability for hybrid war activity around the world. They were technically illegal under Russian law, but all PMCs were subordinate to the Kremlin. In theory, if a PMC leader fell out of favour, he could be arrested and sent to prison.[1] While PMC Wagner was the most famous and visible, the majority kept a low profile.

Allowed to recruit from prisons, by the autumn of 2022 Wagner Group was corps-size (50,000–80,000 men) and provided effective tactical command and control of its assault forces. The internal organization and C2 of its large sub-groups were unclear. Wagner's internal organization used the term 'detachment' to refer to companies, battalions and brigades. The media reported that detachments were as small as platoons with twenty operators and brigades as large as 3,000. Russian Army and Ukrainian battle reports and documents captured from Wagner indicated that Wagner took a page from the First World War German Army and formed stormtrooper assault battalions (detachments).

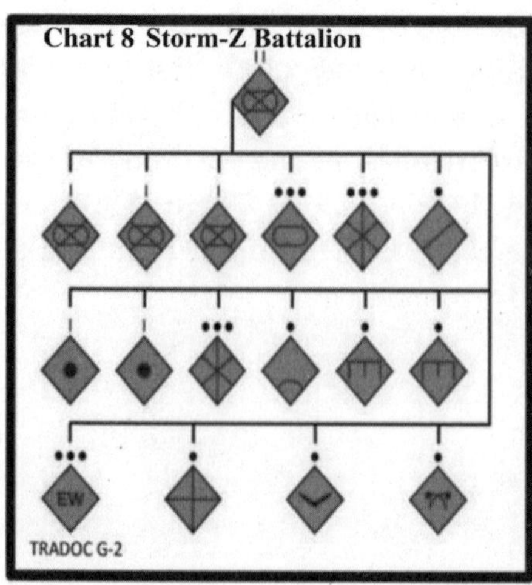

(U) The Storm-Z structure is an attempt to address difficulties experienced by the Russian Army during offensive operations in Ukraine. These units, in both form and function, mirror the assault engineer battalions used by the Soviet Army during WWII. The assault battalion is a battalion in name only, lacking staff and enablers such as sustainment and communications found in the Russian Motor Rifle Battalion or modular BTG. These units are organized around the 10-man capture team. Capture teams are supported by fires and armor organic to the assault company. In both Bakhmut and Advika, assault units have supported platoon- or company-sized advances of better trained and equipped Russian troops.

Source: US Army

Rather than 'wasting' trained contract operators, Wagner rounded out the assault battalions with recruited prisoners. The supporting infantry units were staffed by highly paid and trained Wagnerite mercenaries. The ill-equipped and poorly trained prisoners formed the core of the assault companies, but they were led by experienced contracted 'Wagnerites'.

A Wagner assault battalion (detachment) consisted of a headquarters and combat support company (HQ and CSC) manned mostly by trained Wagnerites, and two to three assault companies. The battalion HQ and CSC included: a tank platoon of three tanks, flamethrower section with twelve shoulder-fired PRO-A thermobaric rocket launchers, one towed D-30 122mm howitzer battery (six guns), one 2S9 self-propelled 120mm mortar battery (six vehicles), fire support group of two 12.7mm heavy machine guns (HMG) and two AGS-17 automatic grenade launchers, an ADA section of two ZU-23 autocannons, a drone section, combat engineer section, sniper/reconnaissance section, mobile electronic warfare section, medical section and vehicle recovery section (BREM-L recovery vehicle).[2]

Each assault company (detachment) contained a command group, two or three assault platoons, an armoured vehicle platoon, artillery platoon, fire support platoon, medical section and UAV/drone team. The assault platoon consisted of 12–15 soldiers led by an officer and was divided into four or five three-man teams: a command team, two tactical teams, an advance/scout team and a reserve fire support team. The armoured vehicle platoon normally included a tank and four BMPs or BMDs. The primary role of these vehicles was manoeuvrable direct fire support, not troop transport. The vehicles could be grouped together or assigned to assault platoons. Captured documents suggest that the armoured vehicles were deployed behind the assault platoons to protect their flanks.

Employing tanks singly instead of in sections of two or platoons of three or four violated the armour doctrine of every major power, including Russia. Numerous videos taken by Ukrainian drones depicting individual Russian tanks speeding to reinforce infantry positions were posted on the internet. In each case the unsupported tank and its crew met their death in a fireball as an ATGM, FPV drone or artillery round destroyed it. Wagner tank crews were better trained than Russian regulars and had a higher survival rate.

Wagner's company fire support group was a mix of two AGS-17s, two HMGs, two ATGMs and a sniper team. The artillery support platoon contained one D-30-towed 122mm howitzer or a 2S9 vehicle and two 82mm or 120mm mortar teams. A single howitzer normally stayed with the company HQ, and each assault platoon received a mortar team. RPO flamethrower teams from battalion were often attached to assault platoons, depending on the tactical situation.

Tactically, artillery fire from supporting artillery battalions covered the assault battalion's movement to contact. Assault platoons took advantage of tree lines and other cover (ditches, depressions, etc.) on the steppes and open fields, and in the ruins of cities, as they advanced on predetermined routes. A Wagner scout team would lead the platoon to locate mines, obstacles and defenders' flanks. Company armoured vehicles protected the flanks of the assault platoons and advanced ahead as the attack rolled forward. Wagner platoon commanders directed mortar fire. The AGS-17s deployed 600–1,700 metres behind the assault platoons and provided high-volume indirect fire and smoke to suppress defenders as the assault closed on trenches, bunkers or buildings.

Once supporting brigade or division artillery fire lifted and shifted toward the Ukrainian second defensive line, supporting fire was provided by RPGs, machine guns, grenade launchers and mortars. Under cover of supporting fire, assault teams stormed the trenches with small arms and grenades. Artillery fire on the deeper Ukrainian defences allowed the Wagner assault platoons to consolidate gains before a Ukrainian counter-attack.[3] A typical Wagner assault battalion attack plan would employ four to six assault platoons on a frontage of about three kilometres (1.8 miles). During a typical attack one assault platoon would gain a foothold in a defensive trench, large industrial building or multi-storey apartment complex. Once established they would be reinforced by Wagner reserves.

Attacks were coordinated by brigade as the assault battalions lacked a reserve. A battalion would only support a successful platoon with its heavy weapons. Assault battalions were followed by contracted Wagner supporting detachments. The supporting infantry detachments probably mustered 20–40 infantry supported by four tanks and/or 30–80 infantry, with two BMPs and/or two APCs. Ukrainian drones observed platoons of fifty Wagnerite mercenaries mounted in trucks deployed as a supporting force. This slow and methodical form of attack cost 4,000 KIA and 35,000 WIA Wagnerites, but had captured most of Bakhmut by 16 May 2023.[4]

Russian special forces were part of the Ministry of Defence and organized under the Military Intelligence Service (GRU). Other ministries, such as the FSB and Rosgvardia (Russian National Guard, an internal paramilitary police force) also had their own special forces units, collectively referred to by the West as 'Spetsnaz'. These units were highly trained, motivated, well equipped and as capable as US, UK and other NATO special operations forces.

Spetsnaz teams were in the first wave of the invasion in February 2022. Organized into special purpose brigades, with sub-units referred to as detachments, these brigades were found in the ground forces, Navy, and intelligence services. While organized and trained for clandestine missions, they were often committed to battle in the early months of the Special Operation as the motorized rifle units failed to achieve their objective. They were heavily engaged in combat in 2022 and 2023 and suffered accordingly.[5] Spetsnaz special capabilities were combat multipliers in the defence against Ukraine's 2023 summer counter-offensive. With their high-tech equipment they were essential in coordinating fire support and jamming Ukrainian drones.

The war quickly devolved into a positional fight, in which infantry in small groups advanced while supported by massive artillery fire. Tactical drones became critical for all branches and factions of the Russian ground forces to locate targets for massed artillery.

Chapter 7

The Ukrainian Armed Forces 2023

Through the sheer tenacity of its people, supported with weapons and ammunition from the West, Ukraine survived a conventional invasion by one of the greatest land powers in the world. With determined defence and a courageous counter-offensive, Ukrainian military forces destroyed the myth of Russian invincibility.

Although it was not without its own problems of corruption, the Ukrainian military united in the face of the Russian invasion. Ukraine had been preparing for war since the Donbas fighting in 2014/15 that had continued at a low intensity up to 2022. Through various programmes such as Partnership for Peace with NATO, US Military and California National Guard, Ukrainian regular ground and air force combat skills were enhanced.[1]

The Ukrainian military was divided administratively between the ground forces, Air Force, National Guard (NGU) and Navy. The ground forces were divided administratively under the Ministry of Defence into the Army, Airborne, Marines and Territorial Defence. Some units of the Special Forces were under the control of Ukrainian Intelligence. The National Guard fell under the Ministry of Interior. The International Legion battalions (worldwide volunteers) were divided between Ukrainian Intelligence and the Ministry of Defence.

Operationally, the ground forces were divided between four regional operational commands (OCs). The OCs provided the operational combat support and combat service support to units assigned to each region. Brigades and battalions were shuffled between OCs as the operational situation dictated. Experienced battle staffs capable of integrating battlefield operational systems (command and control, manoeuvre, fire support, intelligence, air defence, mobility/counter mobility/survivability, combat service support) were initially lacking. OCs provided command and control of combat operations within the four regions of Ukraine. They combined the functions of divisions and corps in a typical NATO force structure. OCs provided combat support and combat service support to manoeuvre units in their area of operations. Their organic combat support units included artillery, anti-air artillery and engineer brigades, signal regiments, reconnaissance intelligence and signal intelligence centres and electronic warfare battalions. Their organic combat service support units included a maintenance regiment, logistics and transportation battalions.

The main theatre of the war during 2023 was managed by OC-East. It had C2 over the Donbas and Zaporizhzhia Sectors and was the strategic and operational main effort. OC-South was a shaping operation, providing C2 for the Kherson/Dnipro Sector. OC-South was a direct threat to the flank of the 58th CAA defending Zaporizhzhia Sector and the entrance to the Crimean Peninsula. OC-Centre was responsible for defending Kyiv and parts of the northern border with Russia and Belarus. OC-West defended the remainder of the Belarus border and training and logistics centres in western Ukraine. The border with Belarus runs through the Pripyat Marshes, and invasion routes through the marshes were limited. The forested marshland, peatbogs, and swamps, even when frozen, hindered the movement of heavy equipment from north or south. These natural obstacles were reinforced with minefields, concrete obstacles and fortifications.[2]

OC-East commanded the Zaporizhzhia, Donetsk and Luhansk Sectors where most of the ground fighting was conducted. It controlled over seventy manoeuvre brigades at any one time. Providing C2 for such a large group would have been a herculean task, without intermediate headquarters to coordinate the operations of brigades fighting in any given regional battle.

OC-East was divided into four tactical groups. Strategic Group Tavrai under command of Brigadier Oleksandr Tarnavsky was the OC's main effort in the Zaporizhzhia Sector. It concentrated on the Orikhiv-Tokmak-Melitopl axis. Tactical Group Donetsk, under General Yuriy Sodol, was the strategic supporting effort, with its tactical main offensive along the Velyka-Novosilka axis while defending along the Avdiivka Sector. Strategic Group Khortezya, under Colonel General Oleksandr Syrskyi, was also a strategic secondary effort, while its tactical main effort was focused on the encirclement and recapture of Bakhmut. Tactical Group Lyman, under Brigadier Volodomyr Shvoral, was tasked with the defence of the Luhansk Sector.[3]

OC-South provided C2 for Tactical Group Kherson, commanded by Brigadier Myklailo Drapatdy, and Odesa Group under Major General Eduard Moskalyov. The Kherson Group held the west bank of the Dnipro River, from where the river entered the destroyed reservoir just south of Zaporizhzhia down to the Black Sea. The Odesa Group secured the grain export ports and protected Air Force ADA assets deployed to the region. It might have also provided some C2 for the aerial and sea drone strikes into Crimea and the eastern Black Sea.[4]

After ten months of high intensity combat, four corps headquarters were organized to provide C2 for the Ukrainian summer 2023 counter-offensive and

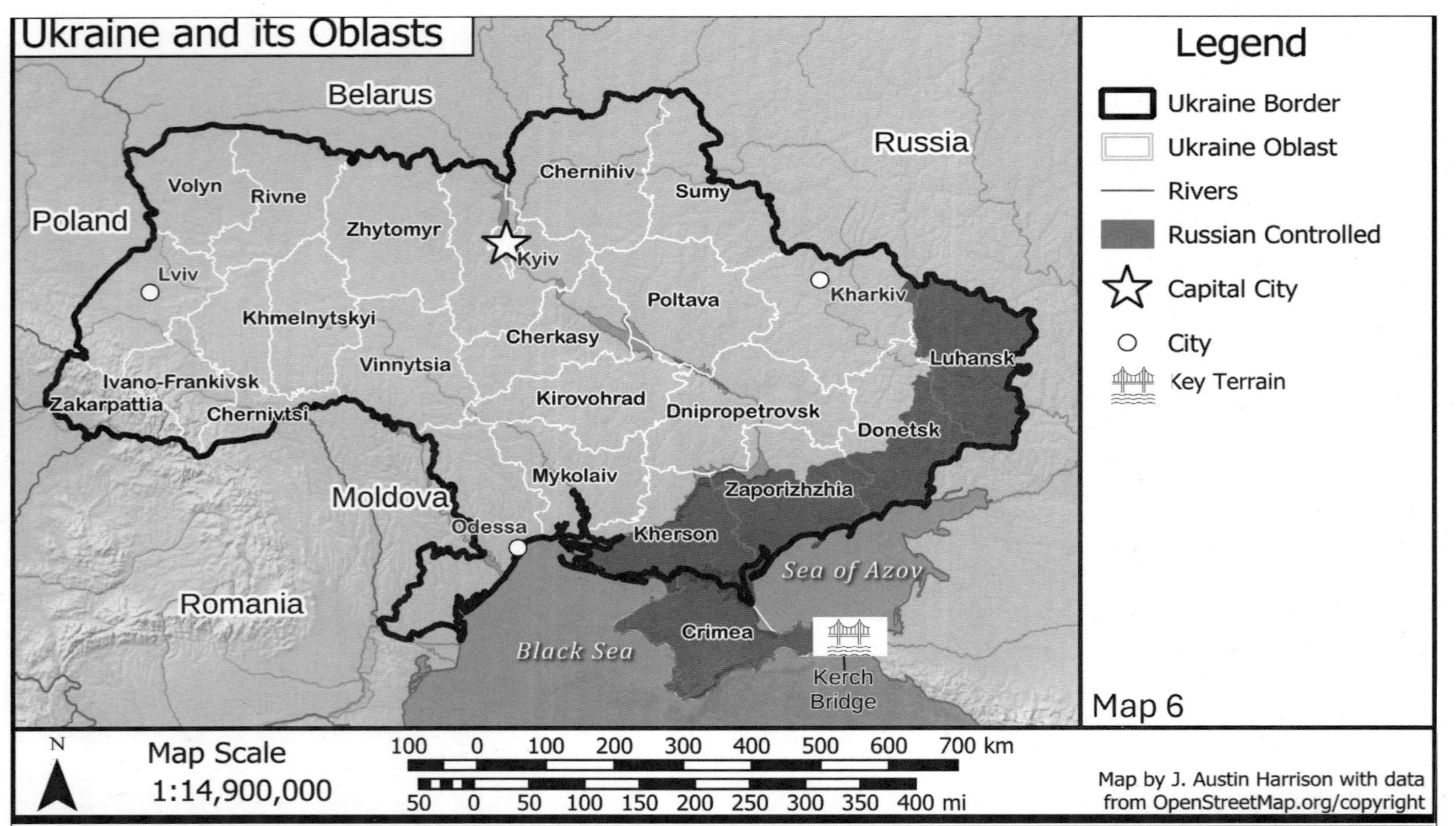
Ukraine and its Oblasts
Belarus
Russia
Poland
Volyn
Rivne
Zhytomyr
Kyiv
Chernihiv
Sumy
Lviv
Kharkiv
Poltava
Khmelnytskyi
Cherkasy
Vinnytsia
Luhansk
Ivano-Frankivsk
Zakarpattia
Chernivtsi
Kirovohrad
Dnipropetrovsk
Donetsk
Mykolaiv
Zaporizhzhia
Moldova
Odessa
Kherson
Sea of Azov
Romania
Crimea
Black Sea
Kerch
Bridge
Legend
Ukraine Border
Ukraine Oblast
Rivers
Russian Controlled
Capital City
City
Key Terrain
Map 6
N
Map Scale
1:14,900,000
100 0 100 200 300 400 500 600 700 km
50 0 50 100 150 200 250 300 350 400 mi
Map by J. Austin Harrison with data
from OpenStreetMap.org/copyright

to serve as intermediate operational headquarters. During the first half of 2023, IX, X, Marine and Airborne Corps were prepared for the counter-offensive.

The composition of IX Corps varied over 2023, averaging four mechanized, one tank, one artillery and one special purpose brigade with support battalions. The composition of X Corps averaged four mechanized brigades with support battalions. The Airborne Group or Maroon Tactical Group (46th Airmobile, 82nd Air Assault, 71st Jaeger Brigade and 132nd Separate Reconnaissance Battalion) was the third corps.[5] The IX and X Corps and Maroon Tactical Group would become the main strike force for the Ukrainian summer counter-offensive.

Reports from the front indicated that the more lightly equipped four Marine brigades (35th, 36th, 37th, 38th) fighting in the same small sector appeared to provide mutual support.[6] Two months into the summer counter-offensive, the Ukrainians massed all four of their Marine Brigades on a 16 km (10 mile) front along the Mokri Yaly River valley. The 35th, 36th, 37th and 38th Marine Brigades were organized and equipped similarly to the ground force's mechanized brigades but were more lightly armed.[7] These Marine Brigades each contained three motorized infantry battalions, a tank company or battalion, an artillery group and combat support and combat service support battalions. The 35th Marine Brigade differed in that it had five motorized infantry battalions instead of three. The newest brigades, 37th and 38th, were created in February 2023 and were the most lightly armed. The 37th was equipped with French AMX-10RC reconnaissance vehicles instead of tanks, and MRAP armoured trucks instead of IFVs or APCs. The 38th was equipped with T-72EA tanks and MARP and HMMWV armoured trucks.

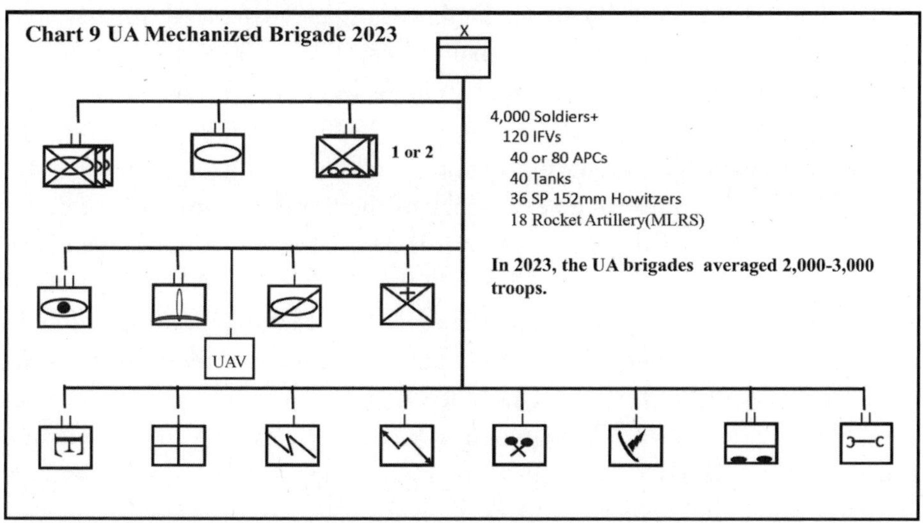

The older 35th was armed with T-80BV, T-64BV and a mix of Soviet-era BMP-1s, MTLBs and western MRAP armoured trucks.[8] With the exception of the 35th, Marine brigades were equipped with lighter-wheeled APCs, some of which were amphibious. In late summer 2023, the Marine Corps was transferred to OC-South and deployed along the Dnipro River near Kherson.

When Russia invaded, the Ukrainian Army fielded twenty-seven active manoeuvre and four artillery brigades. An additional seven manoeuvre and two artillery brigades were in the reserve. The Airborne branch fielded seven manoeuvre brigades and one artillery brigade. The Marines consisted of three manoeuvre brigades, one artillery and one rocket artillery brigade. The National Guard of Ukraine (NGU) fielded one manoeuvre brigade and several detachments deployed across Ukraine. In total these brigades fielded 114 combined arms battalions (CABs), and over thirty-eight artillery battalions, organic to the manoeuvre brigades. The combat battalions were categorized as mechanized infantry, motorized infantry or tank, regardless of which branch of the ground forces the brigade was administratively attached to. In addition, twenty-five Territorial Defence brigades served as auxiliaries and front-line units.

In March 2023, the Ukrainian ground forces (Army, Territorial, National Guard, Airborne, Marine, International Legions, Volunteers and Special Forces) fielded over 115 combat brigades, augmented by over 100 independent battalions. Included in the total were seven tank brigades and sixteen artillery brigades, with most of the motorized and mechanized brigades containing a tank company or battalion along with one to three tactical mortar or artillery battalions.[9]

By 1 January 2023 the Territorial Defence Brigades expanded from twenty-five to thirty-one, plus an additional twenty-five independent battalions. Initially, the Territorial brigades and battalions were lightly armed[10] In theory, the brigades provided rear area security and law enforcement. However, the Kyiv, Chernihiv, Kharkiv, Mariupol, Sumy, Luhansk, Donetsk, Zaporizhzhia and Mykolayiv brigades were in the thick of the fighting from the first day of the invasion. From April 2022 the veteran Territorial light infantry brigades and battalions were deployed to the fighting in the Donbas with ATGMS, grenade launchers and other light infantry weapons. The Territorials initially fought as auxiliaries to the heavier brigades. Both the 110th (Zaporizhzhia Black Cossacks) and 112th Territorial Defence Brigades were noted in dispatches for their fighting ability.[11] Recognizing a weakness in C2, the TDF command established a 'School of Captains' to improve the proficiency of platoon, company and battalion commanders. Captains often commanded battalions.

Private donations improved Territorial soldiers' kit.[12] To all intents and purposes the frontline Territorial brigades were combat veterans and the equal of regular soldiers in all but name. Only nine Territorial brigades were performing rear area security by 2023, mostly assigned to OC-West. The remainder of the Territorials fought as regular combat battalions and brigades, many upgraded to mechanized or motorized formations and equipped accordingly.[13]

The Ukrainian National Guard (NGU) was in the thick of the fighting from the first day of the invasion. Through the efforts of Major General (retd) David Baldwin, former Adjutant General of the State of California and Commander of the California National Guard, the NGU was included in defence planning with the Ministry of Defence before the invasion.[14]

The Ukrainian National Guard organized eight new storm brigades totalling 40,000 soldiers in the winter of 2023 to support the nine new army brigades created for the counter-offensive.[15] These formations included soldiers and police from the National Guard, National Police and State Border Service. Each brigade had a large core of experienced combat veterans who had been fighting on the frontlines since the Russians invaded. Their ranks were filled by volunteers. The brigades were divided into Police and Guard brigades. A volunteer joining the Lyut Brigade became a policeman, those joining the Stalevyi Cordon Brigade served as a border guards, and volunteers with the six remaining brigades became National Guard soldiers. The NGU trained its soldiers. Unlike the California Army National Guard, which had a Partner for Peace relationship with the NGU, Ukraine's Guard soldiers were full-time; before the war they provided internal security and border protection.[16]

Unlike the new Army brigades, the combat veteran Guard officers, sergeants and soldiers conducted the training of new volunteers. These soldiers received several months of training before their units were sent to the frontline. The significant difference between joining the Army and the NGU was that Guard soldiers were in effect joining the Ukrainian civil service. They had opportunity for free education at a university during their term of service, an annual vacation and, as in the Army, earned a pension after twenty-five years.[17]

About 2.5 per cent of each brigade were female soldiers.[18] Police brigade volunteers were required to pass a test on their knowledge of the law.[19] Each brigade took on an honorific such as 'Border of Steel', 'Hurricane', 'Spartan', 'Chervona Kalyna', 'Frontier', Rage, 'Azov' and 'Kara Dag' (a mountain in Crimea). Valerly Padytel, Commander of the Border of Steel Brigade, led Guardsmen in the defence of occupied Mariupol. He was captured but was freed in a prisoner exchange in September 2022.[20]

NGU started recruiting, organizing, and training the new Guard formations in January/February 2023. The brigades differed slightly in their organization.

The average brigade contained an HQ and HQ company, three or four motorized or mechanized infantry battalions, a tank company, artillery, anti-aircraft defence battalions and a reconnaissance company. In addition, each brigade contained combat service and combat support companies.

During the counter-offensive, the Bureviy and Rubizh Brigades were deployed to the Luhansk Sector, while the Spartan, Kara Dag and Chervona Kalyna brigades were deployed as frontline units in OC-East. Other units operated in the Sumy region hunting subversives and Russian infiltrators.[21]

As the battles raged in the autumn of 2022, through winter and into spring 2023, Ukraine prepared for a major spring/summer counter-offensive. In preparation, nine new mechanized or motorized brigades were formed. To equip these brigades the Ukrainians requested 300 modern tanks, 600–700 IFVs and 500 artillery systems from their allies. Even if the requested equipment had been provided promptly, the brigades would still have been equipped with a mix of old Soviet and modern Western weapons. The new brigades were organized like a standard Ukrainian formation. On paper each infantry brigade had three to four mechanized or motorized infantry battalions, one tank, two artillery and one MRLS battalion, with additional combat support and combat service companies and battalions. To fully equip a new brigade required 120–160 IFV/APCs or armoured trucks, 40 tanks, 36 howitzers and 18 MRLS. A tank brigade required 120 tanks, 40 IFVs, 36 howitzers and 18 MRLS. In total, the nine new brigades required 480 tanks, 1,120 IFV/APCs or armoured trucks, 360 howitzers and 178 MRLS. Allied pledges of equipment would satisfy most of these requirements, but a

Chart 10. Ukrainian Brigades Raised for the Counter-offensive

- **116th Mechanized Brigade**: T-64BV Tanks, BMP-1 & *Cougar MRAP* , 2S1 (122mm) and AS-90 Howitzers
- **117th Mechanized Brigade**: *PT-91 (Polish T-72)Tanks*, MT-LB APC, *AS-90* and D30 Howitzers
- **118th Mechanized Brigade:** T-72 Tanks, BMP-1, ***M109 and FH70 Howitzers***
- **32nd Mechanized Brigade:** T-64BV Tanks, *M2 Bradley, M113*, MT-LB, 2S1 Howitzers
- **23rd Mechanized Brigade:** T-64BV Tanks, *MRAPS*, BM-21 MLRS
- **32nd Mechanized Brigade:** *Leopard 2* & 72 Tanks, BMP-2 & ***M113***, M119 Howitzers
- **82nd Airborne Brigade:** *Challenger 2 Tanks, Marder, Stryker, M109 Howitzers*
- **37th Marine Brigade:** *AMX 10 Recon Tanks, MRAPs, D30, M109 Howitzers*
- **47th Mechanized Brigade:** *Leopard 2, S-55s Tanks, M2 Bradley* & BMP-1, *M109 How.*, BM-21 MLRS

Italicize =NATO Supplied. Some of the Soviet era weapons are also NATO supplied.
Source: https://militaryland.net/ukraine/armed-forces/23rd-mechanized-brigade/

high percentage of the equipment did not arrive until after the summer 2023 counter-offensive commenced. With this shortfall in Western equipment, some of the new brigades were equipped with Soviet-era equipment.[22]

Brigades that received NATO equipment and training grabbed the headlines, but the Ukrainians created additional brigades based on their continuing combat experience. The 3rd and 5th Assault Brigades were examples of first-rate combat units formed with minimal training assistance from NATO.

Based upon lessons learned by the hard-fighting Azov Territorial Defence regiment, the 3rd (Azov) Assault Brigade was created on 9 March 2023. The Brigade had a core of experienced combat veterans who had been fighting the Russians since 2014 as an Azov NGU formation.[23] They developed successful infantry and artillery assault tactics, incorporating elements of combined arms tactics, and conducted their own internal training.[24] The 3rd Assault Brigade made world headlines when Bakhmut was captured on 21 May 2023. On the same day the 3rd Assault Brigade attacked the high ground on the southern flank of the city. Using infantry-artillery assault tactics with tanks in support, the Brigade stayed in the headlines by slowly pushing the Russian lines east.

The 3rd Assault Brigade's four mechanized battalions were mounted in US M-113, BMP-2, YPR-765 and NATO MRAP armoured vehicles. Two battalions were named 1st and 2nd Assault Battalions and two were named 1st and 2nd Mechanized Battalions. All four were similarly organized and equipped. The tank battalion included T-90A and M-72M tanks. The brigade contained two air reconnaissance drone units (Terra and Kryla), and a strike drone unit (Hornet).[25]

The 5th Separate Assault Brigade was created in February 2023 when the 5th Assault Regiment and 24th Assault 'Aidar' Battalion were combined. Its commander, Pavlo Palisa, had attended the US Command and General Staff College. The Brigade was organized like the 3rd Separate Assault Brigade with 1st and 2nd Mechanized Battalions, 1st Assault Battalion, 24th Separate Assault 'Aidar' Battalion, Tank Battalion (T-64s), Artillery Group (two SP howitzer and MRLS battalions) and additional combat support and service support battalions and companies.[26] Like the other successful brigades created by combining independent veteran battalions and regiments, the 3rd and 5th Separate Assault Brigades did not directly benefit from NATO training, but successfully employed combined arms tactics.

Other brigades were led by veterans tempered by a year of heavy fighting. A few of the surviving leaders of these brigades had been trained at the US Command and General Staff College or at a base outside of Lviv before the war. The US Army and/or Army National Guards of the various US States trained Ukrainian leaders, especially NCOs, at this centre over the previous ten years. Combining US training with Ukrainian operational procedures and combat experience, successful brigade and battalion commanders adapted quickly to changing battlefield conditions.

On 23 June 2023, the *New York Times* claimed that the nine brigades had been transformed into 'a NATO-standard fighting force' but were having difficulty breaching Russian defences.[27] The naivety of this statement by a major world newspaper underscored the media's delusion as to the training level 40,000 Ukrainian soldiers had received at the NATO training bases throughout Europe. The nine brigades in question were not fully trained to NATO standards.

The NATO training received by Ukrainian soldiers was severely truncated. The 40,000 Ukrainian soldiers received between five and ten weeks of training in a NATO country.[28] The training was excellent and the trainers skilled, but cadre lacked sufficient time to train the Ukrainians properly.

A miscommunication between Ukrainians and NATO training bases resulted in mostly new, untrained soldiers lacking combat experience being sent for training. NATO and allied trainers had expected the Ukrainian soldiers to be combat veterans. This misunderstanding reduced the effectiveness of the training programmes and the combat readiness of the new brigades. The soldiers sent for training were issued complete sets of kit. The Ukrainians praised the hands-on programme that highlighted tactical medical training, something which was virtually unknown in post-Soviet armies. The training for modern warfare failed, however, to take into account that Ukraine was involved in First World War-style trench combat even though equipped with twenty-first century technology. The combat veteran NATO instructors had not experienced a war of attrition. These issues were compounded by the lack of translators with a military background, resulting in communication difficulties.

Additionally, there were some cultural issues. A NATO soldier believes that there will be air support, artillery and de-mining operations before the infantry advances. On the steppes of Ukraine there was insufficient cover and concealment to apply NATO small unit tactics. At the individual soldier level, training emphasis was placed on urban combat rather than trench warfare, assault group tactics or coordination with artillery and drones. Finally, NATO and allied trainers had never operated in an environment where every action was visible to enemy reconnaissance and kamikaze drones.

The length of training received depended upon the job the soldier was assigned. Patriot Missile crews received a 10-week crash course at US Fort Sill, Oklahoma.[29] US M1A1 Abrams tank crews received ten weeks of training. Training included basic weapons instruction and how to maintain and repair equipment during combat operations.[30] Twenty thousand Ukrainians received a five-week course in the UK.[31] In comparison, a British Army recruit goes through fourteen weeks of basic training, a US Marine receives thirteen weeks, a US soldier receives ten, a German soldier eight, and a French soldier twelve. Even without close order drill and other aspects irrelevant to the Ukrainian ground force requirements, five weeks was barely sufficient to impart basic survival skills, let alone the complexities of squad and platoon tactics. In the short time available the UK training programme focused on fieldcraft, weapons skills and tactics. About 11 per cent of the soldiers trained in the UK had prior military experience, and their average age was thirty-four. They were probably the pool from which squad leaders were drawn.[32]

NATO training provided the nine assault brigades with the individual basic skills required to operate their weapons and survive on the battlefield. The training did not bring the new combat brigades to the point where they could be certified as combat ready by NATO standards, or even to the training standards of the Ukrainian combined arms battalions on the eve of the war.

By comparison, during the first quarter of the twenty-first century, a fully trained, equipped and manned federalized US Army National Guard heavy brigade (Bradleys IFVs and Abrams Tanks) post-mobilization processing included six to sixteen weeks of collective combined arms training before deployment to a war zone.[33] In a final comparison, 900 Ukrainian Marine commandos received six months of training from the UK Marine commandos. The Ukrainian commandos came from varied backgrounds, many being civilians with no prior military service. They were fully trained to NATO standards when they returned home.[34]

Drones became vital for groundforce operations. They were critical for reconnaissance, targeting and strike missions at the operational and tactical level. Drone sections and platoons were organic to formations from battery and company to brigade. The battlefield became a chess board, with every major ground movement observable in real time.

The Ukrainians had equipped and fielded eleven UAV Strike Companies by January 2023. The companies did not need specialized armoured vehicles but could be transported in standard civilian pickup trucks or SUVs. While large and small drones were common in all manoeuvre and fire support battalions, the UAV strike companies' mission was to attack individual Russian soldiers and armoured vehicles. The smaller drones were equipped to drop hand and anti-tank grenades, while larger UAVs carried 81/82mm or 120mm mortar rounds.

Small tactical drones were initially nothing more than converted civilian toys, often internationally crowdfunded. As drones came to dominate the battlefield, the Ukrainian defence industry began mass production. The

Minister of Digital Transformation, Mykhailo Fedorov, lifted regulations hindering the development and production of locally made drones.[35]

Counter-drone systems utilized by both sides fell into two general categories, kinetic and non-kinetic. Kinetic systems included everything from standard rifles and machine guns to autocannon and missiles. More sophisticated systems equipped light armoured vehicles with sensors and radars to track and engage drones with autocannon or missiles. Most of these systems, like the *flakpanzers* from Germany, were old Cold War weapons.

Non-kinetic systems disrupted the drones in flight by jamming their control and navigation signals. Small systems could be mounted on vehicles to disrupt the signals of an attacking kamikaze drone. These systems were low-powered, creating a small jamming bubble around a target. Larger systems could jam larger areas, but since they disrupted all frequencies, coordination with the operators of friendly drones was required. They were vulnerable to enemy EW direction systems and, when located, easily targeted by standard artillery ammunition. These systems were extremely expensive and their supply was limited within both side's arsenals. 'Anti-drone' rifles were developed by both sides for use at the tactical level. These short-range non-kinetic systems allowed an individual soldier to disrupt a signal controlling the drone with a directed radio pulse.[36]

On the strategic level, a combination of aerial drones and missiles struck targets in Russian-occupied Ukraine and could also strike deep into Russia as far as Moscow. The Ukrainian Navy in the Black Sea had been reduced to a mosquito fleet of small fast surface vessels donated by allies. It compensated for this deficiency with fast, long-range sea drones. When these were combined with air drone and missile attacks, Russia's Black Sea Fleet suffered severely.

The Ukrainian Air Force (UAAF) established Air Operational Commands with boundaries coinciding with the ground OCs. ADA assists were divided between defending strategic targets such as cities and industrial centres. The ADA defended operational targets including supply depots and command posts. Tactical targets such as troop concentrations were defended by ground forces AD.

Despite the overwhelming numbers of the VKS, the UAAF survived over a year of combat and in 2023 remained a viable deterrent preventing Russia from gaining air dominance over the battlefield. The Ukrainian Air Force was responsible for defending the air over Ukraine, providing ADA coverage and striking strategic targets inside Russia. Russia never achieved air superiority. The UAAF continued to conduct limited strikes in support of ground forces and was able to strike targets deep within Russia with unmanned aerial drones. Lacking modern jet fighters, the UAAF pilots were at a severe disadvantage

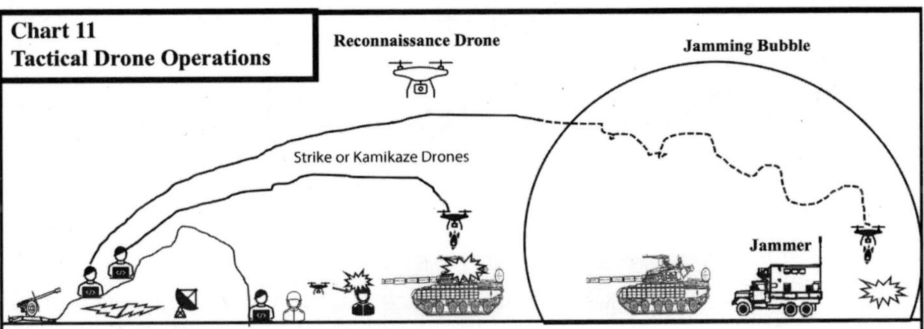

Chart 11
Tactical Drone Operations

1. RU armoured column moves to attack UA positions.
2. UA Reconnaissance Drone detects Russian attack.
3. UA Strike and Kamikaze drones attack RU tanks and infantry
4. RU jammer disables some attacking drones.
5. Direction finding antennae locate jammer and relays coordinates to artillery.
6. UA artillery targets and destroys RU jammer

when faced with Russian interceptors and long-range targeting radars and anti-air missiles. In addition, only the limited number of Su-24 (Fencer) jets in the UAAF could launch long-range Storm Shadow air-to-ground missiles. GPS-guided glide bombs were more accurate than their Russian equivalents, but the UAAF generated fewer sorties per day due to the threat of Russian Su-27 (Flanker) and Su-35 (Flanker-E) interceptors with long-range radars, missiles and advanced electronic defences.

During the second half of the year the US authorized NATO and other allies to provide F-16 jet fighters to Ukraine. This late decision delayed the training of Ukrainian pilots and ground crews, and consequently the aircraft were not delivered until 2024.

At the beginning of the second year of the war the Ukrainian military focused its efforts on obtaining training and weapons from its allies and expanding its ground combat force. As more and more drones entered the battlefield, obtaining operational tactical surprise became impossible. Never before had drones impacted a war to such a degree. The battlefield truly became a chess board, on which every movement by both combatants was instantly observable.

Chapter 8

The Russian Strategic 2023 War Plan

After the initial invasion failed to quickly achieve its objectives, General Sergei Surovikin was appointed commander of Putin's 'Special Operation' in October 2022. He supervised the Russian withdrawal from the regional capital of Kherson to the east bank of the Dnipro River. This action was well-planned and executed under heavy pressure from the Ukrainian counter-offensive. The withdrawal shortened Russia's battle line and freed elite VDV paratroopers and Naval Infantry stationed to defend the Kherson bridgehead. Militarily, it was the correct move and saved some of Russia's best units from isolation and capture. However, politically, liberating Kherson in November 2022 gave the Ukrainians a morale boost and justified the massive expenditure of money and materiel by its allies.

Russia lost three major battles, Kyiv, Kherson and Luhansk, and suffered extremely heavy casualties and losses of equipment. Considering the situation on the ground, General Sergei Surovikin went onto the defensive in all sectors except Bakhmut. Fortifications were built on the front, along the expected axis of advance of a Ukrainian counter-offensive. Some defensive trenches were constructed inside Russia to protect the Motherland. Additional defences were built along the beaches of Crimea. Surovikin was heavily criticised by the worldwide media for taking these precautions.

Wagner Group and VDV units kept the pressure on Bakhmut. While Ukrainians made small advances at Kreminna, Surovikin maintained the missile and drone bombardment of Ukrainian civilian infrastructure. Russian reconstitution efforts proceeded as units were rebuilt with Mobiks. Russia suffered fewer losses in December 2022 as fewer frontal attacks were launched along the frontlines. Surovikin adjusted the frontlines, giving up positions that were exposed and difficult to re-supply. He appeared to be implementing a defensive strategy that was more in line with Russia's actual military capability on the ground.

Surovikin's strategy of defence, reorganization, reconstitution and limited offensive operations against Bukhmut was not in line with the Kremlin's political strategy. Surovikin's rebuilding of the Russian Army appeared to give the initiative to the Ukrainians, and his close relationship with Wagner

Group CEO Yevgeny Prigozhin also undermined the confidence in him of his superiors in the Kremlin.

Prigozhin's mercenaries had fought to capture Bakhmut since the summer of 2022. After recruiting prison inmates, it was estimated that by December 2022 Wagner Group had 50,000–80,000 soldiers fighting in Ukraine, 30 per cent of whom were highly paid contractors.[1] This division-size mercenary group was focused on storming Bakhmut with frontal attacks, resulting in extremely heavy casualties and expenditure of artillery ammunition for gains of territory measured in metres. During the worst days in December, Wagner units would suffer as many as 1,000 casualties a day. It was estimated that by 24 February 2023 Wagner Group had suffered 30,000 casualties, 9,000 of which were KIA, and that 90 per cent of the casualties were suffered by ex-prisoners.[2] By the end of December 2022 Wagner Group and Russian Army units had stalled before the gates of Bakhmut.

General Valery Gerasimov, Chief of Staff of the Russian General Staff, convinced Putin that Surovikin was being too defensive, and that he would not be able to secure the political objective of capturing the Donbas. Putin agreed, and on or about 12 January 2022, Gerasimov replaced Surovikin as Commander of the Special Operation in Ukraine. Gerasimov maintained the strategic bombing campaign and fortification operations, but ground attacks increased, along with increasing numbers of casualties and vehicle and materiel losses.

Gerasimov took command as the Russian 2023 winter offensive commenced. Russia had deployed 320,000 soldiers to Ukraine by January 2023, and had 150,000 Mobiks and volunteers at training sites within Russia.[3] These figures did not include a further 120,000 conscripts training inside Russia. The western media expected a grand mechanized assault like that of February 2022's initial invasion but on a smaller scale. It was envisioned that a pincer movement would aim to cut off the Donbas. The southern arm would attack north from Vulhledar and the northern arm would attack from Luhansk Oblast through Lyman and Izyum, then turn south, linking up with the southern arm near Pokrovsk. Frontal attacks from the Donetsk and Luhansk would pin Ukrainian forces inside a pocket. Renewed attacks toward the cities of Sumy and Kharkiv were anticipated.[4]

The media's predication failed to take into account that while Russia was rich in manpower in January 2023 it was poor in armoured vehicles and trucks.[5] It no longer had the tools for grand sweeping manoeuvres, but it did have the artillery ammunition and manpower for attritional warfare. In January 2023, Gerasimov chose the operational tactic of continuous battle along the front instead of an operational pause to rebuild his brigades. With its superiority in manpower, Russia chose to retain the initiative by continuing to attack with poorly trained formations.

The Russian 2023 winter offensive did not conduct any shaping operations in support of its ground manoeuvres. They did not even attempt deception of their main effort. The ongoing missile and drone bombardment of Ukrainian cities and infrastructure continued unabated, having little impact on the Ukrainian frontline defenders. Periodically a bombardment would destroy a Ukrainian ammunition or supply dump, causing a spectacular explosion captured by the media. Yet these successful strikes failed to undermine the Ukrainian defence of any sector. Russian air operations near the frontline intensified, employing guided gravity bombs. In short, the Russian 2023 winter offensive was a series of uncoordinated frontal attacks throwing battalions and brigades against fortified cities of the Donbas. The defending Ukrainians expended men and ammunition to hold the line and limit the invaders' advance. Even if the Russians had managed a successful penetration, they lacked an exploitation force in reserve to take advance of the breach. Meanwhile, the Ukrainians had established second echelon brigades to contain any penetration.

This operational attrition tactic was first employed on a massive scale during the American Civil War by the Union General Ulysses S. Grant between May 1864 and April 1865. The Union Army had not scored any significant victories, but by a series of inconclusive linked engagements managed to wear down the Confederate Army of Northern Virginia. The overwhelming number of men, weapons and supplies fielded by the Union Army of the Potomac could not be matched by the Confederacy. In coordination with Grant's continuous year-long offensive, Union General William Tecumseh Sherman's army destroyed Confederate logistics. Sherman's army conducted a scorched earth raid through Georgia beginning on 15 November 1864 and ending on 21 December 1864. The Union army burned a swathe 160 km (100 miles) wide and 480 km (298 miles) long, culminating with the capture of the Port of Savannah on 21 December 1864. Sherman's Army turned north on 1 January 1865 and torched a path toward the Carolinas to link up with Grant in Virginia. As he marched, Sherman encountered then overwhelmed Confederate General Joseph E. Johnston's army at the Battle of Bentonville in North Carolina. Defeated, Johnston unconditionally surrendered.

Final defeat of the Confederacy occurred on 26 April 1865, two weeks after Confederate General Robert E. Lee surrendered the Army of Northern Virginia at Appomattox Courthouse (Virginia) on 9 April 1865.[6] It would take the ruined economies of the southern states sixty years to recover.[7]

The operational tactic of continuous battle developed by Grant and Sherman required superior numbers of men and materiel to keep the opponent decisively engaged in a battle of attrition, while simultaneously destroying their logistical support. Imperial Russian and Soviet military academies studied the American Civil War in detail, and lessons learned from that war can be directly traced to the development of Soviet doctrine.[8]

During the First World War Battle of Verdun (21 February to 18 December 1916) the Imperial German Army attempted a similar strategy against the French. The Germans were unable to cut the French supply lines, but the German General Staff assumed that seizing or threatening to capture Verdun would force the French to expend their reserves in a counter-attack to recapture the region. They believed that the French would conduct frontal attacks against the entrenched German infantry, who were supported by artillery. In this insane battle of attrition, the Germans believed they could inflict heavy casualties on the French at a ratio of 5:2. At the end of the battle the French were estimated to have suffered 348,000–378,000 casualties and the Germans 337,000. Experts debate the exact numbers but agree that there were equally tremendous losses on both sides.[9] Eventually defeated, the Germans were forced back to their February 1916 starting lines. Given the German inability to cut the French supply lines, this battle of attrition between two equal adversaries could only end in a stalemate.

Gerasimov's staff was aware of the capabilities of the Russian Army and its auxiliaries. The Battalion Tactical Groups (BTGs) had failed as a tactical combined arms organization. The BTGs were replaced with motorized rifle battalions, the majority of which were not fully equipped with armoured vehicles and tanks. The VDV paratroopers and Naval Infantry brigades had been reconstituted during the first year of the war but appeared to have been re-equipped with sufficient armoured vehicles and tanks. By the beginning of the second year many of these elite formations had again suffered heavy casualties and had again been rebuilt, but with Mobiks, and were only nominally elite. Less prestigious units were motorized brigades in name only, being understrength and lacking sufficient IFVs and APCs to mount all their infantry. The top-tier Russian Army, VDV and Naval Infantry units were no longer fully combat-capable, while Wagner Group detachments remained effectively operating as an assault division, mustering between 50,000 and 80,000 combatants. Needless to say, Wagner Group supplied the main Russian effort during the Russian winter offensive.

With the capability of the Russian ground forces in mind, Gerasimov's staff developed an offensive plan with the limited objective of capturing Luhansk and Donetsk Oblasts, while digging fortifications and defending along the Kherson and Zaporizhzhia Sectors. The main effort remained the politically important capture of Bakhmut. If Wagner and VDV paratroopers could

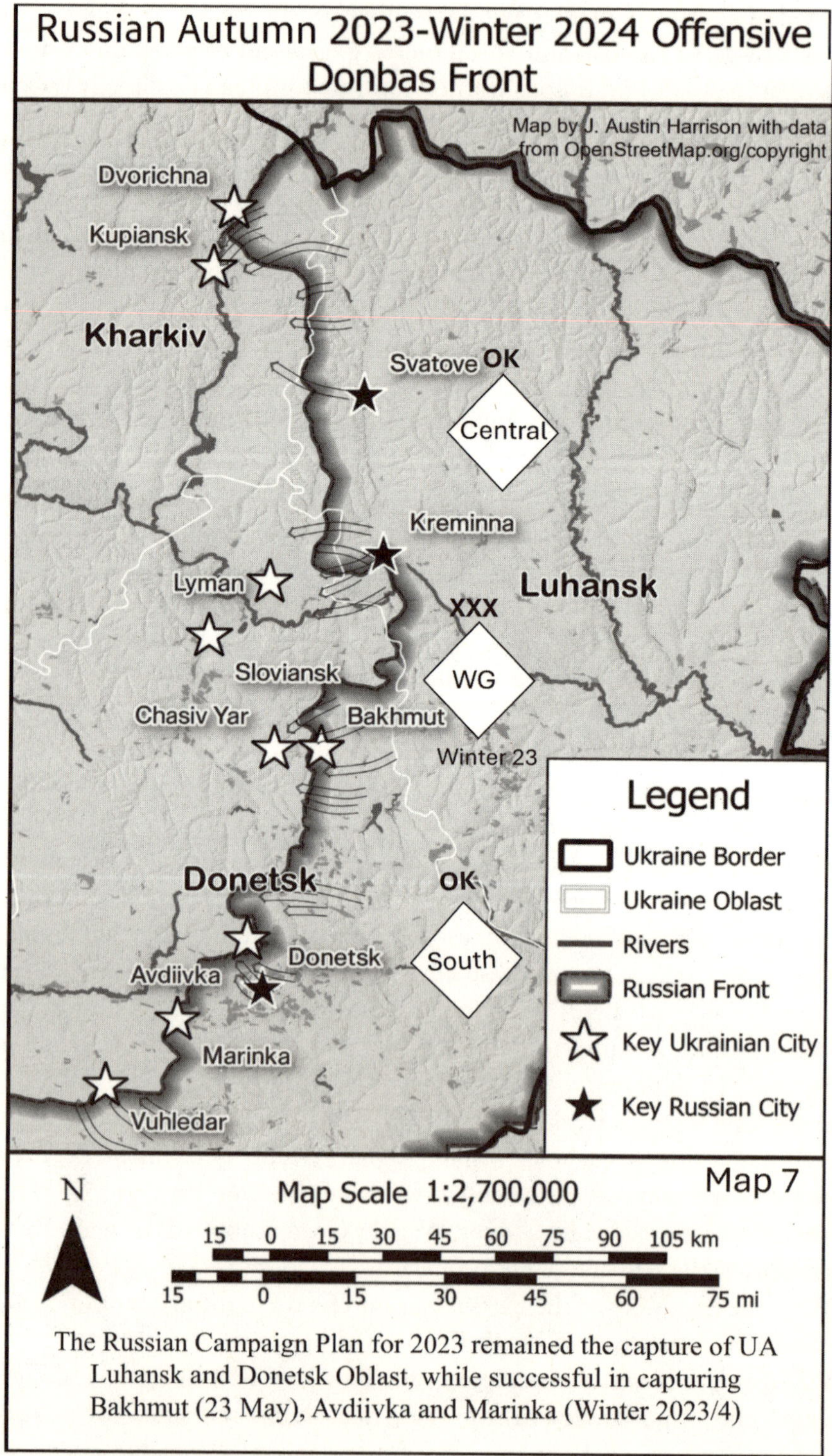

The Russian Campaign Plan for 2023 remained the capture of UA Luhansk and Donetsk Oblast, while successful in capturing Bakhmut (23 May), Avdiivka and Marinka (Winter 2023/4)

promptly capture the town, Russian forces could turn north and unhinge the Ukrainian Kreminna-Svoatove line. In Luhansk Oblast, Gerasimov envisioned OK-West breaking through the Ukrainian Kreminna-Svoatove line to recapture Lyman. He placed fully equipped brigades in the Donetsk Sector aimed at the fortified towns of Avdiivka, Marinka and Vuhledar. If successful during the winter freeze at Vuhledar, Russian mechanized forces would be in position to threaten the rear of Avdiivka 50 km (31 miles) away. They also would be in position to threaten Marinka 23 km (14 miles) to the north.

After ten months of gruelling high-intensity combat the invaders failed to capture any of the fortified towns. Avdiivka is a mere 13 km (8 miles) from Russian-occupied Donetsk City, the capital of Donetsk People's Republic. It was only 6 km (3.7 miles) from Donetsk international airport. Marinka was a mere 3 km (1.8 miles) from the DPR's border.[10]

Gerasimov apparently believed that the winter offensive could capture or destroy these fortified cities by repeating the failed battle plans of the first year by adding glide bombs in support of his ground forces.

Gerasimov shifted supplies and priorities but failed to significantly alter troop deployments. Elite units were assigned assault missions in the various sectors, and regular BARS and Mobik battalions were given defensive and support roles. Gerasimov expected to capture the Donbas with tactics that had failed during the previous ten months. He was dead wrong.

Putin entered January 2023 on the horns of a dilemma. Of his five strategic objectives he had only accomplished one, the establishment of the land bridge between internationally recognized Russian territory and the occupied Crimean Peninsula. Due to the defeats and heavy attrition the Russian military had suffered in 2022, the Kremlin no longer had the ground combat power to conduct major offensive combat operations in all sectors of the battlefield. In hindsight it was clear that Putin and his generals had a realistic understanding of the situation on the ground; however, they lacked a clear picture of their ground forces' capability and failed to appreciate the tenacity of the defenders. They decided to go on the strategic offensive to capture the Donbas while defending the Kherson and Zaporizhzia Sectors.

Having taken over direct command of the theatre in January 2023 with the mission of pushing the Ukrainians back over the administrative borders of Donetsk and Luansk Oblasts by 31 March 2023,[11] Gerasimov announced on 22 December 2022 that his forces would focus their efforts on seizing Donetsk Oblast.

The 2023 winter offensive suffered from a lack of operational planning. The Russian generals apparently lacked the fighting skills of their grandfathers, honed during the Great Patriotic War. Intelligence-gathering and planning, as well as preparation of the battlefield (IPB), were ignored. An effective IPB plan would have collected, organized and processed intelligence utilized in targeting and decision-making. Asset intelligence collection ranged from foot patrols to satellite. The IBP process of templating terrain and enemy capability lead to identification of enemy positions in sufficient detail for targeting. A properly prepared IBP would identify weakness in defences where manoeuvre forces could take advantage. The Russian IPB was flawed, or the results were ignored. Instead of attacking weak spots on the long line of contact, Russian generals ordered direct assaults on fortified cities that they had been attempting to capture for twelve months.

An assault plan for fortified objectives requires: adequate intelligence regarding the fortifications, supporting artillery and air assets, combat engineers to reduce or breach obstacles, chemical obscuration (smoke) concealing breaching teams, and assault force (boots on the ground) to capture the objective. But Russian military culture hindered coordination of these attacks. Attritted battalions, rotated off the line, failed to share their hard-won tactical intelligence with replacements. Under-trained combat engineers were unable to breach the simplest minefields. To make matters worse, they often attempted to breach defences without smoke cover in broad daylight. When engaged, the panicked tank and armoured vehicle crews failed to use their white prosperous (WP) grenades to create smoke clouds. Smoke would have confused FPV drones and ATGM gunners in targeting their vehicles.

During the Second World War the Soviets were masters of smoke operations. They used smoke generators to obscure objectives, river crossings and ground manoeuvres. Soviet and modern Russian doctrine directed that smoke should be used to conceal artillery, command posts, manoeuvres, forward movement to the line of contact, breaching operations and observation posts, and be laid on enemy positions to blind gunners. The blinding smoke screen laid on enemy positions or between combatants was a combination of normal smoke and white or red phosphorus rounds. Delivery of these tactical smoke screens was accomplished by mortars, artillery, rocket launchers or aircraft. The camouflage smoke screens were produced by smoke pots, barrels and smoke generators.[12]

Attacking Russians should have followed Soviet doctrine regarding smoke in order to: cover their movement to the line of contact, cover their breaching of minefields, isolate defending companies and platoons and disrupt the defenders' coordination of interlocking fields of direct fire. Smokescreens three to five times wider than the zone of attack should have been employed to deceive the defenders as to the actual location of the attack. Once obstacles were breached and the assault force was 400–1,000 metres from the defences, smoke should have been lifted so that the assault was unencumbered.[13]

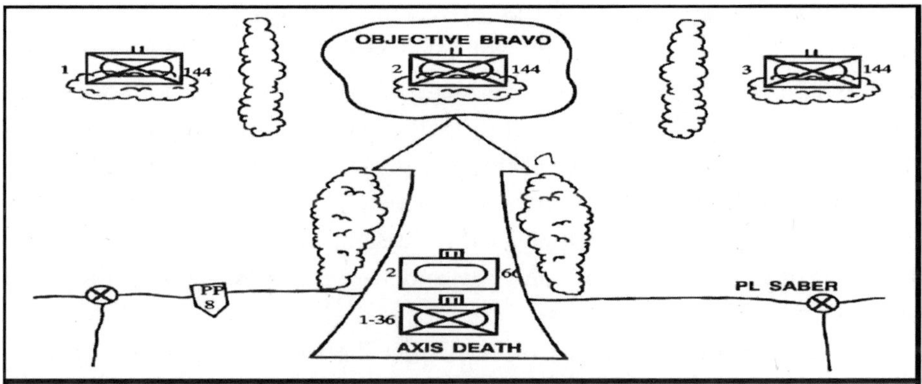

Chart 12 Hypothetical RU BDE Smoke Plan
1. Flank Smoke Screen protects flanks of attacking force and covers movement to contact.
2. Blinding Smoke isolates the strike sector and prevents the defending BNs from massing direct fire and protects breaching teams while reducing obstacles Source: US Army

Despite the Soviet doctrine, the Russians failed to effectively employ smoke to conceal attacks, river crossings, assaults and/or breaching operations. There was some speculation at the time that thermal sights had rendered smoke obsolete. This assumption was false. Western and Russian thermal tank sights can, to some extent, see through smoke. But a great density of particulates (small particles of metal, graphite, etc.) and the thickness of the smoke, coupled with distance to the target and the prevailing weather conditions, all impact the ability to identify targets in or behind the screen. Small particles block the infrared spectrum signature of the target. They can also block laser designators used by some ATGMs and precision artillery shells. Depending upon the type of smoke or particulates, breathing the smoke can cause short and long-term health issues – although consideration for the health of their soldiers rarely impacts Russian planning and operations.[14]

Russian Ivans and their officers stuck out in the open in a minefield during daylight seldom paused to consider the long-term health implications of breathing smoke. Their main concern would have been surviving until sundown. The issue was probably logistics. Either the Russians expended their stockpile of smoke rounds during the first year of the war, or standard shells were given a higher priority than obfuscation rounds.

The failure of Russian armoured vehicle crews to discharge their smoke phosphorus grenades when being attacked was clearly attributable to their lack of training. Fully qualified Western tank crews were rarely allowed to fire phosphorus grenades in training.[15] Even in the heat of battle, well-trained tank crews often neglected to employ their smoke grenades.[16]

The Russian battle plan for the 2023 winter offensive sent down to the brigades and divisions was sloppy and failed to reflect the realities of the first year of fighting. Coordinated smoke plans by the large CAA staffs were not attempted; brigades lacked sufficiently trained staffs to make up the shortfall, nor did they have authority to modify the plan. Putin and his generals failed to provide adequate time to prepare the offensive. Wellington's comment after the Battle of Waterloo could apply to the Russians in the twenty-first century: '[T]hey came on in the same old way and we sent them back in the same old way.'[17]

The 2023 winter offensive can be divided between the planned decisive assaults on the Donetsk Sector and the shaping operation in the Luhansk Sector. The main effort in the Donetsk Sector was by PMC Wagner Group to capture Bakhmut. Major shaping or supporting attacks were aimed at Vuhledar, Marinka, and Avdiivka. Media speculation at the time was that the Russians would execute a pincer movement with the northern arm attacking south from Kerominia (Luhansk Sector) linking up with the southern arm from Vuhledar (Donetsk Sector), while frontal attacks pinned Ukrainian brigades in place in the middle.[18] This over-optimistic projection failed to take into account Ivan's lack of capability as demonstrated during the second half of 2022 and the heavy losses of trained soldiers and equipment.

Chapter 9

Battle for Luhansk Oblast
The Russian 2023 Winter Offensive

Fighting in Luhansk Oblast during 2022 had stabilized along the Kupyansk-Svatove-Kreominia line. The mission of the forces deployed in this Sector was to push the Ukrainians back over the Oskil River and recapture Lyman.

This offensive was a shaping operation, with the appearance of an ill-planned, hasty attack. The Kupyansk-Svatove-Kreminia line had been relatively static in January 2023. Decisive action could have been achieved in the north at Kupyansk and in the south at Kremina. The terrain in both sectors consisted of rolling hills with large tracts of forest interspaced with open fields. Streams and small rivers flowed north to south joining the meandering Siversky-Donets River. Forest canopies provided cover and concealment from the increasing use of drones. Mass attacks were a thing of the past in this sector, and combined arms platoons and companies became the primary assault formations. Periodic winter freezes and thaws rendered vehicle movement difficult, resulting in miserable fighting conditions for the combatants.

The Kremlin's objective was to capture the town of Lyman because it was the gateway to crossing the Siversky-Donets River. Liberated by the

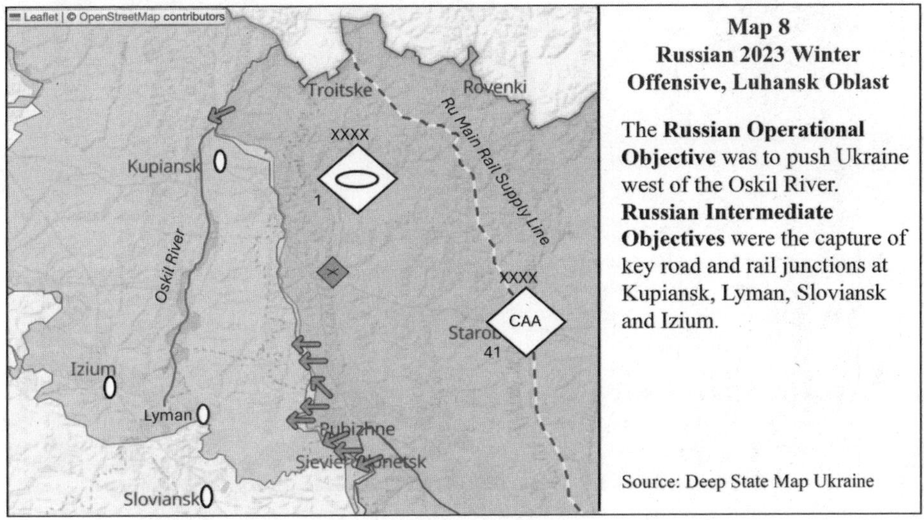

Map 8
Russian 2023 Winter Offensive, Luhansk Oblast

The **Russian Operational Objective** was to push Ukraine west of the Oskil River. **Russian Intermediate Objectives** were the capture of key road and rail junctions at Kupiansk, Lyman, Sloviansk and Izium.

Source: Deep State Map Ukraine

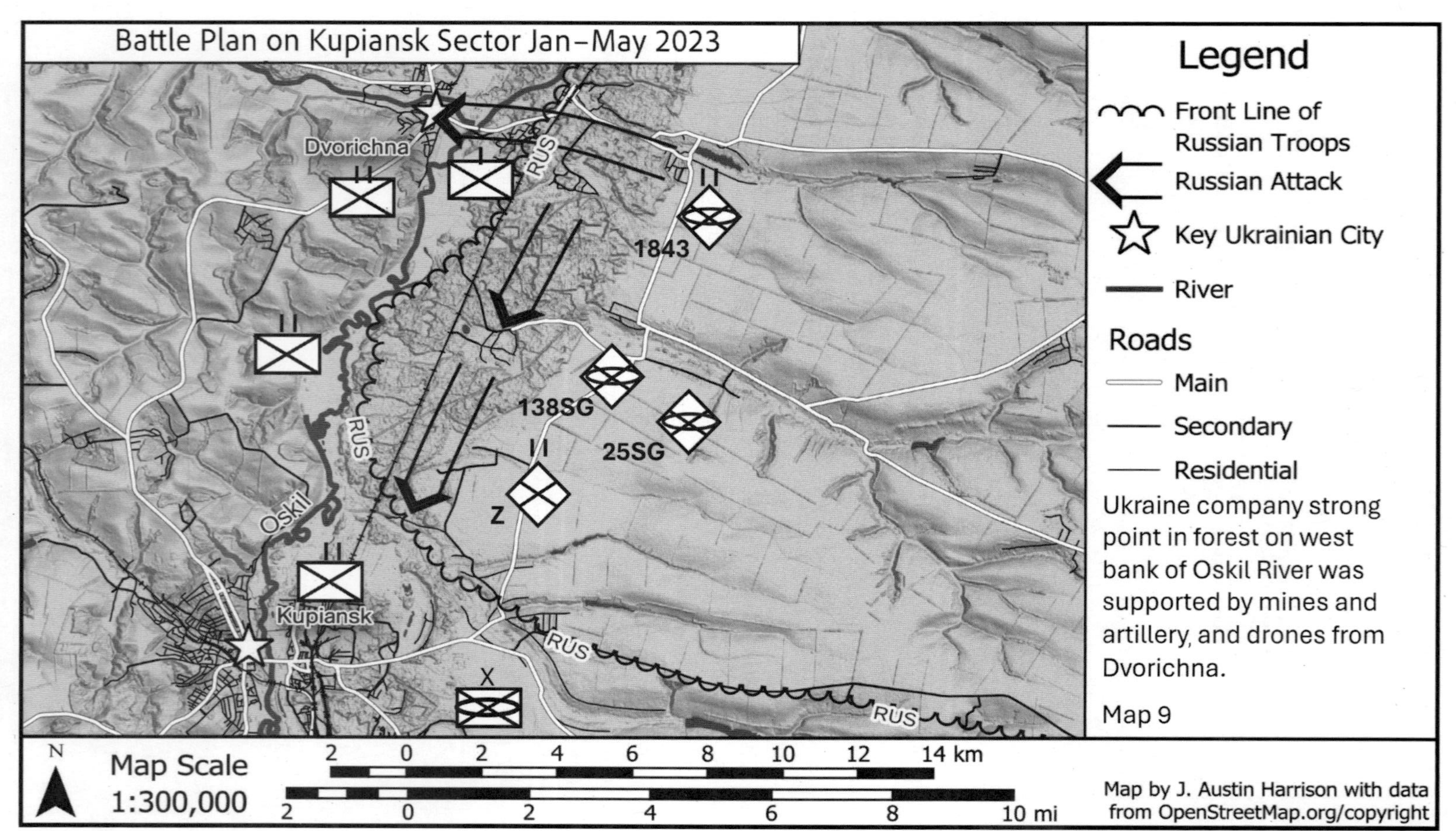
Battle Plan on Kupiansk Sector Jan–May 2023
Dvorichna
RUS
1843
138SG
25SG
Z
X
Oskil
Kupiansk
Legend
Front Line of Russian Troops
Russian Attack
Key Ukrainian City
River
Roads
Main
Secondary
Residential
Ukraine company strong point in forest on west bank of Oskil River was supported by mines and artillery, and drones from Dvorichna.
Map 9
N
Map Scale
1:300,000
2 0 2 4 6 8 10 12 14 km
2 0 2 4 6 8 10 mi
Map by J. Austin Harrison with data from OpenStreetMap.org/copyright

Ukrainians in the summer of 2022, the small city of Lyman was an important transportation hub, and its hard roads linked it with the fortress and supply cities of Sloviansk and Kramatorsk. While the infrastructure of the city had been heavily damaged during the fighting in 2022, it remained a key logistical hub for the Ukrainians in 2023. To capture Lyman, the attack would need to advance 30 km (18 miles) and cross the minor Zherebets River.

During late December 2022 and early January 2023 Ukrainians conducted tactical offensive operations to liberate Kremina. The Russians defended in standard Russian/Soviet three-echelon formation. The first echelon contained two regiments and a brigade (488th Motorized Rifle Regiment, 4th Separate Motorized Rifle Brigade [2nd Army Corps] and 35th Separate Guards Motorized Rifle Brigade).The second echelon contained three brigades (488th Motorized Rifle Regiment, 55th Mountain Motorized Rifle Brigade, a battalion from the 90th Tank Division and 74th Separate Guards Motorized Rifle Brigade) with the 30th Separate Motorized Rifle Brigade held in reserve. Command and control of the defence was probably the 144th Guards Motorized Rifle Division. All formations were under-strength, so a reasonable estimate of combat strength was 10,000.[1] Ukraine massed seven under-strength brigades (approximately 14,000 troops) against this force. The Ukrainians could only creep forward during the heavy fighting in early January 2023 and never reached the town of Kremina.

While the Ukrainians inched toward Kremina, the Russians moved three divisions into Luhansk Oblast. Two VDV air assault divisions and a VDV air assault brigade were allocated to the Kremina axis. A motorized rifle division was sent to join the attack at the Kupyansk axis. Additional independent units like the 13th BAR and unidentified Storm-Z detachments were also deployed to this sector. The combined pre-war combat strength of these formations was near 22,000, but in January 2023 the three divisions and one brigade probably only mustered between 8,000 and 10,000 troops. Thermobaric rocket launchers were deployed to reinforce the artillery previously positioned in the Oblast. The Russian attack commenced at the end of January and lasted until the end of March 2023.

The attack on the Kremina axis was launched from a salient, in an attempt to advance 8 km (5 miles) to reach and cross the Zherebets River. The attack from the northern point of the salient pushed Ukrainian defensive lines back 2 km (1.2 miles), while in the south, attack by the 488th Motorized Rifle Regiment and 234th Air Assault Regiment advanced 2 km (1.2 miles). The Russians attacked all along the sector on 2 February 2023, making slow progress. Despite heavy fighting, by 5 March 2023 the Russian attack stalled after advancing only 5 km (3.1 miles) never reaching the defences along the Zherebets River. Ukrainian counter-attacks halted the Russian advance and regained some ground. After weeks of heavy fighting, the Russians were only able to expand the salient less than 3 km (1.8 miles). The heavy fighting continued throughout May and into June 2023, but the frontlines had stabilized.[2]

Tactically, the frontlines barely moved. The Russians had deployed insufficient combat power to this axis to be able to capture Lyman, let alone conduct a sweeping advance to encircle a large Ukrainian force. However, operationally the offensive was a success. The Russians tied down Ukrainian brigades that could have withdrawn from the line in preparation for the summer counter-offensive. While the Kremina operation failed to gain any territory, it accomplished its mission as a shaping operation for the decisive action against Bakhmut.

The situation in the Kupyansk Sector presented an operational dilemma for the Ukrainians. The town was a major rail hub with five different rail lines intersecting there, one of which led directly into Russia. It was an absolute requirement for Russia to capture the town so that the invasion force could advance into southern Kharkiv Oblast. The town, a crossroads for vehicles and supply convoys operating in the region and critical to the Ukrainian defence and their attempt to liberate occupied northern Luhansk, was occupied quickly by the Russians at the start of the invasion. The pro-Russian mayor Hennadiy Matsehora surrendered Kupiansk without a fight. Despite this quisling's efforts, Ukrainian defenders destroyed a key rail bridge in an attempt to slow the oncoming invaders. It was reported that Matsehora helped the Russians find a bypass. The Ukrainians charged him with treason, but he escaped to Russian territory. The Russians later arrested him in July 2023 for unknown reasons.[3]

Once occupied by the invaders, the town became important as a supply and transportation hub for moving supplies and reinforcements to the front. The town was liberated on 10 September 2022 during the Ukrainian counter-offensive. The defeated Russian forces retreated and established new defensive positions within artillery range of Kupyansk. From these positions they conducted indiscriminate terror bombardments, killing and wounding hundreds of civilians.[4]

The line of contact ran from the Russian border, 32 km (20 miles) south along the Oskil River, turned east just north of the town of Kupyansk and then ran 21 km (13 miles) south-east through open fields and forests. The exact composition of the defending Ukrainian Kyslivka Group during this period is unclear. The 101st, 103rd, and 105th Territorial Defence Brigades were known to be present during this period. In the summer of 2023, the 14th (upgraded TD formation), 32nd, 41st, 43rd and 88th Mechanized Bridges were identified in the group, with the 95th Air Assault and the 3rd Tank Brigade held in reserve.

During the 2023 Russian winter offensive the 1st Tank Army, including the 2nd Motorized Rifle Division, and 138th Separate Guards Motorized Rifle Brigade, was identified as participating in the Russian strike force. Additional motorized rifle brigades and regiments would have taken part in the attacks. More alarming to the Ukrainian defenders were the 100,000 soldiers detected in February 2023 in the Russian Belgorod Oblast. This force was later identified as the newly formed 25th Combined Arms Army, positioned to threaten Kharkiv City and flank the defenders of the Oskil River north of Kupyansk.

The 25th Combined Arms Army (25th CAA) consisted of officers and conscripts from the Irkutsk and Buryatia Oblasts under the command of Major General Andrey Seritsky. While the troops arrived in theatre during the winter of 2023, the formation was announced as fully manned and staffed in May 2023.[5] At full strength the 25th CAA mustered 17,000 combat troops, indicating that its battalions were only a portion of the 100,000 soldiers reported.

The fact that the 25th CAA was in the process of forming, and the remainder may have been conscripts in training, did not lessen the threat it posed to the Ukrainian defenders. In mid-2022 the Russians had thrown large untrained formations into combat. They committed the well-equipped but under-trained 3rd Army Corps' 'volunteer battalions' from the oblasts.[6] Detecting the build-up, Ukrainians countered by establishing a defensive line between the Kupyansk west to Husynka River.[7]

If an attack had launched from the north, the terrain would have funnelled the Russians directly toward Kupyansk and the newly established defence line. However, an attack from Belgorod Oblast never materialized. Instead, 1st Tank Army units attacked into the teeth of the Kupyansk defensive sector. This attack was intended to cut off the Ukrainian Kyslivka Group east and south-east of Kupyansk. Fixing attacks by the 2nd Motorized Rifle Division held the Kyslivka Group in place, while the main effort by the 138th Separate Guards Motorized Rifle Brigade attempted to cut the group's supply lines by attacking toward Kupyansk. The attack was hampered by a small Ukrainian bridgehead on the east bank of the Oskil River that included the village of Hrianykivka in the forest. The Russians planned to advance, taking advantage of the forest to provide cover and concealment. Unfortunately for the Russians, the bridgehead was supported by direct and indirect fire from the higher west bank around the village of Dvoiche.[8] This position enfiladed the axis of

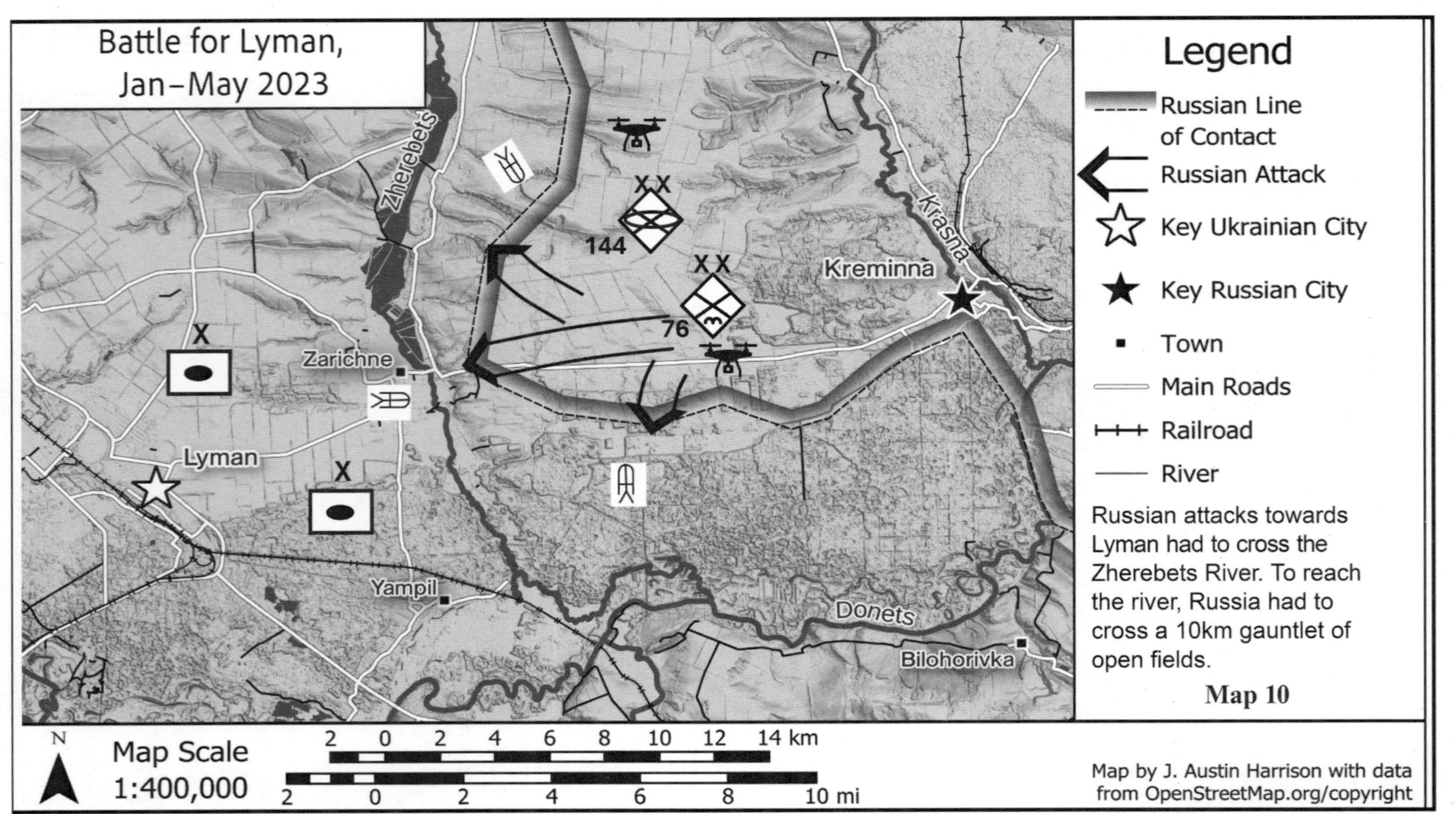

Battle for Lyman,
Jan–May 2023
Zherebets
X
X
XX
XX
144
76
Zarichne
Lyman
Yampil
Kreminna
Krasna
Donets
Bilohorivka
Legend
Russian Line of Contact
Russian Attack
Key Ukrainian City
Key Russian City
Town
Main Roads
Railroad
River
Russian attacks towards Lyman had to cross the Zherebets River. To reach the river, Russia had to cross a 10km gauntlet of open fields.
Map 10
N
Map Scale
1:400,000
2 0 2 4 6 8 10 12 14 km
2 0 2 4 6 8 10 mi
Map by J. Austin Harrison with data from OpenStreetMap.org/copyright

advance south along the river toward Kupyansk. Reinforcing their fire plan, the Ukrainians had mined the forest.[9]

Heavy shelling of the area in March 2023 resulted in a mass evacuation of Ukrainian civilians from Kupyansk and surrounding villages.[10] The Russians conducted 502 artillery strikes and 15 airstrikes against Kupyansk and surrounding areas. The town had a pre-war population of 25,000. In a televised appeal, Oleh Syniehubov, head of the Ukrainian regional administration, urged residents to vacate the town and surrounding villages. The majority of the population left, but some chose to stay. At the time of the evacuation 11,000 people remained, including 812 children and 724 disabled.[11] Many of the elderly and those in poor health were afraid to leave and did not have anywhere to go to. Local authorities and volunteer groups assisted the elderly to move to safer locations.[12 13]

The Russians conducted numerous attacks north of Kupyansk along the Oskil River, supported by a heavy artillery bombardment. They sought to win the east bank of the river and secure their flanks, only to be thrown back by Ukrainian counter-attacks and pinned down in the forest minefields.

The mined forests slowed the Russian attackers, who were then targeted by artillery. The fighting in Hrianykivka on the flank of the Russian attack resulted in a see-saw battle as control of the village shifted between the combatants. While the fighting continued on its flank, the main attack attempted to fight its way through 13 km (8 miles) of farmland and tree lines to Kupyansk. Heavy bombardment, mines and local counter-attacks contained the Russian advance. By the end of March 2023 the Russians had made little headway, and the offensive stalled.

The Russians failed to make any significant territorial gains during their winter offensive. They also failed to cut the Ukrainian supply route. The Russians did manage to fix Ukrainian forces, preventing units from Kyslivka Group shifting to other sectors or being pulled off the line for preparations for an expected summer counter-offensive.[14] The 2023 winter offensive ended in the Kupyansk Sector, but low-level fighting continued until the commencement of the Russian July 2023 summer offensive.

Chapter 10

The Battles of Avdiivka and Marinka Russian 2023 Winter Offensive

The town of Avdiivka is 8 km (5 miles) north-west of the city of Donetsk, the capital of the Donetsk People's Republic, and 5 km (3 miles) from Donetsk Airport.[1] The Ukrainians fortified Avdiivka after the heavy fighting in 2014/15. The newly fortified city was divided into three defensive zones. The northern urban area was dominated by the vast Avdeyevsky Coke Plant and the slag mountain known as the Terrikon. To the south and east were private homes, abandoned due to the fighting. The Soviet-planned civic centre, known as the Ninth Quarter, was located on the south-western side of the city, where multi-storey buildings provided unobstructed observation points to view Donetsk City. Fighting had been constant since the beginning of the war.

By February 2022 Avdiivka was a complex multi-echelon fortress. To make matters worse for the Russians, the town was in artillery range of the city of Donetsk and its airport. During the first ten months of the war the town was destroyed, but the bunkers and trenches held. Bloody frontal assaults by DPR

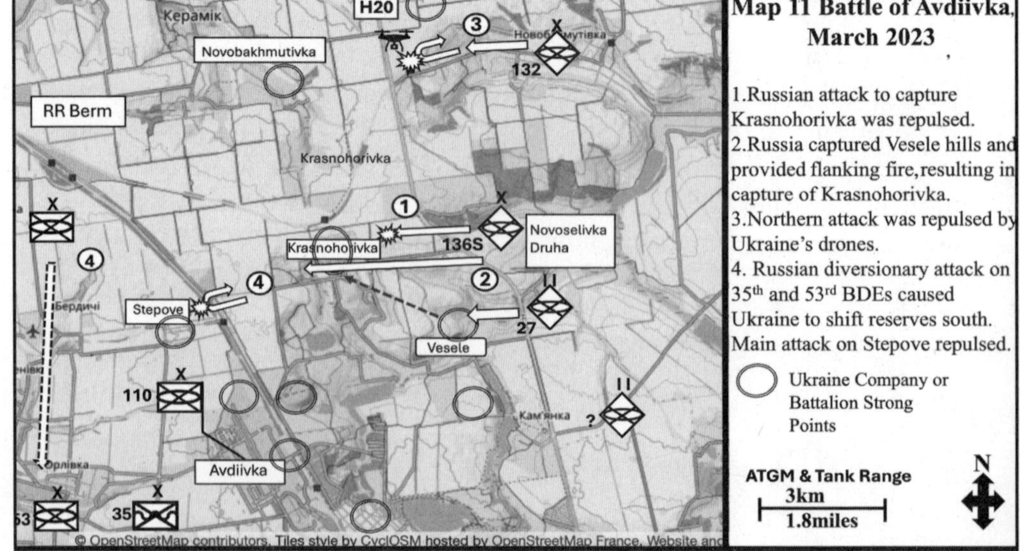

and Russian units completely failed to capture the ruins. Attempts to encircle the town failed, when both arms of the pincer movement were bogged down in complex defences, resulting in slow progress.

Repeated attacks in February 2023 made little progress. However, in early March 2023 the northern arm of the Russian attack was heavily reinforced with new conscript formations. After failing to bypass Krasnohorivka to the north, a battle group consisting of the 136th Separate Motorized Rifle Brigade, 19th Rifle Regiment (DPR), 27 Rifle Battalion and additional unidentified battalions shifted their attack vector and assaulted the ruined town on 1 March 2023. After eight days of heavy fighting the Russians only managed to capture a few buildings on the town's eastern edge. While the first echelon defenders held the town, the second echelon provided direct fire support from the railroad embankment 3 km (1.8 miles) west of Krasnohorivka. From this position, Ukrainian tanks, ATGMs and FPV drones protected the flanks and rear of the defenders in the town. Defensive positions in the hilltop village of Vesele, 3 km (1.8 miles) south-east of Krasnohorivka provided flanking fire on the Russian formations attacking west.

The Russians finally realized that to take Krasnohorivka they had to capture Vesele. On 7 March 2023, a brigade conducted a coordinated frontal and flanking attack on the village. By capturing the hills around Vesele, the Russians then dominated eastern Krasnohorivka. On 11 March 2023, supported by fire positions in the hills, the attackers suppressed defensive fire and advanced into the centre of the town. The Ukrainians conducted a fighting withdrawal to their second echelon defensive line, laying mines as they retreated. After securing the town, the Russian advance continued, supported by air strikes (glide bombs). Heavy armoured direct firefights with the 110th Mechanized Brigade slowed the Russian advance. The capture of Krasnohorivka placed the Russians in position to threaten the supply lines to Avdiivka.

The breach of the less heavily fortified flank of Avdiivka provided the opportunity for an advance. The Russians attacked north and south of Krasnohorivka to widen the breach in the first echelon, then struck north towards the town of Novokalynove to widen the breach in the first echelon of the Ukrainian defence.[2]

Capitalizing on the breach, motorized rifle reserves were rushed to the sector, while Ukrainian Territorial Defence and elite special forces formations, such as the White Wolves, reinforced the defenders. The White Wolves were part of the Ukrainian Security Service (SBU) and since the beginning of the war had employed FPV drones to stalk and kill Russian armour, specializing in night hunts.[3]

The 132nd Separate Motorized Rifle Brigade was assigned the mission of capturing Novokalynove. The Russians took the hills east of the town in preparation for a daylight attack. The night before the Russians advanced, the Wolves conducted a spoiling FPV drone night attack. A few days later, they released a video of the ten Russian tanks and APCs that had been destroyed.[4] While the Russians captured the hills overlooking Novokalynove, the spoiling attack by the White Wolves halted the assault. The open killing fields surrounding the town contained the Russian attack and discouraged any additional attack from this direction.

As the heavy fighting north of Avdiivka continued, the Russian generals sought to create the illusion that they had shifted their main effort to the south. They concentrated the 111th Separate Rifle Regiment, 9th Separate Regiment of Naval Infantry, 1st Separate Motorized Rifle Brigade, 87th Rifle Regiment and 117th Motorized Rifle Regiment (DPR) and other unidentified units in the vicinity of Vodiane.

Heavy fighting flared up in the south on 10 March 2023, and it appeared the Russians had shifted their main effort to the southern arm of the pincer. Russian tanks tried to outflank the 35th Marine Brigade defending Sieverne as infantry conducted a frontal attack. The Marines destroyed several tanks and armoured vehicles in the flanking force, blunting the attack. After several days of heavy fighting the 53rd Mechanized Brigade on the Marines' western flank failed to stop a similar Russian armoured flanking force. It appeared that the Russian breakthrough caused the Ukrainians to send their Avdiivka tactical reserves to reinforce their southern flank.

The southern attack was only a Russian shaping operation, with the goal of forcing the Ukrainian reserves to commit against the southern attack. When the Ukrainian reserves were committed south, the motorized rifle battalions in the north attacked toward the key road junction of Stepove. In middle to late March 2023 the Russians crossed the rail embankment 500 metres east of Stepove with a battalion of fifteen tanks, nine BMPs and 300–500 Ivans, capturing the eastern buildings. The combatants hotly contested the town, but ultimately the Russians were repulsed with heavy casualties and the battalion was nearly destroyed.[5]

To prevent a breakthrough and in an effort to stabilize the situation, the Ukrainians committed a reinforced tank battalion from operational reserves and counter-attacked in late March and early April 2023. With heavy fire support by artillery, FPV drones and air strikes (gliding bombs), the armoured counter-attack successfully pushed the Russians out of Stepove and back over the rail embankment.[6]

Heavy fighting continued in June 2023, as the Ukrainian ground offensive was launched. The 114th Motorized Rifle Brigade captured Krasonhorivka after intense combat and cut the H20 highway. Possession of the town was critical since the H20 served as a Ukrainian supply line. The town provided the Russians with a covered assembly or staging area to mass combat formations for the planned offensive in October 2023.

The Battle of Marinka

The Battle of Marinka was a Russian secondary supporting attack with the objective of pinning down Ukrainian brigades badly needed in other sectors. The town of Marinka sits on a critical road junction dominating a main axis of advance from the DPR into Ukraine. Situated close to the DPR border, Marinka was heavily fortified. Fighting in the region had been continuous since 2014. Falsely claimed by the Russians to have been captured early in the war, Ukrainian defenders held the city, throwing the Russian assaults back in house-to-house fighting. By winter 2023 the city had been reduced to rubble, but the defenders held on.

Skirmishes in the Marinka area continued during the autumn and winter of 2023. Attempts by the Russian 150th Motorized Rifle Division to encircle the ruined city failed, and it resorted to repeated frontal attacks. Outnumbered 6-1 in artillery and 4-1 in infantry, the defending 79th (Cyborgs) Mechanized Brigade repulsed repeated frontal attacks by the under-trained Russians in close combat.[7] Despite the heavy fighting in and around Marinka throughout the year, it remained a supporting effort for the Russians. Between March and September 2023 the Russians eventually captured half of the town, but the decisive battle for the Donetsk Oblast was fought at Avddiivka.

Chapter 11

The Battle of Vuhledar. The Russian Winter Offensive, January–April 2023

The city of Vuhledar had a pre-war population of 15,000. It is 100 km (60 miles) south of Bakhmut and 75 km (46 miles) north of the port city of Mariupol. Strategically, it was located at the junction of the western Donetsk and the eastern Zaporizhzhia Oblasts. It is 24 km (15 miles) north-west of the town of Volnovakha, where the only railway linked Crimea with internationally recognized Russia. The rail line was within artillery range of Vuhledar. Unlike Bakhmut, the capture of Vuhledar would have both an operational and strategic influence on the outcome of the war. Capture of the town would have made Russian logistics in this sector much simpler. Ukrainian artillery, firing precision ammunition, routinely targeted Russian supply trains, threatening Russian ability to transfer manpower and armoured vehicles into and out of the sector. When HIMARS were factored in, the Russians were forced to use a secondary road along the coast to transport replacements by bus into Western Zaporizhzhia Oblast. The secondary road was just out of HIMARS range.

There were two major coalmines just outside the town with coal reserves estimated to be 200 million tons. Control of the coal was important to both sides. Electricity generated by the coal provided 50 per cent of Ukraine's power prior to the invasion, the rest being imported from Russia and Poland. The mines were state-owned and provided a major source of income for the Ukrainian government.

The town was strongly fortified as a result of the fighting in 2014, and over the following eight years trenches and firing positions had been constructed. The town is located on the empty steppes, and high-rise apartment complexes dominated the surrounding terrain. None of the possible approaches from any direction provided any cover or concealment, except for a tree line near the hamlet of Pavlovka and two tree lines on the east and west of the town. A network of trenches and tank and artillery firing positions defended all approaches to the town.[1]

The Russians attempted unsuccessfully to capture Vuhledar in March–October 2022. The first assaults were repulsed on 13/14 March 2022, and the front stabilized just south of Vuhledar through March and early April 2022. Between 6 and 7 April the town was heavily shelled and a ground assault was repulsed. On 16 May DPR and Russian troops again attempted to take the town by assault and failed. The town was shelled throughout the summer, and a number of half-hearted attacks were repulsed. Russian and DPR troops attacked the town of Pavkivka just south of Vuhledar defended by the 72nd Mechanized Brigade, during the night of 28/29 October. The heavy artillery battle raged until 15 November.[2]

The 155th and 40th Separate Naval Brigades spearheaded the attack on Pavkivka. The Russian Naval Infantry lost over 300 men and half of their T-80 tanks, BMPs and BTRs during the first four days of fighting.[3] Pavlivka was captured on 14 November 2022, but heavy losses by the Naval Infantry made it a pyrrhic victory at best. As the battle for Pavlivka played out, Russian artillery targeted Vuhledar's civilian infrastructure on 2 November 2022. With the capture of Pavlivka the Russians occupied the south bank of the small Kashlahach River facing 2–4 km (1.2–2.4 miles) of open fields to reach Vuhledar.[4] Vuhledar had been heavily shelled, including bombardment by 2S4 Tyulpan self-propelled 240mm mortars. The onslaught continued throughout December 2022. Without being pulled out of the lines, the Naval Infantry Brigades were rebuilt with Mobiks and volunteer battalions from the Russian oblasts.

Colonel Vladyslav Bayak's 72nd Mechanized Brigade, supported by the 55th Artillery Brigade, remained the primary defensive formations in 2023. They were reinforced with the 48th Rifle Battalion (58th Mechanized Brigade), 68th Jaeger Brigade and Kastus Kalinouski Regiment (Belarusian volunteers). Kastus Kalinouski was a Belarusian and Polish national hero who led the January 1863 uprising against the Russian Empire in Belarus and Lithuania.[5] The Regiment was brigade-size with three infantry battalions, a UAV company dubbed 'Nikita Kryvtsov' and combat service support companies and detachments.[6]

The 68th Jaeger Mechanized Infantry Brigade contained four infantry battalions, a tank battalion (T-72s) and field artillery regiment (two battalions) and the full range of combat support and combat service support battalions and companies. Jaeger (Jäger) is the German word for hunter. The brigades with Jaeger in their title (61st, 68th and 72nd) were considered medium weight formations between the Territorial light and Army heavy brigades. The 68th was formed in April 2022, and its infantry battalions were mounted in civilian pickups and US MaxxPro wheeled APCs (MRAPS), while its MRLS batteries included pickup-mounted launchers.[7]

The 72nd Mechanized Brigade was one of the major formations defending Kyiv at the beginning of the war. It consisted of three mechanized infantry battalions (BMPs and MTLBs), three motorized infantry battalions, a tank battalion (T-64s and T-72s), an artillery regiment of two self-propelled artillery battalions (2S1 [122mm], 2S3 [152mm], US M109A3 [155mm]), a BM-21 multiple-rocket battalion and an anti-tank artillery battalion (100mm anti-tank gun). The Ukrainians were supported by American M777 and French Caesar howitzers. The brigade was transferred to the Donbas, where it participated in the Battle of Bakhmut before being transferred to Vuhledar.

The 55th Artillery Brigade was organized into four artillery and one anti-tank battalions. Its combat support units consisted of an artillery reconnaissance battalion, NBC company, counter-battery radar company, an engineer company and combat service support including medical, logistics and maintenance companies. Its firing batteries consisted of several towed and semi-towed guns, including US M777 (155mm), French Caesar (155mm), Soviet 2A36 Giatsint-B (152mm), 2AMsta-B (152mm) howitzers and T-12 100mm anti-tank guns. Except for the truck-mounted French Caesar, the remaining howitzers were towed by MTLB APCs.[8]

The Russian offensive operation may have been supervised by the 42nd Motorized Rifle Division, but the commander on the ground was General Rustam Muradov. He commanded the equivalent of a reinforced division.[9] On paper, the force massed against Vuhledar consisted of some of the best units in the Russian order of battle: the 155th Naval Infantry Brigade, 40th Naval Infantry Brigade, 14th GRU Spetsnaz Brigade and the PMC Patriot battalion. Before the war, a Naval Infantry Brigade consisted of 2,500 personnel, divided into a headquarters, two naval infantry battalions, reconnaissance (airborne) battalion, tank battalion, sniper company, SP howitzer battalion, MLRS battalion and flamethrower company, along with combat support and combat service support battalions and companies. Each of the three infantry battalions mustered 500 soldiers mounted on an assortment of BTRs and MT-LB APCs and BMP IFVs, and mortar platoons with 2S1 self-propelled 120mm mortars.[10]

Details on the 14th GRU Spetsnaz Brigade are limited, but it was reportedly divided into four detachments. Smaller and better-trained than other elite AFR units, it appeared that 1,200 Ivans were detailed to this attack as infantry.[11] The equivalent of the US 75th Ranger Regiment or British 16th Air Assault Brigade, their normal missions included battlefield reconnaissance, raids behind enemy lines and training guerrillas.[12] The fact that they deployed as standard infantry in at least one attack demonstrated the importance of capturing Vuhledar to the OK-South to protect the Russian rail supply line.

The Naval Infantry Brigades were fully equipped and probably near 100 per cent strength. Additional independent battalions, such as the Volunteer Tartar Alga Battalion and Kaskad Battalion (DPR), were assigned to the three main assault brigades. Additional unidentified formations held the right and left flanks of the assault force, but their combat capability was extremely limited.

Many of the early casualties were from the Tartar Alga Battalion. This Muslim battalion was a BAR unit recruited from Tatarstan Oblast, one of the poorest regions in Russia. The battalion had been formed in June 2022 and each volunteer was paid the equivalent of $2,250 per month. While willing to fight, many of the soldiers did not speak or understand Russian.

The 155th Naval Infantry Brigade suffered heavy casualties during its shaping operation to capture Pavlivka just south of Vuhledar in 2022 and had been rebuilt at least twice. Its losses had been made good with Mobiks. The 40th Naval Infantry also consisted of many newly mobilized replacements. The two under-trained Naval Infantry brigades were given the complicated mission of assaulting a fortified position on a higher elevation across 2–4 km (1.2–2.4 miles) of open ground.

Behind this assault group, held in tactical reserve were: the 78th Motorized Rifle Regiment, 136th Separate Guards Motorized Rifle Brigade, 72nd Separate Motorized Rifle Brigade and 123rd Rifle Regiment (DPR). At full strength this reserve force would have represented 8,000–10,000 men, 90 tanks and 120 organic howitzers and MRLS. The initial Naval Infantry assault force of two reinforced brigades would have mustered 6,000 men, 60 tanks, 240 APCs and IFVs, with 100 howitzers and MRLs.

General Rustam Muradov's battle plan was to attack Vuhledar from both flanks with a fixing attack supported by fire positions along the Kashlahach River. The 14th GRU Spetsnaz Brigade, under command of Colonel Sergey Polyakov, was assigned the mission of attacking Vuhledar from the south-west. The 155th Naval Infantry Brigade was to flank Vuhledar from the south-east and capture the coalmines.

General Muradov's shaping operations commenced on the night of 24 January 2023. The 155th, supported by the Kaskad Battalion (DPR), pushed the Ukrainian combat outpost from along the Kashlahach River into the fortifications around Vuhledar. Driving the Ukrainians from the Kashlahach River was important to the Russians because they needed the cover and concealment of the vegetation and riverbank to establish an attack position at which to mass their troops. The distance between cover and concealment of

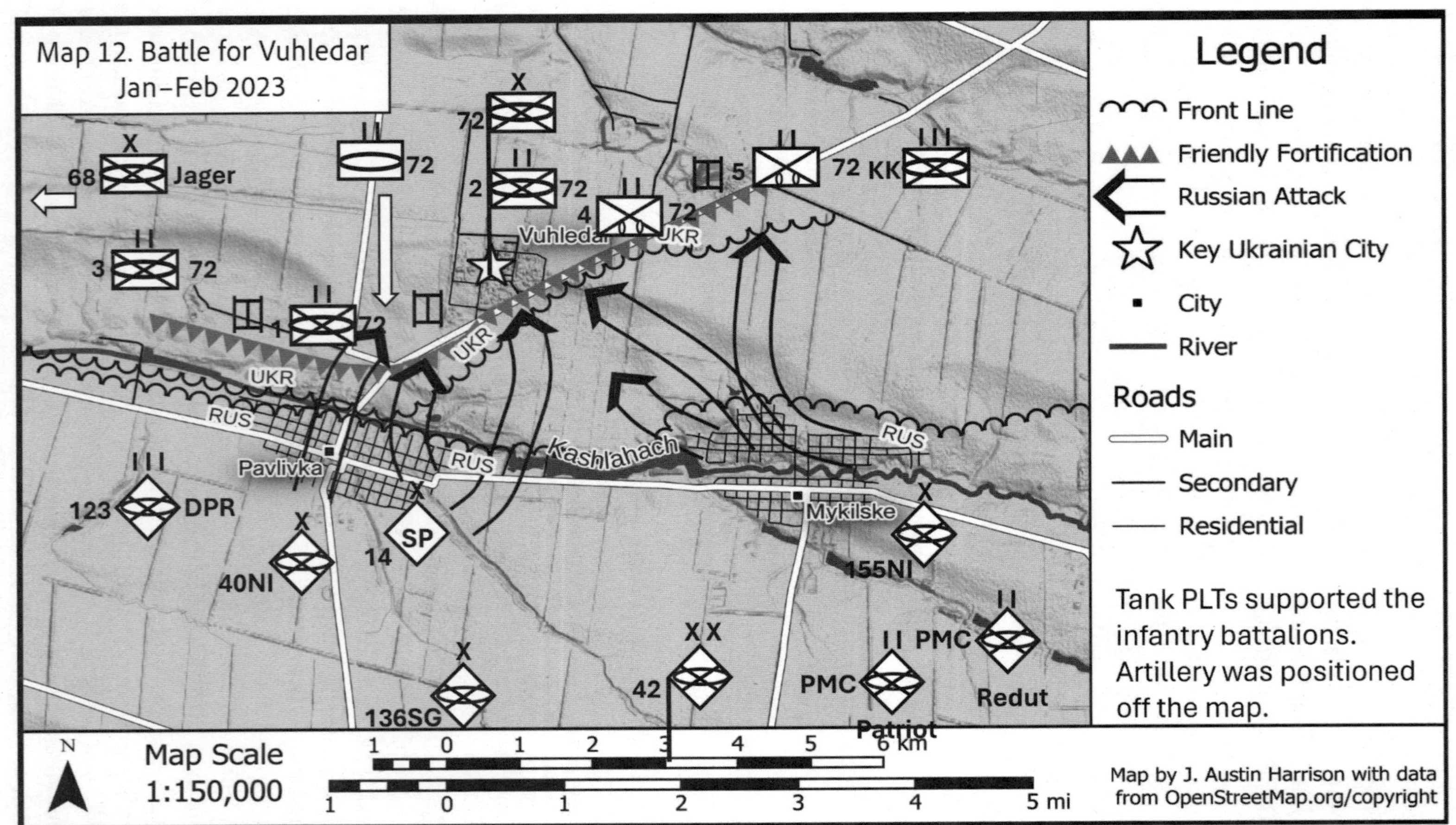

Map 12. Battle for Vuhledar
Jan–Feb 2023
68 Jager
3 72
72
72
2 72
1 72
4 72
5
72 KK
Vuhledar
UKR
RUS
Pavlivka
Kashlahach
Mykilske
123 DPR
40NI
14 SP
136SG
42
155NI
PMC
Patriot
PMC
Redut
Legend
Front Line
Friendly Fortification
Russian Attack
Key Ukrainian City
City
River
Roads
Main
Secondary
Residential
Tank PLTs supported the infantry battalions. Artillery was positioned off the map.
Map Scale
1:150,000
6 km
5 mi
Map by J. Austin Harrison with data from OpenStreetMap.org/copyright

the riverbanks and Vuhledar was only 2–4 km (1.2–2.5 miles) of open fields.[13] Muradov planned to use TOS-1 thermobaric rocket launchers as part of the bombardment of the town and outlying fortifications.

TOS-1 (Buratino) series flame weapons were multiple rocket launchers mounted on a T-72/90 tank chassis. The weapon was designed to target and burn fortifications, enemy soldiers, light equipment and buildings. If it could not burn the fortifications, it was designed to consume oxygen and suffocate the defenders. This is a terror weapon, banned under international rules of war. It was first used in combat by the Russians in Afghanistan (1980s) and again during the Second Chechen War. It was rumoured to have been employed by the Iraqi Army at the Battle of Jurf Al Sakhar (24 October 2014).[14] For a large MRLS, the TOS-1 (Buratino) had a short range of only 500 metres to 3 kms (1.8 miles), while the TOS-1A was reported to have a maximum range of 10 km (6 miles). To be effective against Vuhledar the TO-1 and 1As needed to be positioned in the small Kashlahach River valley.

On 24 January 2023, the 155th Naval Infantry and 14th GRU Spetsnaz Brigades, supported by the Cascad (DPR) Battalion, launched major assaults across the open fields without smoke concealment. The Russians attacked in division strength, with concentrated artillery fire on key strongpoints, advancing on several battalion axes. They successfully pushed the defenders from combat outposts located in hamlets around the town's main defensive line. Due to heavy artillery fire, it took two days for Ukrainian reserves to reinforce the first defensive echelon, which forced the Russians to give ground.

Operators from the 14th GRU Spetsnaz Brigade broke through Ukrainian defences south-west of Vuhledar and entered buildings outside the fortifications. A counter-attack quickly pushed them back. Ukrainian troops along the security line of contact retreated into the fortifications. The Russians followed up, and a series of company and platoon firefights developed in the fields around the perimeter of the city. The Ukrainian withdrawal of their combat outposts drew the Russians into prearranged kill zones, or to use the Soviet term, 'fire sacks'. Ukrainian artillery fire stalled the Russian advance. The Russians suffered over 300 casualties in these skirmishes and failed to gain a toehold in Vuhledar between 23 and 28 January. Russian companies and platoons did, however, successfully push the Ukrainians away from the Kashlahach river valley.[15] When this small valley was no longer threatened by direct tank or ATGM fire, the Russians deployed TOS-1 thermobaric rocket launchers there on 27 January.[16]

Reinforced with thermobaric artillery, the Russians resumed their bombardment of Ukrainian positions. The Ukrainians countered with increased drone reconnaissance. They identified where Russian forces were massing and where their reconnaissance troops were active. Based upon their IPB, they accurately templated the probable axis of advance. Under cover of darkness, Ukrainian combat engineers mined the fields through which the Russians were expected to attack, and the roads were left open to funnel the Russian assault battalions into kill zones. Once the battlefield was prepared, the Ukrainians waited for the attack. The Russian assault troops faced crossing between 2 and 5 km (1.2–3 miles) of open fields to reach the edge of the Ukrainian fortifications.

On 6 February, Deputy Battalion Commander Bairak recalled watching the first Russian column of fifteen tanks and armoured vehicles advance into the ambush. This was the first of a series of attacks over the next few days that repeated the same tactical errors over the same open terrain. The Russians advanced in daylight without the benefit of a smokescreen. Small Ukrainian hunter-killer teams entered the security zone between combatants and established firing positions in tree lines for ATGMs. These teams blocked the column by destroying the lead vehicle. Follow-on vehicles failed to fire smoke grenades to cover their manoeuvre. The headless column attempted to bypass the destroyed lead vehicle by leaving the open road and ploughing through the fields. Several hit the land mines and were destroyed. Pre-registered artillery engaged the halted columns destroying many, while simultaneously delivering more mines behind the Russians, cutting off their retreat. A Russian battalion managed to close to within 3 km (1.8 miles) of the eastern coalmines and entered the kill zone formed by Ukrainian tanks hiding in the tree line. Between the tanks' direct fire and supporting artillery fire the Russian tanks were destroyed or disabled. Surviving under-trained and inexperienced Mobik tank crews retreated into the newly laid minefields.

After the initial assaults the Russians repeatedly attacked over the same ground multiple times a day. Ukrainian T-64 tank commander Hrebenok rolled out of his hide position during the height of the battle and engaged Russian tanks at least four times per day. During the last major engagement he was alerted to move from his hide position and occupy his turret-down position. A column of sixteen Russian tanks halted in a turret-down support fire position 5 km (3 miles) from the kill zone, beyond standard direct fire range (3 km/1.8 miles). Hrebenok coordinated semi-direct fire with drone operators, but fortunately for the Russians, this novel tactic failed. The high velocity 125mm tank cannon could not engage a target on a reverse slope or a tank in a hull or turret-down position.[17] At the same time, and for the same reasons, the Russians could not successfully engage Hrebenok's tank. Basically, one Ukrainian tank pinned down an entire Russian tank battalion.

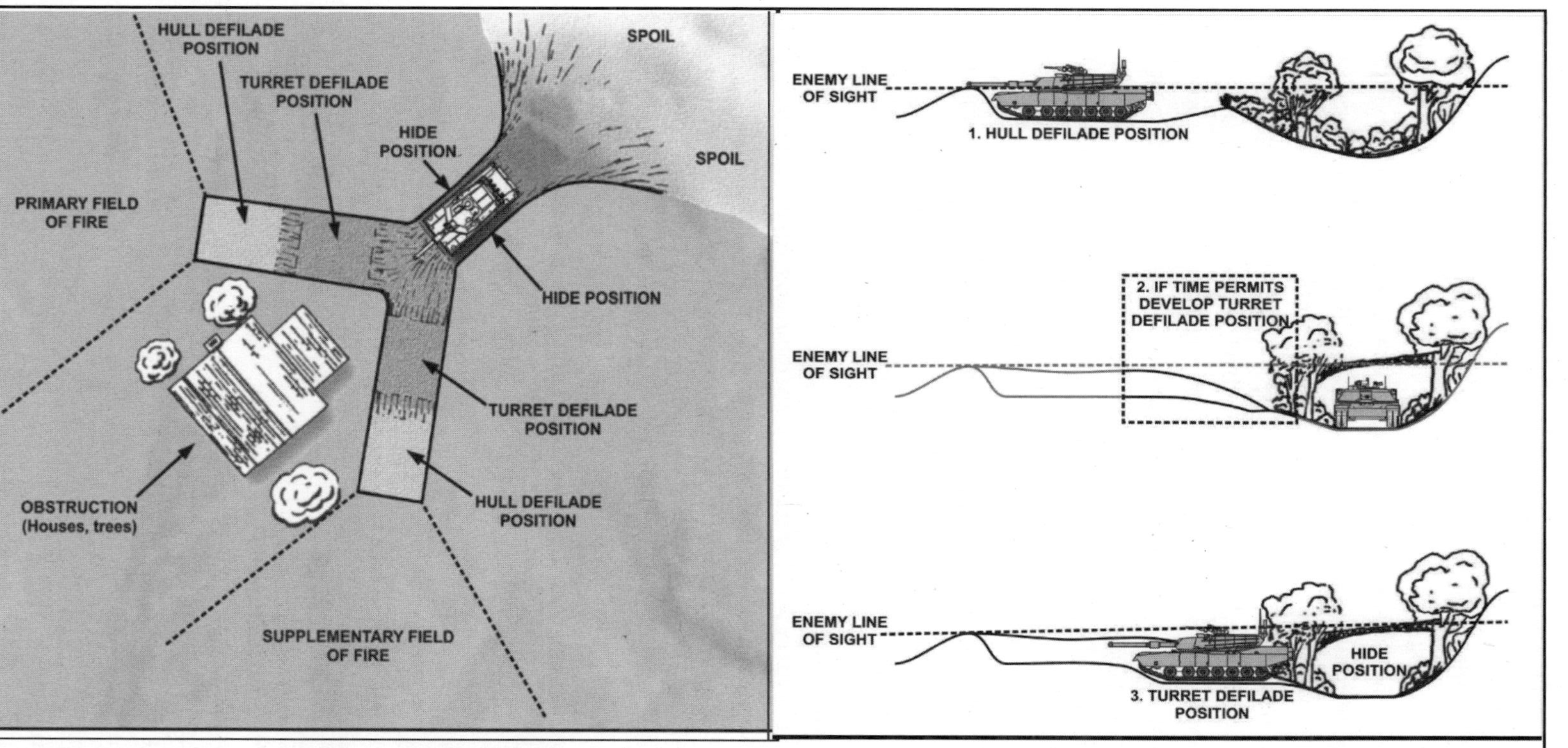

Chart 13 Hull, Turret Down and Hide Positions.
A Tank or Armoured vehicle fighting positions required cover and concealment to survive. Normally each vehicle had primary, alternative (not shown) and supplementary firing positions.

The Russian battalion did not share intelligence concerning the effectiveness of the Ukrainian kill zone. As a result, newly arrived formations of armoured vehicles entered the kill zone just like their predecessors. The Ukrainian artillery fired scatterable anti-tank mines to close the roads and lanes, forcing the Russians into the minefields. As the Russians were forced to break contact, the retreating armoured vehicles failed to deploy smoke grenades. Their brigade also failed to fire artillery smoke to cover the retreat.

During one of the attacks a Russian company briefly captured several dachas on the eastern and southern edge of Vuhledar. A Ukrainian counter-attack by fire forced the company to withdraw. After three days of heavy fighting the 155th Naval Infantry Brigade lost 130 armoured vehicles and 36 tanks.[18]

Despite the losses of three motorized rifle battalions' and one tank battalion's worth of equipment, the Russians continued the battle for three more weeks. As new battalions arrived to reinforce the battle group they were apparently not briefed on the Ukrainian tactics or locations of kill zones. Despite the initial slaughter suffered by assaulting Russian battalions, the Naval Infantry and Spetsnaz were ordered to continue the assault, reinforced by the 72nd Separate Motorized Rifle Brigade.

Throughout February 2023 battalions were reduced to platoon and company size but continued to attack without covering smoke along the same routes, through graveyards of Russian tanks and armoured vehicles. Attempting to bypass the wreckage, they hit mines or were destroyed by ATGMs, FPV drones or artillery. Panicked survivors pulled back along the approach road and were hit by newly laid artillery mines.

In mid-March it was reported that the Russians were short of ammunition. Competition between the Army and Wagner for artillery ammunition had reached the media.

The Russians spent the entire month of March 2023 reorganizing and rebuilding the 155th Naval Infantry Brigade with conscripts, while exchanging artillery fire and FPV drone strikes. Skirmishing continued, and a Ukrainian spoiling attack pushed the Russians back to Kashlahach River and the villages of Pavlivka and Myskilske. The main Ukrainian attack force withdrew, deploying observation posts in the new security zone amongst the newly liberated tree line and villages. Skirmishing continued between the combatants until May 2023.[19]

Analysis of the winter 2023 Battle of Vuhledar and lessons learned underscores the extreme complexity of modern war at the lowest level: squad and vehicle crew. The difficulty of weaving together battlefield operating systems of combined arms warfare was mindboggling to the point of paralysis for the uninitiated. The handicap of partially trained crews, squads, platoons and companies could have been compensated for with trained and flexible battalion, brigade and division staffs. Fortunately for the Ukrainians, the Russian staff lacked experience and was under-strength and untrained in coordinating combined arms attacks.

The Battle of Vuhledar highlighted glaring problems in Russian tactics and procedures. Their battalions did not share intelligence on the Ukrainian tactics. Neither infantry nor armour FPV drones coordinated with the Russian fire control net. Lack of responsive artillery support for ground manoeuvre battalions doomed their attacks. The Naval Infantry was elite in name only. The brigades had been rebuilt and re-armed several times but lacked sufficient training time to build effective crews, squads, platoons, companies and/or staffs. Poorly trained and inexperienced company grade officers made basic mistakes in failing to consider the open terrain littered with anti-tank mines. A company could have generated smokescreens with their armoured vehicle exhausts along with their forward-facing smoke grenades. The use of vehicle-generated smokescreens seems to have been a lost Russian art. After issuing the plan for attack, battalion, brigade and division staffs failed to monitor the battle and failed to develop alternative courses of action. Newly rebuilt battalions were rushed into battle with staffs unable to coordinate even the basic elements for an assault on a fortified position.

The really criminal negligence occurred within the brigade and division staffs. The obvious lack of smoke to cover the manoeuvring units, insufficient reconnaissance, defective organization of the assault force, and insufficient or totally absent air support compounded the problem. The staffs' most glaring defect was their lack of flexibility to alter tactics and procedures in face of the Ivans' daily death toll.[20]

At the end of March 2023, due to his failure to capture Vuhledar, General Muradov was relieved of his command by OK-East. The blame for the near destruction of the 155th Naval Infantry Brigade was levelled at Muradov by the *Moscow Times*.[21] Muradov's and his subordinate senior commanders' inability to adapt quickly to a fluid battlefield doomed thousands of Ivans to an early grave. Even more unforgivable, his failure at Vuhledar illuminated Wagner's future bloody successes at Bakhmut, bringing discredit to the Russia Army on the world stage.

Chapter 12

The Battle of Bakhmut. The Russian Winter Offensive January–May 2023

When the Russians invaded, the city of Bakhmut was in the Ukrainian second operational defensive belt, nearly 30 km (18 miles) behind the first defensive belt along the border with the DPR. The fortified towns and cities along the DPR border were anchored on Popasna, which was captured by Wagner Group on 7 May 2022. After months of heavy fighting through fortified villages, the Russians advanced to within 5 km (3 miles) of Bakhmut where the attack stalled. To regain momentum, in October 2022 PMC Wagner was assigned to reinforce the attack and to capture the fortified city.

Bakhmut was a fortress in the Ukrainian first defensive belt for Donbas. To the east of the city, the Bakhmi River represented a major obstacle, covered by heavy direct and indirect fire. The fortified town of Khromove, 5 km (3 miles) west of Bakhmut was situated on a ridge running south-west to north-east dominating all routes from the city into the middle of Ukraine. Six kilometres (3.7 miles) west of Khromove was the fortified city of Chasiv Yar and another complex series of hills and ridges running south-west to north-east. Approximately 25 km (15 miles) behind these fortified towns and cities was the Ukrainian second operational defensive belt, anchored on the fortified cites of Sloviansk, Kramatorsk and Druzhkivka along the Kazennyi Torets River. The ridges west of the river valley dominated the lower ground on the east of the river. The capture of Bakhmut would not provide any real tactical or operational advantage, but possession of the city became a political symbol of success for both combatants.

With the successful September 2022 Ukrainian counter-offensive in Kharkiv, Russia re-prioritized its objectives and focused on the capture of Bakhmut for the rest of the year. If Bakhmut had been captured in May, it would have led to the capture of Kramatorsk and/or Slovyansk, isolating four Ukrainian brigades in the Donbas pocket. The failure of the Russians to capture these cities by May 2022 rendered Bakhmut irrelevant as the pocket

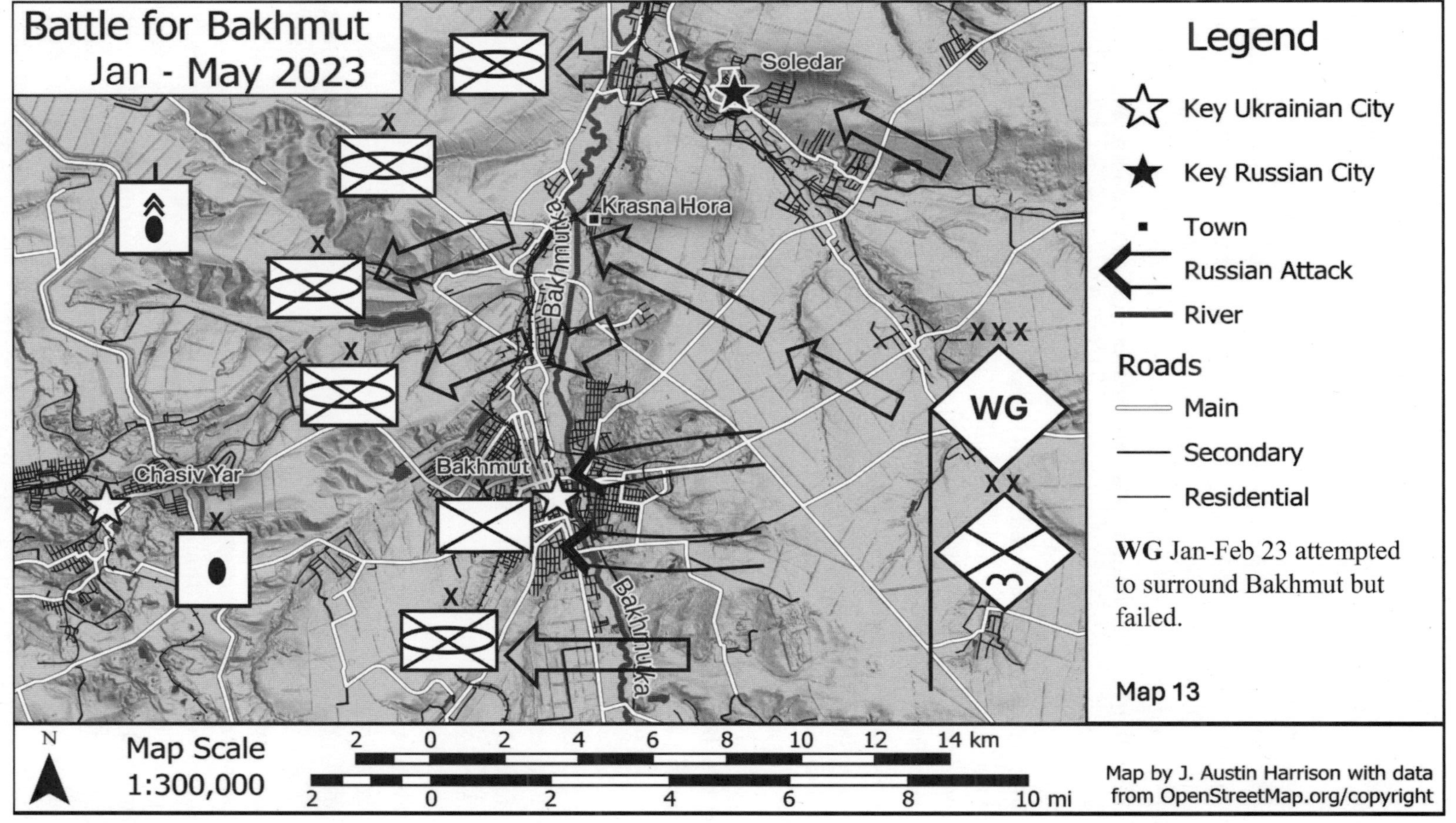

Battle for Bakhmut
Jan - May 2023
Soledar
Krasna Hora
Bakhmutka
Bakhmut
Chasiv Yar
WG
Legend
Key Ukrainian City
Key Russian City
Town
Russian Attack
River
Roads
Main
Secondary
Residential
WG Jan-Feb 23 attempted to surround Bakhmut but failed.
Map 13
N
Map Scale
1:300,000
2 0 2 4 6 8 10 12 14 km
2 0 2 4 6 8 10 mi
Map by J. Austin Harrison with data from OpenStreetMap.org/copyright

had been reduced and the four defending brigades escaped. The city went from being key territory to just another of many fortified cities along Ukraine's first defensive belt.[1]

Bakhmut became important again in August 2022, not for its military significance, but for propaganda value in the fight to capture the Ukrainian Donetsk Oblast. Putin needed a propaganda victory to offset major military defeats, and capturing Bakhmut became a symbolic objective.

The Battle of Bakhmut was renewed in summer/autumn 2022. Putin assigned his most successful combat unit, PMC Wagner, to capture the city. Prigozhin, Wagner Group's CEO, stated that his goal was to turn Bakhmut into a modern 'Verdun' and bleed Ukrainian forces dry through attrition. Ironically, however, like Verdun in 1916, it was Prigozhin's mercenaries and supporting Russian soldiers who suffered extremely heavy casualties, at a higher rate than the Ukrainian defenders.

The renewed Battle of Bakhmut commenced on 1 August 2022, when Wagnerites and DPR militia launched a series of battalion-size attacks against villages south and east of the city. Airstrikes and artillery bombarded the city as the ground forces slowly advanced. The intensity of the attacks surprised the Ukrainians, because the city was heavily fortified and defended by two brigades. FPV drones provided Ukrainian commanders with real-time situational awareness, enabling them to detect the massing of Russian forces. They assumed the Wagnerites would bypass and attempt to encircle the city, expecting the Russians to attack the villages of Soledar to the north and Zaitseve and Opytne to the south.[2] Instead, the Russian main effort consisted of a series of frontal attacks along the strongest section of the Bakhmut front defended by the 93rd Mechanized and 58th Motorized Brigades.

The frontal attacks on Bakhmut were the result of Prigozhin wanting to prove to Putin and military leaders that his mercenaries were better trained and more capable than the Russian Army, which had retreated from Kherson. Prigozhin was Putin's friend and politically connected to General Sergei Surovikin, Chief of Operations, who gave him a free hand to take Bakhmut.

The approaches to Bakhmut were covered by villages, fortified into strong points, with interlocking fields of fire. Assaulting battalions, companies, platoon and squad storm groups were subjected to flanking fire from the strong points and frontal fire from Bakhmut. A coordinated fire plan was required to suppress the strong points and allow the Russians to reach the defenders in the city. Unfortunately for the assault forces, the Wagnerites lacked the skill required to closely coordinate artillery and mortar fires with attacking infantry. Lacking night vision goggles (NVGs), Russian infantry and mercenaries often attacked in daylight. The resulting ground attacks inched forward slowly, suffering heavy losses. Fighting continued throughout December 2022 as both sides dug trenches, while heavy shelling and artillery duels became a daily occurrence.

To feed Wagner Group's need for cannon fodder, Prigozhin was authorized to recruit from Russian prisons in July 2022. By October 2022 approximately 20,000 felons had been recruited, and by January 2023 Wagner Group mustered between 50,000 and 80,000 operatives, two thirds of them recruited from prisons.[3] Prigozhin was not picky. Murderers, rapists, kidnappers and even tax evaders were qualified to volunteer. The new Wagnerites were sent to the front after only two to three weeks of training in infantry assault tactics. Wagner Group was the size of a NATO army corps by January 2023.

With this influx of manpower during months of heavy fighting, Wagner Group adapted their assaults to mirror German First World War storm tactics. These succeeded in breaking through Allied trench lines in 1918 but failed to reach Paris. Prigozhin shifted tactics during the autumn of 2022, and by the beginning of the second year the corps-size Wagner Group controlled 130 km (81 miles) of frontline.

Prigozhin changed tactics again in January 2023 as winter weather altered combat conditions. While frontal assaults on Bakhmut continued, Wagner's main effort was an attempt to encircle the beleaguered city. The city of Soledar 13 km (8 miles) north-east of Bakhmut now became Wagner's target.

Soledar guarded the northern flank of Bakhmut. The town had a pre-war population of 10,490 and was important for its salt mines, the tunnels of which ran under the town. At one time the mine produced 95 per cent of Ukraine's salt, but by 2021 production had stopped. Salt mining had been replaced by mine tourism. Thousands of visitors toured the vast underground city, in which some chambers were so vast that hot air balloon rides were introduced.[4] A group of lakes lay around the town, reducing the avenues of attack.

Shelling of the region began on 3 August 2022. Russian attacks around Soledar continued through the second half of 2022, but slackened as Russia became obsessed with capturing Bakhmut. By December 2022 Russian artillery had reduced the town to rubble, although the mine tunnels allowed the Ukrainians to supply their strong points in the ruins.

Russian troops captured the village of Bakhmutske on 27 December 2022, opening Soledar to attack from the south and east. Wagner Group detachments spearheaded the attack, while the 46th and 77th Airmobile Brigades defended the city and its surroundings. One hundred metres underground, the 200 km (120 miles) of tunnels allowed defenders to move within the defensive perimeter in relative safety.[5]

The Russian assault slugged its way forward, capturing the Dekonska Railway Station on the southern outskirts of the town on 4 January 2023. Between 10 and 13 January Russian media daily claimed the town had been taken, yet the 46th Paratroopers doggedly held on even after their brigade commander, Colonel Yuriy Yurchik, had been killed. As well as allowing the defenders to forward supplies, the tunnels beneath the city enabled them to evacuate the wounded. The defenders also used these tunnels to mount counter-attacks.[6] However, despite the tenacity of the defenders and the Russian heavy losses, Soledar was confirmed captured on 16 January 2023.[7]

With the fall of Soledar, Wagner detachments and Russian forces made slow but steady progress, capturing the high ground along the northern and southern flanks of Bakhmut in an attempt to encircle the city. By March 2023, supply lines into the city were under threat of daily artillery bombardment, and the defenders received fire from three sides. Western commentators and government officials were recommending that President Zelensky withdraw his forces from the city.

General Oleksadr Syrskyi, commander of Ukrainian ground forces and a Soviet-style general with a reputation as a hard driving aggressive commander, was responsible for defence of the city. His nickname was 'Butcher', earned for the heavy losses under his command while defending Bakhmut. Oddly, his family resided inside Russia. He visited Bakhmut in late February and early March and relayed his decision to defend to President Zelensky and General Zaluzhnyi. Syrskyi favoured a more Soviet tactic of locking the Wagnerites into an urban fight.

When the Russians and Wagnerites attacked Ukrainian positions in open country, the loss ratio favoured the defenders by a considerable margin, often between 3:1 and 10:1. In house-to-house fighting the casualty ratio was often even. To save manpower, General Zaluzhnyi favoured fighting in open country, bur Zelensky sided with Syrskyi. He viewed the fight to save Bakhmut as a political necessity.

Despite being surrounded on three sides, Syrskyi's soldiers organized a defence of Bakhmut to contest every inch. Unbeknown to the Russians and the West, Bakhmut also had a series of tunnels that were used to supply the defenders. Despite these tunnels, the Ukrainians within the city often suffered from a shortage of ammunition.[8]

On 11 January 2023 General Surovikin was replaced by General Gerasimov. Gerasimov was no friend of Prigozhin, took issue with his attack on the competence of the Russian Army and started reducing Wagner's allotment of ammunition. In March 2023 Prigozhin publicly complained about ammunition shortages, alleging that his operatives were receiving only 10 per cent of their requirements. Prigozhin blamed Defence Minister Sergei Shoigu and Chief of Staff Valery Gerasimov for reducing supplies and ammunition.[9] This political struggle continued into May 2023. The issue was over who would claim credit for capturing the city: Wagner Group or the Army. If Wagner Group captured Bakhmut, the Army would be discredited.[10] While political infighting persisted, Wagner Group and VDV paratrooper frontal assaults on Bakhmut and the high ground on both flanks continued.

In late March 2023, Ukrainian defenders turned sections of Bakhmut into kill zones. Snipers deployed to high-rise buildings in the city centre, while Wagnerites were confined to one-storey buildings in the suburbs. Firing over the heads of Ukrainian defenders, snipers trapped Wagnerites in buildings which were then targeted with artillery.[11]

On 29 March, defending snipers created kill zones behind Ukrainian lines. As Wagnerites breached the lines, they were engaged by the snipers positioned in the high-rise buildings. Once under concentrated sniper fire, Wagnerites took cover in one-storey buildings at the edge of the city. Trapped in buildings rigged for demolition, the Wagnerite assault wave was destroyed as they were bombarded by artillery.[12] Despite the high casualties and novel Ukrainian tactics, Wagnerites continued to grind forward. As casualties mounted, Defence Minister General Shoigu recruited from Russian prisons to form Storm Z units, but cut Prigozhin off from recruiting felons. Prigozhin was forced to recall contract mercenaries fighting in other countries to reinforce his dwindling assault force in Ukraine.[13]

On 1 April, the Ukrainians launched counter-attacks against both arms of the Russian pincer attempting to encircle Bakhmut. The Russians had captured

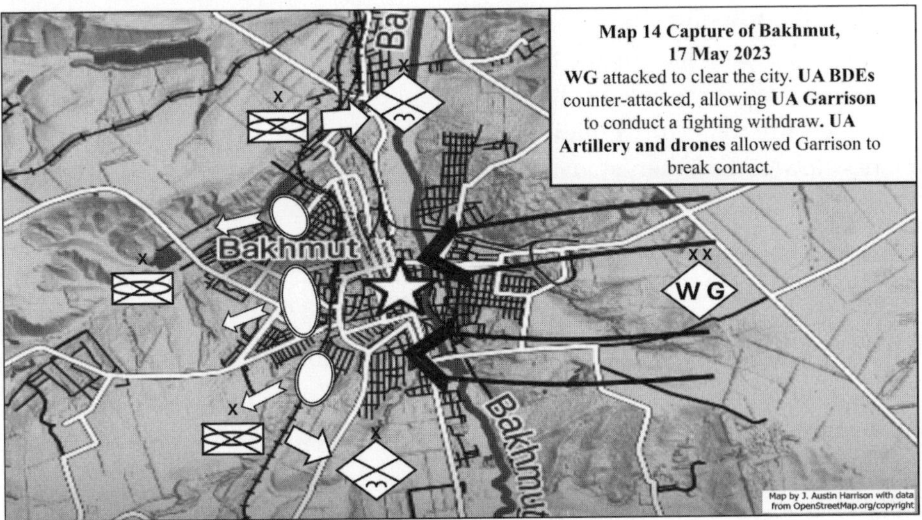

Map 14 Capture of Bakhmut, 17 May 2023
WG attacked to clear the city. **UA BDEs** counter-attacked, allowing **UA Garrison** to conduct a fighting withdraw. **UA Artillery and drones** allowed Garrison to break contact.

the high ground on both sides of the town. Attacking the northern arm of the pincer, a Ukrainian armoured assault company drove down the Sloviansk highway and pushed the Russians off a key hill dominating a supply road into the city. The capture of the hill prevented Russian ATGM teams from hitting supply vehicles on the highway. Another armoured counter-attack by two tanks and an IFV led by a tank battalion commander destroyed a Wagnerite assault squad that had captured a trench. Out of ammunition, the battalion commander crushed the Wagnerites in the trench by repeatedly driving over it with his tank. Other counter-attacks north of Bakhmut threatened Wagner's flanks, forcing Prigozhin to request assistance from the Army. By 3 April 2023 the Ukrainian counter-attack was halted by heavy snowfall. The Russians' attempted encirclement of Bakhmut had failed.[14] However, they still controlled the high ground north and south of the town, threatening the supply lines into the city.

During early April 2023, the Russian effort against Bakhmut was reorganized and was more closely coordinated with VDV. The Wagner Group continued to make the main effort, focused on capturing the city by frontal assault, but their sector of responsibility was reduced from 130 km to 5 km. VDV paratrooper regiments and brigades deployed as supporting attacks protecting Wagnerite flanks from Ukrainian counter-attacks.[15]

Despite the snow, massive artillery bombardment, supported by infantry assaults, forced the Ukrainians inside the city to fall back slowly towards the west. Every time the defenders were forced to give up a fortified building they mined it heavily. As the Wagnerites occupied a building, it was blown up. On 3 April 2023 the ruins of the city hall were captured, and Wagner and Russian flags were raised over it. The 93rd Mechanized Brigade conducted active defence spoiling attacks, supported by massed artillery and drones, and held the southern part of the town.[16] Armoured raids, in which two or three tanks emerged from hide positions to support defending infantry, used direct main gun fire to destroy buildings where Wagnerites had taken refuge. These tactics slowed the Wagner advance but did not stop it.

By 14 April Wagnerites had captured the city administration building and by 15 April they controlled 80 per cent of the city. Prigozhin's mercenary division was totally focused on capturing Bakhmut, and the Ukrainians were slowly being pushed westward. On the northern edge of the city, the VDV 106th Air Assault Division cut the M03 highway toward Orikhovo-Vasylivka.

By mid-April OC-West concluded it could not hold Bakhmut. The Ukrainians developed a fighting withdrawal plan that involved counter-attacks on the forces defending Wagner's northern and southern flanks. Ten brigades participated and each one deployed a battalion in defences in and around the city. The battalions rotated approximately every two weeks. The remainder of the brigades held the flanks of the city and formed a second defensive echelon along the high ground to the west. In support of its ground manoeuvre forces Ukraine deployed five artillery brigades to support the defenders and provide counter-battery fire.

Wagner Group massed its remaining forces along a 5 km (3 mile) front within the city. To support Wagnerite assault groups against the positions in the western high-rise buildings and industrial complex Prigozhin moved his supporting artillery, including short-range thermobaric launchers, to within 10 km (6 miles) of the city centre. Ukrainians mined their positions and registered each location with their artillery, causing Wagnerites to become paranoid about occupying abandoned positions for fear they would explode.[17]

On the evening of Friday, 5 May, the Russians bombarded the Ukrainian positions in Bakhmut with white phosphorus and incendiary ammunition. These attacks burned down buildings to destroy fortified positions, as well as tanks unfortunately parked next to buildings under camouflage nets for concealment.[18]

By early May 2023 the Ukrainians had lost control of 85 per cent of the city, and six battalions defended the remaining 15 per cent. Approximately 1,000 Ukrainian soldiers held the front line. The defensive positions were organized in depth in a heavily industrialized area. Large multi-storey factory complexes and warehouses were grouped into defensive sectors: left (north) centre and right (south). The defenders consisted of a task force of three regular dismounted motorized or mechanized battalions and three Territorial light infantry battalions. All were veteran units, but the regular battalions were better trained and equipped than the Territorials.

The surviving Wagnerites massed along a 5 km (3 mile) front to conduct frontal assaults against the industrial fortresses. VDV paratroopers were pulled out of the salients north and south of the city and massed in a second assault echelon behind the Wagnerite formations. The VDV battalions were replaced with regular Russian battalions that occupied combat outposts along the line of contact.

While it is unclear as to when the VDV pulled out, on 6/7 May combat patrols of the 3rd (UA) Azov Assault Brigade attacked the combat outposts south of Bakhmut held by Russian regular soldiers. After a 12-hour firefight, the defenders broke and fled. After weathering a Russian artillery strike, the 3rd (UA) Assault Brigade advanced on 8 May 2023 in three columns of tanks and M113 APCs. Once within earshot of the 6th and 8th companies of the 72nd Motorized Rifle Brigade, a close-range firefight ensued. Most of the two Russian companies retreated, while a few strongpoints held. The Ukrainians shouted to the Russians to 'Surrender you fools, you morons!' Ukrainian APCs outflanked the Russians and ordered them again to surrender. Five surrendered, and those who continued fighting were killed or ran into the forest.[19]

On 8 May Ukrainians conducted massive HIMARS strikes against Russian and Wagner logistics and command posts, and on troops concentrated in the rear of the Bakhmut sector. These strikes were followed by a ground attack on 9 May by the 3rd (UA) Assault Brigade. After defeating the Russian forces in the security zone, the assault routed more defenders. As their southern flank collapsed, Wagner sent reinforcements to hold the line along the Bakhmut Creek. The attack continued to gain ground on 10 May, forcing Wagner to shift additional reserves in an attempt to contain the assault. The 3rd (Wagner) Assault Battalion reinforced the area and in the ensuing heavy fighting reportedly lost 500 mercenaries.[20]

On 10 May another Ukrainian brigade advanced along two axes through the forests north of Bakhmut. Their objective was to capture the high ground dominating the northern MSR into Bakhmut. By noon the 4th Motorized Rifle Brigade defending the forest had run short of ammunition and pulled back from outlying positions. This retrograde movement resulted in at least one battalion abandoning a heavily fortified trench line. On 11 May the Ukrainians commenced probing attacks and discovered two weak points, then attacked in force. This attack from the north and south threatened to cut the southern arm of the Russian pincer that had failed to encircle Bakhmut.[21]

The Ukrainian attack on the northern arm of the pincer followed the same tactics. Russian defences were probed for a weakness, and a gap was found between the small village of Bohdanivka and a stream in the 9th Motorized Rifle Brigade's first echelon. As more Ukrainians advanced through the gap, the Russians were forced to pull their first echelon back. Preparing for a major attack on Bakhmut from the north, the Russians had moved munitions and weapons forward. As they conducted a hasty withdrawal, these supplies and weapons were captured.[22] These Ukrainian brigade-size attacks on the flanks of the Russian Bakhmut battle group caused Prigozhin's Wagner Group some concern, but they redoubled their assault.

Prophetically, after viewing the situation in the Donbas Sector, Prigozhin publicly warned the Kremlin that Belgorod Oblast was under threat from Ukrainian ground attack. In a panic, Russian military bloggers repeated the warning. The bloggers reported Ukrainian mechanized columns near the Russian border on the highway leading toward Belgorod in Russia. Other rumours surfaced that Ukrainians had liberated several small towns, had conducted a chemical attack and were preparing to cross the Dnipro River in force.[23] There was talk of a deployment of the anti-Putin expatriate Free

Russian Legion and Russian Volunteer Corps into covert assembly areas near the Russian border on roads leading toward Belgorod. Sensing a disinformation campaign, the Kremlin did not reinforce the border guards in Belgorod.

Between 8 and 10 May 2023 Prigozhin blamed the 72nd Motorized Rifle Brigade for losing three square kilometres, resulting in the death of 500 Wagnerites sent to reinforce them. Prigozhin publicly voiced these allegations throughout March, April and May 2023. His criticism focused on two primary issues: his unheeded warning about the scale of a future Ukrainian spring/summer counter-offensive, and the lack of material support for Wagner Group, especially the lack of ammunition. Prigozhin did not spare Putin or other Kremlin leaders such as Shoigu. Chechen military leader Ramzan Kadyrov, whose troops fought alongside the Wagnerites, publicly criticized Progozhin.[24] Pro-Russian bloggers warned that infighting among Russia's military leaders could only negatively impact Ivan's morale.

Russian pro-war bloggers were quick to claim the local counter-attacks were in fact the start of Ukraine's counter-offensive. They missed the fact that the attack south of Bakhmut was carried out by the 3rd Azov Assault Brigade, which occupied a frontline position and was not part of the strategic reserve. The brigade commander, Andriy Biletsky, indicated that the defensive phase of the Battle for Bakhmut had ended,while local counter-attacks could isolate Russians and Wagnerites in the city. The Ukrainian Adam Tactical Group launched drones to support the soldiers as they assaulted the Russian security zone combat outposts. The Ukrainian advance threatened to cut off the salient south of Bakhmut and isolate a Russian brigade.[25]

The phasing of ground operations in Bakhmut placed the Russians on the horns of a dilemma. If the Russian Bakhmut battle group was reinforced, it would divert reserves, weakening the defence of supply routes into Crimea. While the fog of war descended over the battlefield, Prigozhin maintained his focus on the political benefits of capturing Bakhmut. As his flanks appeared to be failing, his assault force was backed up by VDV battalions in the second echelon, a few kilometres to his rear.

While the local counter-attacks were successful, Wagnerites continued hammering the 127th Territorial Defence Brigade positions within Bakhmut. Between 5 and 6 May 2023 the Russians conducted four unsuccessful attacks over the ground and the dead bodies of the previous attack. The 127th Brigade Commander, Colonel Roman Hryshchenko, only forty-one years old, counted forty-eight incoming shells fired on his position while he was giving a phone interview to a reporter. His headquarters was in the basement of a high-rise building. During the fighting the nine-storey building lost its five top floors. The day after the interview, Wagnerites claimed to have captured the first and second storeys of the building. Territorial soldiers counter-attacked, fighting within 5 feet of the Wagnerites, and recaptured it. After killing or ejecting the invaders, the defenders were hammered by Russian artillery. Despite Wagner's claim that they were short of artillery shells, Hryshchenko reported that he did not notice a reduction in the volume fired onto his position.[26]

Fighting for the three western industrialized areas was intense. Covering fire from outside the city allowed the final six battalions (1,000 men) to break contact and escape capture. On 21 May Prigozhin claimed the town had been captured. Heavy fighting continued along the western edge of the city, and on both flanks, but the Battle of Bakhmut was over.

On 25 May 2023 Prigozhin released a video explaining the situation after Bakhmut had been captured. He disclosed that the Wagner Group would be replaced by the Russian Army on 1 June 2023. The responsibility for the Bakhmut sector now shifted from Wagner Group to the Russian Army, but the shift in responsibility did not stop the fighting. The loss of Bakhmut made little tactical difference. The Ukrainians held the high ground west of the city, and skirmishing along the line of contact and exchanges of artillery fire continued for months.[27]

Prigozhin reported at the beginning of the Battle for Bakhmut that the Wagner Group mustered 35,000 professional mercenaries, and after recruiting 50,000 prison inmates, it fielded 85,000 men. It had increased from division to corps size. In eight months of intense combat, the Group had suffered 10,000 inmates KIA and 10,000 professional Wagnerites KIA and 20,000 WIA. It was unusual for a Russian commander to publicly disclose casualties, and his figures were immediately challenged by former Russian officer and military blogger Igor Gerkin. Gerkin pointed out that since only 25,000 inmates had received pardons, the remaining 25,000 felons were KIA. He speculated that real casualties were 50 per cent higher than reported by Wagner. He concluded that a more accurate figure was 25,000 felons and 15,000 professionals KIA. Putin claimed that the overall ratio of WIA to KIA was 2:1, meaning that over 40,000 Wagnerites were KIA.That would have placed Wagner Group's total casualties at 80,000. Based on these numbers, the Wagner Group started 2023 with 85,000 troops, the size of an army corps, but by the end of the Battle for Bakhmut only 5,000 combatants, or the equivalent of one brigade, remained present for duty.[28] The disturbing fact about these casualty rates was the abnormally high ratio of WIA to KIA. The accepted loss ratio was 1 KIA to 3 or 5 WIA. Prigozhin's statement underscored Ukrainian accounts that Wagner provided poor recovery of seriously wounded mercenaries and poor medical treatment.

These extremely high casualty rates explain Prigozhin's steadily reduced area of responsibility as the 2023 winter offensive progressed. In January 2023, Wagner Group was responsible for 85 km (53 miles) of front. By May 2023 its sector had been reduced to 5 km (3 miles) solely within Bakhmut. This may have been why Gerkin told Prigozhin to 'keep his mouth shut and stop talking about losses'.[29]

After finally capturing Bakhmut, Prigozhin asserted that Putin's Special Operation was a complete failure and that Russia had failed to achieve its objectives. The invasion had solidified Ukrainian national identity and legitimized Ukraine as a sovereign nation. Ukrainian armed forces had become more powerful and better equipped with Western weapons than before the war. The US and NATO had ramped up weapon production while 'denazification had completely failed'. If Russia did not transition onto a full war footing, the war could be lost.[30] His observations were accurate.

After capturing Bakhmut, Wagner was pulled out of the line for rest and refit, and the Russian Army occupied the city. The 4th Separate Motorized Brigade held the low ridge 2 km (1.2 miles) west of Klishchiivka. The 57th Separate Motorized Rifle Brigade replaced Wagner Group in Bakhmut and on the high ground north of the city. The 217th Airborne Regiment (98th Airborne Division) and 137th Guards Airborne Regiment (106th Airborne Division) were positioned in a second defensive line 4 km (2.4 miles) behind the frontline.[31]

The capture of Bakhmut was the culmination of the Russian 2023 winter offensive, however it did not end the fighting. Skirmishes continued along the line of contact. Successful local Ukrainian counter-attacks north and south of the city ended with the fighting withdrawal of the Ukrainian garrison. The Russians lacked an exploitation force to continue the attack to the next Ukrainian fortified city complex at Chasiv Yar, located on high ground 10 km (6 miles) west of Bakhmut. Capturing it was beyond the capability of Russian forces in the area.

At best the Battle of Bakhmut was a 'Pyrrhic victory' for the Russians. After the capture of the city the Russians were no closer to capturing the rest of the Donbas.

Chapter 13

The Russian 2023 Winter Offensive Lessons Learned

Colonel Viktor Kevliuk of the Ukrainian Centre for Defence Strategies hypothesised that the objective of General Gerasimov's offensive was to launch local attacks along the entire line from Kuyyansk, Lyman, Bakhmut, Avdiivka and Marinka to Vuhledar. The intent of numerous local attacks was to identify weak areas in the Ukrainian defences. This would force the Ukrainians to spend resources and deploy reserves, and create conditions for the eventual capture of Luhansk and Donetsk Oblasts. In a second phase, later in the year, the general offensive would strive to capture two cities, Slovyansk and Kramatorsk. Taking all of Donbas was not possible without first capturing these two cities, since they controlled the gateway to the rest of Ukraine.[1]

Russia had previous experience of success conducting a general offensive along an entire front. By 1916, the Imperial Russian Army had sufficiently recovered from the early military disasters of the First World War (1914 and 1915) to wrest the initiative from Germany and Austria-Hungary. At this point in the war, the Eastern Front stretched from Riga in the north to the Romanian border in the south. The Russian Army enjoyed superior numbers, with 1,732,000 men against the Austro-German combined force of 1,061,000. Taking advantage of their numerical superiority, the Imperial Russian Army planned a major offensive across the entire theatre of operations. The Russian high command organized its offensive in three fronts, or army groups, entitled North, Western and South-Western. The battle plan was for the Western Front to carry out the main offensive effort, while the South-Western Front conducted a supporting attack. The South-Western Front was to draw the Austro-German reserves from where they were opposing the Western Front's zone of attack.

The offensive commenced 4 June 1916 and culminated on 20 September 1916. General Brusilov's plan of attack, like Gerasimov's, was unorthodox. Instead of massing his combat power in a single narrow attack zone, Brusilov directed each of his four armies, and each of their corps, to prepare an attack zone. The result of this battle plan was that the South-Western Front attacked along the entire length of its 450 km (279 miles) front line. With multiple main attacks and numerous supporting attacks, the Austro-German armies were unable to deploy sufficient reserves to counter the Russian breakthrough. Penetrations developed along the frontlines, and local exploitation forces penetrated the Austro-German line and collapsed the front. The Imperial Russians recaptured 25,000 square kilometres, pushing the Austro-Germans back to the Carpathian Mountains. The Austro-Germans took over 800,000 casualties, while the Imperial Russians suffered over 700,000.

Gerasimov's plan mirrored Brusilov's. The Russian Army's efforts were not concentrated but spread along the Donbas Front. The Army was, of course, in competition with Wagner Group, and Wagner concentrated more combat power on the Bakhmut Sector than the Army did on any of its four zones of attack. Gerasimov assumed one of his attack vectors would be successful.

Despite Gerasimov's plan, the 2023 winter offensive, like the initial Special Operation, was not an overwhelming success. It did demonstrate the Russian military's ability to adapt to changing battlefield conditions, but while the change in battlefield tactics, techniques and procedures (TTPs) led to minor battlefield successes, they were paid for with heavy casualties.

With the failure of the battalion tactical groups (BTGs), motorized rifle battalions became the standard infantry formation in all ground branches including PMCs. Mobilizing manpower was easy, but training and equipping replacements was difficult. The lack of trainers and kit made it impossible to produce fully qualified soldiers and battalions in the limited training time available. As a result, in January 2023, four classes of infantry developed: line, assault, specialized and disposable. Line infantry consisted of second

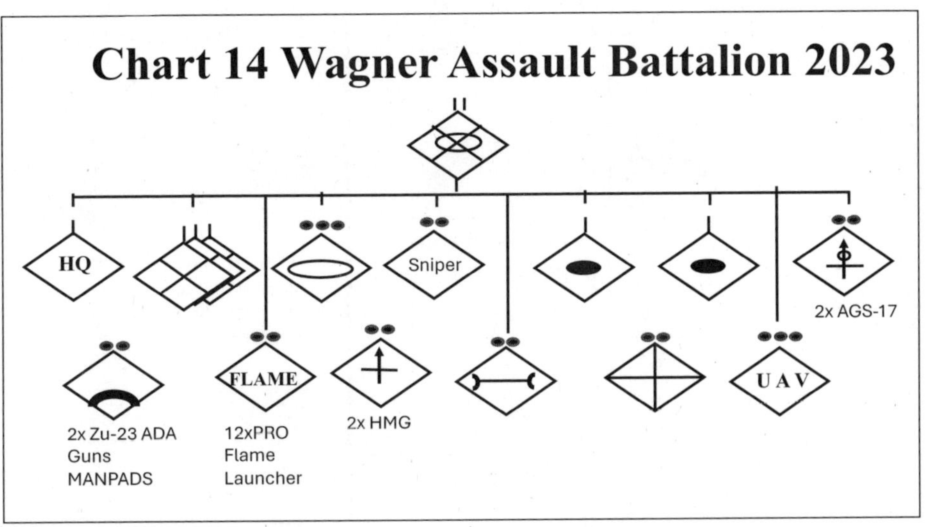

class formations organized to hold ground and conduct defensive operations. Disposable infantry included PMC Wagner and Army Storm Z inmate detachments and battalions. These prison recruits continuously skirmished with Ukraine battle positions and led the assaults to locate weak points in Ukrainian lines. Once a Ukrainian position was captured or breached, assault infantry exploited the situation.

Motorized rifle battalions, known as Storm-Z detachments, integrated lessons learned by Wagner Group. Combined arms rifle platoons of fifteen soldiers were formed. An armoured vehicle section (two tanks or IFVs) provided direct fire support, normally positioned on the flanks. The Storm-Z detachments combined regular and convict platoons, the inmates serving as 'disposable infantry'. Battalion-size Storm-Z detachments were organized into three 100-man companies with organic drone sections. They led attacks in the first echelon, with regular battalions following in the second echelon.[2] Many Storm-Z detachments/battalions were attached to motorized rifle or tank regiments and brigades.

Specialized infantry provided fire support with battalion mortars, heavy machine guns and shoulder-fired thermobaric rocket launchers. They also operated tactical drones. The TTPs that employed these classes of infantry slowly gained ground but took heavy casualties, with the highest rate among the disposable infantry. It is not surprising that the Russian infantry suffered from low morale, poor unit cohesion and lack of inter-battalion/company cooperation.[3]

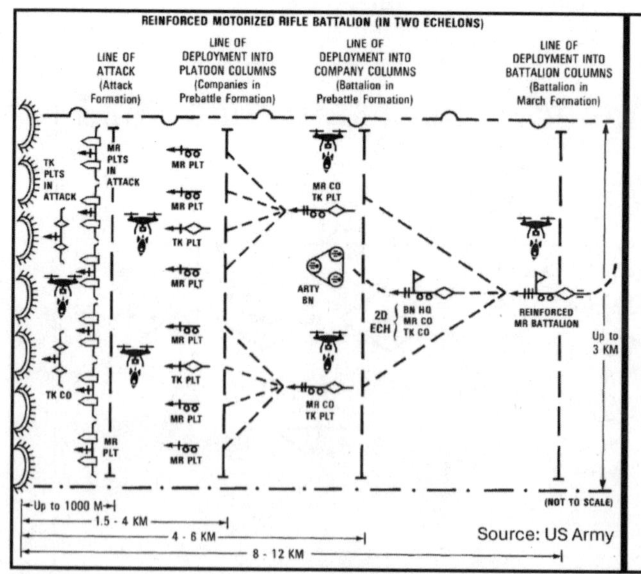

Chart 15 Russian/Soviet Movement To Contact Battalion to Platoon

Soviet/Russian tactics never envisioned their attacking battalion and company columns to come under direct fire before reaching 4km from the line of contact. It was expected that AD would keep enemy air at bay, while the attack advanced.

In 2023, swarms of FPV Drones conducted spoiling attacks on company and larger columns as they approached their Line of Deployment.

Soviet-style massed armour operations were employed by reinforced motorized rifle battalions, but less frequently than in 2022. Media reports from the front often misinterpreted the events on the ground as company columns conducting isolated attacks. When the data on the Battle of Vuhledar was examined, it was seen that multiple motorized rifle company size columns entered the open fields simultaneously. The distance between columns was significantly wider than pre-war doctrine dictated.

The tanks in the columns were not there to break through Ukrainian lines; rather they occupied support by fire positions prior to the infantry assault. From here they provided accurate direct fire onto Ukrainian positions. In closed terrain, tanks advanced singularly or in pairs to support platoon-size assault units. Russians employed thermal camouflage and other modifications on their armoured vehicles. These protective counter-measures reduced the tanks' thermal signature, making it harder for them to be targeted by ATGMs beyond 1,400 metres.

Combat engineers had difficulty breaching Ukrainian minefields and obstacles. Mine clearing crews were poorly trained. Mine clearing vehicles were often disabled in the middle of minefields, blocking the following attack columns, and stranding them in open fields. While unsuccessful at clearing minefields and obstacles, the combat engineers were excellent on the defensive, constructing concrete reinforced trenches, bunkers, anti-tank obstacles and minefields.

Russian artillery improved its targeting cycle by necessity. The success of HIMARS strikes on ammunition depots and C2 infrastructure in the rear left the Russians relatively short of the ammunition required for mass fire Soviet/Russian-style tactics. The Russian solution was closer integration of multiple drones in the targeting cycle. They improved their ability to displace after fire missions. This slightly reduced the effectiveness of Ukrainian counter-battery fire. The ammunition shortfall resulted in a shift from relying on 152mm howitzers to 120mm mortars. While weak at counter-battery fire, Russian artillery units relied on loitering kamikaze drones to strike Ukrainian howitzers.[4]

Leadership at platoon, company and battalion level remained weak. Initiative was not encouraged. Assaults were repeated over the same ground through the wrecked vehicles and dead bodies left by previous attacks. Battalion and brigade staffs failed to learn from prior failures. Russian commanders in the field rarely developed alternative courses of action or improved fire support plans. The poor leadership resulted in needlessly heavy casualties and rarely moved the line of contact.

After ten months of ineffective operations, the Russian Air Force was unable to achieve air supremacy in support of ground operations. The Russian Air

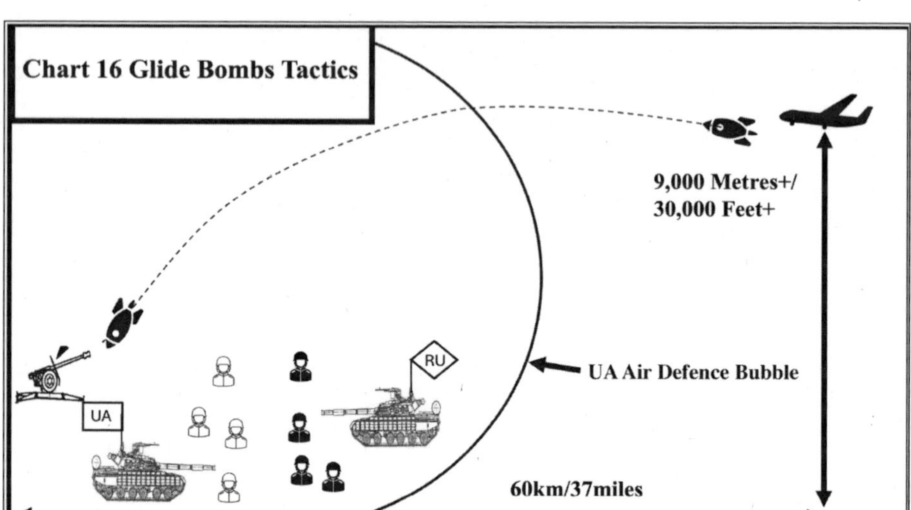

Force developed TTPs to support ground troops with gravity-guided bombs. During the 2023 winter offensive, fighter jets flying at a medium altitude 70 km (43 miles) from the front lines employed FAB-500 (500 kg/1,102 lb) glide bombs. Russia had a large stockpile of FB-500 gravity bombs that were upgraded with cheap glide kits. Firing 70 km (43 miles) from the frontlines, Ukrainian AD and old Soviet era fighter jets could not effectively engage. Larger 1,500 kg (3,306 lb) bombs would eventually be equipped with cheap glide kits.[5] While not highly accurate precision weapons, the glide bombs helped to suppress Ukrainian fortifications.

The Russians did learn from their failures during the 2023 winter offensive. To improve company and battalion leadership and C2 for assault operations, battalions, regiments and brigades should have been pulled out of the line to train, but political pressure from Putin denied his generals the luxury of doing so. During the first half of 2023 new battalions were formed in anticipation of the Ukrainian counter-offensive and the planned Russian offensive of autumn 2023.

Focused on the political goals at stake in the Battle of Bakhmut, the Ukrainians lost momentum in preparing for their counter-offensive. Highly motivated veteran brigades were deployed in the supporting attacks at Bakhmut instead of leading the Ukrainian main counter-offensive effort towards Tokmat. The 2023 winter offensive gained little ground but developed into a successful campaign of attrition and prevented Ukrainian brigades from rotating out of the line for rest and refit. The cost in both manpower and munitions was hardly worth the minor success of the offensive.

Chapter 14

Lend-Lease
January 2023–October 2023

Putin's invasion of Ukraine raised the question of escalation management between the four regional nuclear powers (US, Russia, UK and France). US President Biden made it clear that America supported Ukrainian sovereignty and independence, even though the country was not a member of NATO. Other NATO members quickly, by word or deed, supported Biden's stance. Biden was determined to avoid a war between NATO and Russia and to prevent escalation into a Third World War, while simultaneously aiding Ukraine to defend itself and repel the Russian invasion.[1]

There was no historical precedent to guide Biden and NATO leaders on how to provide aid to Ukraine while avoiding escalation, but Biden made the West's position clear at the beginning of Russia's invasion. The US and NATO did not seek war with Russia. He indicated that so long as the US and its allies were not attacked, the US would not directly engage in the conflict. US troops would not fight in Ukraine and Russian forces would not be attacked worldwide. The US would not attempt to bring about Putin's ouster or overthrow the Russian government. The US would not encourage or enable Ukraine to strike beyond its internationally recognized borders, which included Crimea.[2] The final parameter was a warning aimed directly at Putin: any use of nuclear weapons, on any scale, was unacceptable. If Russia employed nuclear weapons, there would be severe consequences. These considerations determined the level of military support and type of equipment to be provided.

Debates at the highest level of NATO member governments often delayed the decision to provide critically needed advanced military equipment, weapons, precision long-range artillery rockets and missiles. As each weapons system was provided, Putin responded with warnings and nuclear 'sabre rattling', but did not escalate. Unfortunately for Ukraine, political handwringing over whether to provide advanced military equipment and what type of equipment to provide ultimately delayed providing anything at all. During 2022/23, Western allies were not generally forthcoming with their support, and only sent sufficient advanced equipment and supplies to stave off defeat but not enough to liberate Russian-occupied Ukraine.

The media reported that total US aid to Ukraine for financial year 2022/23 was $75.4 billion dollars.[3] Humanitarian support accounted for $2.7 billion (4 per cent of total aid) and included emergency food, health care, refugee support and other humanitarian aid. Financial support accounted for $26.4 billion and included budgetary aid through Economic Support Funds, loans and other economic support.

Total US military support was $46.3 billion (61 per cent of the total) and was divided between weapons and equipment, security assistance, grants and loans. Security assistance in the amount of $18.3 billion (24 per cent of total) covered the cost of training, equipment, weapons, logistics and other assistance provided through the Ukrainian Security Assistance Initiative. Weapons and equipment from the US Department of Defense stockpile were valued at $23.5 billion (31 per cent of total). They were provided pursuant to presidential drawdown authority. The actual value was computed with 'Pentagon Math', actual in place value vs. replacement value. Weapons such as M1A1 Abrams Tanks, M2/3 Bradley OD IFVs (Operation Desert Storm) and M113 APCs were purchased by US taxpayers three to five decades before being provided to Ukraine. When sent to Ukraine, these vehicles were not scheduled to be replaced. The US Government Accounting office found that the Pentagon had overvalued the armoured vehicles, weapons and ammunition provided by $6 billion. If this 'clerical error' had gone undiscovered, it would have greatly reduced actual vehicles, weapons, and ammunition sent to Ukraine by over 25 per cent.[4] Finally, $4.5 billion (6 per cent of total) came in grants and loans through the Foreign Military Financing Program. Ukraine was authorized to purchase weapons and equipment through this programme directly from US defence industries, right off the assembly line.[5]

The US sent more than a hundred times more heavy weapons to the Allies in the Second World War than it has sent to Ukraine in the current Russian-Ukrainian War. Between 1941-1945 the US sent 25,000 tanks and 15,000 airplanes to the UK alone. Ukraine has received 500 tanks, thousands of IFVs, APCs and howitzers, but less than 100 MLRS and HIMARS. Obviously, the modern weapons were more complex and expensive to produce than their Second World War counterparts.

The UK committed £4.6 billion in military assistance, £2.3 billion in 2022 and another £2.3 billion in 2023, and also hosted a training programme for Ukrainian soldiers, supported by allies, with the goal of training 30,000 men by the end of 2023. This training package included pilot training for jet fighters.[6] The EU committed €4.6 billion, including €1 billion to reimburse countries that provided emergency re-supply of Ukrainian artillery ammunition.

In 2022, Germany had a more complex problem than just assisting Ukraine. Ensnared in Putin's petrochemical dependency, Germany had to immediately develop alternative sources of oil while doing its share to support Ukraine. During 2022, Germany provided €264 billion in domestic subsidies to cover the spike in energy costs. It also created a special fund of €100 billion to rebuild the German armed forces.[7] French assistance to Ukraine during 2022 came to over €50 billion. France provided €3.5 billion in military aid through the European Peace Facility which was 20 per cent of its total contribution.[8]

Compared to the Second World War Land-Lease programme, aid to Ukraine was not as extensive as portrayed by the media. The cost and technological sophistication of weapons has greatly increased over the last seventy years, making a comparison by dollar value unrealistic. The best measure, therefore, was to compare donor gross domestic product (GDP) to historical data. The US support to the UK during the Second World War was 2.6 per cent of US GDP, while support to the USSR was 1.2 per cent.[9] The US spent a hundred times more on heavy weapons and supplies provided to the Allies in the Second World War than it did to support Ukrainian military operations during the first two years of Putin's Special Operation.

US military aid to Ukraine during financial years 2022 and 2023 was 0.21 per cent of US GDP. The UK spent 0.18 per cent of its GDP.[10] Germany spent three times more to liberate Kuwait in the 1990s than it spent in 2023 on aid to Ukraine. Countries paying the cost of liberating Kuwait provided a fraction of that amount in aid to Ukraine. As examples, Germany spent 0.55 per cent of its GDP on Kuwait and only 0.17 per cent in support of Ukraine. Japan and South Korea each spent 0.02 per cent of their GDP on Kuwait and 0.01 per cent for Ukraine.[11]

The total amount of aid provided by Ukraine's worldwide allies amounted to approximately 80 per cent of the US contribution.[12] When measured by GDP, the former Warsaw Pact states (former Soviet Republics of Eastern Europe) provided the greatest level of support. They also comprised eight of the top ten countries hosting Ukrainian refugees.[13]

Elon Musk bought Twitter for $44 billion;[14] President Biden's original student debt relief would have cost $30 billion yearly for a decade.[15] When compared to a high-profile social media purchase and a proposed government debt relief programme, the $46 billion in military aid to Ukraine was a bargain to stop Russian aggression. This was especially true when one considers that all the tanks, IFVs, APCs and other equipment provided were decades old, mothballed in warehouses, and had been paid for before the twenty-first century. Most of the hardware provided by NATO members and other allies dated from the Cold War (1947–1991) had also been transferred from storage and was no longer in service.

While the US, UK, Poland, Germany and France provided the lion's share of aid, all NATO and EU countries, and many democratic countries in the Pacific, provided extensive forms of aid. Contributions from many small countries such Latvia, Estonia and Lithuania appeared tiny, but they actually contributed a higher percentage of their GDP than many larger more industrialised states. Many of the smaller European countries bordering Ukraine were also instrumental in helping Ukrainian refugees and the cost of this was not reflected in their aid figures. This aid was of vital importance to morale in supporting Ukraine's defence and was critical for Ukraine's 2023 counter-offensive.[16] All this support was primarily reactive, not proactive.

One of Napoleon's most famous maxims was: 'You can ask me for anything you like, except time.'[17] Every US, UK, French and German general, active or retired, knew the level of support and weapons Ukraine needed in February 2022 to defeat Russia and liberate its occupied territory. The time required to train and equip new Ukrainian assault brigades for the task was hardly a state secret. Despite this knowledge, NATO was deadlocked concerning the number and type of weapons and equipment they were willing to provide. NATO members feared that providing modern technology would result in nuclear escalation.[18] The result was reactive support for Ukraine's war effort instead of proactive. NATO's politicking, indecision and procrastination prevented a timely transfer of advanced, sophisticated weapons and equipment, especially tanks, jet fighters and modern tactical long-range missiles.

The 2022 aid packages were ultimately tailored by NATO's perception of the situation on the ground and Ukraine's requests, rather than by its future requirements. Weapons and equipment provided during Phase 1 of the Lend-Lease programme (February-April 2022) were of the type Ukrainian soldiers and militia could use with little or no training. Major items sent by the US by 15 March 2022 included 800 Stinger MANPADs, 2,000 Javelins, 6,000 AT-4s and 1,000 other man-transportable anti-armour systems. Previous shipments included 600 Stingers and 2,600 Javelins, four counter-mortar and four counter-artillery radar systems, satellite imagery and computers, along with EW, C2 equipment, light tactical vehicles, small arms, ammunition and body armour.[19] The UK shipped individual equipment, small arms, NLAW anti-tank missiles, MANPADs and ammunition. The Poles and other former Soviet Republics and former Warsaw Pact members transferred much-needed Soviet-era tanks, self-propelled howitzers and mobile rocket launchers. The equipment provided was all simple to operate, or at least so basic that a soldier or militiaman could learn to operate it after a few hours of instruction readily available on YouTube.

Germany faced initial political divisions within its government. Since the Second World War the country had followed a policy of never sending weapons to a combat zone. Germany reversed this policy on 26 February 2022 and announced it would send Ukraine 1,000 anti-tank weapons and 500 Stinger MANPADs. It also authorized the Netherlands to ship 500 rocket propelled grenades and Estonia to send nine Soviet-era howitzers, despite both weapons containing components made in Germany.[20] Once this political hurdle was removed, Germany began to provide substantial military aid in all categories except tanks.[21]

Early in 2022, President Zelensky's requests for heavy equipment included T-72 tanks, S-300 SAM/Buk air defence systems or Western equivalents, Multiple Launch Rocket Systems (MLRS) or American High Mobility Artillery Rocket Systems (HIMARS), military aircraft and NATO 155mm howitzers.[22] Both MRLS and HIMARS fired the same guided rockets, with a range of 80 km (50 miles). A request for the Army Tactical Missile System (ATACMS) with a range of 300 km (190 miles) was denied because these would have provided Ukraine with the ability to strike within 'Mother Russia', fuelling fears of escalation.[23]

After victory in the Battle for Kyiv, Ukraine's requirements changed. The Battle for the Donbas was fought on the steppes of eastern Ukraine and had become an artillery duel. Ukraine required modern artillery and counter-battery radars. Original NATO members did not have the Soviet-made ammunition requested by Ukraine, and instead provided NATO artillery that fired standard and precision 155mm munitions.[24] These NATO howitzers did not give Ukraine the ability to outrange Russian artillery, but did allow precision strikes against ammunition, fuel depots and command posts.[25]

In response to President Zelensky's request, original NATO members (US, France, Germany, the UK, Canada and the Netherlands) quickly dispatched eight-plus battalions of modern 155mm towed and self-propelled howitzers, along with counter-battery and counter-mortar radar systems and thousands of artillery shells.[26] While authorizing HIMARS and MRLS to be transferred to Ukraine, President Biden limited the ammunition to smaller rockets, with a range of 80 km (50 miles). He feared that the long-range ATACAMS would escalate the war if Ukrainians fired into Russia. The HIMARS and MRLS forced Russia to relocate its railhead supply depots back into pre-war recognized Russian territory. Russia was then forced to rely on its limited supply of cargo and fuel trucks to meet its supply requirements.

In 2022/23, NATO sent several thousand light armoured vehicles, consisting of IFVs (BMPs), APCs (M-113s and BTRs), and more modern vehicles such as the German PbV-501s.[27] NATO members equipped with old Soviet equipment (Poland, Czech Republic, Germany, Slovakia, etc.) opened their Cold War storage depots and sent replacement weapons to Ukraine with 152mm and 122mm ammunition. Cold War stocks of operational T-72 Tanks were shipped to Ukraine on 24 February 2022 by the Czech Republic. Other countries quickly followed the Czech example.[28]

Requests for relatively modern or Cold War NATO tanks were denied at this time. In April 2022, members of the German government planned to provide two battalion sets of older Leopard IA5 tanks (a total of 88) with their 105mm guns, and 100 old Marder IFVs.[29] The defence contractor Rheinmetall was ready to refurbish these vehicles for combat and to add twenty new Leopard II tanks to the shipment. If the deal had gone through at the time, Germany would have been the first NATO country to provide Ukraine with both obsolete and modern tanks. However, German Chancellor Olaf Scholz blocked the transfer.[30]

There was much internal criticism of Chancellor Scholz's action. Germany had invoked a contract clause that precluded other countries from transferring German-made tanks to Ukraine. While blocking the transfer of main battle tanks, Chancellor Scholz did send other heavy armoured vehicles, such as the Flakpanzer Gepard and Panzer Howitzer 2000. Germany became the third-largest supplier of weapons to Ukraine, at the time excluding modern tanks.[31]

Chancellor Scholz's government offered several logistical and political explanations for refusing to provide tanks. Modern battle tanks such as the M1A1 Abrams or the German Leopard II had not been provided to Ukraine.[32] Both Biden and Scholz remained steadfast on this issue for fear of escalation.

Many excuses were provided by the US and Germany. The objections focused on training, logistics and lack of maintenance infrastructure. Yet Germany provided eighteen Panzer Howitzer 2000s (on modern Leopard II tank hulls) that needed to be removed to a NATO country for depot level repairs and maintenance.[33] The logistical and maintenance problems obviously could have been addressed, leaving the real stumbling block a political one.

Chancellor Scholz's government took the position that since no other country had delivered modern tanks, Germany would not be the first to do so.[34] Germany had business interests tied to Russian natural gas, and each new weapon supplied to Ukraine constituted a threat to their continuance. Scholz's government also took the position that NATO and allied countries armed with Leopard II tanks were contractually prohibited from transferring these weapons to Ukraine. The issue was a realistic fear that providing such deadly armaments would escalate the conflict.[35]

In response to Germany's reluctance to provide tanks, a coalition of countries formed to pressure Scholz into changing his policy. The campaign was aimed at embarrassing Germany for not readily providing the badly-needed Leopard II tanks to Ukraine. The campaign was launched by two Finnish politicians and led to a coalition of countries armed with Leopard IIs aiming to furnish Ukraine with a tank brigade of 90–100 tanks. Pro-Ukrainian civil demonstrations erupted throughout Germany and across Europe. The call to action was 'Free the Leopards'.[36] The impasse between Biden and Scholz lasted into January 2023.[37]

To mount a successful counter-attack in the spring and summer of 2023, Ukraine requested 300 modern tanks, 600–700 modern IFVs, 500 SP howitzers and US F-16 fighter jets or the equivalent. This equipment would have been sufficient to equip eight to ten tank battalions, eighteen mechanized infantry battalions and twenty-seven artillery battalions, which could be organized into one armour, eight mechanized infantry and three artillery brigades.[38] A mechanized force the size of three NATO divisions would be a decisive force during the fighting in 2023.

Scholz's administration hesitated to supply German-made modern weapons until other members of the alliance were willing to supply similar weapons. Germany was specifically reluctant to provide the eighty obsolete Leopard I tanks sitting in a Rheinmetall factory warehouse since April 2022. Within the alliance, only Germany, France, the UK and the US produced modern tanks fitted with a main gun capable of firing NATO standard 120mm ammunition.

France cracked the political logjam on 4 January 2023 by announcing it would provide Ukraine with forty AMX-10 RC wheeled armoured reconnaissance vehicles. Billed as a 'light tank', the AMX-10 was a lightly armoured wheeled reconnaissance fighting vehicle. It was armed with the 105mm main gun, like the gun on the German Leopard I tank. It was designed to support lighter armoured scout cars.[39] Literally hours after France's announcement, the Biden and Scholz administrations announced they would provide IFVs. Germany agreed to provide 100 Marder IFVs, while the US announced that it would provide 109 Bradley IFVs and eventually included 100 Stryker APCs.[40]

Rheinmetall was authorized to refurbish the Marders sitting in its warehouse since spring 2022. The Marder had been heavily modified over the decades. Its primary armament was a 20mm auto-cannon and a 7.62mm machine gun, but it could be equipped with a MILAN ATGM. In addition to its three-man crew, the Marder could carry six or seven soldiers. Combat loaded, it weighed

30 tons and had a top speed of 65 kph (40 mph). It had been combat tested in Kosovo and Afghanistan.

The US Bradley M2/3 (Operation Desert Storm) OD IFV's primary armament was a 25mm chain gun with a coaxial 7.62mm MG, and a TOW II ATGM. It weighed 30 tons combat loaded and had a top speed of 56 kph (35 mph). The Bradley ODs served in the Gulf War (1990–91), the Iraqi War (2003–11) and peacekeeping operations in Kosovo. The Bradley IFVs destroyed more Iraqi tanks in the Gulf War than the M1A1 Abrams.[41] As the US Army upgraded its Bradley, the OD version had been sitting in warehouses for nearly twenty years.

The American Stykers were eight-wheeled APCs that could travel at 95 kph (60 mph). They carried a crew of three and could transport a squad of nine soldiers. They were armed with a heavy machine gun or automatic grenade launcher. When employed properly, these IFVs and APCs would provide Ukraine with a tactical advantage in the offensive.

The Bradley and Marder offered more reconnaissance capabilities with their enhanced optics and other sensors. Significantly better-armoured than the Soviet BTRs and BMPs, they might encourage Ukrainian soldiers to ride inside, protected from artillery, rather than atop in case of IED mines. Due to the threat of land mines, both Ukrainian and Russian infantry had developed the habit of riding on the outside of their armoured vehicles to avoid being trapped inside.

British Prime Minister Rishi Sunak broke the impasse on 14 January 2023 by taking the lead in announcing that Great Britain would provide fourteen Challenger 2 modern tanks and thirty AS-90 155mm self-propelled howitzers. Britain only had 250 Challenger 2 tanks in total. The announcement greatly enhanced the type of military aid, providing offensive weapons that would assist Ukraine to regain its occupied territory.[42]

Britain's announcement increased pressure on Washington and Berlin to follow its lead. With the political pressure mounting from all sides, President Biden announced on 25 January 2023 that the US would send thirty-one M1A1 Abrams tanks to Ukraine.[43] On the same day, Germany announced it would send fourteen Leopard II 2A6 tanks and most importantly authorized other countries to send their tanks, even though they contained parts manufactured in Germany, ending months of debate.[44] Other allies quickly followed suit, and twelve countries ultimately agreed to supply Ukraine with a total of 100 Leopard II tanks, the equivalent of three battalions or one brigade.

The Challenger 2, M1A1 Abrams and Leopard II A4 and 2A6 tanks had similar advanced optics, thermal sights and the same NATO standard 120mm main gun. They fired accurately to 4,000 metres and had protected ammunition compartments within their hulls and turrets. All three tanks were far superior in every category to the former Soviet era T-54/55, T-62, T-64, T-72, T-80 and T-90 tanks in use by both combatants. The Challenger 2 tank was a heavily armoured and highly mobile vehicle powered by a diesel engine. Armed with a 120mm main gun and two 7.62mm machine guns, it entered service in 1994 and had undergone a series of upgrades over the years. It had seen combat service in Bosnia, Kosovo and Iraq.

The Leopard II first rolled off the assembly line in 1979. It had been upgraded several times, and by 2023 had earned the reputation of being the best main battle tank in the world. Even the older models had superior optics and thermal sights to any tank serving on the Ukrainian battlefield at the time. Combat loaded it weighted 55 tons, and powered by a diesel engine it had a maximum speed of 70 kph (44 mph).

Perhaps most significantly, the tanks from all three countries were armed with a 120mm NATO standard cannon and a coaxial 7.62 machine gun. The 120mm gun was particularly important as it allowed Ukraine to fire the large available stockpiles of NATO ammunition. This was critical because by January 2023 the Ukrainian supply of Soviet 125mm ammunition was dwindling.

Supplying Ukraine with three different heavy battle tanks was problematic, even though the Challenger 2, Leopard 2 series and the M1A1 all fired NATO ammunition. The tanks did not have interchangeable parts. Three separate logistics chains were required to support these heavy armoured vehicles. Three different depot level maintenance faculties were thus required and were created in neighbouring NATO countries.[45]

In addition to modern tanks, Ukraine received 100 Leopard 1A5 tanks, armed with the old NATO standard 105mm main gun, from Germany, Denmark and the Netherlands. Germany had an additional 178 Leopard 1A5s in its warehouses. The Leopard 1A5 is a good tank, and its 105mm main gun was effective against older Russian/Soviet-model tanks and armoured vehicles.[46] In addition to various types of Sabot (armour-piercing fin-stabilized, discarding-sabot – APFSDS) rounds, the 105mm fired high explosive anti-tank (HEAT) and high explosive (HE) rounds.[47] In the Cold War the 105mm ammunition loadout of a tank could include high explosive-plastic/high explosive smash head (HE-P/HESH) and anti-personnel (beehive) rounds. Both types of ammunition could still be found lingering in the ammunition stockpiles of countries using US or European tanks with 105mm main guns.[48]

Ukraine did not receive all the heavy weapons in the quantity requested to support its 2023 spring/summer counter-offensive, but it did receive enough armoured manoeuvre vehicles required to maintain its defence. It also did not receive sufficient armoured combat engineering vehicles or minefield breaching equipment to fully support the counter-offensive.

Of equal importance were the large number of drones, guidance and tracking radars, anti-radar missiles and precision guided munitions of all types, as well as combat and service support equipment, that were requested by and provided for the Ukrainian logistics system.[49]

The US quickly provided a 'thirty-one tank training set' and accelerated the timeline to ship M1A1 Abrams.The Abrams intended for Ukraine was not shipped to Europe until late in 2023.[50] The thirty-one M1A1 Abrams tank training set arrived at Grafenwoehr Training Area in Germany during May 2023.[51] This battalion set was not intended for combat. Although promised, the M1A1 battalion did not arrive in time for the Ukrainian summer 2023 counter-offensive.

By April 2023, two months before the summer counter-offensive commenced, Ukraine had received 230 tanks, and 1,550 IFVs and APCs and other equipment, and stood up more than nine new mechanized infantry brigades.

The new brigades were equipped with a mix of new Western armoured vehicles and upgraded Soviet equipment. As an example, the tank battalions in the 47th Assault Brigade received twenty-eight upgraded ex-Slovakian M-55s (old Soviet T-54/55 tanks) with Israeli electronics, and old British NATO standard 105mm guns. The brigade's three mechanized infantry battalions received several of the US M-2 Bradley IFVs to supplement its older armoured vehicles. Tactically, the M-55 tanks' limited effective range of 2 km (1.2 miles) was enhanced by the Bradley's TOW II (Tube-Launched Optically Wire Guided Missile) downward-blasting warhead with a range of nearly 4 km (2.8 miles). The 30-ton Bradley carried an infantry squad of six, who disembarked to secure ground and assault bunkers or fortified buildings.[52]

The US and other Ukrainian allies were reluctant to supply long-range missiles capable of striking targets inside Russia, fearing that such strikes would be a dangerous escalation in the conflict. After almost a year of denying Ukraine's request for long-range rockets to attack Russian logistics and C2 in the deep rear, Britain finally led the allies in agreeing to supply Ukraine with long-range missiles.

On 11 May 2023, the UK Defence Secretary confirmed the decision to arm Ukraine with the Storm Shadow air-to-ground cruise missile (a French/British weapon). The Storm Shadow had a range of 250 km (155 miles) and were difficult to detect by Russian air defence. On the same day, Polish officials confirmed the transfer of fourteen MiG-29 jet fighters. This combination of weapons systems allowed Ukraine to strike logistical and C2 targets deep in the Russian rear, excluding the Kerch Strait bridge leading to Crimea 246 km

Chart 17 F-16 vs Su-34

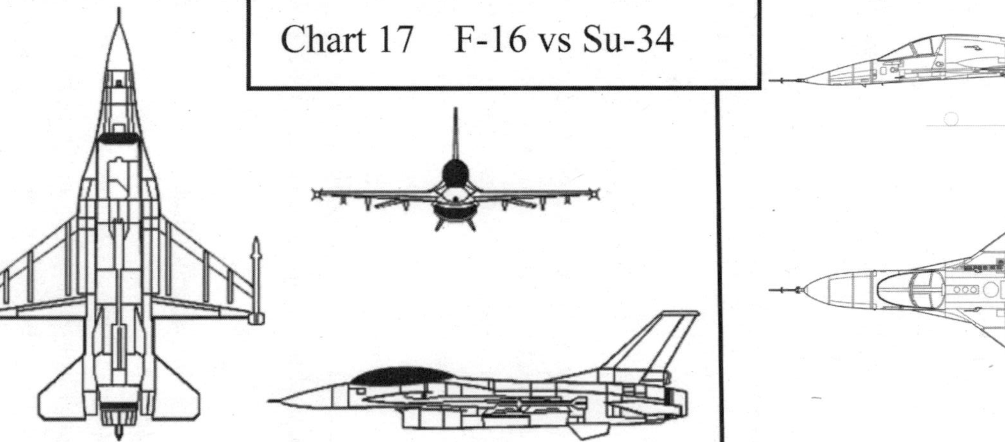

US General Dynamics F-16 Fighting Falcon
All weather, medium range fighter-bomber
Max Speed: Mach 1.89 (1,247mph, Mach 2.05 (1,353mph) at 40,000feet.
Range: 3,220km (2,000 miles)
Ceiling: 40,000feet +
Armament: 4535kg (10,000 pounds), air to air and air to ground, anti-ship munitions from 11 hard points
Radar Range: 294km (184miles) estimate

Source: US Air Force, General Dynamics

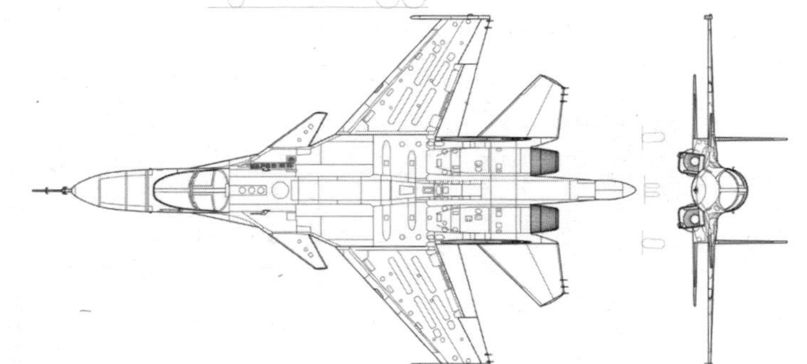

Sukhoi Su-34 NATO Name Fullback
All weather, medium range fighter-bomber.
Max Speed Mach 1.89 (1,247mph, Mach 2.05 (1,353mph) at 40,000feet)
Range: 4,000km (2,500miles)
Ceiling: 40,000 feet +
Armament: air to air, air to ground standoff missiles and glide bombs. 4,000kg (8,818 pound)
Radar Range: 200-250km (120-160mile) estimate.

Source: Diagram Kaboldy, data Business Insider,

(152 miles) from the frontlines. The bridge was certainly a high value, but one that realistically could not yet be targeted with a high probability of success.[53]

The UK Secretary of Defence, Ben Wallace, confirming that Britain would supply Ukraine with Storm Shadow cruise missiles, stated that the missiles would assist Ukraine to push Russian forces from its sovereign territory. The decision to provide these long-range missiles was influenced by the continuing Russian bombing of civilian infrastructure. Wallace considered that the delivery of the long-range missiles was an appropriate response to Russian bombing with the sole purpose of terrorizing Ukrainian civilians.[54] Storm Shadows would provide the long-range precision capability to strike Russian ammunition depots, command posts, airstrips and even ships in the Black Sea Fleet. When Ukraine obtained long-range missiles, Sevastopol ceased to be a safe port for the Russian Navy.

The Storm Shadows are air-to-ground missiles, and Ukrainian Su-24 and 27 jet aircraft were adapted to carry and launch them. The challenge was that although Ukrainian aircraft could carry and launch the missile, they were technically unable to programme it while in flight. Ground crews were required to programme the missile prior to take-off, meaning there was no ability to guide the missile in flight or change the target. The missiles weighed 1,315 kg (2,900 lbs) each and were much too heavy for the more advanced Ukrainian MiG-29s and Su-25s.[55] The Ukrainians desperately needed US F-16s, or similar NATO jet fighters, to employ these weapons to their full potential.

For eighteen months the Biden Administration rejected Ukrainian requests for F-16 fighter jets, then in August 2023, the President relented and authorized third party transfers of the aircraft.[56] This reactive (rather than proactive) decision was announced after the Ukrainian counter-offensive became bogged down in the 58th CAA's fortifications. Upon finally hearing Biden's consent to provide long range missiles, General Zaluzhnyii commented that the F-16s were 'less helpful' than if they had been delivered in 2022. During the eighteen months of media hype and public debate about arming Ukrainian with F-16s, the Russian air defence had been able to prepare for the appearance of the F-16 fighters in the skies over Ukraine.[57]

The Biden Administration followed internal guidelines when it came to providing modern weapons to Ukraine. The priority was to take care not to escalate the conflict, while at the same time providing Ukraine with the military aid needed for the current fight. In providing aid, Biden also had to keep an eye on his funding limitations. The choice either was to provide lots of older weapon systems and ammunition, i.e. 'more bang for the buck', or to provide fewer modern weapons. Clearly, the first option would have more impact on the battlefield, considering that Ukraine was running low on ammunition, and it was the option Biden chose.

By August 2023, after eighteen months of war, the escalation argument was becoming hollow. With each introduction of a modern weapon system, Putin's rhetoric rattled the nuclear sabre, but then moved on to other subjects.[58] By the second half of 2023, the Biden Administration was confident that providing F-16s to Ukraine would not escalate the war. The issue remained the cost of providing the aircraft.

Biden appeared to the world to have unlimited funds available pursuant to his Presidential drawdown authority. This was an illusion. Modern high-tech weapons and equipment are extremely expensive. Providing F-16s to Ukraine would have greatly depleted Biden's available funds to aid Ukraine's defence, without significantly improving the situation on the ground. The most recent F-16E and F-16F upgraded models cost between $25 and $30 million. Earlier models such as the F-16A&B were approximately $13 million, and F-16C&D models cost $20 million. Improvements, ground equipment and the maintenance package on the latest models increased the cost to $60–70 million per aircraft.[59] In 2023 the cost of a US-manufactured 155mm artillery shell was $2,171. One F-16, with support package, thus cost the same as 27,637 basic 155mm artillery shells. Would General Zaluzhnyii prefer one F-16 jet fighter or a month's supply of artillery shells? Biden answered the question for him: one month's worth of artillery ammunition. Ultimately, the cost did not prevent the US from pondering how to fulfil both requirements in the future: both ammunition and modern fighter jets.

During the winter of 2023, the US Air Force hosted two veteran Ukrainian pilots to train on F-16 flight simulators. The twelve-day evaluation indicated that the two pilots needed new technical skills to master Western cockpit instruments. Based on the results, the US determined that Ukrainian pilots with proficiency in English could be trained to fly F-16s in four to five months.[60] Pilot and ground crew training would take months, but it was 'doable' within the administration's budget if NATO members assisted. Providing the F-16 aircraft was not in Biden's budget.

The solution to budget problems was to encourage NATO members to provide the hardware and support. More than 4,600 F-16s had been manufactured in the US by Lockheed Martin. By the beginning of 2024 there were 2,796 worldwide in service, including those in the air forces of a dozen different countries. Over 162 F-16s were on order with Lockheed Martin. In 2024 there were over 516 F-16s serving in NATO air fleets, with 936 operated by the US Air Force. Shortly after Biden's August 2023 announcement authorizing allies to provide Ukraine with F-16s, Norway, the Netherlands and Denmark announced their intention to donate their F-16s to Ukraine.[61] The Netherlands alone pledged forty-two aircraft as it was planning to phase the fighter out of its air force. Denmark pledged nineteen jets.[62]

The downside of relying upon the F-16s was that they required seven to eight months of training for pilots and ground crews. Training was conducted in the US, Denmark, Romania and Greece. Maintenance on all jet aircraft is time-consuming and complicated, and the F-16 was no exception. It was estimated that due to the required maintenance schedule an individual aircraft would only be flyable 25–50 per cent of the time. Each fighter required twenty maintenance hours for every one hour of flight time. From an air wing of sixty F-16s, only twenty-five would be flyable at any given time.[63] Despite best efforts of Ukraine's allies, the F-16 air group would be unavailable to defend the skies over Ukraine before late 2024.

While the F-16 was not a wonder weapon, it levelled the playing field in the skies. The F-16 replaced Ukraine's ageing and thinning fleet of MiG-29s, Su-24s and Su-25s, whose short-range radars placed them at a severe disadvantage when confronting modern Russian aircraft. These old Soviet-era fighters came on line during the Cold War. The F-16 was also a Cold War aircraft, introduced in the late 1970s, but as time passed it had been upgraded to be a multi-role jet fighter. By the First Gulf War (1991) it was flying ground attack missions with missiles, bombs and anti-radiation missiles. Upgrades during the twenty-first century had made the F-16 a dangerous adversary.

The most importan characteristic of the F-16 was that it could employ the entire array of NATO precision air-to-ground missiles to their full potential. It carried more weapons than the ageing Ukrainian Soviet jet aircraft. Its advanced radar allowed the pilot to control its missiles, like the Storm Shadow, during flight. Its AGM-88 Anti-Radiation Missiles (HARM) could target ground AD radars and ground-based drone jammers.[64]

The F-16's long-range air-to-air missiles reduced the effectiveness of Russian fighters launching glide bombs against ground targets. Equipped with the AN/APG-66 radar, it was able to track and engage air and ground targets past 100 km (60 miles).[65] Armed with the AIM-120 Advanced Medium-Range Air to Air Missile (AMRAAM), the F-16 could track and engage multiple targets beyond visual range. The missile autonomously tracked moving targets with onboard radar.[66]

The F-16 multi-role jet fighter enabled Ukraine to defend its skies. The training of personnel in allied countries brought Ukraine politically closer to NATO members. With Western aircraft, the Ukrainian Air Force would eventually be able to integrate with NATO's European defence. In the short term the agreement to provide F-16s to Ukraine was a political defeat for Putin.

The massive amount of equipment, materiel and supplies provided by its allies masked the fact that Ukraine lacked the capacity to wage a successful counter-offensive in the summer of 2023. The very limited amount of support provided gave the Ukrainians hope, but sadly, hope is not a battlefield operational system. Delayed delivery of pledged support was critical. Reactive support versus proactive support often guaranteed failure.

Chapter 15

Non-Government Military Support Crowdfunding Goes to War

International support for Ukraine crossed borders and included outspoken pro-Ukraine individuals and groups in countries that may have remained neutral in the conflict, or which saw an opportunity to profit from the war by buying cheap Russian oil. During the twentieth century, individual efforts to support a country fighting for independence were generally limited to monetary contributions to international humanitarian organizations like the Red Cross, Red Crescent or Doctors Without Borders.

Individual citizens purchasing military equipment for their own military was not unheard-of. The concept of families buying additional kit for their soldiers going off to war is centuries-old. During the twentieth century private groups often organized to fund the purchase of modern weapons. As an example, during the Second World War the British 'Spitfire Fund' raised £12,600 (£490,000 or $590,000 in today's value) to purchase the best fighter aircraft for the Royal Air Force.[1]

Seventy years later, with the invention of the internet and crowdfunding, things changed. Crowdfunding harnesses the power of social media networks on the internet to provide individuals with the means to raise funds, donate to charities and even help to overcome personal hardship. The core principle of crowdfunding is simple: if every member of a community contributes a small sum, large projects can be funded.[2] It has successfully raised funds for charities and other worthy causes, but has also been a method of raising money to finance projects and start up businesses for profit.[3]

The first recorded modern crowdfunding occurred in 1997 in Britain, when a rock band funded a reunion tour through online donations from fans. In 2000 'ArtistShare' became the first dedicated crowdfunding online platform. Other organizations and companies quickly developed. By 2009 crowdfunding had become a major funding source, and big business raised over $530 million. Crowdfunding raised $1.5 billion in 2011 and $2.5 billion in 2012 for various causes. The next year, US President Barack Obama signed the 'Jumpstart Our Business Startups Act' (JOBS), reducing regulations on small business and legalizing equity crowdfunding. Crowdfunding continued

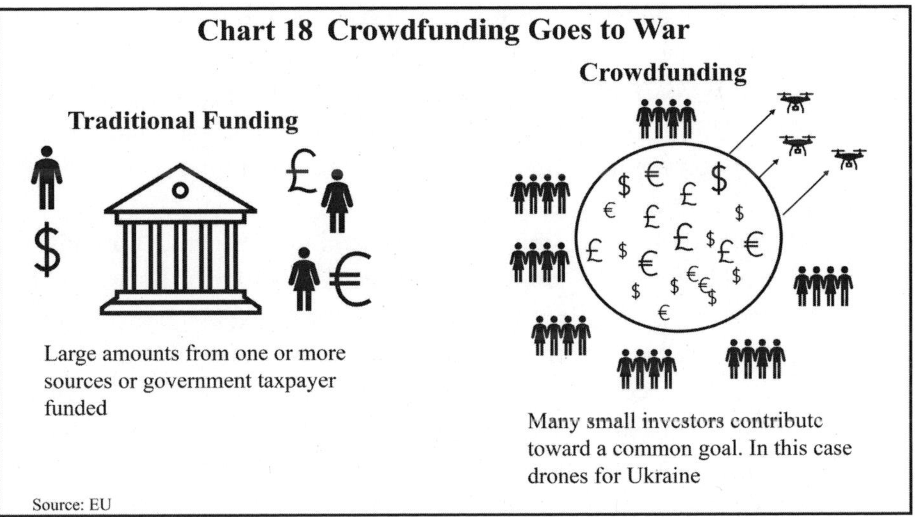

to grow worldwide, and new companies like 'Kickstarter' simplified the process, allowing more individuals and small businesses to take advantage of this powerful fundraising engine.[4]

There are seven types of crowdfunding legally recognized internationally, of which only four were relevant to supporting Ukraine. 'Peer to Peer Lending' allows internet investors to contribute money to a company with the understanding they will be paid back. 'Equity Crowdfunding' allows an individual to buy a share of a business in return for interest on the amount invested. 'Reward-Based Crowdfunding' enables individuals to donate whatever sum they wish to a project or business, with the expectation of receiving a non-financial reward in the form of goods or services. The reward may be of nominal value, such as a patch or lapel pin. Individuals participating in donation-based crowdfunding generally donate a small amount for a specific charitable project and do not receive any product or compensation in return.[5]

There are inherent risks with crowdfunding as there is no guarantee that sufficient funds will actually be invested to achieve group goals. Underestimating the cost of a project has been a major problem. Finally, fraud and/or unintentionally breaking national or international laws were ever-present concerns. There is little or no legal oversight on crowdfunding. International laws regulating crowdfunding are still evolving. The lack of regulation created a perfect environment for fraud and data mining.[6] As an example, a project advertised as raising funds for schoolbooks for a specific country may actually have been collecting funds to purchase weapons for a terrorist group.

After the unjustified Russian invasion of Ukraine, the international civilian community immediately rallied to the side of the defenders. International celebrities such as Mark Hamill (Luke Skywalker) publicly purchased drones, while former California Governor Arnold Schwarzenegger posted a speech on the internet condemning the invasion and offering moral support to the beleaguered Ukrainian fighters.[7]

In the heat of combat the Ukrainian military expanded rapidly as volunteers quickly filled the ranks of the Territorial Defence Battalions and excess volunteers were organized into ad hoc militia battalions. The Ukrainian Ministry of Defence had stockpiled assault rifles in Kyiv and other major cities but was short of basic equipment, from helmets and body armour to canteens and first aid kits. Civilian crowdfunding groups formed both inside Ukraine and internationally to meet the needs of soldiers and refugees.

Crowdfunding quickly became extremely important to the early Ukrainian war effort. A vast donor network was quickly organized to provide everything from boots to tanks. Since the beginning of the war individuals throughout the world have joined together to contribute. Small sums added together have provided hundreds of millions of dollars to purchase all types of items from night vision devices and medical supplies to expensive naval drones.[8] Some organizations like 'SignMyRocket' allowed donors to have their name inscribed on an artillery shell for $150. For $2,000 your name would be written on a grenade dropped from a Mavic 3 FPV drone.[9] While crowdfunding supplemented all categories of military and humanitarian assistance to Ukraine, it was the procurement of first-person drones (FPV drones) that made the headlines.

Private contributions from different crowdfunding sites raised millions in 2022 to buy off-the-shelf drones, while other sites funded the development of sea drones. Crowdfunding purchased civilian hobby FPV drones costing between $700 and $1,000, and these were converted to carry hand grenades or rocket-propelled anti-tank grenades. The grenades were dropped as bombs or crashed into the side or rear of an armoured vehicle.[10] Throughout the first year of the war, crowdfunding supplemented the purchase of off-the-shelf drones with high-tech enhancements such as thermal imagers.

Private contributions to the war effort remained important throughout the second year of the war. There were many small private organizations augmenting Ukrainian government procurement. A case in point was the 69th Sniffing Brigade, an Estonian private organization. This focused on purchasing trucks, while coordinating with other smaller organizations to fill the trucks with badly needed supplies. The 69th Sniffing Brigade collected €2.5m and purchased 152 pickup trucks loaded with medical supplies, delivered directly to sixteen different Ukrainian brigades. The trucks travelled in convoy from Estonia to Kyiv. Configured as ambulances and utilized for medical evacuations once unloaded, these trucks contained much needed medical supplies as well as privately purchased Kamikaze drones destined for a specific Special Forces Drone unit. Arthur Rehi, who conducted the fundraisers for these drones, accompanied the 69th Sniffing Brigade convoys from Estonia to Kyiv to document the deliveries. Each small drone cost about $700 and could easily hunt down an individual Ivan or destroy a logistics vehicle.[11]

The Lithuanian 'Song of Drones' campaign raised €300,000 and purchased 500 small kamikaze drones for Ukraine.[12] 'Operation Unity', a Ukrainian government campaign launched on 14 August 2023, sought enough funds ($6 million) to purchase 10,000 drones. The first $1 million was raised within 24 hours.[13] The joint project with 'Come Back Alive Foundation', United 24 and Monobank quickly reached their goal, and the 10,000 FPV drones were issued to fifty-three units in the Marine Corps, Ground, Air Assault, Special Forces and Territorial Defence, NGU, Security and Police forces. The warheads for the drones were manufactured by the Ukrainian defence industry, and they were equipped with a daytime camera and thermal imaging for night-time operations.[14]

The 2022 crowdfunding campaign was extremely important to the development and fielding of naval drones. United 24 and other organizations were instrumental in mounting the campaign to build 100 naval drones at $250,000 each. Each naval drone was 18 ft long and carried a payload of 199 kg (440 lbs), with a speed of 80 kph (50 mph) and a range of 804 km (500 miles).[15] In 2023, the naval drones, along with air drones and Storm Shadow missiles, were instrumental in defeating the Russian fleet in the western Black Sea.

The great advantage of crowdfunding was that as soon as it became obvious that cheap off-the-shelf hobby drones had value on the battlefield, they were immediately provided. Donors did not have to go through government bureaucracy, budgetary or appropriations committees or funding decisions. The downside of small civilian hobby drones was the inability to continuously replace them as large numbers of FPV drones were destroyed daily. As 2023 progressed, Russian drone and anti-drone operations became more sophisticated, and the cheaper civilian drones became less effective. As Russian EW jamming operations became more effective, Ukraine needed thousands of FPV drones per month, equipped with anti-jamming systems.

Drone operators reported that in most ground battles small civilian drones dropping explosive charges accounted for one in every three Russian tanks, IFV and logistics trucks destroyed. Between June and August 2023 crowdfunded drones ($500–$5,000) were responsible for destroying a total of 1,200 Russian heavy weapons and supply vehicles. Chinese Mavic and DJI drones proved to be the most effective. By October 2023 vehicles destroyed by crowdfunded drones included 208 tanks, 272 APCs and 331 artillery systems. By the end of 2023 all brigades had drone sections, and some brigades, lacking approved positions for more drone operators, created additional sections by listing operators as cooks, clerks and administrators. The 92nd Mechanized Infantry Brigade's Drone Group 'Code 9.2' was credited with defeating a Russian attack on 10 December 2023 in the eastern Bakhmut Sector. Drone operators expertly flew hobby drones to first hover over, then drop grenades into, the open hatches of new Russian BTR-82 APCs.[16]

Seeing the value of the FPV drones, by the end of 2023 the Kremlin had bought tens of thousands of Chinese hobby drones and converted them in Russian factories. Crowdfunded drones could not match the volume of those purchased by Russia, and Ukrainian drone operators urged their government to fund the purchase of more.[17]

Russia also quickly took advantage of crowdfunding to support its armed forces. Russian grassroot groups such as 'Help Our Soldiers' and 'We Don't Give up on Our Own' quickly organized to supply kit to soldiers. This was critical for Ivan, since upon mobilization the Kremlin's military warehouses lacked sufficient kit to equip every soldier. Families were eager to contribute funds to outfit their sons and husbands. Everything from body armour to medical supplies, cold weather gear and even basics like tea and coffee were funded and sent to the front.[18]

While crowdfunding military equipment to Ukraine was important, in the long term it could not produce the volume of expendable kit and weapons needed in modern war. As drones became critical for military operations, thousands were lost every month. The Ukrainian government eventually stepped in to manage production. Crowdfunding of equipment and supplies allowed the international community to directly support Ukraine. Crowdfunding immediately provided drones, as soon as their potential for combat was realized. There was no waiting for government studies, bureaucracy, budgetary and appropriation committees to determine the value of cheap off-the-shelf drones on the battlefield. Individuals could take direct action to demonstrate their support of Ukraine without leaving home. The old proverb, 'The only thing necessary for the triumph of evil is for good men to do nothing', holds true.[19] Crowdfunding was the tool for any individual, no matter how humble, to contribute to a fund to provide effective weapons to stop a Russian tank or sink a warship.

The private sector quickly mobilized support for Ukraine at the grassroots level. Tiny companies, such as Victoria Miniatures of Australia, mobilized their customers to give donations to Ukrainian relief efforts. Non-Government Organizations (NGOs) such as Save the Children, Doctors Without Borders and the Red Cross, to name just a few, quickly mobilized too.[20]

However, the most critical support for military operations came, surprisingly, from Elon Musk, the richest man on the planet, and his Starlink satellite constellation. Like Sir Lancelot, Musk charged into the fray. Russian EW was jamming Ukrainian C2 at all levels, but within days of the invasion Musk shipped thousands of his Starlink terminals to Ukraine, re-establishing tactical, operational and strategic C2 throughout the theatre of war. As the war progressed, Starlink became pivotal in the coordination of drone strikes.[21]

Like Lancelot, however, Musk was a knight with flaws. After a conversation with a Russian official, he became worried that an attack on Crimea could spiral into a nuclear conflict. As a result, in the middle of a sea drone attack during September 2022, Musk deactivated Starlink satellite service near the coast of Crimea. This not only thwarted the attack on the Black Sea Fleet but allowed the Russians to capture advanced Ukrainian sea drones provided by crowdfunding. A year later, Musk defended his action in a tweet, saying 'If I had agreed to [Ukraine's] request, then SpaceX would be complicit in a major act of war and conflict escalation.'[22]

Musk's statement drew an angry response from Mykhailo Podpyak, an adviser to President Zelensky. Podpyak stated that Musk's interference had allowed the Black Sea Fleet to continue firing cruise missiles at Ukrainian cities, killing hundreds of civilians, including children. 'This is the price . . . of ignorance and big ego.'[23]

A SpaceX executive told Ukrainian officials in February 2023 that action had been taken to curtail Kyiv's ability to control long-range drone strikes into Russia. Musk was able to act independently because he was not a US defence contractor. He obviously made decisions and took action that did not align with official US policy. Concerned about being over-dependent on Musk's Starlink, Ukraine consulted with other satellite providers, but discovered that for all intent and purposes Musk had a monopoly in the market. As negotiations proceeded, it appeared that Musk was less worried about escalating the war than keen to turn a profit on his product, once thought to have been magnanimously provided. He pressured Washington for a contract and payment for Starlink access.

At the beginning of June 2023, SpaceX received a Pentagon contract to provide Starlink satellite communication to Ukraine, something which Musk had sought since October 2022.[24] As of June 2023 he became a US Department of Defense Contractor, and pursuant to contract the US pays him $20 million a month to maintain Ukraine's support.[25]

Like Lancelot's, Musk's armour was tarnished. No longer a trusted ally of Ukraine, he simply became a mercenary. In February 2024 Ukrainian intelligence discovered that Russia had purchased Starlink terminals in Arab countries and they had been deployed to Ukraine. Musk denied selling terminals and access to Russia, and both he and the Kremlin denied that Russia had deployed Starlink satellite terminals, but Ukrainian intelligence discovered that Russian forces increasingly communicated via Starlink while fighting in Ukraine.[26]

The denial from both parties was hollow. The Ukrainians captured Starlink terminals in Russian positions, and Russian state media broadcast videos of Russian soldiers unpacking new Starlink terminals and activating them. Russian activation of Starlink terminals inside occupied Ukraine should have been easily detected by Musk. It is simply inconceivable that Musk did not know the Russian invaders were accessing his Starlink system.

Chapter 16

Cyber War

The Third World War started in February 2022, after Russia's invasion of Ukraine unleased the largest cyber war in history. Cyber warfare is the deliberate use of computer technology to strategically disrupt, influence or otherwise interfere with another state for a military purpose. As the worldwide internet has become more and more widely available it has literally infiltrated every aspect of daily life. Utilization and hacking of data bases containing confidential information became the norm for governments and businesses. The news media became just as much digital-age junkies as government and business. Fake news, often presented by once reputable sources, became undiscernible from reality, with little or no fact checking by the public to ensure accuracy. With the invasion, Russia increased its cyber-attacks on the US, other NATO members, the EU and Ukraine's allied countries around the world. To insure against a crippling loss of confidence, cyber attack and defence became every country's most closely held secret. As a result, there was limited information about the occurrence of cyber attacks available in unclassified sources. The Russian-Ukrainian War demonstrated that there was no clear demarcation in cyberspace between war and peace. Ukraine had made significant investments in cyber security since the Russian annexation of Crimea in 2014, but Russian cyber attacks continued to exact a significant toll.

Historically, Russia has used common but effective cyber tactics to gain access to targeted networks. They were much the same as the tactics employed by petty criminals to hack data bases for financial gain. These tactics included phishing, spearfishing, credential or data harvesting, brute force, and password spray techniques against weak internet security. They took advantage of simple passwords and unsuspecting employees to gain access to a network. Once in, they moved laterally through the network to establish a presence in order to exfiltrate and/or manipulate data. Like an undercover sleeper agent, hacker access and manipulations often laid dormant within malware for weeks or months until triggered. The resulting hack intrusion enabled Russia to acquire classified information, chart communication infrastructure, and read emails, military plans and technology.[1]

The US joint doctrine defines cyberspace operations as the 'employment of cyberspace capabilities where the primary purpose is to achieve objectives in and through cyberspace'. Defence in cyberspace requires expanding public-private partnerships and collaboration with government, alongside pooled data to identify attack patterns and trends.[2]

From a military perspective, countries seek to defend their own networks, while infiltrating enemy networks through the different layers of cyberspace (i.e., physical, logical and personal). Achieving access to an opponent's data network became an intelligence advantage or means of delivering malware attacks. Malware, or malicious software, often takes the form of inserting a 'worm' or a 'virus' to interfere with a computer program, or 'spyware' which allows the hacker access to the data. It is often more advantageous to simply access or enter an opponent's data than to destroy it. Degrading an adversary's C2 network could risk losing access to valuable intelligence on enemy operations and communications. As a result, the cyberspace attacker, or 'hacker', must determine whether it is more valuable to read the opponent's data and gain an intelligence advantage, or whether the advantage lies in disrupting and/or degrading an adversary's network to unhinge a defence, slow down a counteraction or damage his economy.

The advantage of cyber operations in attacking an enemy is anonymity. The fact that there is a legion of criminal hackers operating in cyberspace allows an attacking country to hide and offer plausible deniability. As cyber warfare developed, so did technology to detect and uncover the actual perpetrators of an attack.

In 2007, Russia launched a massive 'denial-of-service' operation to punish Estonia after the country removed a Russian monument known as the Bronze Soldier. While it is unknown exactly what was denied, Russia was in a position to cut off any service in Estonia supported by the internet or computer technology. During the invasion of Georgia in 2008, Russia used cyber attacks to disrupt the defender's C2. Russia targeted Kyiv's power supply in 2014 and 2015, perhaps to test Ukraine's cyber security, but the attack reportedly had limited effects. Cyber attacks and promotion of 'fake news' against the US had some limited success in undermining confidence in the 2016 presidential election. Subsequent lawsuits by Dominion as manufacturer of the voting machines used in the election revealed the cyber attacks and fake news reported by Fox News. In a settlement vindicating the election process Fox News agreed to pay $787 million.

In 2020 Russia utilized a combination of espionage and criminal malware produced by the hacker group 'Cozy Bear' to both collect data and insert malicious code into Microsoft servers. In 2021, criminal actors known as

'Darkside' inserted ransomware against Colonial Pipeline, the system which transported fuel used across the US East Coast.[3] Between 2000 and 2020 there have been thirty known cyber attacks between Ukraine and Russia. Of these, twenty-eight were initiated by the Russians. Most of the targets were private non-state actors, but three were against military targets. The limited results of these attacks may indicate that Ukraine's cyber defences were difficult to penetrate. The cyber war between Russia and Ukraine has been a continuous yet unpublicized conflict since 2014.

Less than an hour before the invasion, Russian hackers targeted Ukrainian and US infrastructure. The hackers were partially successful in blocking the US satellite company Viasat's internet services to Europe. Thousands of internet customers in Europe lost internet access. Viasat KA-SAT modems became inoperable in Ukraine due to the introduction of malware into the system.[4] Remote control of 5,800 wind turbines across Central Europe was impacted.[5] The attack interfered with Ukraine's ability to defend itself, but the international community did not directly blame the attack on Russia until May 2022. The actual perpetrator was well hidden behind a screen of criminal hackers and diversions. It took weeks for cyber investigators to identify Russia as the culprit.[6]

As a result of these early cyber attacks, the US Cybersecurity and Infrastructure Agency and the Ukrainian State Service of Special Communication and Information Protection of Ukraine signed a Memorandum of Cooperation (MoC) to share cybersecurity priorities. This MoC allowed closer cooperation between the allied cyber warriors against their common enemy, Russia, resulting in shared tactics, techniques, and procedures (TTP).

Russian cyber attacks against NATO members have been constant. After submitting bids to join NATO, Finland and Sweden reported a rise in cyber ransomware attacks in suspected retaliation for their anti-Russia, pro-NATO stance. A ransomware attack is when a hacker breaches the security of a data base and prevents access by the owner unless/until a specific sum is paid. If the demanded ransom is not delivered in full, the hacker threatens to destroy the data. The silent cyber war between Russia and NATO has been ongoing, but remains mostly out of the headlines. One hack targeted the Turkish component of the Rapid Deployment Corps. Another attacked two dozen embassies in Kyiv. The attacks increased after European and US governments expelled Russian agents.[7]

In the second half of 2023 the Russian hacker groups known as 'The Dukes', 'CozyBear' and 'Midnight Blizzard' targeted US servers. These attacks have caused US Agencies to upgrade their TTPs.[8]

During its eight-year cyber war with Russia, Ukraine has developed its resilience to cyber attack. Their TTPs improved defences to secure networks, hunt for and expel malicious cyber intruders, counter-attack surface monitoring, and provide intelligence on cyber threats to improve protection of critical infrastructure. One of the most important Ukrainian TTPs dictated the development and employment of procedures to quickly recover from a Russian attack on critical infrastructure.[9]

The private sector has teamed up with Ukraine, NATO and allies in the cyber war. A dozen companies have donated thousands of hours, and millions of dollars' worth of equipment to help Ukrainian defenders. Volunteer cyber experts have joined with the Ukrainian government. Greg Rattray and Matthew Murry, former US experts on cyber security, assisted CRDF Global to help upgrade Ukraine's cyber security.[10]

As military operations go, cyber conflict remains the most secretive. Neither combatant publishes the successes or failures of infiltrations, because hacks are more effective if they remain undiscovered. An undiscovered hack cannot be corrected.

Some are known, however. Ukraine counter-intelligence published a report identifying a range of malware used by Russian intelligence to attack Android devices, as used by Ukrainian soldiers to plan and execute combat missions. The Russian unit 'Sandworm' (military unit 74455) was identified as conducting the cyber attack. Russians used captured Android devices from the battlefield to introduce malware into the network, to execute passive (intelligence gathering) or active (disabling C2) attacks.[11]

In November 2022 the Russian cyber unit 'Frozen Barents' attacked the Caspian Pipeline Consortium, which carries oil from Kazakhstan to the Black Sea, and in December 2022 the unit targeted Ukrainian defence industry and military email. This was part of a sustained effort to disrupt energy companies in Europe. The attacks expanded to affect energy companies in Eastern Europe in 2023.[12]

Kremlin cyber units actively disseminate the Russian narrative on Putin's Special Operation via social media. 'Frozen Barents' targeted users of popular social media platforms such as Telegram and Patreon. They successfully infiltrated Patreon and removed two anti-Russian bloggers from the network for referring to Russia as 'occupiers'.[13] Cyber attacks often begin by sending emails seeking personal data. The emails look legitimate and are often successful in obtaining passwords, bank account numbers, social security numbers and other confidential information from naïve users. This is referred to as 'data mining' or phishing. Phishing campaigns via SMS email spoofed Telegram to steal credentials, targeting users following anti-Russian channels.

It created online personae to create and disseminate the Russian narrative. The GRU (Russian military intelligence) YouTube Cyber Army site is a good example of an online persona.[14]

It is difficult to accurately assess the impact of the Russian cyber campaign on the war effort. It is unknown whether Russia's cyber war efforts contributed to the deadlock in the US Congress over aid to Ukraine. It may be years before that information becomes available. If Russia continues its illegal war and/or its illegal occupation of Ukraine, the prospect remains that cyber operations will escalate. Even if Russia ended the ground war and was ultimately forced to withdraw from Ukraine, the high-intensity cyber war against Ukraine and the West would continue.[15] It has become totally possible to achieve the goals of war in cyberspace while retaining total and plausible deniability. It has suddenly become possible to win a war without risking the loss of men or equipment. It has become possible to wreck the economy of an opponent and to undermine the ability of a country to defend itself. It has become possible to turn allies against one another and destroy the infrastructure of both. Control of cyberspace poses a real and continuing risk in future warfare.

Chapter 17

The Campaign Plan to Liberate Ukraine Spring–Summer 2023

Ukraine's preparation for this campaign was extensively covered by the world media, much like the preliminaries of the Football World Cup competition or the US NFL/AFC Superbowl. There were three integrated components to the campaign which incorporated all land, sea and air branches of the Ukrainian armed forces. The media focused over-much on the ground elements, where armoured forces were expected to cut through Russian defences and seize deep objectives.

The campaign had four strategic objectives. Initial drone strikes into the Russian heartland aimed to force the redeployment of limited Russian AD systems from the front to defend deep air bases, supply depots and Moscow itself. Secondly, FPV drone, air and commando raids were to reduce the effectiveness of Russian AD in and around the Crimean Peninsula; this would interdict the supply lines to the 58th CAA and the Kherson Sector. Thirdly, drone and air strikes were to be conducted against the Russian Fleet, forcing it to redeploy to the eastern Black Sea. This would secure sea lanes in the western Black Sea for merchant ships transporting Ukrainian grain to world

Chart 19 Ukrainian Summer 2023 Counter-offensive Order of Battle

• Main Effort: Orikhiv Axis

IX Corps, ME
- 33rd Mechanized Brigade
- 47th Mechanized Brigade
- 67th Mechanized Brigade

X Corps, ME Reserve
- 116th Mechanized Brigade
- 117th Mechanized Brigade
- 118th Mechanized Brigade

Maroon (Airborne) Corps, ME Reserve
- 46th Airmobile Brigade
- 82nd Air Assault Brigade
- 71st Jager Brigade
- 132nd Separate Recon Battalion

• Supporting Effort: Velyka Novosilka

Marine Corps, SE
- 35 Marine Brigade
- 36 Marine Brigade
- 37 Marine Brigade
- 38 Marine Brigade

Reserve
- 33rd Mechanized Brigade
- 53rd Mechanized Brigade
- 46th Air Assault Brigade
- 71st Jager Air Assault Brigade
- 1st Tank Brigade

Both axis were supported by Territorial , National Guard, Combat Support and Combat Service Support Brigades and battalions.

markets. Finally, Ukraine needed to sever the land bridge between Crimea and mainland Russia.

The main effort of the ground counter-offensive on the Orikhiv axis in the Zaporizhzhia Oblast needed to advance 28 km (17 miles) to its tactical objective, Tomak, and 85 km (53 miles) to the operational objective of Melitopol. Capturing Tomak would have allowed HIMARS to effectively cut the coast supply road between Rostov-on-Don and Melitopol. To achieve this tactical objective, Ukrainian ground units only had to advance 20 km (12 miles).[1]

The media expected a repeat of the blitzkrieg Kharkiv counter-offensive, ignoring the slow, methodical Kherson counter-offensive against Russia's best soldiers, paratroopers and Naval Infantry. The upcoming battle was portrayed much like a professional football team playing a small university; the Ukrainians were projected to blitz through the Russians.

This pre-game hype ignored critical facts that the Ukrainians' ground offensive had to deal with. Their ground forces faced a similar situation to the Allies on D-Day (6 June 1944), or the Germans trying to breach the Russian defences at the Battle of Kursk (4 July–23 August 1943).

The Allies had spent three years preparing for their D-Day assault on 'Fortress Europe'. The invasion force, consisting of both green and veteran soldiers, spent years training and preparing for the invasion. They were supported by overwhelming air superiority and massive naval gunfire. They faced well-led, albeit second-rate, Nazi troops in heavily fortified positions, with good inland defensive terrain.[2] After thirty days of heavy fighting, the Allies were contained in the Normandy Beachhead 80 km (50 miles) wide and 48 km (20 miles) deep. On 25 July 1944, the Allies executed 'Operation Cobra'. Six hundred Allied fighter bombers hit Nazi strongpoints on a 270-mile-wide strip, followed by 1,800 heavy bombers, with 3,000 tons of ordnance that carpet-bombed a narrow section of the front. By 1100 hours, Allied infantry began to move into the 8 km (5 mile) wide gap. The Nazis' line collapsed by 28 July 1944 as US P-47 and UK Typhoon fighter-bombers swept over their rear, hunting for reserve formations. By 1 August 1944, seven divisions of General George S Patton's 3rd US Army were in the German rear, racing for Paris. On 25 August, the Third US, First Canadian and Third British Armies had reached the Seine.[3] To breach the Nazi front the Allies required overwhelming air superiority and superior combat engineering support, assets which the Ukrainians unfortunately lacked.

The Ukrainians faced a situation similar to that the Nazis encountered at the Battle of Kursk (1943). The Nazis had massed their heavy panzer divisions in an attempt to cut off the Russian salient around the city of Kursk, but the Nazi attack was delayed, allowing the Soviets to develop a defence in depth along the salient and to deploy heavy anti-tank minefields along the base of the salient. The minefields were covered by interlocking fields of fire from Soviet anti-tank guns. The Germans spent five months preparing for the attack, and poor weather pushed the start date from the spring to the summer. Other factors resulted in a delay deploying new 'wonder weapons' such as Tiger I heavy tanks, Panther medium tanks and Ferdinand (Elephant) heavy tank destroyers.[4] The Soviets took advantage of the delay to strengthen their defences and conduct training. Three defensive belts were constructed, with massive minefields and thousands of tanks in reserve. The battle began on 3 July and ended on 12 July 1943, with the Nazi panzer armies soundly defeated. Heavy fighting continued into August 1943, but the Nazis had lost the strategic initiative on the Eastern Front for the rest of the war.[5]

Unnoticed except by a few experts, Ukrainian shaping operations began on or about 19 April 2023, with an uptick in the targeting of Russian tactical artillery. From late April 2023, the Russians lost, on average, more than twenty artillery systems a day. To support the shaping operations, the UK again led the way and in May 2023 provided long-range Shadow missiles. On 22 June 2023 one missile struck the strategically important Kerch Strait Bridge connecting Crimea with Russian-occupied southern Ukraine.[6]

Operational long-range weapons increased Ukraine's ability to target Russian supply depots and command posts, starving Russian tactical artillery of ammunition and reducing the Russians' superiority in tubed artillery.[7]

One of the early, novel shaping operations was an attack on the Motherland by the Russian Volunteer Corps (RVC) and Freedom of Russia Legion (FRL). These far-right Russian national units were fighting to free Russia from Putin's autocratic rule. Both units were supplied by and operated under Ukrainian command.[8]

On 22 May 2023, the two anti-Putin Russian detachments conducted a raid across the Russian border into Belgorod Oblast. One raiding group crossed the border, riding two tanks and nine APCs full of anti-Putin Russian soldiers. As the raid unfolded, the FRL posted videos and photos of their operators in front of road signs announcing the Russian village of Bezlyudovka. The raiders established checkpoints and restricted movement, requiring civilians to produce proof of identity. On 23 May 2023, FRL videos depicted a drone strike on the city of Bolograd. The raid lasted 24 hours and fulfilled a Prigozin prophecy that Ukraine would send ground troops into Belgorod Oblast. Ukrainian officials denied direct involvement in the raid; however, it was clear that they had provided armoured vehicles and support to the RVC and FRL. The raid caused panic among Russian civilians in the region, and the 74th

Motorized Rifle Brigade (41st CAA OK-Centre) was dispatched to counter the incursion.[9]

Russian 'milbloggers' were outspoken social media war correspondents who reported on and supported the war but criticized Russia's faltering operations, demanding more drastic action. Most were temporarily distracted from reporting about the glorious capture of Bakhmut by the incursion, and they filled Russian information space with panicked messages of an impending Ukrainian invasion. Prigozhin, and nationalist milblogger Igor Girkin had warned about a possible incursion weeks before the raid, and Prigozhin seized upon the opportunity to criticize Defence Minister Shoigu and General Gerasimov for failing to strengthen border security.

Igor Girkin was arrested for his criticism of Putin's handling of the war and for referring to the Russian leader as a 'lowlife and a cowardly bum'. He criticized Putin for not being ruthless enough in Ukraine. Girkin reported that Russia was '[O]n the cusp of very grave internal political changes of a catastrophic character'. He was arrested, tried, convicted for advocating extremism and sentenced to four years in prison. The 25 January 2024 sentence also barred Girkin from the internet.[10] A former FSB officer and ex-military commander, Girkin played a crucial role in Russia's annexation of Crimea and in the early stages of the Donbas invasion. He had been linked to the downing of Malaysia Airline Flight MH17 in July 2014, and since the invasion of Ukraine he had become a prominent Russian milblogger with 500,000 followers on Telegram.

A second incursion, coinciding with the beginning of the Ukrainian ground offensive, was more serious. The Russians had deployed the 245th Guards Motor Rifle Regiment to protect the approaches to Belgorod, and other Russian units moved into the Oblast assigned to the new 25th CAA. On 1 June 2023 the FRL and RVC, together with the Belarusian volunteer Terror Battalion, again crossed into Belgorod Oblast and occupied a few villages. The raiders crossed the border in the Shebekinsky District of Belgorod Oblast in three company-size columns, equipped with tanks, APCs and Grad Mobile Rocket Launchers. The FRL and RVC reached the village of Shbekino 4 km (2.5 miles) and the village of Tavolzhanka 8 km (5 miles) from the border. The raiders moved swiftly, disrupting the defenders in the region and destroying Russian installations. Russian Colonel Andrey Stesev, who was killed in a skirmish on 5 June, was the commander of the ad hoc Belgorod Task Force, organized to drive the raiders back into Ukraine. The raiders were still in control of Novaya Tavolzhanka on 8 June, but on 15 June Russian troops re-entered the village. The situation was confused. The Russians evacuated 6,500 civilians from the area, then fired thermobaric artillery against suspected raiders or anti-Putin partisan positions within the Oblast.

Under fire, the FRL and RVC withdrew from Russian territory toward the end of June 2023. A total of fourteen Russian soldiers were reported killed in the raids, and twelve were reportedly captured.[11]

The raid succeeded in stealing the headlines from Prigozhin's victory at Bakhmut. The FRL and RVC had embarrassed the Russian Army and Putin, but the raids failed to encourage them to shift forces to defend Belgorod. While the raids were occurring, the Russians were massing troops in the Oblast, in preparation for spoiling attacks in Luhansk Oblast later that summer. In July–December 2023, skirmishes were still taking place in Belgorod Oblast, but they did not result in any important gains for either side.

Chapter 18

Ukrainian Strategic Drone Campaign

The Ukrainians surprised Russia and the world on 3 May 2023 by conducting a drone strike on the Kremlin. A follow-up strike then landed near the Moscow international airport. Moscow was subjected to a total of six additional drone strikes during May and July 2023.

The initial strikes could be compared to the Doolittle Raid on Tokyo in 1942, which occurred five months after the US Fleet was crippled at Pearl Harbor. As Japan advanced through the Western Pacific, capturing US territories and victoriously expanding into China, the US found itself at a severe disadvantage. Surprising the world at 1200 hours on 18 April 1942, Colonel James H. Doolittle led sixteen land-based B-25 medium bombers out of the Pacific Ocean and conducted a 30-second bombing raid on Tokyo. After dropping their bomb load, causing minimal damage, most of the bombers disappeared over the horizon toward mainland China. American morale soared when news of the raid was published. The origin of the raiders was withheld from US official news reports; President Roosevelt responded to questions by indicating that the raiders had taken off from a mythical 'Shangri-La'. The Imperial Japanese Navy correctly assumed the land-based bombers must have been launched from aircraft carriers. Japanese warship and naval aircraft commanders 'lost face' and were 'mad as hornets' for failing to prevent the attack on their homeland's capital and having failed to locate the US aircraft carriers. The foxes eluded the hounds, and the aircraft carriers USS *Hornet* and *Enterprise* disappeared into the vastness of the Pacific. Despite the morale boost it gave to the US, the raid had little impact on the war. US heavy bomber armadas would not return for the main attack on Japan for another two years. Like the Japanese Emperor, Putin was annoyed by the drone strike on the Kremlin, and it resulted in a redeployment of air defence assets. Unlike the Japanese, Putin did not have to wait two years for the Ukrainians to return.

The retaliatory Ukrainian drone bombing campaign supporting the ground counter-offensive began in earnest as a pinprick in May 2023. After the counter-offensive culminated in December 2023 it became a sword thrust, incorporating drone, cruise missiles, commando and anti-Putin partisan raids. The objective was to disrupt Russian logistics in Mother Russia, the invaders'

Ukrainian drone strikes on Russian oil

Ukraine's fight against Russia's invasion has entered a new phase, pitting homegrown drone technology against Russian oil facilities

300km
185 miles

FINLAND
Baltic Sea
ESTONIA
LATVIA
LITHUANIA
RUS.
BELARUS
POLAND
UKRAINE
Kyiv
MOLDOVA
ROMANIA
BULGARIA
TÜRKIYE
GEORGIA
AZERBAIJAN
KAZAKHSTAN
RUSSIA
Moscow
Black Sea
Caspian Sea
Russian-held territory

Kirishi *Mar 12-13*
Ust-Luga *Jan 21*
Yanos *Jan 29*
Norsi *Mar 12*
Ryazan *Mar 13*
Pervyi Zavod *Mar 15*
Kuibyshev *Mar 16*
Syzran *Mar 16*
Novokuibyshev *Mar 16*
Volgograd *Feb 3*
Novoshakhtinsk *Mar 13*
Slavyansk *Mar 17*
Afipsky *Feb 9*
Ilsky *Feb 9*
Tuapse *Jan 25*

REFINERIES ATTACKED *(Jan 21-Mar 17, 2024)*

Operations disrupted: Attacks disrupt production at sites representing at least 14% of Russia's total refining capacity

Operations restored

Not damaged

Status unknown

Source: Bloomberg

deep rear. Unlike the Russians, however, the Ukrainians' policy was to strike targets of military significance and/or economic facilities supporting the war effort. When civilian areas were hit, it was normally the result of collateral damage caused by Russian AD firing at or destroying Ukrainian drones.

The initial Ukrainian drone attacks against Russia's deep rear took Putin by surprise. Fearful of escalating the war, the US and NATO had refrained from providing Ukraine with weapons capable of striking outside its internationally recognized borders. But Crimea was considered a part of Ukraine and was therefore a legitimate target. During the first year and a half of the war, the invaders deliberately bombed Ukrainian civilians, port facilities and energy installations without fear of retaliation. They often defaulted to bombing with the goal of creating terror among the civilian population rather than targeting legitimate military targets. On 3 May 2023, it became clear to Russia that NATO restrictions did not extend to strikes by Ukrainian weapons.[1]

Taking advantage of this strategic reality, Ukraine created a drone defence industry overnight. Initially, the build-up was immediate and spontaneous, without any government institution or department managing the development of Ukraine's domestic drone industry, although Minister Mykhailo Fedorov of the Ministry of Digital Transformation eventually oversaw it. More than 200 small manufacturing companies began mass-producing drones by the end of 2023. Ultimately, over 100,000 drones of all types were produced and sent to the front. This was in addition to the significant number of crowdfunded drones still being provided. For the most part, manufacture of drones relied on foreign components, many from China.[2] China happily provided parts to both Ukraine and Russia, for a price. Ukrainian defence industries projected that by the end of 2024 they would produce 10,000 long-range drones, such as the AQ-400 with a range of 900 km (559 miles), capable of carrying a warhead of 43 kg (95 lbs). Ukrainian industries produced a total of twelve different long-range drones of varying costs and with varying capabilities.[3]

Between 3 May and July 2023 Moscow was attacked six times. While the damage was insignificant, it put the Russian population on notice of possible things to come. It was two years between Doolittle's 'mosquito' raid over Tokyo in 1942 and the June 1944–August 1945 US Army Air Force bombing campaign that devastated the Japanese home islands. Like the Doolittle Raid, attacks on Moscow distracted and embarrassed Russian military commanders but actually caused minor damage. Russian combat air patrols were probably diverted to cover the air approaches to Moscow and a few ADA batteries diverted to Moscow. As a shaping operation it was ineffective.

Ukrainian drones penetrated Russian air space, striking airbases and ammunition storage depots deep within Russia and making headlines worldwide. In mid-May 2023, the first use of Storm Shadow precision missiles targeted troop concentrations and warehouses in Luhansk. ADM-160 decoy missiles tricked Russian AD and the Storm Shadows were able to reach their target. These missiles had the ability to strike targets in the deep rear, well inside the Russian homeland; however, due to political limitations, they were confined to targets in occupied Ukrainian territory.

Drones struck Russian military equipment in the Bryansk Oblast inside Russian territory, just north-west of Kyiv.[4] Drones also crossed the border on 24 May 2023, attacking targets inside Belgorod Oblast in support of the FRL and RVC raids. These small tactical drones dropped hand grenades on Russian defenders, while larger kamikaze drones struck deeper into the Oblast.[5]

On 22 May 2023, Storm Shadow missiles struck a military airfield near Berdyansk and Mariupol, inside occupied Ukraine. Other missile attacks struck warehouses near Donetsk.

On 31 May 2023 Ukraine conducted a massive drone strike on Moscow, targeting the engineer battalion base located in the south-western suburbs. This was in retaliation for the massive and unjustified Shahed kamikaze drone attacks on Kyiv. At least thirty-four drones were launched at Moscow. The Russian media claimed that only eight reached the target area, and all were destroyed. However, locals filming the strikes verified that some of the drones hit their target. Five were neutralized by EW weapons that hijacked the drones' GPS guidance system. The hijacked drones fell into Rubliovka, an elite residential neighbourhood, where residents were annoyed. A famous Russian ballet dancer made a video complaining about the noise and explosions, and, ironically, her complaints annoyed ordinary Russians. Their amusement at elites being 'inconvenienced' became such a serious issue that Russian state media addressed it; Russian news hosts broadcast that the reaction was unacceptable, and the ridicule should be considered treason.[6]

The Ukrainian drone bombing campaign continued throughout the summer and autumn of 2023. Moscow was attacked over thirty times, and additional targets between the capital and the Ukrainian border were hit thirty-one times. Troop concentrations, supply and C2 headquarters in Belgorod Oblast were targeted a total of thirty times. Ukrainian long-range strikes into Russia became so frequent that they rarely made worldwide headlines.

In December 2023, the Ukrainian targeting priority changed. While the attacks on military, airfields, supply depots and transportation hubs had caused damage, especially to the Russian Air Force, the impact was only tactical. What was needed was a strategic impact. The targeting priority shifted to Russia's forty-four oil and gas refineries and critical coastal transfer terminals. Despite the sanctions, Russia continued to sell petrochemicals on the world market, and damage to oil and gas facilities could not be easily repaired. Before the war, the Russian energy industry was over-reliant on Western technologies. Sanctions prohibited access to these, and rebuilding, replacing or repairing any gas, oil or refining facility was difficult.

Ukraine's long-range strike potential was limited when compared to Russia's. Focusing on Russia's 'Achilles Heel', the importance of gas and oil on the battlefield as well as to its overall economy, promised a better return on investment. Additionally, instead of relying primarily on drone attacks, the newly prioritized operations included direct action by commandos and anti-Putin Russian partisans.[7]

Ukraine conducted a series of strategic strikes in early December 2023, seriously impacting Russian petrochemical operations and logistics. Ammunition and supplies from China and North Korea were shipped by rail, and the supply route was forced to pass through the Sveromuysky Tunnel or along a secondary bypass over a 35-metre-high bridge. The Tunnel is in Buryatia Oblast in southern Siberia, 6,554 km (4,072 miles) east of Kharkiv. Ukrainian commandos or anti-Russian partisans attacked both routes. The first attack damaged the Sveromuysky Tunnel. Four train cars in a train of fifty carrying diesel and aviation fuel exploded as they passed through the tunnel. The explosion caused a chain reaction and sixteen more cars exploded. Heavily damaged, the tunnel was out of commission for a considerable period. A second fuel train on the bridge's back-up rail line was then attacked, and six cars were blown up as the train passed over the bridge. The bridge itself was heavily damaged, but unfortunately, it was later discovered that the North Korean artillery ammunition had already been moved into theatre.

As the commando raids commenced, drone attacks continued. In January 2024, two Ukrainian drones struck the Ust-Luga petrochemical terminal on the Gulf of Finland in the outskirts of St Petersburg. Local Russian civilian videos, uploaded to the internet, assisted the Ukrainians to assess damage. One day before that attack, a drone struck a major oil-loading terminal in St Petersburg, causing heavy damage.[8]

At the same time long-range drones attacked a warehouse in Bryansk where Iranian drones were being assembled or stored. Bryansk is 308 km (191 miles) north of Sumy, Ukraine. Residents filmed multiple drones attacking and ultimately destroying the warehouse. A combination of drones and Storm Shadow missiles penetrated Russian AD in Crimea to strike the airfield at Saky, damaging numerous aircraft on the runway.

Continuing the attack on strategic targets, long-range drones hit an aviation factory in Smolensk, 310 km (192 miles) north of the Ukrainian border. Local residents again unknowingly helped with battle damage assessment by filming the explosion and damage to the factory. The tractor factory in Chelyabinsk Oblast (Siberia) was deemed a strategic target. The city is 2,166 km (1,345 miles) east of Kharkiv. Residents once again unintentionally assisted the Ukrainians by posting videos of the explosion and resulting damage to the factory. Simultaneously with these strategic attacks within Russia, fires broke out in markets and shopping centres in Moscow, St Petersburg and Rostov-on-Don. Russian authorities blamed the fires on electrical short circuits.[9]

Additional oil infrastructure was targeted and destroyed in February 2023 by long-range drones. A number of sources in Kyiv explained the strategy: by destroying oil refineries supporting the Kremlin's military industrial complex, Ukraine not only cut off logistics and fuel to the front, it also damaged Russia's national economy.[10]

Russia's drone and missile bombardment of Ukrainian cities was as much about terrorizing civilians as it was about destroying Ukrainian military and industrial targets. In comparison, Ukraine's strategic drone campaign focused on destruction of military targets and the erosion of Russia's ability to wage war. Despite Ukraine's increased long-range drone production, their campaign only damaged Russian warmaking infrastructure, but it was unable in 2023 to decisively destroy it.

Stryker APC from the 1st Battalion, 185th Infantry, California Army National Guard on manoeuvres near the Suwalki Gap. (*SSGT Matthew Schoofs, CAARNG*)

Ukrainian commercial FBV drone with anti-tank grenade taped to the underside. Field expedient kamikaze drone. (*Ukraine General Staff Facebook page*)

FBV drone dropping anti-armour grenade on Russian tank recovering and towing a disabled tank. (*Ukraine General Staff Facebook page*)

Crowdfunded commercial FPV drone being launched on reconnaissance mission. (*Ukraine General Staff Facebook page*)

Russian tank with anti-drone and ATGM cage. (*Ukraine General Staff Facebook page*)

Sea Baby long-range high-speed naval attack drone. (*Ukraine General Staff Facebook page*)

Russian Patrol Ship Sergey targeted by Ukrainian sea drone. (*Ukraine General Staff and Militarnyi, https://mil.in.ua/en/news/video-of-the-destruction-of-the-russian-ship-sergey-kotov-was-released/*)

Hi-tech Ukrainian anti-drone rifle. (*Ukraine General Staff Facebook page*)

Ukrainian mobile anti-drone teams were critical in protecting combat service operations in the rear and deep rear. (*Ukraine General Staff Facebook page*)

Australia developed cardboard kamikaze drones in support of Ukraine's defence. This low-cost drone was nearly invisible to Russian radar. (*Militarnyi, https://mil.in.ua/en/tag/war-with-russia/?page=114*)

First launch of Ukrainian ATACMS. These missile systems were provided too late and in insufficient numbers to impact the Ukrainian counter-offensive. (*Militarnyi, https://mil.in.ua/en/news/ukrainian-military-showcased-last-year-s-atacms-launches/*)

Patriot anti-air missile launcher. The US Patriot and other modern hi-tech anti-air systems were key to the defence of Ukraine's civil and industrial infrastructure. In late 2023 and early 2024 roving Patriot batteries reduced the effectiveness of Russian glide bomb attacks on Ukrainian defensive positions. (*UA General Staff*)

Ukrainian tank equipped with mine ploughs. These tanks were employed to ensure lanes in minefields created by line charges were clear of mines. (*Ukraine General Staff Facebook page*)

US M1A1 Abrams tanks arrived too late to participate in Ukraine's summer/autumn 2023 counter-offensive. They were instrumental in the rearguard actions which enabled the Ukrainian defenders of Avdiivka to withdraw to the defensive line 10 km (6 miles) west of the city. (*Ukraine General Staff Facebook page*)

Ukrainian Marines, trained by UK and Norway, conducted raids along the Dnipro River and the west coast of the Crimean Peninsula. (*Ukraine General Staff Facebook page*)

Crowdfunded pick-up trucks from the 'Come Back Alive Foundation' were armed with HMGs for roving anti-drone patrols. (*https://mil.in.ua/en/news/mobile-aa-fire-teams-received-pickup-trucks-from-the-come-back-alive-foundation-and-ukrnafta/*)

Chapter 19

Russian Strategic Bombing Campaign

Moscow's stockpile of missiles dwindled, but Putin continued the strategy of terrorizing the Ukrainian people in an attempt to erode their will to resist. Fighting over the budget to continue aid to Ukraine, President Biden reminded Congress and the world that after two years of fighting, Putin's objective remained unchanged: the obliteration of Ukraine and subjugation of its people.[1]

It was no surprise that on 21 September 2023 Russia resumed its bombing campaign, focusing on Ukraine's energy infrastructure and the terrorizing of civilians. On that date forty-three cruise missiles and drones were launched toward Ukrainian cities. Ukrainian AD shot down a total of thirty-six, while eight got through and hit energy faculties in central and western Ukraine. The Russians had targeted the electricity grid the previous winter in an effort to freeze Ukrainian civilians into surrender. They hoped to achieve their goal with a repeat attack on civilian heating oil facilities.

The earlier campaign disrupted Ukrainian communities, cutting off civilian access to heat and electricity for extended periods during an extremely cold winter. The bombardment damaged 61 per cent of Ukraine's electricity generating capacity. A humanitarian catastrophe was averted thanks solely to the bravery and dedication of state electrical workers. The electricity grid had not been completely repaired, as replacement parts and transformers were in short supply. Damage to the grid was estimated at over $8.8 billion, but electricity company CEOs had prepared for Putin's 2023 onslaught.[2]

During the bombing campaign between February 2022 and December 2023 Russia launched 7,400 long range missiles and 3,900 Shahed drones against Ukraine.[3] Having depleted its missile stocks, Russia acquired these Iranian–made waepons, long-range loitering kamikaze drones. Small, and with a smaller warhead than the cruise and ballistic missiles, they quickly became a critical part of Russia's bombing campaign. The drones were relatively cheap, and Iran authorized Russia to produce them domestically. A large plant was built in Russian Tatarstan and when in full production was able to produce 200 Shahed drones per month.[4]

Between 29 December 2023 and 5 January 2024 Russia launched 500 missiles and drones at targets across Ukraine. In 2023 there were three to six attacks per month. The attacks included legitimate military and defence industry locations along with purely civilian targets, to terrorize the Ukrainians, such as hospitals, residential buildings and shopping malls.[5]

The combination of missile and drone attacks was orchestrated to overwhelm Ukrainian AD capabilities. The initial wave of long-range drones forced defenders to launch intercepting missiles. Once the defensive launchers were depleted, a second wave of attacking missiles passed through the AD umbrella before the defenders could reload. Despite variations of these tactics, Ukrainian AD batteries managed to shoot down 70–80 per cent of the incoming drones and missiles.

The Ukrainian AD missiles had been provided mostly by the US. Missile reserves became dangerously low in January and February 2024 because Congress was deadlocked over passage of an appropriation bill which included military aid to Ukraine. Due to this shortage, Ukrainian generals were probably forced to concentrate their dwindling supply of missiles to defend the most critical targets. This left much of the country undefended and could have led to thousands of unnecessary civilian casualties. With the US distracted by internal politics, Germany sent Ukraine an additional Patriot system, and the UK provided 200 air defence missiles.[6]

Russia conducted five major missile and drone attacks on Ukrainian cities during 2023, causing over 100 civilian casualties. On 14 January 2023, a Russian supersonic missile hit an apartment building in the city of Dnipro, killing forty-five people including six children. The number of wounded was unreported. On the night of 28 April 2023, another apartment block in the city of Uman was hit, killing twenty-one, including three children. Again, the number of wounded was unreported. The Russians claimed they were targeting a military barracks.

On 6 September 2023, sixteen people were killed when a Russian missile struck a busy market in Kostiantynivka. Russia falsely claimed it was a Ukrainian missile that did the damage. On 5 October 2023, a Russian rocket killed fifty-one people in a café in the village of Hroza. The café was hosting a wake following a funeral. On 29 December 2023, Russia launched 122 missiles and many drones against military and civilian targets across Ukraine. The barrage killed twenty-four civilians and wounded 130 more, even though Ukrainian AD shot down most of the missiles and drones.[7] Most, if not all, of these five major strategic attacks were considered war crimes under international law since they specifically targeted civilian sites. Some of the missiles in this attack violated Polish airspace, but the only response was a protest by NATO and Poland.[8] Like the attacks in 2022, the Russian 2023 strategic campaign against the Ukrainian infrastructure was inconclusive. It failed to disable the Ukrainian electricity grid, it failed to prevent supplies and ammunition from reaching the front line and it failed to undermine the determination of the Ukrainian people to resist.

Chapter 20

Ukrainian Ground Counter-offensive 4 June–5 July 2023

Hoping to repeat their 2022 successful counter-offensive, the Ukrainians executed a similar campaign in 2023. The main effort of the ground force was to cut the Crimean land bridge and liberate occupied southern Ukraine, including Crimea. The Ukrainians did not have the benefit of overwhelming air superiority, or even local air superiority. They were outnumbered by Russian artillery, aided by drones to improve its counter-battery reaction time, while Russian aircraft actively flew air interdiction missions, and kamikaze drones loitered over the battlefield seeking Ukrainian targets.

Germany's delay in 'releasing the Leopards' and supplying equipment required for the counter-offensive resulted in truncated training programmes for Ukrainian vehicle crews and infantry squads. The NATO training previously conducted failed to recognize relevant battlefield conditions and requirements. Ukrainian squads, platoons and companies should have been

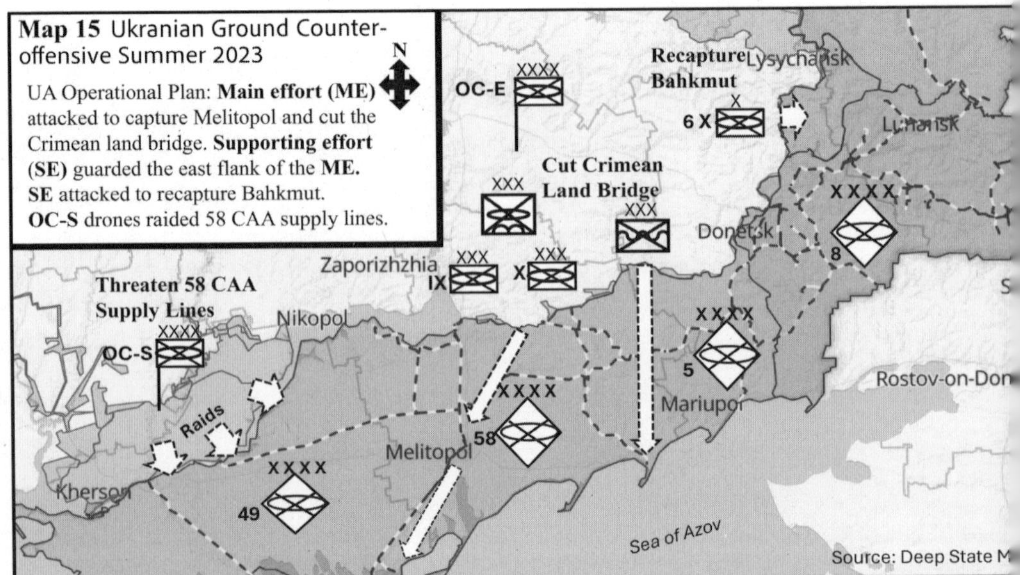

trained in the use of combined arms tactics to storm heavily fortified positions and in the reduction of minefields. In attacking heavily entrenched Russian defence positions the Ukrainians faced a task much like the US Marines invading Imperial Japanese fortified islands during the Second World War.

During the winter and spring of 2023, NATO and Allies debated on whether to 'release the Leopards' and long-range ATACMs and similar missiles to Ukraine. While the debate continued into spring 2023, the Russians anticipated that Zaporizhia and Kherson Oblasts would be the target of Ukraine's 2023 summer counter-offensive. As a result, they were deeply entrenched. Their fortified zone would come to be known as the 'Surovikin Defensive Line'.[1]

Surovikin served as the commander of Russian forces in the Special Operation between late 2022 and early 2023. He was a career soldier and combat veteran of Afghanistan, where he served as a special forces commando. He also fought in the Second Chechen War and in Syria. During his tour of duty in Syria, Western media nicknamed him 'General Armageddon' for his brutal tactics against civilian targets.

In order to improve his defensive position, Surovikin reduced offensive operations in January 2023 and rebuilt his shattered battalions. Dissatisfied with Surovikin's defensive policies, Putin and General Shoigu gave command of the Special Operation to Chief of the General Staff General Valery Gerasimov on 8 January 2023. Despite this change in operational leadership, Major General Ivan Ivanovich Popov, Commander of the OK-South 58th CAA, and other commanders of defensive sectors were provided with heavy engineering entrenching equipment to turn hastily constructed defences into major fortifications.[2]

The 'Surovikin Defensive Line' was a 2,000 km (1,242 mile) long fortified zone running from the Russian border in Luhansk Oblast in the north to Kherson Oblast in the south. In some parts of Zaporizhzhia and Kherson Oblast the defences were 30 km (18 miles) deep. In many areas the line was developed in accordance with Soviet doctrine, consisting of a security zone and two defensive echelons. After six months of effort between January and June 2023, the security zone was transformed into a defensive echelon, with combat outposts interlinked with direct and indirect fires, minefields and pre-planned counter-attack routes. The most extensively fortified sectors were in Zaporizhzhia, followed by Kherson, Donetsk and Luhansk Oblasts. Each defensive echelon was a complex of infantry trenches, anti-personnel and anti-tank minefields, anti-tank ditches, dragon's teeth and elevated earthen berms for tank firing positions.[3]

Soviet/Russian doctrine dictated that minefields should be 120 metres deep. NATO (MICLIC) and Soviet (UR-77) line charges, towed behind armoured vehicles, could clear a line through a minefield 6 metres wide and 120 metres long. With this capability in mind, the Russians laid minefields 500 metres deep. Ukraine would need to deploy several line charges to breach these minefields and open a lane 6 metres wide and 500 metres long for its armoured vehicles. Clearing minefields was an extremely dangerous operation as the Ukrainians would be subjected to direct and indirect fire and loitering kamikaze drones. Disabling even a single vehicle in the lane would trap a column in the open, in the middle of a minefield, exposing the rest of the column to deadly fire. The Russians had insufficient mines to lay them in the density dictated by the doctrine, so they deployed them in irregular patterns, often laying multiple mines on top of each other to ensure mine-clearing vehicles would be disabled.[4]

The Russian defensive zone was not created by simply building a wall hundreds of kilometres long like the Great Wall of China or Hadrian's Wall. Like NATO, the Russians utilized the terrain in constructing defences. Defensive sectors were organized at every level on the battlefield from battalion to army, based upon projected enemy avenues of approach, key terrain, observation, field of fire, obstacles and cover and concealment.

The first step was to identify the Ukrainian avenues of approach. Ukraine's strategic objectives in the south were to capture the road and rail junctions at Tokmak, Melitopol, Kamianka, and the port cities of Berdiansk, Yalta and Mariupol. Capturing these operational objectives would achieve the strategic objective of cutting the land bridge to Crimea. The objectives and expected

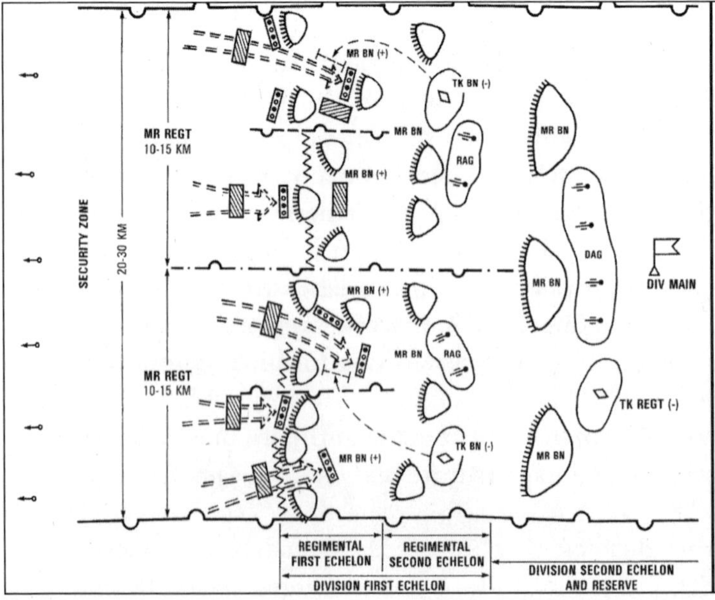

Chart 21 Russian Defensive Structure

The Russian Army applied a successful defensive developed during WWII. In the **security zone** and **first and second echelons** a series of platoon and company **strong points** were **interlocked** with direct and indirect **fire plans**.

This Soviet defensive template was essentially a 21st century Russian division defence once the Russian reinstated division C2 of the separate MRB and MRRs in 2022.

The surprise for UA and NATO was the Russians employed an **Active Defence** in the **security zone**.

axis of attack were no secret. The southern front ran through steppes and fields with undulating open terrain, small rivers and only a few bridges and hard all-weather surface roads. This terrain reduced Ukraine's options for a major offensive. Once the avenues of approach were identified, key terrain features dominating the axis were identified and fortified.

With the key terrain identified, Russian planners projected the Ukrainian scheme of manoeuvre. Intelligence planning sections at army, brigade and battalion levels all studied the enemy's method of fighting and determined the probable course of action. Once planning was completed, probably in the autumn of 2022, combat, combat support and combat service support planners completed defensive preparations. Russian operational defence commanders for southern Ukraine had eight months, from November 2022 to June 2023, to dig in, construct obstacles, train soldiers and stockpile supplies. The 58th CAA and 5th CAA generals planned to execute an active defence in the security zone. This was often referred to in the media as an 'elastic defence'.

The terrain along the Zaporizhia Sector favoured the defender. Steppes and open fields provided the Russians with the ability to observe Ukrainian attackers approaching the Russian defences from 10 to 15 km (6 to 9 miles) away. Tree lines along fields and streams provided cover and concealment that were incorporated into the defences. The steppes and open fields created an illusion that the ground was flat. In fact, it was rolling hillside with numerous intervisibility lines, allowing numerous hide positions for tanks and ATGMs. Controlling the relative high ground, often only 3–5 metres higher than the surrounding steppes and fields, provided defensible terrain for platoon and company strong points. Russian reconnaissance drones coordinated massed artillery fire, preventing the attacker from concentrating battalion-size tank and IFV assaults.

The Russians planned an active defence that included operational shaping operations and tactical counter-attacks. Russian aircraft, especially attack helicopters, were an active part of the defence. Tactical drones provided reconnaissance and directed and adjusted artillery fire.

If the Ukrainians had broken through the Zaporizhzhia defences, another defensive zone defended the entrance to the Crimean Peninsula. While at first blush the defensive zone appeared to be static, it actually functioned as an active defence.

Major General Popov's troops were primarily Mobik battalions or replacements who had arrived in theatre between December 2022 and February 2023, after only a few weeks training. The Zaporizhzhia and Kherson Sectors were relatively quiet during the Russian 2023 winter offensive, providing the Mobiks with an additional four months of on-the-job training in defensive operations before the Ukrainian ground counter-offensive commenced in June 2023.

The fighting was expected to be most intense along the trench lines that could be spotted from space crossing the open steppes. Unexpectedly, however, the heaviest fighting occurred along the tree lines which provided cover and concealment for the defending Russians. These trees had been planted by Ukrainian farmers in an effort to break up the winds that sweep across the steppes. Most of the tree lines run north to south, dividing the steppes into large compartments and having a similar impact on military operations to the 'bocage' (hedgerows) in June 1944 in Normandy, where each 'bocage' had to be cleared by the Allies, slowing their rate of advance. These tree line fortified positions enhanced the Russian active defence within the security zone.

The Russian defence was organized with four operational groupings. Furthest south, Group Dnipro defended the Dnipro River line from the middle of the eastern half of the Nova Kakhovka Reservoir to the Black Sea and the main avenues into the Crimean Peninsula. It appeared that the 49th CAA provided C2 for the Sector, with the 29th and 22nd Army Corps (Naval Infantry) providing intermediate C2. In January 2023, defenders of the Dnipro River line included the 25th Spetsnaz Regiment, 810th Naval Infantry Brigade, 385th Territorial Motorized Rifle Regiment, 1821st Territorial Motorized Rifle Regiment, 11th Motorized Rifle Regiment, 127th Motorized Rifle Regiment, Don Cossack Battalion (volunteers) and the Alga Battalion of volunteers. The 103rd Motorized Rifle Regiment formed a second operational echelon with the 7th Mountain Air Assault Division as the Operational Reserve. Except for the Spetsnaz and Naval Infantry, the remaining fourteen battalions of the first echelon were third-rate units.[5]

The 58th, 35th and 36th CAAs provided C2, and defended the eastern half of the Nova Kakhovka Reservoir to the town of Vuhledar. The boundaries between CAAs were unclear. It was clear that General Ivan Popov's 58th CAA defended the Novodanylivka-Robbtyne axis, where it was projected the main Ukrainian offensive would strike. This axis led to the first intermediate objective at the road and rail junction of Tokmak 30 km (18 miles) behind Russian lines.[6] The composition of the defenders included Spetsnaz, Naval infantry, VDV paratroopers and regular army (including BARS and volunteer battalions).

At the tactical level, Russian artillery pre-registered fire on their own positions, so if the Ukrainians were able to capture the positions, Russian artillery could accurately target them. The Ukrainian counter-action to this tactic was to subject Russian artillery to counter-battery fire. The assaulting Ukrainian infantry quickly adapted by advancing from captured trenches forward to dig other fighting positions. To protect their artillery, the Russians prepared their trenches for demolition. The plan was to withdraw from a trench if it was captured by the Ukrainians and blow it up, rather than try to defend at close quarters.[7]

OK-Centre was assigned to defend a sector fromVuhledar east then north along the Donetsk Peoples' Republic border. The 8th CAA provided overall C2, with the 1st (former DPR), 2nd (former LPR) Army Corps, 14th and 68th Motorized Rifle Divisions and Wagner Group providing intermediate C2. The composition of the defenders included Spetsnaz and regular army, including BARS and volunteers, and mercenary battalions.

OSK West defended Luhansk Oblast and included the 1st Tank Army, 41st, 20th and 2nd CAAs and the 11th Army Corps. In the Belgorod region the 6th CAA was in position to block a Ukrainian attack into Russia itself. In the spring of 2023, the new 25th CAA was also located near Belgorod. Composition of the defenders included Spetsnaz, Naval Infantry, VDV paratroopers and regular army, including BARS and volunteer battalions.

The Zaporizhzhia Sector became the primary battle zone. The defences were organized in three echelons. Between January and June 2023 the security zone was reinforced and developed into a defensive echelon. Without the aid of heavy excavating equipment, but taking advantage of the tree lines for cover and concealment, a complex series of trenches, minefields, combat outposts and anti-tank ditches reinforced with dragon's teeth were created. These positions were built across the projected axis of advance of the main Ukrainian attack.

The first defence echelon was constructed with heavy entrenching vehicles and stretched 150 km (93 miles) from the town of Vasylivka, near the Kahovka Reservoir on the Dnipro River, to Novopetrykivka on the Donesk Oblast border. Artillery was positioned 15–30 km (9–18 miles) to the rear, near the beginning of the second echelon. The second echelon was a longer line running 130 km (80 miles) and stretching east from Orlyansketo Vuhledar. This echelon would serve as a base for counter-attacking the flanks of Ukrainian units if they succeeded in penetrating the first echelon. The third echelon was a series of disconnected strong points organized around large towns, controlling major road and railroad junctions. Not as robust as the first and second echelons, these strong points could slow a major Ukrainian penetration.[8] Augmenting these obvious defences within each echelon were fortified tree lines, which were heavily fortified, requiring the Ukrainians to storm each one with dismounted infantry.[9] These fortifications were as extensive and complex as those employed by the Soviets during the Second World War.

The much-anticipated Ukrainian ground counter-offensive along the southern front commenced on 3 June 2023. The Ukrainians were organized

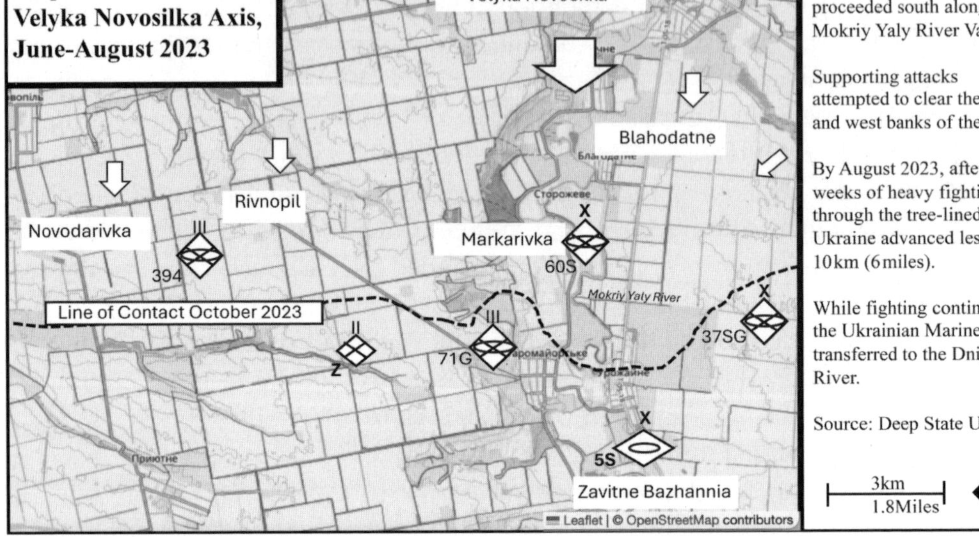

into division-size ground attacks on four main axes from the Dnipro River in the west to Vuhledar in the east. Three of the attacks were shaping operations intended to fix Russian defenders in place. Each of the shaping/supporting attack formations included an armoured reserve to take advantage of any breakthrough that might materialize.

On 3 June 2023, the 37th Marine Brigade attacked on the east of the sector with the objective of capturing the town of Novodonetske in the Donetsk Oblast. This sector was defended by the 131st Motorized Rifle Regiment (DPR) and 100th Separate Motorized Rifle Brigade (DPR). The 37th Marine Brigade was part of a division-size task force conducting a shaping operation. The Marines were not equipped with tanks; however, the 3rd Tank Brigade was in the division TF reserve. The 2,000 Marines were mounted in 17-Ton M-ATVs or MRAP armoured trucks and were supported by French AMX-10RC reconnaissance vehicles that provided direct fire support.[10] The Marine armoured trucks and recon vehicles were lightly armoured, so they remained in 'support by fire position', while the Marine infantry used the tree lines along the fields as cover to close with Russian positions. The Marine attacks ended on 6 June 2023, but Novodonetske remained in Russian hands. Despite constant skirmishing, the frontline remained stable. During the fighting, four AMX-10 reconnaissance vehicles were knocked out; one destroyed, two abandoned and one captured, and twelve MRAP armoured trucks were knocked out, eight destroyed, three damaged and one captured.[11] As a result of these skirmishes, the division task force was determined to be too lightly equipped to launch a major assault on this axis during June/July 2023.

A second shaping operation's axis of advance went through the village of Novopil, about a kilometre north of Russian-held Novodarivka. A Territorial Defence Brigade (probably Zaporizhzhian Separate Territorial Defence Brigade) was dug in along the tree lines and had been in place for months. Ukraine had deployed two mechanized brigades for this attack.

The Russians defended the sector with a dismounted motorized rifle battalion. One company defended the village of Novodarivka, a second defended the village of Rivnopil, while the third held the gap between the two. A tank company was held in reserve. The approaches to both villages were heavily mined. Russian EW was able to periodically prevent Ukrainian drone reconnaissance of the Russian positions. For some unknown reason the EW unit failed to continually jam the frequencies in this sector, and this allowed Ukrainian drones to build an accurate picture of the Russian defences.[12]

During the shaping operations (April/May 2023) in the Rivnopil area the Ukrainians won the counter-battery battle. The longer-range Ukrainian batteries of M777 155mm towed howitzers forced the Russian artillery to displace, to positions deeper in their rear. The normal TTP for Ukrainian batteries was to displace within 2–15 minutes of completion of a mission. The limited Russian counter-battery radar capacity, and the shorter range of their howitzers forced the Russians to deploy their artillery positions further to the

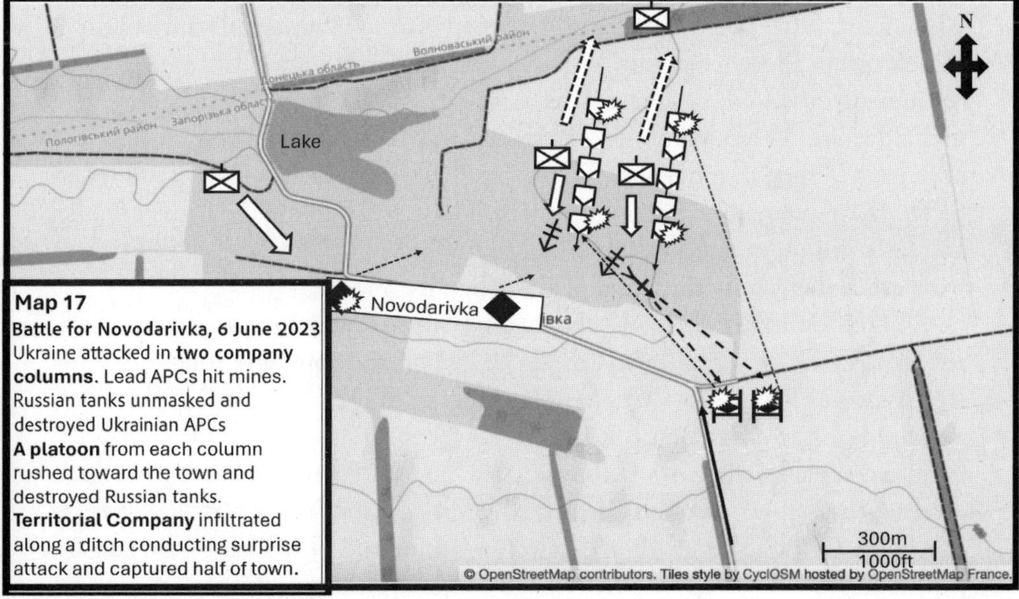

Map 17
Battle for Novodarivka, 6 June 2023
Ukraine attacked in **two company columns**. Lead APCs hit mines. Russian tanks unmasked and destroyed Ukrainian APCs
A platoon from each column rushed toward the town and destroyed Russian tanks.
Territorial Company infiltrated along a ditch conducting surprise attack and captured half of town.

rear. Ukrainian towed artillery had longer range and did not need to displace as often, which allowed them to fire more missions in a 24-hour period. The Ukrainian artillery bombardment was supplemented with drones dropping converted rocket-propelled grenades (RPGs) onto Russian vehicles; but when Russian jammers were active, the hunter-killer drones were not sent aloft. In one engagement, when EW operators were lax, drones carrying four RPGs destroyed or damaged seven Russian tanks.[13]

The Ukrainians attacked the villages of Novodarivka, and Rivnopilon in the night of 3 June 2023. There was some concern about the bogginess of the ground due to recent rain, but it was decided to attack at dawn. The initial breach of defences was planned to occur in the vicinity of Novodarivka, because the minefield there was less dense, and the combatants were closer to each other. The village had been reduced to rubble, but the ruins were linear, running east to west, and made excellent defensive positions.[14] To all intents and purposes, the Ukrainians launched a frontal attack.

On the morning of 4 June 2023, two UR-77 Meteorite line charges blew two 6-metre-wide lanes from the Ukrainian tree line to Novodarivka. Under cover of artillery fire, a company mounted in UK MaxPro MRAPs was led into the east lane by two tanks. Halfway through the minefield, several MRAPs bogged down in the mud. The leading tanks had churned up the muddy lanes, making them nearly impassable for the wheeled MRAPs. The route forward was blocked, and the MRAPs could not bypass the mired vehicles due to the mines. With the column halted in the middle of the minefield, a Russian tank platoon (two tanks) rolled out of their hide positions and engaged the Ukrainians. The Ukrainian tanks returned fire at 800m, but the column's vehicles were all knocked out. The Ukrainian infantry in the front half of the column dismounted, rushed to the edge of Novodarivka and established a toehold there. The remaining infantry toward the rear of the column made it back to the Ukrainian tree line. The troops that reached the village had carried SPR-9 73mm recoilless rifles with them. The crews flanked the Russian tanks and knocked them out. With the tanks knocked out, the Ukrainian casualties were evacuated across the mine field to friendly lines.

While the first company was bogged down, a second company entered the western lane. The ground was firmer, but when the company rolled into the lane a second Russian tank platoon (two tanks) moved from its hide position and fired on the advancing column. Observed via a drone feed, the Ukrainian battalion engaged the tanks with artillery. Under direct fire, the second column increased its speed through the lane, but in the confusion it deviated from the cleared route, and all the vehicles were knocked out. The infantry again divided, with half going into the village and half back into the forest.

As the Ukrainian infantry entered eastern Novodarivka, the Russians fell back to strongpoints east of the village. In order to reinforce their toehold in the village, the Ukrainian battalion commander sent a dismounted infantry platoon along the lanes in the minefields. This reinforcing platoon advanced toward the village, taking advantage of the knocked-out vehicles as cover. Russian artillery was suppressed with counter-battery fire, protecting the platoon. A second platoon attacked the western part of the village after advancing through dense foliage. This platoon entered the village and, after heavy fighting, secured the crossroads that split the village in half. It took an additional week of heavy fighting to capture the village ruins.

With the capture of Novodarivka, the Ukrainians focused on the village of Rivnopil. The village included a series of tree lines that ran north and south, threatening the Ukrainian armoured advance with flank shots from ATGMs. The Ukrainians had lost two companies of vehicles taking Novodarivka, but thanks to advanced Western vehicle armour, casualties had been relatively light during the engagement in the minefields. The loss rate of Western-supplied equipment could not be sustained, so the Ukrainians changed tactics.

The attack on Rivnopil was led by Territorial light infantry, probably from the Zaporizhzhia Separate Territorial Defence Brigade. The Territorials were supported by two tanks and an artillery battery from a different brigade. The attack commenced with artillery suppressing Russian positions. The two tanks moved into support by fire positions, moving in and out of cover while firing on Russian positions.

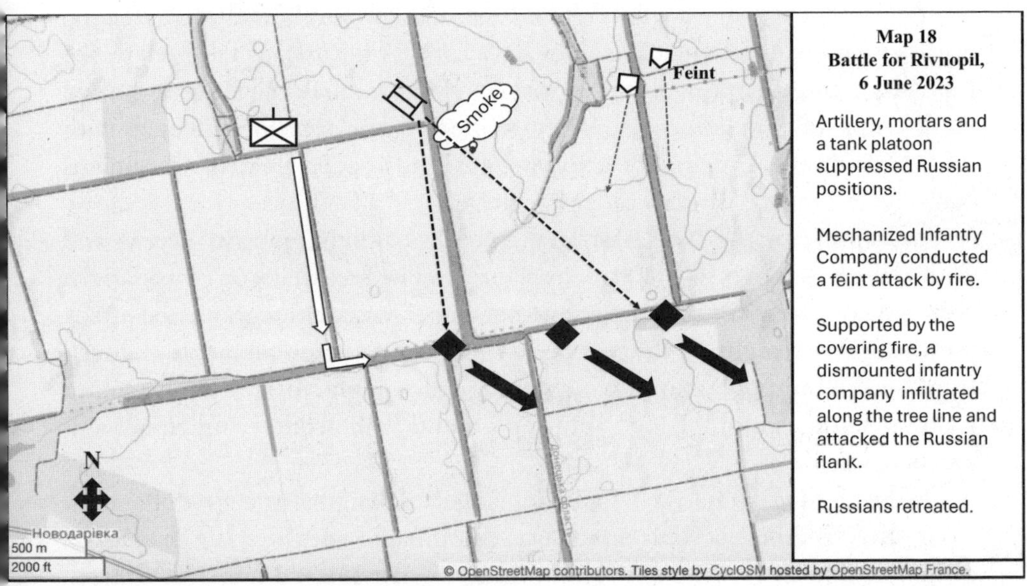

Map 18
Battle for Rivnopil, 6 June 2023

Artillery, mortars and a tank platoon suppressed Russian positions.

Mechanized Infantry Company conducted a feint attack by fire.

Supported by the covering fire, a dismounted infantry company infiltrated along the tree line and attacked the Russian flank.

Russians retreated.

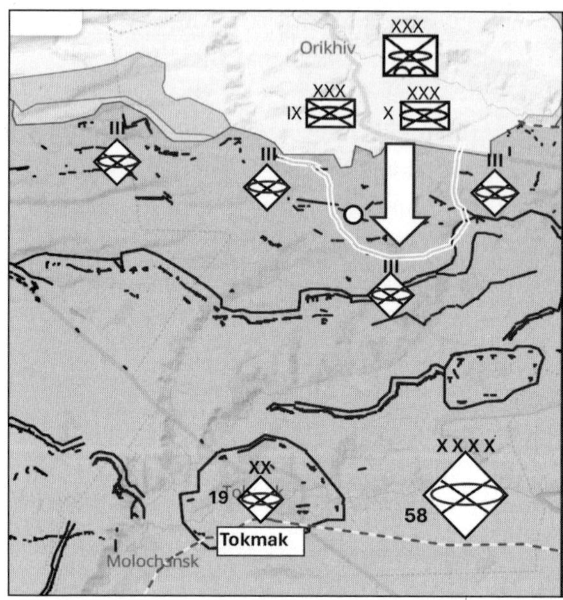

Map 19 Ukrainian Counter-offensive Decisive Operations June–October 2023

Ukraine planned to attack and cut the Crimean land bridge by advancing 81 km (50 miles) to capture Melitopol.
The intermediate objective was to advance 35 km (21 miles) and capture Tokmak, HQ of the 19th MRD. Ukraine committed IX, X and Maroon Corps to the operation. If Tokmak could be captured, HIMARS rockets could interdict the supply routes to Melitopol.
In June 2023, 58th CAA defended the sector with four Motorized Rifle Regiments (MRRs). By October 2023, seventeen MRRs, including 76th VDV Airborne Division defended the sector. The active defence of the 58th CAA, with air support, prevented a Ukraine breakthrough.

Source: Deep State Map, OpenStreetMap@copyright

The Russians fixated on the two Ukrainian tanks, while Ukrainian artillery delivered a smokescreen obscuring their support by fire position. Distracted by the tanks, the Russians failed to notice that a Territorial platoon had infiltrated the tree line west of their positions. The Russians had thinned their lines to reinforce their eastern positions facing the tanks. Enfilading the defenders' position from the west, the Territorials advanced by fire and manoeuvre. They reached the village and dug in beyond the Russian positions (which had been pre-targeted by Russian artillery). The Territorials were relieved by a following brigade that secured the village a few days later. The Russians fell back out of the village and established their positions along a canal, blowing up several small dams to flood the area. They reinforced the tree-line defence with ATGM positions. Lacking the ability to cross the flooded area, the Ukrainians consolidated their position inside the village.

The capture of the Novodarivka-Rivnopil positions took two weeks and pushed the Russians back 1,200 metres (1 mile). The first attack on Novodarivka cost two companies of vehicles, while personnel losses throughout the attack on Rivnopil were light. In the two weeks of fighting, Ukrainian tactics changed from high tempo operations, which expended equipment at a rapid rate, to a slower tempo, emphasizing capturing ground while conserving equipment and personnel.[15]

On the night of 4 June, the Ukrainians launched their main decisive operation along the Orikhiv axis. This attack was coordinated with shaping operations across the frontlines along and within the Zaporizhzhia and Donetsk Oblasts.

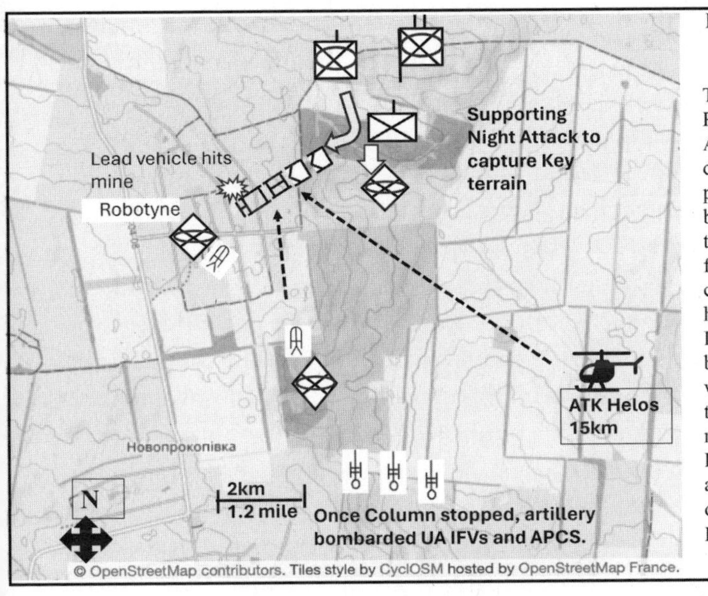

Map 20 First Battle for Robotyne, 8 June 2023

The 47th BDE attacked to capture the Russian-occupied town of Robotyne. A Ukrainian company conducted a dismounted night attack to secure position to protect the main attack. A battalion of the 47th passed through this company and attacked the town from the east. Detecting the armoured column, Russia called for attack helicopters. Ukrainian task force of Leopard 2s, IFVs and APCs was led by special Leopard 2 mine-clearing vehicles. These struck mines, halting the column which bunched up in the middle of the minefield.
Russian massed fire from ATGMs, artillery and attack helicopters destroyed Leopard 2s and M2 Bradleys.

Approximately ten brigades equipped with Western and Soviet-era equipment were massed in the vicinity of Orikhiv. The initial counter-offensive was mainly focused on the Orikhiv and Vielya-Novosilka axes and shaping or supporting attacks along the Zaporizhzhia and Vuhlehdar axes.[16]

On 8 June the main Ukrainian attack was launched on the Melitopol axis of advance, with Roboryne the initial objective and Tokmak the intermediate one. A Ukrainian division-size task force consisting of the 33rd Mechanized and 47th Assault Brigades rolled south from their assembly area near Mala Tokmachka towards Russian-held Roboryne. This axis was defended by the 70th and 291st Motorized Rifle Regiments, stiffened by two Spetsnaz brigades and supported by attack helicopters firing over the defenders, taking advantage of their 10 km (6 mile) range.

The 47th Mechanized Brigade probably the best-equipped of the nine new combat manoeuvre formations, spearheaded the main effort. Its armoured vehicles included Leopard II tanks and Bradley IFVs. A limited number of heavy combat engineering vehicles based on tank chassis were attached. Its infantry were well equipped with night vision googles. Situated on high ground, Roboryne dominated the Ukrainian main axis of advance. It was probably defended by the 291st Guards Motorized Rifle Regiment, supported by the 70th Motorized Rifle Regiment that was forward-deployed in the security zone fortifications. The 1430th Motorized Rifle Regiment held a reserve position in the first echelon trenches.

The overall details of the Ukrainian multiple brigade attack are unclear. The 33rd Mechanized Brigade and a second unidentified brigade conducted fixing attacks on both flanks of the 47th Mechanized Brigade. Two infantry battalions of the 47th Mechanized Brigade were mounted in ninety-nine US M2 Bradley IFVs. Its tank battalion included Leopard II tanks and mine-clearing combat engineer vehicles. The 33rd Mechanized Brigade's tank battalion was equipped with thirty-two Leopard II tanks.[17]

The 47th Mechanized Brigade's battle plan assigned a reinforced mechanized battalion to assault Roboryne from the east. A second battalion probably suppressed the Russian defenders with direct fire. The assaulting battalion conducted a dismounted infantry company night 'movement to contact' to capture a Russian combat outpost. The infantry crept forward at night, occupied an attack position near the Russians and waited for dawn, then conducted a surprise attack, storming and capturing the outpost. With the outpost in Ukrainian hands, the southern flanks of the main attack were protected. A reinforced mechanized company following the infantry advanced south along the route that had been cleared and secured the night before. Just before reaching the outpost, it turned west. The column broke cover from the tree line and entered the minefield protecting Roboryne's eastern flank.

The Ukrainian column was led by a breaching team, consisting of Finnish Leopard II R mine-clearing tanks and Leopard IIs. An assault team followed close behind. The following assault team, consisting of a mechanized infantry company mounted in Bradley IFVs and MaxxPro MRAP armoured trucks, followed behind in single file. The Russians detected the breaching team as they broke cover. Observing the developing Ukrainian attack, the Russian defenders of Roboryne probably called for attack helicopter support.

The mine ploughs on the lead combat engineering vehicles missed several mines. As a result, a few Bradleys and Leopards triggered the mines and were disabled in their tracks, halting the column. The partially trained, inexperienced Ukrainian crews in the centre and rear of the column continued their advance, and the column bunched up. The Russians rained down artillery once the column became stationary, and Russian Ka-52 attack helicopters arrived on station and commenced firing ATGM fire from 10 km (6 miles). The Russians pummelled the halted column for two hours while Ukrainian crews and infantry bailed out of their disabled vehicles. As the fire lifted, a second Bradley company roared in, rescuing the survivors and bringing them back to safety. When the engagement ended, twenty-five Ukrainian vehicles, (seventeen Bradleys, four Leopard II A6 Tanks, three Leopard 2Rs and one Armoured Recovery Vehicle) had been damaged or totally destroyed.[18] The disaster could have been even worse for the Ukrainians. Western combat vehicles are designed with crew survivability in mind, and while their vehicles were disabled or destroyed, most of the crews survived. Private Serhiy's Bradley hit a mine, and the vehicle was heavily damaged; the crew and infantry were certainly rattled but happy to have survived the explosion with only minor injuries.[19]

Continuing attacks over the following week by three brigades failed to capture the fortified town of Robotyne. The three brigades suffered heavy casualties, and large amounts of Western equipment were damaged or destroyed. Minor damage to Leopards and Bradleys (tracks and road wheels) were repaired behind the frontlines in assembly areas. The damaged Leopard IIs were evacuated to repair depots in the Polish cities of Gilwice and Poznan, and the US quickly shipped replacement vehicles to Ukraine.[20] The US sent ninety-nine replacement Bradleys to Ukraine in June 2023.[21] Ten Leopard II tanks and mine-clearing tanks were knocked out; three were destroyed and seven damaged beyond repair.[22]

The combatants fought a series of see-saw engagements on the Vielya-Novosilka axis during the same timeframe. These engagements resulted in the liberation of several villages, and the frontlines were slowly pushed south. The opponents also skirmished along the line of contact on the Vuhledar axis, but there the front lines remained unchanged.

OC-South had captured several islands on the lower Dnipro River in the Dnipro Sector, and artillery duels became a routine occurrence. To the Ukrainians' surprise, the Russians destroyed the Noova Kakhovka Dam on 5 June 2023, flooding the lower Dnipro River Valley to the Black Sea.

This defensive shaping operation protected the 58th CAA western flank and would prevent a major Ukrainian attack in this sector for the remainder of the year. The explosion at Nova Kakhovka destroyed the dam and power station, and the water flooded 139 square kilometres. Destroying a purely civilian water/power installation that did not have any military importance and releasing the force of devastating floodwaters was clearly a war crime pursuant to the International Law of War.[23] The resulting flood prevented the Ukrainians from crossing the Dnipro River in significant force; providing a reprieve for regiments of the 22nd Army Corps and 7th Mountain Air Assault Division, which were transferred from the Dnipro River line to reinforce the 58th CAA's defence along the Zaporizhzhia Sector.

The extent of flooding surprised the Russians. In order to maintain operational security, the defenders occupying the first echelon defences along the river had presumably not been informed that the dam was going to be blown up. On lower ground than the Ukrainian western bank, the Russian defences were flooded and washed away. Russian soldiers, who had not been warned about the flood or given orders on how to proceed in the aftermath, escaped as best they could.[24] One squad was spotted using blue and yellow (Ukraine's national colours) recreational kayaks from a water park to paddle to safety.[25]

NATO tactics during the initial phase of the counter-offensive proved unsuccessful. The counter-offensive resulted in heavy casualties and the loss of 20 per cent of Western heavy armour. Unlike the Russians, when faced with battlefield reverses the Ukrainians took a tactical pause and assessed the reasons for their lack of success. The failure to make significant progress in recapturing the Zaporizhzhia Oblast was duly noted in the press. The Western press loves an underdog when he is winning but hesitates to continue support when he is not.

Russia likely destroyed Ukrainian dam

Evidence suggests that Russia blew up the Kakhovka dam that collapsed on June 6 in a Russian-controlled area of Ukraine, according to analysis by the New York Times

Jun 6, 2023: Seismic stations in Ukraine and Romania detect signs of large explosions at 02:35 and 02:54. Witnesses in area hear large blasts between 02:15 and 03:00

Just before dam gives way, U.S. intelligence satellites capture infrared heat signals that also indicate explosion

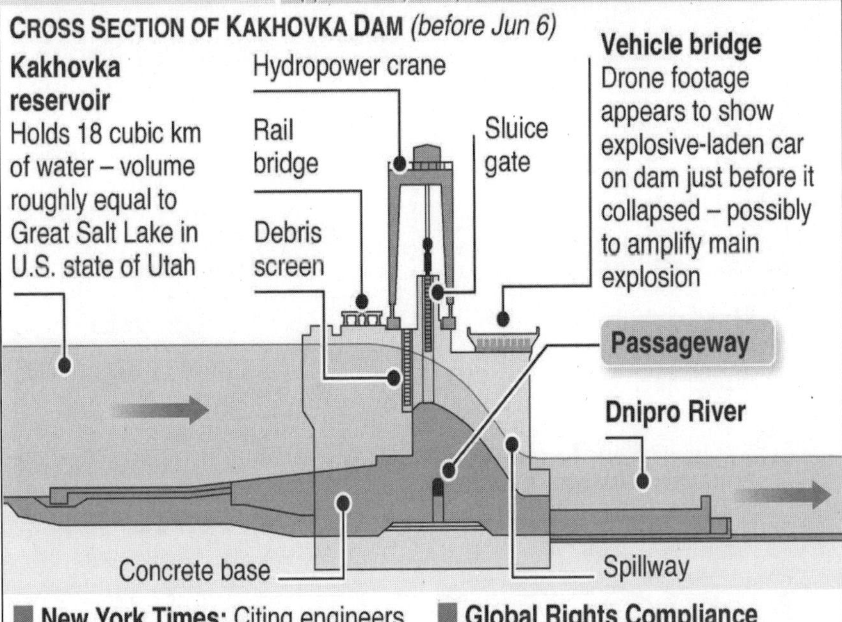

New York Times: Citing engineers and explosive experts, investigation found evidence suggesting explosive charge detonated in passageway, destroying dam on Jun 6

Global Rights Compliance Separate team of legal experts assisting Ukraine's investigation said in initial findings that Russia was "highly likely" to have destroyed dam

Sources: New York Times, Reuters

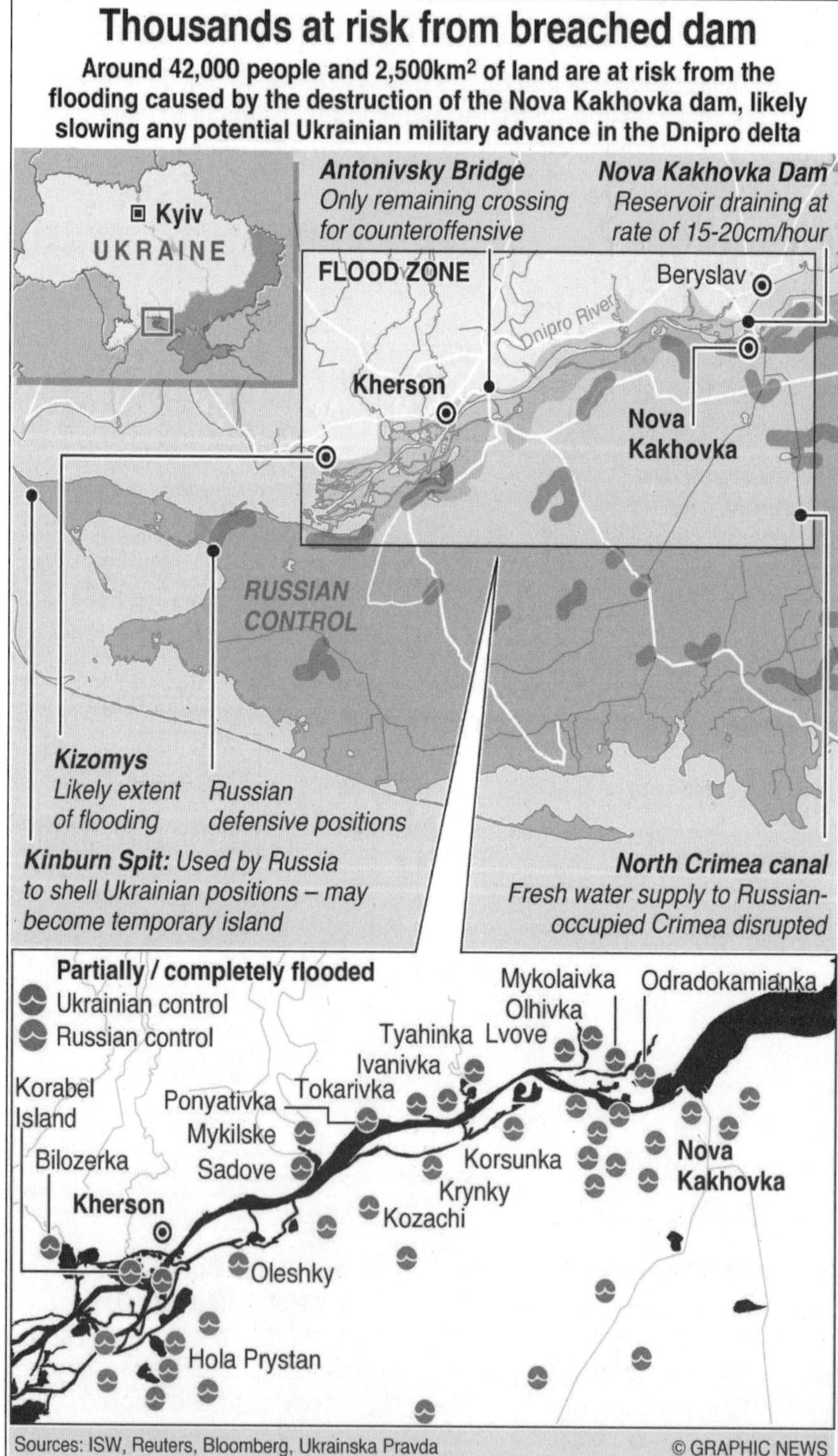
Thousands at risk from breached dam
Around 42,000 people and 2,500km² of land are at risk from the flooding caused by the destruction of the Nova Kakhovka dam, likely slowing any potential Ukrainian military advance in the Dnipro delta
Kyiv
UKRAINE
Antonivsky Bridge
Only remaining crossing for counteroffensive
Nova Kakhovka Dam
Reservoir draining at rate of 15-20cm/hour
FLOOD ZONE
Beryslav
Dnipro River
Kherson
Nova Kakhovka
RUSSIAN CONTROL
Kizomys
Likely extent of flooding
Russian defensive positions
Kinburn Spit: Used by Russia to shell Ukrainian positions – may become temporary island
North Crimea canal
Fresh water supply to Russian-occupied Crimea disrupted
Partially / completely flooded
Ukrainian control
Russian control
Mykolaivka
Odradokamianka
Olhivka
Tyahinka
Lvove
Ivanivka
Korabel Island
Ponyativka
Tokarivka
Mykilske
Sadove
Korsunka
Nova Kakhovka
Bilozerka
Krynky
Kherson
Kozachi
Oleshky
Hola Prystan
Sources: ISW, Reuters, Bloomberg, Ukrainska Pravda
© GRAPHIC NEWS

Chapter 21

Ukrainian Counter-offensive Ground Operations, July–October 2023

The tactics employed in June 2023 by Ukraine on the three axes of attack failed to achieve decisive results. The attack along the Bakhmut axis was led by the 3rd and 5th Assault Brigades and was mostly conducted by battalions that had not benefited from NATO training. While a few of their commanders had received some US and/or NATO training before the invasion, most of the officers and soldiers were trained by Ukrainian combat veterans. The IX and X Corps assigned to the Zaporizhzha and Velkyka-Novosilka axis had received NATO training, but the rank and file lacked combat experience.

The Velyk-Novosilka supporting axis of advance followed the Mokriy River Valley south toward the town of Zavitne Bazhanna. This sector was defended by the 127th Motorized Rifle Division. To protect the Ukrainian advance, the high ground on both sides of the river needed to be secured. To the west, in the first echelon of defence, Novodanrivka and Rivnopil had been secured in June 2023. The 134th Motorized Rifle Regiment (127th MRD) retreated south to Pryiutne, but the 37th Separate Guards Motorized Rifle Brigade and UI Separate Guards Motorized Rifle Brigade held the river valley, and the 131st Regiment (DPR) held the higher ground on the east, with their defence centred on the village of Novodonetsk. Behind the units, in the second echelon of defence, the 394th Motorized Rifle Regiment held the west side of the river valley, while the 136th Motorized Rifle Regiment held the centre and the 125th Separate Motorized Rifle Brigade held the right. The 5th Separate Tank Brigade and a battalion from the 111th Separate Rifle Regiment were in reserve.[1]

Between 15 July and 5 August 2023 the Ukrainians attacked along the western ridge of the Mokriy River Valley, toward the village of Pryiutne. The main attack advanced south along the valley towards the village of Zavitne Bazhanna. Marines from three brigades and tanks from the operational reserves captured the village of Urozhayne on 27 July. The 1st Tank and 31st Mechanized Brigades replaced the Marines and prepared to attack towards Zavitne Bazhannia.

Ukrainian reconnaissance drones flying over the battlefield could not miss the flow of new battalions entering the Mokriy River Valley. Based upon the influx of newly arriving Russian battalions, the 128th Territorial Brigade reinforced the defenders of the village of Staromaiorske. On 15 August, elements of the 1st Tank and 31st Mechanized Brigades attacked from the village of Urozhaine as their first step in the advance toward Zavitne Bazhannia. The distance between Urozhaine and Russian-held Zavitne Bazhannia was only 3 km (1.8 miles). The two villages were at extreme tank main gun and ATGM range. A heavy firefight ensured, and the Ukrainians made almost no progress down the river valley. The ground that was gained was shortly recaptured by a counter-attack from the 60th Separate Motorized Rifle Brigade. The Russians used glide bombs during the fight to hit Ukrainian rear areas.[2]

The 127th Motorized Rifle Division was reinforced between 19 and 21 August by three additional motorized rifle regiments. The reinforcements occupied the high ground on both sides of the river with a defence in depth. The Russian reinforcement rendered any chance of a breakthrough on the Velyk-Novosilka axis unlikely. By the end of August that supporting attack ended. Skirmishing continued across the tree line-studded fields, but the frontlines stabilized.

The Ukrainians conducted a supporting attack on the Bakhmut axis with two objectives. The first was to recapture the ruined city of Bakhmut itself. The second was to tie down as many Russian forces in the immediate area as possible. Given all the fanfare Russian media had previously sounded after the

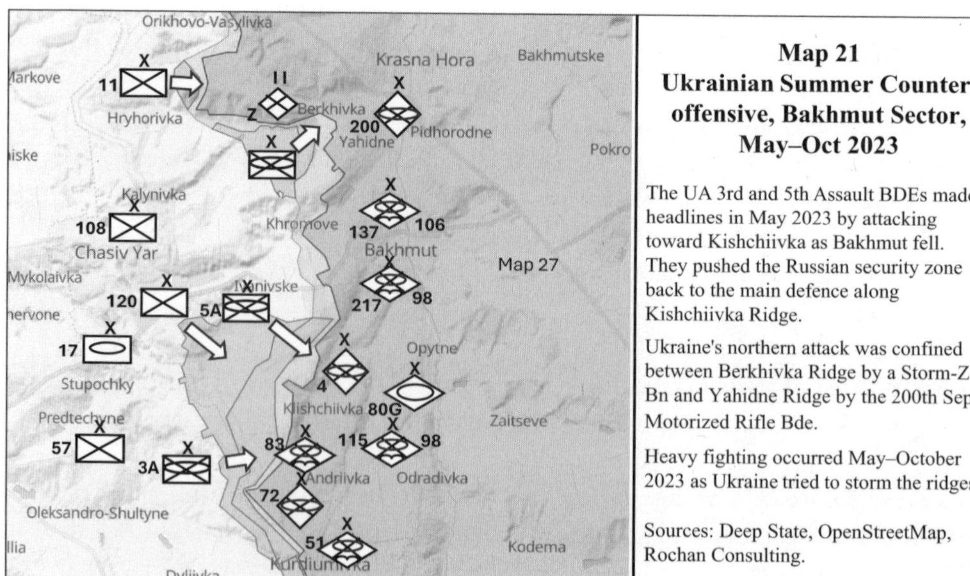

Map 21
Ukrainian Summer Counter-offensive, Bakhmut Sector, May–Oct 2023

The UA 3rd and 5th Assault BDEs made headlines in May 2023 by attacking toward Kishchiivka as Bakhmut fell. They pushed the Russian security zone back to the main defence along Kishchiivka Ridge.

Ukraine's northern attack was confined between Berkhivka Ridge by a Storm-Z Bn and Yahidne Ridge by the 200th Sep Motorized Rifle Bde.

Heavy fighting occurred May–October 2023 as Ukraine tried to storm the ridges.

Sources: Deep State, OpenStreetMap, Rochan Consulting.

capture of Bakhmut, its recapture would be a loss of face for Putin and for the Russian Army.

Local counter-attacks started on the flanks of the city before Wagner Group raised their flag over the City Centre on 21 May 2023. By the time Wagner pulled out of the city, battles were raging north and south of the city, as Ukraine attempted to capture the dominating high ground. From 12 to 30 May 2023, the 3rd and 5th Assault Brigades pushed the Russian security zone back towards the village of Klishchiivka.[3] Tank raids moved forward to suppress Russian positions, covering their infantry's assault. The Russians were forced back to a low ridge just a few hundred metres west of Klishchiivka. The southern ridge on the approach to Klishchiivka was defended by the 4th Separate Motorized Rifle Brigade. Its southern flank was covered by the 72nd Separate Motorized Rifle Brigade. The 137th Guard Airborne Regiment (106th ABD) and the 217 Airborne Regiment (98th ABD) were in a reserve position 5 km (3.1 miles) north-west of Klishchiivka, with the 57th Separate Motorized Rifle Brigade defending Bakhmut.

On the northern side of Bakhumt, the Ukrainians attacked up a valley toward the village of Berkhivka. The Berkhivka Reservoir at the northern edge of the valley protected approaches to the Russian-held ridge on the north. The southern ridge was dominated by the village of Yahidne. At its narrowest point the ridges were only 2 km (1.2 miles) apart. The northern ridge was defended by the 9th Motorized Rifle Regiment (18th MRD) and the 200th Separate Motorized Rifle Brigade.

General Oleksandr Syskyi's strike force consisted of the 80th Air Assault Brigade, the 3rd and 5th Assault Brigades, the 95th Air Assault Brigade and the Liut Offensive Guard Brigade. Additional brigades were present but had not been mentioned in dispatches.

On 6 June, after two weeks of heavy fighting, the 3rd Assault Brigade advanced 3 km (1.8 miles) but halted at the base of the ridge east of Klishchiivka. By 10 June, the 4th Separate Motorized Rifle Brigade replaced the 72nd Separate Motorized Rifle Brigade. On 12 June, the 80th Guard Tank Red Banner Regiment reinforced the 4th Separate Motorized Rifle Brigade.

The northern attack encountered heavy resistance as it attempted to bypass the Berkhivka Reservoir. Subjected to crossfire from both ridges, the Ukrainians were only able to advance a few metres per day, and the attack stalled. Despite heavy fighting near the Reservoir, the Russians retained possession of the ridges throughout 2023.

On 23 June, the defenders on the Klishchiivka ridge were reinforced with the 83rd Separate Guards Air Assault Brigade. On 25 June, Ukrainian attempts to outflank the southern ridge were stopped by the 51st Guards Airborne

Regiment (106th ABD). On 1 July, the 4th SMRB was rotated out of the line and replaced with the 72nd SMRBD. On 4 July the defenders were also reinforced by the 11th SMRB.

The opponents remained locked in combat along the Klishchiivka ridge. On 17 September, Ukraine's Interior Minister, Iho Klymenko, and General Syskyi claimed Klishchiivka was cleared of Russians. President Zelensky congratulated the 80th Air Assault Brigade, 5th Assault Brigade, 95th Air Assault Brigade and the Liut Offensive Guard Brigade for their heroic part in capturing the town.[4] Heavy fighting continued into October 2023 without any decisive results. By late October 2023, Ukrainian formations began reporting logistic issues; mortar and artillery rounds were in short supply. This was not surprising, as the Zaporizhzhia axis was the priority.

The small tactical victory at Klishchiivka failed to lead to operational success. President Zelensky's announcement and celebration was only a publicity stunt. It took an additional four months of heavy fighting for the counter-offensive to advance 500 metres and cross a small ridge to capture an unimportant town. For better or worse, the tactical victory cemented President Zelensky's and General Syskyi's relationship, which led to Syskyi being elevated to Commander of Ukrainian Military Forces at the beginning of 2024.

The main show on which Ukrainians, NATO and the world were focused was the Zaporizhzhia axis. General Tarnavsky appeared to command this operation. Ukraine had massed most of its new brigades in the IX and X Corps and Maroon Tactical Group on this axis.

The destruction of the Nova Kakhovka dam and power plant on 6 June produced an insurmountable obstacle for a Ukrainian armoured attack to overcome. With the river in full flood, the 58th CAA's western flank was secured from a major Ukrainian attack. The flooded lower Dnipro River failed to prevent Ukrainian commando raids across the river into Russian-occupied Kherson Oblast, but these attacks, from June through October 2023, constituted minor annoyances. Safe from a major ground attack in its deep rear, Russia shifted its elite paratroopers from Kherson into occupied Zaporizhzhia. The swampy and muddy ground along the Dnipro River line, caused by draining the lake behind the Nova Kakhovka dam, ensured that the Russians were safe from a division-size assault crossing the river in 2023.

By the middle of June 2023, IX Corps brigades on the Zaporizhzhia sector changed tactics. For two weeks the Ukrainians attempted to replicate NATO tactics while lacking air superiority or long range ATACMS missiles. These frontal attacks were launched from one tree line to the next, across minefields. The results were unacceptably heavy casualties and the loss of 20 per cent of

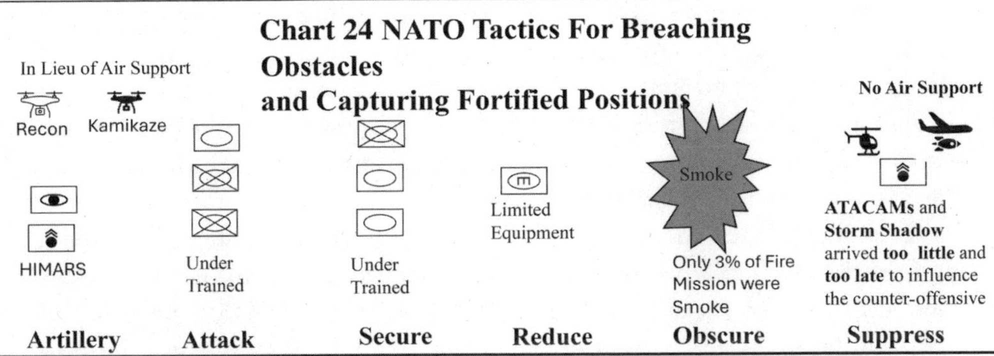

To breach obstacles and capture complex defensive position, NATO forces **Suppress** enemy forces, **Obscure** the attacking force, **Reduce** the obstacles, **Secure** the breach site and **Attack** the position. Artillery, aircraft, attack helicopters, ATACMs and drones **suppress** enemy tactical and operational forces. Artillery fires smoke to **Obscure** the breaching force. The breaching force tanks and IFV **secure** the site while Combat Engineers **reduce** the obstacles. The **attack** force captures the enemy position. **Ukrainian Forces were not supplied with sufficient equipment or training to successfully employ NATO Tactics**

Sources: Colonel Markus Reisner, Austrian Army
https://www.youtube.com/watch?v=EWjMr3RZ8Ss&t=1251s, US Army FM 71-1 Tank and Mechanized Task Force.

Ukraine's Western-supplied weapons and armoured vehicles.[5] The simplest way to visualize the newly adopted tactics is to imagine a chess board.

Like the 'bocage' (hedgerow) country in Normandy in 1944, the Zaporizhzhia and Velkyka-Novosilka axis was laid out along open fields, surrounded by tree lines. In the initial days of the counter-offensive the Ukrainians applied NATO tactics and conducted frontal attacks from one field to the next. They apparently lacked an effective artillery fire plan to deploy smoke to obscure

their advance or break up the Russian coordinated fire plan. There was little evidence of armoured vehicles in support by fire positions to provide covering fire to breaching and assaulting units as they attempted to cross the open fields. Company and battalion columns were often trapped in the open, where Russian ATGMs, helicopter gunships, mines and artillery inflicted heavy casualties on men and equipment.[6]

After a short tactical pause, the Ukrainians reverted to tactics, techniques, and procedures developed over the previous eighteen months of war. Attacks were organized by small platoon assault groups, coordinated at company and battalion level. Assault groups would advance in and along the tree lines to attack Russian positions. Once a position was captured, IFV, APCs or MRAPs utilized the cleared tree line to rotate the assault group with a Territorial platoon. The assault group would rest and re-arm. When the attack was to resume, the Territorials were replaced with the assault group. These tactics resulted in slow and methodical advances. Vehicle losses were reduced, but personnel casualties remained high.[7]

The change in tactics failed to address the problem of how to block Russian reconnaissance. Escaping observation, even at the squad level, had proved nearly impossible. The battlefield had become transparent due to the hundreds of FPV drones launched daily by both sides.[8]

In July 2023 most of the strategic and operational reserve brigades remained ready to exploit any breakthrough, while frontline brigades focused on small unit tactics to identify weak spots. The new Ukrainian attrition operational tactics were designed to bleed Russian forward supply depots of artillery ammunition and other supplies, while minimizing Ukrainian casualties. The Ukrainians understood the maxim, 'Expend ordnance to minimize the loss of soldiers.'

The village of Robotyne, located on high ground, dominated the main Ukrainian axis of advance through the Russian security zone towards the tactical objective of Tokmak. The 58th CAA's active defence had been focused on holding Robotyne since June 2023.

Russian frontline positions were a series of strong points, not a continuous line. There were gaps that allowed for infiltration. In a turning movement, the attacker avoids the enemy's principal defensive position by seizing objectives behind his current position or by seizing objectives that threaten his lines of communication and supply. The defender's options are: hold position and be cut off, retreat or divert reserves to meet the threat.[9]

Throughout July and August 2023, the 47th Mechanized Brigade's mission was to capture the village of Robotyne. This NATO-trained brigade began the counter-offensive armed with three M2 Bradley Battalions (ninety-nine vehicles). Approximately thirty of its Bradleys had been damaged or destroyed during the fighting in June 2023. With the change in tactics, the M2s were used to transport soldiers to the front and evacuate wounded. Learning from their failures in July 2023, the Ukrainians employed M2 Bradley WP smoke grenades to cover the deployment of the infantry squads.

The 47th Mechanized Brigade was supported by the 65th Mechanized Brigade. The 65th Mechanized Brigade was armed with T-72 tanks and Dutch YPR-765 APCs, but were not NATO-trained. The YPR-765 was armed with a US .50 calibre M2 heavy machine gun. Carrying a squad of seven, the YPR-765 performed like the US M-113 APC. The Dutch donated 196 YPR-765s to Ukraine.

Between 24 and 28 July 2023, the 65th Mechanized Brigade launched a supporting attack along the ridge west of the village of Robotyne, while the 47th Mechanized Brigade launched the main attack to flank the village through the valley, east of the town. The area was defended by the 1439th Motorized Rifle Regiment and the 71st Guards Motorized Rifle Regiment. After capturing a Russian trench line, one battalion of the 47th Mechanized Brigade attacked the village.[10] A second battalion attacked east along the trenches to widen the penetration. A third battalion pushed the Russians south 5 km (3 miles), but the attack was ultimately halted due to heavy rain.[11] The 65th Mechanized Brigade unsuccessfully conducted two supporting attacks against the 291st Guards Motorized Rifle Regiment's position in the hills west of Robotyne. Both attacks were driven back by heavy Russian anti-tank fire. Suffering heavy casualties, the brigade was rotated to the rear to rebuild.

The late July 2023 attack was billed as a breakthrough by the media and bloggers. It was not. It pushed the Russian security zone back 5 km (3 miles), creating a salient 6 km (3.7 miles) deep and 10 km (6 miles) wide. Four Russian regiments and a BARs battalion held the high ground surrounding the Ukrainian salient in the valley. They were supported by two separate special purpose battalions with drones and EW equipment. The cost of this June 2023 advance was that the 65th Mechanized Brigade was rendered combat-ineffective.

Minor skirmishes took place daily over the next two weeks, with the frontlines shifting by a few metres each day. The Russians reinforced the defenders with the 218th Tank Regiment and BAR battalions. Finally, in late August 2023, the Ukrainians commenced another big push by conducting probing attacks along the Russian lines near Robotyne.

Taking advantage of its infantry equipped with night vision googles and Bradleys equipped with thermal sights, the 47th Brigade attacked Robotyne in the dark of night on 22 August 2023. The 47th Brigade Bradleys transported infantry to attack positions on the flanks of the village. The Bradleys suppressed the Russian defenders with their autocannon while the infantry stormed the village. The Bradleys fired white phosphorus (WP) smoke grenades to screen the assaulting infantry and degrade the Russians' limited night vision targeting capabilities. When the infantry assault was delayed by Russian strong points, Bradleys were called forward to reduce the position with autocannons. The Bradleys again fired smoke grenades to cover their withdrawal from the village before Russian artillery could react.

The Russian infantry was pushed into the southern part of the village, where they held. A heavy Russian artillery bombardment prepared the way for a Russian infantry counter-attack, supported by T-90M tanks. The Ukrainians were pushed back to the northern part of the village. Ukrainian tanks and Bradleys were called forward again, and the Russian attack was halted and pushed back. Ukrainian drones may have been active during the fight and the Bradleys' ATGMs may have been the key in defeating the T-90Ms assault.[12] Following the retreating Russians, the Ukrainians captured the southern part of the town and on 23 August soldiers from the 47th Mechanized Brigade raised the Ukrainian flag.[13] The next day, 24 August, was Ukrainian Independence Day. In celebration, a dozen successful drone and artillery strikes damaged or destroyed four Russian command posts, ten troop concentrations, four air defence systems and two artillery systems in the area. Most importantly, HIMARS hammered the 58th CAAs supply depots in Tokmak, which was the supply centre for the 58th CAA defending Robotyne.[14] With Robotyne finally secured, the Ukrainians took advantage of the confusion caused by the strike on the command post and advanced towards the village of Novoprokopivka.

On 23 August, the 47th Mechanized Brigade (IX Corps) was rotated out of the line. In the two months of heavy fighting, it had suffered heavy casualties and the loss of fifty of its ninety-nine Bradleys. The capture of Robotyne was touted as a breakthrough, but it was not. As the 47th Mechanized Brigade was raising the Ukrainian flag over Robotyne, the 58th CAA was receiving reinforcements. The high ground around the salient was held by seven motorized rifle regiments, six BAR battalions, the 810th Naval Infantry Brigade and the 108th Airborne Assault Regiment. These formations were supported by a reserve of two motorized rifle regiments and one tank regiment, a total of approximately 25,000 combat troops.

The IX Corps' lack of success resulted in its being replaced on the front line by the X Corps and the Maroon Tactical Group. The X Corps contained the NATO-trained 116th, 117th and 118th Mechanized Corps, and the Maroon Tactical Group contained the NATO-trained 46th, 82nd Air Mobile Brigades, the 72nd Jaeger, the Scala Recon Battalion from the 3rd Spartan Brigade and the 15th Karadag Brigade, supported by the 44th Artillery Brigade. The X Corps arrived on the front line on 7 August 2023.

Skirmishing between the fresh opposing forces commenced almost immediately. FPV drones conducted reconnaissance, directed artillery and attacked vehicles and troops. Between 31 August and 12 September, Ukrainians made incremental gains in see-saw skirmishes, while the Russians committed the 76th Air Assault Division to the battle. After a month of heavy fighting the situation remained unchanged: the Russians still held the high ground and Ukrainians the low ground. The salient in which the Ukrainians found themselves was only 10 km (6 miles) deep and 10 km (6 miles) wide.

Unhappy with how the counter-offensive was proceeding, Biden informed Zelensky in late September 2023 that he would provide ATACMS in the future, and in October Biden's administration authorized ATACMS to be provided to Ukraine.[15] Delivery of new advanced Western weapons was normally announced in the press, but the delivery date for the ATACMS was kept private and they were delivered in secret. The first surprise ATACMS fire mission on 17 October 2023 hit two Russian airfields in occupied Ukraine and destroyed nine attack helicopters. Additional ATACMS missions followed, until finally the Russians were forced to withdraw their attack helicopters to bases further into the rear. The additional distance to fly to the frontline reduced the length of time Russian attack helicopters could remain on station supporting ground troops.

While some versions of ATACMS had a range of 300 km (180 miles), Biden only authorized the shorter-range cluster munition version to be sent. These Block I tactical missiles had a maximum range of 160 km (100 miles). The Biden Administration was concerned that providing long-range ATACMS would have enabled Ukraine to strike within Mother Russia, which would have expanded the war. Biden was also hesitant about providing Ukraine with the MGM-168A ATACMS Block IVA missiles, equipped with a 500lb warhead and having a range of 300 km (186 miles).[16] Such a powerful, long-range missile could destroy or heavily damage the Kerch Bridge, Putin's pride and joy.

The Biden Administration sent the M39 Block I ATACMS missiles with a much more limited range of 25–165 km (15–100 miles). These carried a payload of 950 anti-personnel bomblets. The Block I was made in the 1990s and was no longer in production. The US had produced approximately 1,650 Block I missiles, but several hundred had been fired during Operation Desert Storm and Operation Iraqi Freedom.[17]

Unfortunately, the ATACMS provided were too little and too late. Block I cluster missiles would have had a decisive impact on the battlefield when the

Russians were reinforcing the 58th CAA in July and August 2023. Assembly areas for motorized rifle regiments would have been perfect targets for Block I cluster missiles, even though the Kerch Strait Bridge remained out of range. The road and rail bridges connecting the Crimean Peninsula within occupied Ukraine were in range, but cluster missiles could not damage these structures significantly. Block I cluster missiles could harass supply trains and destroy trucks along the coast road, out of range of normal HIMARS rockets. The limited number of ATACMs supplied were better utilized, forcing Russian attack helicopter bases back from the frontlines.

The heavy fighting continued to the end of October 2023. More elite paratrooper regiments joined the fight. Russian counter-attacks were quietly reduced, but Ukraine's not very impressive ground counter-offensive seemed to fizzle out. The twelve brigades (nine NATO- and three Ukrainian-trained) committed to the three operations had all sustained heavy casualties and significant equipment losses. Tokmak and Melitopol were not in danger of being captured. Cutting the land bridge to Crimea and liberating the peninsula seemed only an impossible dream. The main attack on the Zaporizhzhia and Velkyka-Novosilka axis advanced 10 km (6 miles), liberating one village and 76 square kilometres of open fields. The counter-attack along the supporting axis Velkyka-Novosilka penetrated 11 km (6.8 miles,) liberating eight villages, and 244 square kilometres of open fields. Most importantly, the counter-attack along the Bakhmut axis failed to take the city of Bakhmut, even though it did succeed in liberating thirteen smaller villages.[18] By the end of October 2023,

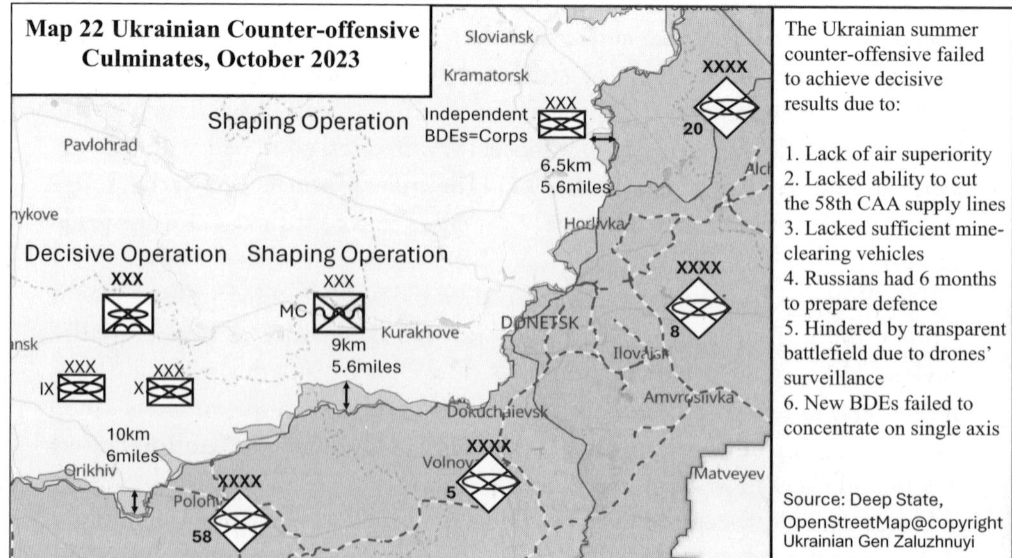

General Zaluzhnyii acknowledged that the counter-offensive had reached a dead end.

General Zaluzhnyii published an essay and granted an interview with *The Economist*, making it clear that as Commander of Ukrainian Military Forces he was responsible for the counter-offensive's failure to achieve its objectives. After five months of fighting, Ukraine had advanced only 17 km (10 miles). After ten months of intense fighting around Bakhmut they had failed to liberate the city, and had made only insignificant gains in empty hilly terrain. Zaluzhnyii believed that he could defeat Russia through attrition, but despite suffering 150,000 casualties Russia was as strong as ever. According to the NATO training manual, the Ukrainian Army should have been able to breach Russian defences and advance 30 km (18.6 miles) per day. Four months should have been sufficient time to reach Crimea. Instead, his troops had got stuck in minefields around Bakhmut, and Western equipment had been pummelled by Russian artillery and drones. Inexperienced brigades immediately ran into trouble.

'First, I thought there was something wrong with our commanders', Zaluzhnyii said, 'so I changed some of them. Then I thought our soldiers are not fit for purpose, so I moved soldiers in some brigades.'[19]

When this failed, he told his staff to break out a Soviet Staff Study entitled 'Breaching Fortified Defence Lines'. Published in 1941, and written by Soviet Major General P. S. Smirmov, it analysed battles from the First World War. Halfway through the book, Zaluzhnyii realized he was facing the same problems as his First World War predecessors. Technological developments had confounded both the Russian and Ukrainian leaders, and neither had a clue what to do. Twenty-first-century technology had made the battlefield transparent. Drones, electronic warfare, anti-artillery (counter-battery radar), de-mining equipment and robotics had changed the route to victory on the battlefield.[20]

While not blaming Biden for the failed counter-offensive, Zaluzhnyii stated that the US and NATO were overly reluctant to supply Ukraine with their latest technology and modern weapons. Biden had early on stated that the US objectives at the start of the war were to ensure Ukraine was not defeated, and that the US was not dragged into the war. The result was that arms supplied to Ukraine were sufficient to sustain Ukraine's war effort but insufficient to deliver victory.[21]

Zaluzhnyii expressed gratitude for the support provided, yet the delay in supplying ATCMS, modern tanks and jet fighters allowed Russia to regroup and establish defences after the successful Kharkiv and Kerson counter-offensives in 2022. While frustrated with the delay in receiving modern weapons, he acknowledged that the war could not be won with outdated weapons and methods. Due to advances in technology, sea and air drones are now decisive on the modern battlefield. Equally important is the development of electronic warfare capable of interfering with effective use of battle drones.

We had truly entered the dawn of drone warfare.

Chapter 22

Wagner's Revolt
22–25 June 2023

Historically, the priority of an emperor, dictator or tyrant has always been to remain in power. The welfare of the people comes a distant second, so distant that it is acceptable to expend the lives of hundreds and thousands of soldiers to create the illusion of victory from a failed policy. Napoleon has often been quoted as saying, 'Never interrupt your enemy when he is making a mistake.' Seeming to take counsel from the master strategist, General Zaluzhnyi's attacks on the Russian lines seem to have reduced in intensity between 22 and 26 June 2023.[1]

There had been friction between Yevgeny Prigozhin, Wagner's CEO, and the Russian Minister of Defence General Shoigu since the start of the Battle of Bakhmut in the summer of 2022. Prigozhin's belligerent manner in publicly promoting Wagner Group's minor successes at the expense of the Russian Army's significant defeats did not sit well with Shoigu. Putin appeared to have been satisfied with Prigozhin's bellicose manner, since it counterbalanced Shoigu's political power.

In October 2022, Prigozhin publicly criticized the Russian military leadership for retreating from the city of Lyman. In November 2022, Prigozhin publicly boasted about successfully interfering in the US Congressional midterm elections – a boast that was unconfirmed. The midterm elections were crucial as the Republicans were much friendlier to Putin and had just gained a majority in the House of Representatives. The election results seemed to harbinger a future decline of financial support for Ukraine. By January 2023, the friction developed into a feud. General Surovikin, a Prigozhin supporter, was replaced by General Valery Gerasimov, an officer loyal to Shoigu. As Chief of the Russian Armed Forces, General Gerasimov was given direct control of the Special Operation. Shoigu recognized Prigozhin as a threat to the power and influence of the Russian military in general and more specifically to his personal authority and influence with Putin. Unfortunately for Ivan, Gerasimov was a bureaucratic soldier, promoted to his level of incompetence, similarly to Field Marshal Semyon Mikhailovich Budenny during the Second World War. Like Budenny, Gerasimov lacked the strategic expertise to command the Special Operation. His greatest attribute was that he was unquestioningly loyal to Putin.

As the Battle of Bakhmut raged in February 2023, Prigozhin publicly alleged that the Wagner Group was being slowly starved of supplies, especially artillery ammunition. Whether this was true or not, massive artillery support was critical to Wagnerite tactics. Putin stepped in several times, publicly ordering Gerasimov to increase military supplies to Prigozhin's troops. Prigozhin afterwards responded that the supplies finally provided were often degraded due to improper storage, or amounted to only a fraction of what was required.[2] Prigozhin released a video in early May 2023 depicting him standing amongst the dead bodies of dozens of his mercenary soldiers. He blamed Shoigu and Gerasimov for the death of tens of thousands of 'Wagnerites'.

'We are lacking 70 per cent of the needed ammunition', he said. 'Shoigu, Gerasimov where is the ammunition? . . . The blood is still fresh . . . They came here as volunteers and are dying so you can sit like fatcats in your luxury offices.'[3]

Prigozhin charged that the military leadership was corrupt and incompetent. It was clear that Shoigu and Gerasimov were jealous of Priozhin's influence with Putin and the success of Wagnerites on the battlefield. Prigozhin ultimately threatened to pull his soldiers out of the fight if the supply situation did not improve by 10 May 2023. He sent an open letter to Shoigu accusing the General Staff of sending only 32 per cent of the required ammunition since October 2022.[4]

Prigozhin publicly warned Putin in late March 2023 that Ukraine was going to strike the Belgorod Oblast. Ignoring his warning, Russian commanders decided to defend the sector with border guards and police, but they were no match for the heavily armed anti-Putin forces of the Legion of Free Russians and Russian Volunteer Corps. The raid was successful, publicly embarrassing the Russian Army.

Prigozhin's troops remained in the fight and on 21 May 2023 captured the ruined town of Bakhmut in the Donetsk Oblast. While Prigozhin gave most of the credit for capturing the town to his mercenaries, he did mention the support of the VDV. He also indicated that Wagner Group would transfer control of Bakhmut to the Russian Army by 1 June 2023.[5]

Tension between Wagner Group and the Army came to a head in early June 2023. Lieutenant Colonel Roman Venevitin, Commander of the 72nd Motorized Brigade, mined the road used by Wagner Group to withdraw from Bakhmut. The Wagnerites discovered the mines and detained Venevitin. Confessing on video, Venevitin said he hated the Wagner Group and was drunk when he gave the order to mine the road. Prigozhin alleged the order to mine the road came directly from General Gerasimov.[6]

Critical of the Army's failure to act in response to Prigozhin's early warning of the attack on Belgorod Oblast, Wagner group hacked Russian media channels on 7 June 2023 and posted a video address from Prigozhin. His address and comments were almost like a campaign speech. He concluded that only he could protect Russia, that the top military 'brass' was incompetent and that while Wagner was capturing Bakhmut, the generals were asleep at the switch on Belgorod.[7]

On 11 June 2023 General Shoigu decreed all military volunteer formations were to sign contracts with the MoD. Wagnerites viewed this as an attempt to bring Wagner Group under Russian Army control. Prigozhin refused to follow Shoigu's order, as did the Wagnerites.[8] On 23 June 2023 Prigozhin claimed that AFR helicopters had conducted missile attacks on a Wagner camp in eastern Ukraine near the Russian border. He alleged that Shoigu directly supervised the strikes from OK-South HQ in Rostov-on-Don. The attack was followed by another video posted on social media by Prigozhin in which he stated that Putin's Special Operation was based on false intelligence from the Ministry of Defence. Prigozhin concluded that; neither Ukraine nor NATO were preparing to attack Russia, so the invasion was founded on Shoigu's ambition to become as famous as Field Marshal Zhukov (the hero of the Great Patriotic War), and that greedy Russian oligarchs had promoted the invasion as they sought the spoils of war. The oligarchs planned to place Putin's Ukrainian friend and relative oligarch Vktor Medvedchuk as the new president of Ukraine.[9] With Medvedchuk in office, the oligarchs could control all Ukrainian businesses and natural resources. Prigozhin continued stating that mind-boggling corruption within the Russian Army had resulted in it being unprepared for the invasion, resulting in a catastrophe and the loss of thousands of soldiers before the gates of Kyiv. He emphasized that Shoigu and Gerasimov should be prosecuted for creating genocide. It was unclear if the genocide Prigozhin referred to was the loss of thousands of Russian soldiers or the war crimes committed against the Ukrainian people. While his allegations were well publicised by the international media, they contradicted the narrative which Putin's media was broadcasting to the Russian people.

Four hours later, Prigozhin posted yet another video on social media, depicting a strike on a Wagner Camp.[10] Shortly after the air strike and Prigozhin's broadcasts, the MoD announced it had launched a criminal investigation against Prigozhin for instigating a coup.[11] This was the last straw for Prigozhin. He took command and led his detachments of several thousand men from their Ukrainian camps towards Rostov-on-Don inside Mother Russia.

General Sergei Survikin and Chief of General Staff General Alekseev were Prigozhin's friends. Both had helped him establish Wagner Group and both now publicly appealed for him to stand down. Their pleas were ignored. The Kremlin had tolerated Prigozhin's antics for months but had finally lost patience. On the morning of Saturday, 24 June 2023, Prosecutor General Igor Krasnov announced that Prigozhin was being investigated on charges that carried a maximum prison sentence of twenty years.[12] Shortly thereafter, TASS, the Russian State News Agency, reported that Prigozhin had been charged with a violation of Article 279 of the Russian Criminal Code: 'Inciting Armed Revolt'.[13]

Wagner troops reached Rostov-on-Don and seized control of several military sites. After securing OK-South headquarters and posting Wagner operatives to supervise air operations, Prigozhin prepared to march on Moscow. As the Wagner convoys started north, Putin finally went on the air, declaring Prigozhin's actions a 'stab in the back'.

In response, Prigozhin announced he was marching north with 25,000 operatives and that he had not instigated a 'military coup' but a 'March for Justice'.[14] In the early morning of 24 June 2023 Wagner forces began their march toward Moscow. As the columns passed through villages, Russians poured out onto the street to wave, smile and photograph Prigozhin. Russian military bloggers reported that three columns consisting of 4,000 combat-hardened operators, armed with 350 military vehicles including tanks, IFVs, APCs, artillery, captured US MRAPs, MANPADS and Pantsir ADA systems were observed heading for Moscow. Encountering minimal opposition from local police or other Russian ground forces, the column rolled north.[15]

The Russian Air Force flew into action to stop the convoy. In a running fight Russian helicopter gunships attacked the columns. The Wagnerites defended themselves, and the Russians lost seven aircraft in the battle, including a Ka 52 attack helicopter, a fixed wing Ilyushin Il-22VZPU airborne command aircraft, three Mi-8MTPR electronic warfare helicopters and a standard Mi-8 and Mi-35M attack helicopter. An estimated fifteen Russian airmen were KIA.[16]

The Russian strike package in response to Prigozhin's 'March for Justice' demonstrated that the Russian Air Force had improved its tactics since the beginning of the Special Operation. The size of the strike was unclear, but it was well organized, and the force contained 'wild weasels' (Mi-8MTPR) to jam Wagnerite anti-air radars and three different Russian attack helicopter units, with a forward air controller coordinating the effort, and it effectively stopped the mutiny in its tracks.[17] Russian aircraft attacked Wagner units during the March and elsewhere, in the Rostov-on-Don area. To counter Wagnerite control of Rostov Oblast, Chechen units were ordered in to threaten the mutineers' flank.[18]

The lead column of mutineers reached Krasnoe, Litetsk Oblast, at 1750 on 24 June 2023 where it halted. The adversaries then entered into negotiations for a peaceful solution brokered by Belarus President Alexander Lukashenko. Putin, Lukashenko and Prigozhin were friendly and had been on good terms for over twenty years. As a result of the negotiations, Prigozhin agreed to leave Russia for Belarus and end the armed March for Justice. In exchange, charges against him and the Wagnerites were dismissed. The Wagnerite operatives were to sign contracts with the Russian MoD. Prigozhin's convict operatives were incorporated into Storm-Z units within the Russian Army, but his well-paid professional mercenaries did not sign the proffered contracts, preferring to remain independent. Wagnerites withdrew from Rostov-on-Don and returned to their camps in Ukraine.[19]

Prigozhin's threats and actions were the result of competing military power structures that had emerged during the Special Operation.

It was never Putin's intention for Wagner Group to grow into a major military organization. The Group, along with the other PMCs, was created to promote Russian worldwide economic and political interests. Prigozhin had controlled and enforced Russian foreign policy in Africa. Russian oligarchs used Wagnerites to prop up brutal governments in Mali, Sudan, Libya and the Central African Republic (CAR) in exchange for a free hand for Wagner to plunder the valuable mineral riches of these countries. CAR President Faustin-Archange Touadera relied upon Wagnerites to stop coups toppling his government. Wagner Group accomplished its ends through violence and disinformation, while being paid off through shell corporations that obscured the exploitation of CAR's mineral wealth. These riches funded Prigozhin's corps-size military operations in Ukraine.[20]

Potential problems caused by one country having two competitive armies, one government and the other private, had previously been identified by the Kremlin, but each level of command had apparently decided it was a problem to be solved by someone else – a 'let them sort it out' philosophy.[21] The potential for conflict and disaster was ignored and it festered. Encouraging creation and utilization of private military companies outside the administration of the Ministry of Defence was inherent to Putin's hybrid warfare strategy. It was never envisaged that PMCs would replace the Russian Army or become brigade-, division- or corps-size conventional military units. The failure of the BTGs and motorized rifle battalions to achieve results in urban combat, and the MoD's attempt to hide their high casualty rates, created the conditions for the Wagner Group to expand. Wagner's well-publicized success on the battlefield threatened the power and influence of Russian Army generals, and Prigozhin's popularity increasingly became a threat to Putin's own. Wagner Group ultimately consisted of 25,000 skilled combat veterans, almost two divisions, under the command of a possible rival to Putin's rule.[22] The issue was almost sorted out at the point of a bayonet. Prigozhin had to go, at least he had to appear gone, as did anyone else in power who was seen as supporting him or sympathizing with his views. Putin purged more than a few Russian Army generals who apparently met that criterion.

The FSB alleged General Surovikin was aware of the revolt prior to Prigozhin's March for Justice. Surovikin disappeared shortly after his public plea to Prigozhin to halt the revolt. While still out of public view, it was announced on 24 August 2023 that he had been relieved of command of the Russian Air Force and transferred out of the military into an administrative position in the Ministry of Defence. He remained out of the public eye for another month, and it was rumoured by his inner circle of officers that he had been arrested and possibly executed for treason. However, he reappeared in September 2023 and was subsequently reported as being in charge of the Russian mission to acquire former Soviet-era weapons from Algeria.[23]

On 11 July 2023 the 58th CAA headquarters at the Dune Hotel in Berdyansk was hit by a Storm Shadow missile, killing Lieutenant General Oleg Tsokov, but missing its intended target, Major General Popov.[24] After the attack, the frustrated Popov criticized his superiors in a presumably private conversation. Unfortunately for him, his political enemies taped his comments, and on the evening of 12 July, Andrey Guruly, Deputy Head of the Duma, released an audio recording of General Popov's statement, in which the General accused his higher command of 'treacherously and vilely decapitating the army at the most difficult and tense moment'. Popov emphasized that the lack of counter-battery radars and the absence of artillery drone reconnaissance stations had resulted in mass casualties from Ukrainian artillery fire. Popov had informed Gerasimov that units of the 58th CAA needed to be rotated after weeks of heavy fighting and suffering many casualties. Not surprisingly, General Popov was relieved of command. His dismissal came three weeks after the Wagner mutiny. Popov had risen from platoon commander to army command. He was known for tactics which aimed to avoid unnecessary casualties. Unlike most Russian commanders, he interacted with his soldiers and was very popular with Ivan. The dismissal of a successful general concerned with Ivan's wellbeing undermined Gerasimov's reputation.Gerasimov was already being criticized for the failure of the Russian Army on the battlefield. Sergei Markov, a pro-Kremlin analysist, noted that Popov's statements mirrored those of Prigozhin during his mutiny.[25]

On 15 July 2023, Major General Vladimir Seliverstov, Commanding General of the 106th Guards Airborne Division, was relieved of command. The 106th had fought alongside Wagner Group during the battle for Bakhmut, and General Seliverstov was a known friend of Prigozhin.[26] Following the munity, thirteen senior military officers were detained, and fifteen others were relieved from duty. The detained officers had apparently lost the Kremlin's confidence and were no longer trusted.[27]

This was not the first purge of senior military leaders during the Special Operation, selected as scapegoats for Russia's failure to obtain a quick victory. Putin, Shoigu and Gerasimov sacked Russian Ground Forces General Alexander Dvornkov in autumn 2022. Commander of the VDV Colonel General Andrey Serdyukov was also relieved of command during the same period. The justification for the action was the heavy losses suffered by VDV Paratroopers. Colonel General Alexander Zhuravlev, Commander of the Western Military District, responsible for the Kharkiv front, was also relieved.[28]

On 23 August 2023, Yevgeny Prigozhin boarded a small Wagner-owned private jet, planning to fly from Moscow to St Petersburg. Among the seven passengers were the senior staff of the Wagner Group. A second executive Wagner jet accompanied the aircraft. The transponder signal from Prigozhin's jet unexpectedly disappeared just a few minutes after take-off. The plane had been hit by a Russian surface-to-air missile, and it crashed 100 km (60 miles) from Moscow, killing all ten people on board. The second aircraft returned to Moscow, where all onboard were arrested.

Emergency personnel initially found only eight bodies. It was not known whether Prigozhin had actually been on board, even though he was listed on the manifest. Shortly after the crash was reported, Russian state media confirmed Prigozhin had been on board and had been killed.[29] As news of the crash circulated, Putin was speaking at a memorial event commemorating the 1943 Battle of Kursk and hailing the heroes of Russia's Special Operation in Ukraine.[30] Prior to the reported crash, Prigozhin's whereabouts were unclear. At various times he had been reported in Belarus, Africa and Moscow. Shortly after the news hit the media, Wagner bloggers claimed the jet had been shot down by Russian air defence. A video of a small jet plummeting down with a smoke trail was quickly published on YouTube.[31] Videos from the crash site confirmed the jet had been shot down by a Russian surface-to-air missile.

On 24 August, Russian state media reported that the cause of the crash was a bomb on board Prigozhin's aircraft. They confirmed that Prigozhin, his right-hand man Dmytro Utkin and Wagner Head of Security Valery Chekalov had all been killed in the crash. Putin went on the air expressing his condolences to the families of those who had died. He indicated that even though Prigozhin had a 'troubled fate he was a very useful person who helped Russia achieve a lot of goals.'[32]

Surviving Wagner Group leadership vowed revenge for the assassination of Yevgeny Prigozhin. According to Russian news agencies, Wagnerites blame Putin and Shoigu for their leader's death.[33]

The assassination of Yevgeny Prigozhin was no surprise to students of Russian history. It was expected. What was unexpected was that it took nearly two months for Putin to eliminate Prigozhin. Soviet and Russian dictators have a long history of assassinating their opponents. Starting with Leon Trotsky in 1928, Stalin and his successors used assassination as a tool to hold on to power. Between 2006 and August 2023, former FSB officer Putin has been linked to the assassination of no fewer than thirteen high-profile opponents, including the 16 February 2024 murder of Alexei Navalny while in prison.[34] Over 150 assassinations or attempted assassinations have occurred since the founding of the Russian Federation, most during Putin's time in power.[35] Opponents like Navalny are routinely sentenced to long prison terms, while others have oddly developed a terrible habit of falling out of hotel windows.[36] For Putin to maintain his power, the crisis generated by his Special Operation could only end one way: the elimination of Prigozhin from the chess board.

Chapter 23

NATO Expansion, Russian Containment and the New Cold War

As Ukrainian shaping operations got underway in April 2023, Russia's Special Operation reignited the Cold War. Putin's goal of recreating a buffer zone backfired, resulting in the expansion of NATO and encouraging member states to increase their military budgets. NATO provided billions of dollars, euros and pounds in military and economic aid to Ukraine. NATO built up its military forces along the Russian and Belarusian borders with Poland. By January 2023, for all practical purposes, the new porous 'Iron Curtain' ran through Estonia, Latvia, Lithuania, Poland, Slovakia and Romania to the Black Sea.

Through the winter and spring of 2023, NATO members publicly debated critical issues, including whether to provide main battle tanks and F-16 jet fighters to Ukraine, and whether applications for membership by Finland and Sweden should be granted. Turkey was initially the sole member objecting to both applications. After protracted negotiations, Turkey ultimately

Map 23 NATO Expansion

The Baltic Sea became a 'NATO lake' when Sweden and Finland joined. Putin's aggressive policy drove both neutral countries into the alliance, greatly complicating his attempt to dominate the region.

Sweden's and Finland's formidable military and industrial base reinforces NATO's northern flank. They provide forward air bases to counter any Russian threat to NATO members Estonia, Latvia and Lithuania.

NATO Member

Russia

Russian Ally

Source: US CIA Briefing Map

relented and withdrew its objection to Finland's application, and on 4 April 2023 it joined the alliance to become its thirty-first member. Just before the NATO summit at Vilnius, Lithuania on 11/12 July 2023, Turkey withdrew its objections to Sweden's application, and Sweden became NATO's thirty-second member. Meanwhile, Hungary's pro-Putin Prime Minister Orbán blocked Sweden's application. However, Sweden had initially refused to sell its modern jet fighters to Hungary, and after extensive negotiations between Sweden, Hungary and NATO members, Sweden agreed to sell the aircraft, and Hungary saw the obvious advantages of allowing Sweden to join.

The addition of Finland and Sweden as NATO members resulted in the expansion of the line of contact between the alliance and Russia by 1,340 km (832 miles). The border between Finland and Russia was mostly sparsely populated swamps, forests, bogs and tundra. The terrain was considered easy to penetrate by commandos, especially during winter, and impossible to defend. This new NATO border threatened the only supply route to Severomorsk on the Kola Peninsula, the location of Russia's main naval and submarine base in the Artcic Ocean. In March 2023, Finland began construction of a barrier wall along the southern border with Russia. When completed in 2027, it will stretch up to 260 km (160 miles). The original purpose of the wall, constructed along the most populated part of the border, was for civilian traffic control and to prevent illegal entry into Finland.[1] It will no doubt serve Finland well in case of future Russian aggression.

Sweden's acceptance resulted in NATO control of the Baltic Sea, limiting Russia to a narrow sea lane from St Petersburg to Kaliningrad Oblast, reducing naval access to the Oblast from Russia and Belarus. More critically, the important Baltic Sea naval base in the Oblast is surrounded on three sides by Poland and Lithuania, both NATO members, greatly restricting land access. In the case of future conflict with Russia, Kaliningrad would be left with the narrow sea lane from St Petersburg as its sole supply route.

The NATO meeting at Vilnius addressed several key issues concerning the unjustified and illegal Russian invasion of Ukraine and hybrid warfare focused on alliance members. Disruption of European, North Atlantic and worldwide security was also on the agenda. NATO members reaffirmed their commitment to increase defence spending to a minimum of 2 per cent of individual Gross Domestic Product (GDB) and to support NATO military operations. They agreed to an increased presence along the alliance's eastern flank and to support the territorial integrity and sovereignty of non-member states Ukraine, Moldova, and Georgia. NATO fully supported Ukraine's right to choose its security arrangement. It was acknowledged that Ukraine's future was in NATO, that Ukrainian reforms had moved beyond needing a 'Membership

Action Plan' and that Ukraine had become increasingly interoperable and politically aligned with the alliance.[2] In other words, there was a place for Ukraine as a NATO member when the current war concluded. It was clear from the closing communiqué that NATO was aware that current Ukrainian membership would instigate a general war between Russia and NATO. The conclusion was that to avoid triggering Article 5 of NATO's mutual defence agreement, it was best to delay ratification of Ukraine's membership.

Allied efforts in support of Ukraine were viewed by Russia as an expansion of the conflict. Russia's strategic political goals in this proxy war were to undermine international support for Ukraine's defence and to destabilize supporting countries, particularly the US, with the expectation that a change in national leaders would help achieve Putin's goals. The military strategy to support this political strategy was a return to a 1950 Cold War type of operations on the ground, air and sea.

Between 22 April and 23 June 2023, a total of 34,000 troops from NATO and Allied countries participated in a series of multinational field exercises under the umbrella of 'Defender Europe 23'. The purpose of the exercise was to build readiness in a complex, joint, multinational environment and improve interoperability between the various armies. A combination of command post and field exercises in ten countries included units from the 1st German-Netherlands Corps, NATO's Rapid Deployment Corps in Italy and the 208th Digital Liaison Detachment, along with forward deployed NATO battlegroups.[3] The exercise was designed to demonstrate the US ability to rapidly deploy combat-ready forces and equipment to assure its commitment to the defence of NATO and other European allies. An additional 7,000 US troops deployed for the exercises and they drew 13,000 pieces of equipment from pre-positioned stock.[4]

The US participants included the headquarters of the 34th Red Bull Infantry Division (Minnesota Army National Guard) and its 2nd Battalion 135th Infantry Regiment, based in Udbina, Croatia, that controlled 8,000 personnel from ten different countries. The ten battalions were organized into Task Force South in Albania, Task Force Black Sea in Bulgaria and the Croatian Army Lead Task Force North located in Croatia at Slunj Range.[5]

As part of these exercises, Germany hosted twenty-five countries to participate in 'Air Defender 23', when 10,000 personnel and 250 aircraft participated in Command Post Exercises (CPXs) and flight operations. The intent of the exercise was to broadcast a clear message that NATO was ready to defend every inch of Allied territory and air space.[6]

A Russian fighter jet fired a missile at a British surveillance aircraft in October 2022. The jet was flying over international waters in the Black Sea.

Luckily, the missile malfunctioned. According to US Intelligence, the Russian pilot misinterpreted the communication from his radar operator and ground control, and apparently believed he had been authorized to fire. Prior to this incident, NATO aircraft routinely flew patrols over the Black Sea, 20 km (12 miles) from the Crimea coast, which is recognized as international air space. The US Secretary of Defense imposed a new 74 km (46 mile) stand-off for American aircraft. Between 29 September 2022 and 22 February 2023 UK, French and US jets reacted to six incidents of Russian aircraft dangerously approaching from within six nautical miles to just 100 feet of their patrolling aircraft.[7] Russian fighters had flown dangerously close to US aircraft in Syria and had come close to violating air space limits in the Baltic and on the US Alaskan Coast. In March 2023, a Russian fighter jet struck a US surveillance drone, causing it to crash into the Black Sea. The unarmed MQ-9 Reaper was 120 km (75 miles) south-west of the Crimean Peninsula. On 5 July 2023 Russian jet fighters over Syria dropped flares on a US MQ-Reaper Drone, damaging its wing. These incidents were the exception to previous encounters between skilled, professional NATO and Russian pilots.[8] NATO members decided to treat these potential violations of Article 5 as accidents or errors.

Russia's cancellation of a deal that would have allowed commercial sea transport of Ukrainian grain to a hungry world was followed by repeated Russian violations of NATO air space as they bombed ports to prevent grain shipments. On 1 August 2023 two Belarusian helicopters violated Polish air space. On 2 August 2023 Russian cruise missiles violated Romanian air space

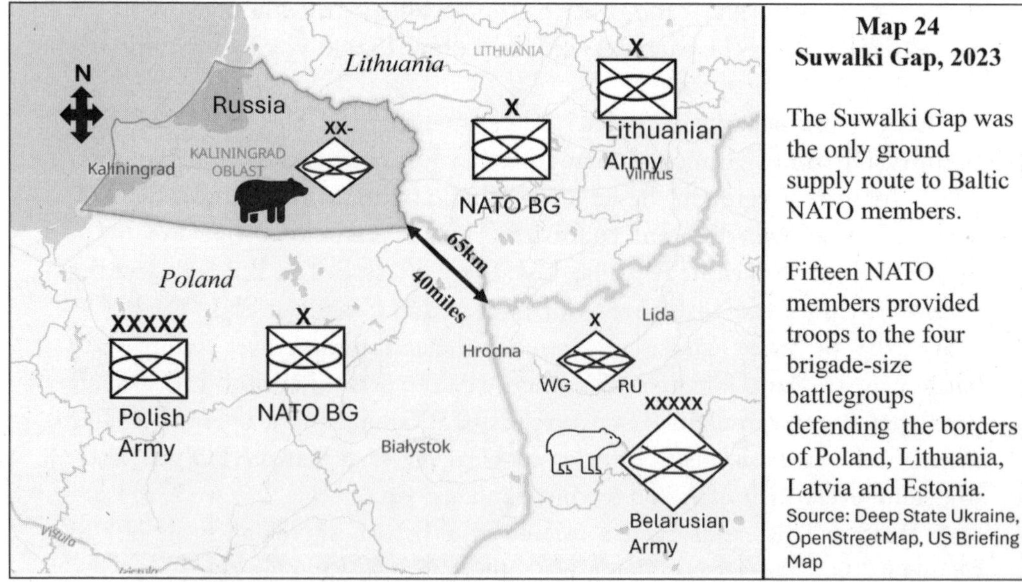

Map 24
Suwalki Gap, 2023

The Suwalki Gap was the only ground supply route to Baltic NATO members.

Fifteen NATO members provided troops to the four brigade-size battlegroups defending the borders of Poland, Lithuania, Latvia and Estonia.

Source: Deep State Ukraine, OpenStreetMap, US Briefing Map

as they manoeuvred to strike grain storage facilities at the small Ukrainian Danube port of Izmail to enforce the blockade of Kyiv's grain exports.[9] NATO officials initially denied publicly that the intrusions had occurred, but photographs taken by villagers and posted on social media and published in the news media depicted the overflight. NATO's response was once again to treat the hostile violations as unintentional.

On land, Russia chose to pressure NATO at the Suwalki Gap. Russia requires control of the Gap because it is the shortest and most direct land route to its naval base at Kaliningrad Oblast. Russia's naval base is completely landlocked. The Gap, sometimes referred to as the Corridor, runs through Poland and Lithuania, and it is seriously anticipated by NATO that Russia will at some point attempt to gain control of it. On 29 July 2023 Wagner Group deployed a detachment of approximately 100 operators within Belarus, near the borders of the two NATO members.[10] The Suwalki Corridor is a sparsely populated, swampy, forested area 65 km (40 miles) long, from the Kaliningrad Oblast to Belarus. Russian-Belarusian activity in this area could have easily violated Polish or Lithuanian sovereignty, which would have triggered NATO's Article 5. If the activity had developed into trespass, it would have led to a general world war. It has always been a flashpoint where NATO expects Russia to continually test its resolve. As a result, over the years NATO has developed plans and conducted numerous war games based upon a theoretical Russian attempt to capture the Gap and gain land access to the Kaliningrad Oblast.[11]

If Russia captured the Corridor, it would sever all land access from Poland to the Baltic States and make it impossible for NATO to reinforce its Baltic State members. It would also threaten Polish sovereignty and territorial integrity. In this context, a comparison between the 'Polish Corridor' once separating East Prussia from Nazi Germany and the Suwalki Gap holds powerful symbolism for the region. Nazi Germany invaded Poland to capture the Polish Corridor and unite East Prussia with the rest of Germany. Similarly, by invading Poland to capture the Gap, Putin could unite the naval base at Kaliningrad Oblast with his puppet in Belarus.[12] With this historical context in mind, it is not surprising that the appearance of Wagner Group in the region created a media storm. The Group was the primary tool of Russia's hybrid warfare, and Poland feared an imminent attack, but this did not materialize in 2023.[13]

Based on the terrain in the Suwalki Corridor and similar areas along the Polish-Belarusian border, Poland's Territorial Defence Force formed an experimental cavalry reconnaissance company. It was thought that horses could move more easily than heavy vehicles in the flat, swampy, forested terrain, and they could live off the land for short periods. The cavalry was tested during a crisis on the Belarus border when the unit deployed as a reaction force. Unlike heavy military vehicles or even motorcycles and ATVs, horses proved to be good at operating in wooded areas with wet soil. Between 23 and 30 July 2023 British cavalry soldiers from the Royal Lancers trained with the Polish cavalry. As accomplished horsemen, the British soldiers joined the Poles in various drills and cross-country rides.[14]

The Suwalki Corridor became the new Fulda Gap of Cold War fame. The difference was the terrain. The Fulda Gap was a tankers' dream terrain, while the Suwalki Corridor would be a nightmare for heavy tanks, armoured vehicles and supply trucks. Unlike the Fulda Gap, the Suwalki Corridor had few hard surface roads, and supplying light infantry forces would be extremely difficult.

In response to Wagner operatives arriving in Belarus, Poland deployed 1,000 troops to the Corridor. The NATO multinational Iron Wolf Mechanized Infantry Brigade was based in Poland near the region, and a second NATO brigade in Lithuania was also put on alert status. The US California Army National Guard 1-185th Infantry Regiment (Stryker) based at Orszyz, near the Corridor, was also alerted.[15]

Putin's invasion of Ukraine resulted in the expansion of NATO membership along Russia's border, the very thing he feared. Along with increased membership, NATO improved its readiness to protect member nations, increasing production of military equipment, ammunition and supplies. Most importantly, Putin's aggression prompted NATO to prepare the way for Ukraine to join the alliance. NATO expanded its capabilities by conducting field exercises on a scale not seen since the Cold War in the 1980s. All these results seem to be the exact opposite of what Putin hoped to achieve by invading Ukraine.

Chapter 24

The Short-Lived Grain Deal

Ukraine was the breadbasket for Africa, Asia and the Middle East. Some of the poorest countries in the world, like Bangladesh, depended on affordable Ukrainian grain, but Putin's Special Operation severely disrupted scheduled grain shipments. Prior to the war, 90 per cent of Ukraine's agricultural exports were shipped from Ukrainian ports on the Black Sea. Pre-war, in 2021, Ukraine exported 20 million metric tonnes of wheat and 25 million metric tonnes of corn.[1] Ukraine directly supplied 725,000 tonnes to the United Nation's World Food Programme, distributed as humanitarian aid to Afghanistan, Djbouti, Ethiopia, Kenya, Somalia, Sudan and Yemen. Prior to February 2022 the World Food Programme procured 89 per cent of its wheat from Ukraine. To put this in perspective, one ship carrying 37,000 tonnes of wheat provided much needed food to 4 million people throughout the world.[2]

The invasion brought the export of grain from Ukraine to a standstill.[3] The Russian Fleet blockaded Ukrainian Black Sea ports for over four months. By May 2022, Ukraine had expanded its overland routes but was only able to transport a significantly smaller amount. With Ukrainian grain off the market, worldwide grain prices spiked. The rise in prices negatively impacted Third World countries, many of which were Russian allies. Beginning in March 2022, the leaders of Egypt, Iran, Saudi Arabia and African countries started clamouring for relief. With world opinion turning against Russia, Putin was ready to make a deal.

In response to international pressure, the United Nations and Turkish President Recep Tayyip Erdogan brokered an agreement between the belligerents on 22 July 2022. The agreement provided that Russia would allow grain shipments from three Ukrainian Black Sea ports: Odesa, Chernomosrk, and Yuzhny/Pivdennyi.[4]

Moscow had two reasons for signing the agreement. First, it would allow some grain shipments to reach its allies in the Middle East and Africa. Receipt of the grain would help prop up Russian allies with unstable governments. Second, unblocking Ukrainian seaports would allow Russia to export its fertilizer via a pipeline that ran through the Ukrainian ports. Easing sanctions against Russian products such as fertilizer was not initially part of the deal allowing grain shipments. However, Russia would not have signed the Grain Deal without having its exports protected as well. The extra clause was successfully negotiated with the US and EU. To put this in perspective, Russia earned $11 billion from exports in 2021. Previously imposed sanctions on the Russian Agricultural Bank (Rosselkozbank) had to be eased in order to accommodate payment for the exported goods, and this became part of the grain deal.[5]

The deal resulted in millions of tons of Ukrainian gain reaching world markets.[6] Under the terms of the agreement, Ukrainian patrol cutters escorted ships carrying the grain. Russia agreed not to attack the ships or any port infrastructure. Turkey, Russia and the UN committed to inspecting the ships to ensure they were not smuggling weapons.

Russia's expectation for the grain deal never fully materialized. Moscow wanted Rosselkozbank reconnected to the international SWIFT payment system, established by the international banking system for the global financial community to securely move money. Rosselkozbank had been cut off from SWIFT in June 2022, and the EU indicated that it would not consider its reinstatement. UN officials developed a way to work around this roadblock with approval from the Biden administration, and utilized US bank J P Morgan Chase & Co to process some of the payments. In addition, the UN worked with the African Export-Import Bank (Afreximbank) as a platform for processing Russian exports of grain and fertilizer to Africa. As part of the agreement, Russia was able to resume its Black Sea ammonia/fertilizer exports via a pipeline from the Russian port at Togliatt to the Ukrainian port of Pivdennyi. The pipeline had pumped 2.5 million tons of ammonia per year before it was shut down due to the war.

In May 2023 Russia unilaterally threatened to abandon the deal unless certain additional demands were met. According to TASS, the grain was headed to developed countries, instead of the world's poorest as intended. Kremlin spokesman Dmitry Peskov said Russia was ready to renew the agreement if its additional demands having to do with payment and banking of oil revenues previously sanctioned were granted.[7] The parties did not agree, and the grain deal was not renewed.

Russian officials began to slow inspection rates, reducing the flow of grain ships from forty to ten a month.[8] Russia claimed that terminating the deal would not impact the price of grain on the world market, because Moscow would make up for the lost Ukrainian grain. This disingenuous propaganda ignored market reality, and a week after cancelling the deal, the price of various grains increased by 10–15 per cent. Any reduction in the world's grain supplies results in increased prices, while any significant increase brings the price down.

Wealthy countries had little problem paying the increased cost, but poor third world countries could not absorb the significant increase.[9]

Russia's actions and strategy were focused on undermining international support for Ukraine by denying its ability to satisfy contract obligations, and more importantly by denying Ukraine the economic returns from selling its grain on the world market. The strategy backfired as it caused many UN members, and others that had previously remained neutral, to condemn Russia's actions. The African Union called on Russia to resume the grain deal. The Chinese went on record stating that the deal should be implemented in a balanced, comprehensive and effective manner, while urging peace talks. The Chinese statement was convoluted, but as a major importer of Ukrainian grain, China wanted the commodity to flow.

As a major trade partner, Turkey had not imposed as many sanctions on Russia as the rest of NATO or the EU. However, Turkish weapons had been supplied en masse to Ukraine. Days before Russia pulled out of the grain deal, President Erdogan publicly announced that he and Putin had agreed that the deal would continue. Putin embarrassed Erdogan on the world stage shortly thereafter by walking away from the deal.

Moscow needed to win the war of world opinion and undermine international support for Ukraine. Withdrawing from the deal and immediately attacking port facilities and grain storage, destroying thousands of tons of grain, had a significant negative impact on world opinion. Russia's actions forced Ukraine to use alternative methods of shipping grain to the world market through NATO allies, slowing and reducing the amounts provided, but not stopping exports altogether. Putin's actions also seem to have influenced NATO in easing restrictions on and objections to Ukraine conducting deep strikes into Russia. After Russia's withdrawal from the grain deal and its subsequent attacks on Ukrainian port facilities, non-NATO-supplied drone attacks on Moscow became routine.

The EU, Ukraine, and NATO were not surprised that Putin pulled out of the grain deal. They expected it at some point and had planned accordingly. The primary ground line of transport, as an alternative to the Black Sea ports, was the 'Danube route' through Romania. The Romanian port of Constanta, at the mouth of the Danube, handled 15 million tons of grain in the first half of 2023, double the volume it handled in 2022. Moving grain via rail to the Croatian ports on the Adriatic, or to the Baltic Sea ports, were other options. Transporting grain through Europe's extensive river-canal system could also be expanded. However all these alternatives increased the cost of shipping the grain.

Two major events that occurred in June 2023 probably contributed to undermining the grain deal. On 5 June 2023, the Russians destroyed the Kakhovka Dam, flooding the lower Dnipro River Valley to the Black Sea. Shortly thereafter, on 7 June 2023, the Russian ammonia pipeline to the Ukrainian port of Pivdennyi was destroyed. The Ukrainians claimed that a Russian missile hit the pipeline; the Russians claimed the Ukrainians caused the damage.[10] Intentional or not, the destruction resulted in a significant loss of revenue to Russia.

Putin cancelled the grain deal on 17 July 2023, and on 18 July 2023 Russia attacked Odesa's grain storage facility, destroying 60,000 tonnes of grain. On 20 July 2023, the Russian MoD announced the closure of maritime humanitarian corridors in the Black Sea, and declared that all vessels sailing the waters toward Ukrainian ports would be regarded as potential carriers of military cargo. Later that same day, the Ukrainian MoD announced that all vessels in the Black Sea heading to Russian ports would be considered to be carrying military cargo, with the associated risks. These competing declarations authorized ships in the Black Sea to be boarded and searched, and if flying the flag of a combatant, seized as a war prize.[11]

With the grain deal protection gone, the simplest method of exporting grain and testing Russia's resolve would have been to sail a neutral ship though the Black Sea to Odesa. The problem was insurance. To counter Russia's threatening declaration, Ukraine established a fund of $543 million to compensate civilian ships for any damage they suffered at Ukrainian ports. A mid-size container

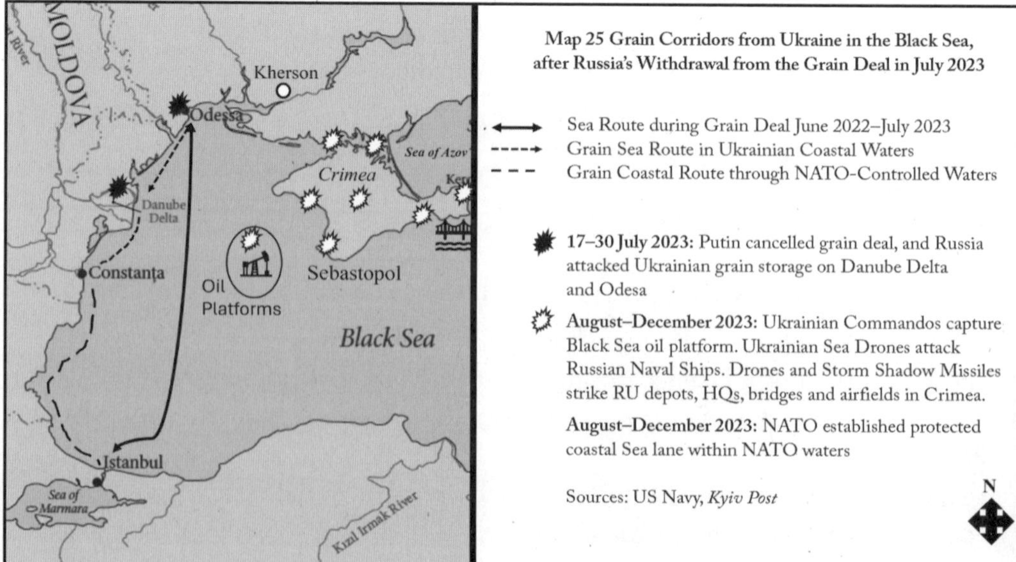

Map 25 Grain Corridors from Ukraine in the Black Sea, after Russia's Withdrawal from the Grain Deal in July 2023

ship costs between $50 and $200 million to build.[12] Modern cargo ships are large, and absent a hit below the waterline by a torpedo, can only be damaged by a drone or small missile strike. Lloyd's of London and fourteen other insurers partnered with the Ukrainian government to offer war risk insurance premiums, gambling that Russia would not directly attack unarmed neutral ships carrying non-military cargos.[13] The relatively small war zone covered by the insurance was the sailing distance from NATO/Romanian waters to Odesa: 173 km (107 miles).[14]

Russia's response to international actions was limited. If it attempted a blockade of Odesa it would need to move surface warships within range of Ukrainian littoral anti-ship missiles and aerial drones. Russia could have attacked or harassed merchant ships with missiles, but Ukraine indicated that it would in return attack Russian merchant ships. Attacking neutral shipping in international waters would very likely have expanded the war. Russia's gambit, of cancelling the grain deal in the hope that the international community would comply with its demands, failed. The failure resulted in Russia losing control of the Western Black Sea as NATO stepped in to assist in establishing a protected shipping lane.

Chapter 25

The Battle of the Black Sea

Between the beginning of Putin's Special Operation in February 2022 and December 2023 Russia suffered the loss of sixteen ships and large patrol craft, eleven of which were confirmed by photographic evidence by Oryx. The guided missile cruiser *Moskava*, landing ships *Saratov*, *Minsk*, *Torchka*, *Olenegorsky Gornyak*, and submarine *Rostov-on-Don* were irreplaceable.[1]

The Black Sea Fleet had accomplished its operational and strategic missions by the end of March 2022. It had participated in the initial bombardment during the first days of the Special Operation. It had effectively blockaded the Ukrainian coast, destroyed Ukraine's Navy, and was providing AD for Russian invaders marching toward Odesa and besieging Mariupol.

The Black Sea Fleet was re-supplied by sea from the Don River and Rostov-on-Don. It also received supplies from mainland Russia over the Kerch Strait Bridge, which was the sole land access to the supply Fleet. The bridge became an obvious target of immense value for Ukraine. If it could be damaged or destroyed this would severely limit Russia's ability to re-supply the Fleet. The first attack on the bridge was carried out by a truck bomb on 8 October 2022. It was put temporarily out of use, but was eventually repaired.

By March 2023, Russia's Black Sea Fleet had gone from being an unchallenged force dominating the Black Sea to a target of opportunity for Ukrainian defenders. Likewise, the Fleet's supply route became an important target. NATO-provided missiles hit a Raptor-class assault boat, the Alligator-class landing ship *Saratov* and two additional Ropucha-class landing ships, all of which were supporting the Mariupol siege. In April 2022, two Neptune anti-ship missiles slammed into Russia's flag ship cruiser *Moskva*, sinking her. The *Moskva* had been providing AD for the 58th CAA and 22nd Corps as they marched toward Odesa. The rescue tug *Vasility Bekh* was reported destroyed in June 2022. These unexpected naval reverses caused the Russians to pull their ships blockading Odesa and the western Ukrainian coast back to the illusory safety of Fleet Headquarters in Sevastopol.[2]

With the total loss of its surface ships and patrol boats at the beginning of the Special Operation, the Ukrainian Navy and Air Force had been forced, by necessity, to apply the theory of 'littoral defence'. As events unfolded, it became apparent that the Ukrainian Ministry of Defence had not planned to implement a littoral defence. However, as allies provided standard anti-ship weapons, Ukraine was able to pose unique challenges to the Black Sea Fleet. It became equally apparent that the Russian Admiralty was unprepared to fight a littoral campaign.

Combat by naval, air and ground amphibious forces in coastal areas is known as 'littoral warfare'. Naval operations in littorals have much in common with open sea or blue water combat. Both rely on radar and sonar to detect incoming aircraft and missiles. Most warships rely on high-volume autocannon like the US Phalanx and the Russian Kashtan. Both of these close-in weapon systems (CIWS) were designed to automatically defend against incoming aircraft, missiles and small boats at very short range.

Littoral actions are normally tactical rather than operational. Due to rapidly changing circumstances and the pace of events in a tactical situation, combat in littorals requires a decentralized C2. A littoral defender can deny the enemy use of an area by deploying land-based aircraft, missiles, drones, diesel-electric attack submarines, small fast coastal attack craft, mobile missile batteries and sea mines. A blue water fleet, with long range capability, can normally retreat into the vast ocean to limit the effectiveness of an attack from a littoral defensive position.[3]

The blue water Black Sea Fleet was faced with diverse threats. In the relatively small and largely landlocked Black Sea, the Russian ships could not retreat far enough to distance themselves from long-range Ukrainian air and sea drones. To complicate matters, the Black Sea was crowded with a great many neutral commercial vessels, small fishing boats, high-speed pleasure craft, billionaires' yachts and large container ships. Sifting though the radar clutter to identify high-speed Ukrainian sea drones was nearly impossible. In comparison to wide open blue water operations, reaction time to sea and air drone attacks was much shorter. Attacking sea drones were often undetected until they made their final attack run. In most published videos from attacking sea drones closing on Russian ships, the ship's Kashtan CIWS autocannon seems to have been switched off. If activated, the autocannon should have automatically destroyed the attacking drone, but if the ship was in port the autocannon would have been a danger to other possibly innocent civilian or merchant craft.

The grain deal previously negotiated provided a small window for grain to be safely exported from three Ukrainian sea ports. The deal did not impact the war, which continued unabated. Pursuing its attack on the Black Sea Fleet, Ukraine deployed aerial and naval drones towards Sevastopol and launched

Harpoon missiles at a Russian military supply ship moored at Snake Island, destroying it. As tiny strategic Snake Island became untenable, the Russians again withdrew back to Sevastopol.

In September 2022, the Ukrainians launched British cruise missiles at the Black Sea Fleet Headquarters and ships anchored at Sevastopol. Russian submarines redeployed to the eastern Black Sea. In October 2022, Ukraine launched nine naval drones against Sevastopol.

The new Russian flagship *Admiral Makarov* was damaged at the end of the month. The drone attacks ultimately proved Sevastopol was no longer a safe harbour, and major elements of the Black Sea Fleet were withdrawn to Novorossiysk, 434 km (270 miles) from Odesa. Having expended their supply of naval drones, Ukrainians started a crowdfunding campaign to purchase 100 maritime drones.[4]

By December 2022, the Ukrainian MoD determined that an aerial and sea drone campaign followed by a successful ground operation could successfully defeat the Black Sea Fleet and threaten Russian control of the Crimean Peninsula. In addition, a mosquito fleet of fast zodiac-type boats could covertly convey commandos onto the Peninsula and threaten vulnerable AD systems. In preparation for a January 2023 maritime offensive, 900 Ukrainian Marines arrived in the UK for a six-month commando training programme conducted by the UK 42nd and 47th Commando Raiding Groups, the 24th Commando Engineers, the 29th Commando Artillery and the Netherlands Marines.[5]

January and February 2023 were relatively quiet on the front as both sides assessed their position. Musk was playing politics with the Biden administration and, ostensibly fearing an escalation of the war, denied use of his Starlink system for drone attacks on or near Crimea.[6] Despite this complication, drone strikes continued against Russian naval targets.

Between February and June 2023, Ukraine increased drone and missile strikes against Russian ground lines of supply and communication throughout Crimea and Zaporizhzhia. A major shift in the naval war occurred on 28 February 2023, when Ukrainian drones struck the Russian eastern Black Sea strategic port of Tuapse, 434 km (270 miles) from Ukrainian-held territory north of Russian-occupied Mariupol. The port was a major oil terminal, south of the Russian naval base at Novossiysk and north of the city of Sochi. The attack was a warning to the Black Sea Fleet that with only a recovering 'mosquito navy', Ukraine could threaten Russian naval and merchant maritime activity throughout the Black Sea.

Unable to directly challenge Russia's surface fleet, Ukraine focused on increasing its fleet of unmanned kamikaze surface vessels (USV). Sea drones were difficult to detect by Russian radar, and because of their relatively small

Ukraine increases use of "kamikaze" drones
Kyiv is stepping up attacks against Russian warships with the use of domestically produced sea drones, which have crippled Moscow's naval capability in the Black Sea
MAGURA V5
Cruise speed: 40km/h
Burst speed: 78km/h
Range: 800km
Weight: Up to 1,000kg
Battery life: 60 hours
Reported price: $250,000
Controlled remotely by satellite communication or radio network
Engine
Electric or hybrid
Sensor pod
GPS and infrared camera
Payload
320kg of explosives
Operator:
Controls drone via console
Impact fuse
Height above waterline: 0.5m
1.5m
5.5m
SUNK BY SEA DRONES
1 Oct 29, 2022: Frigate Admiral Makarov
2 May 24, 2023: Intelligence-gathering ship Ivan Khurs
3 Aug 4: Landing ship Olenegorsky Gornyak
4 Feb 1, 2024: Missile corvette Ivanovets
5 Feb 14: Landing ship Caesar Kunikov
6 Mar 5: Patrol ship Sergei Kotov
UKRAINE
Russian control
ROMANIA
CRIMEA
RUSSIA
Sevastopol
Novorossiysk
BLACK SEA
Bosphorus
100km
60 miles
TURKEY
Sources: AP, Reuters, Spetstechnoekport
Picture: Ministry of Defence of Ukraine © GRAPHIC NEWS

size were hard to target at long range. However, controlling the drones and locating camouflaged targets was difficult due to their narrow field of view.

The Ukrainians fielded several types of sea drones. Two models of new naval drones had an extended range: the 'Sea Baby' carried 850 kg (1,800 lbs) of explosives with an operational range of 800 km (500 miles); the smaller 'Magura' V5 Sea drone was 5.5 metres long, with an operational range of 800 km (500 miles) and a burst speed of 42 kmph (26 mph).[7] Simple earlier designs, known as kamikaze naval drones or just naval drones, were similar to Canadian Seadoo jet skis.[8] Equipped with over 100 of various types of extended-range sea drones, Ukraine vigorously pursued its drone campaign against Russian maritime forces.

At 0330 on 23 April 2023, naval sea drones attacked the Black Sea Fleet base in Sevastopol, causing minor damage.[9] On 7 May 2023 ten naval drones again attacked Sevastopol. While the attacks were repulsed, they gave notice of Ukraine's newfound capabilities to the Russian admirals. During the same month, the Russian warship *Ivan Khurs* was attacked by drones, but successfully defended itself. In June 2023, another warship, *Priazovye*, was attacked by six high-speed naval drones, but also defended itself successfully.[10] These annoying naval drone attacks on Russian ports and warships allowed the Ukrainians to test Moscow's Black Sea defences and were followed by another strategic strike damaging the Kerch Strait Bridge.

Surprisingly, the Russians published a graph depicting the twenty layers of protective weapons and equipment positioned to defend the bridge. These layers included satellite surveillance, combat air patrols, ADA, security cameras, combat swimmers, patrol boats and even trained dolphins.[11] With all these high-tech defences, the Russians neglected to deploy simple 'torpedo nets', or barriers around the bridge pillars, and on 17 July 2023 two Ukrainian naval drones struck the Kerch Strait Bridge pillars. They were detected at the last minute, but the defending machine gunners failed to hit the fast-moving drones. Two people were killed in the blast, and the road over the bridge was once again damaged. The bridge was unable to support road traffic, but the rail line remined open. At the time it was projected that the bridge would not be fully operational until November 2023.[12]

The sea drones were reportedly launched from either the western Black Sea Coast or from Snake Island. Four high-speed marine objects had been observed travelling along the Crimean coast several hours prior to the attack on the bridge. One of the two drones attacking the bridge was launched from the Russian-occupied Azov Sea. It was speculated that a 'Q-Ship' was allowed into the Azov Sea and launched the naval drone. 'Q-Ships' are warships masquerading as merchantmen. In this case it was probably a merchant ship, carrying at least one naval drone.[13]

Damage to the Kerch Strait Bridge was spectacular and made headlines worldwide, but ultimately it proved a difficult target to destroy. It was a very well-engineered and built structure, designed to withstand substantial pressure from extreme sea currents. The bridge is massive, designed and built to sustain both rail and road traffic, with pillars sunk to a depth of 100 metres into the sea floor. The remote location of the bridge behind Russian lines made it difficult to target, but it was a critical key structure in the Russian supply line to Zaporizhzhia and Crimea as well as the Black Sea Fleet, and it provided a potential escape route should a Russian occupation force ever be cornered in Crimea. Finally, as Putin's pet project, it was a symbol of Russian prestige and power.[14]

On 17/18 July 2023, Russians attacked the Ukrainian port of Odesa's grain storage and grain terminal with sixty-three missiles and drones. The attack destroyed 40,0000 tons of grain destined for Africa, China and Israel and damaged the grain terminals.[15] Following the attack, Russia announced that any ships headed for Ukrainian ports would be viewed as potentially carrying military cargo. An executive from the US Agency for International Development, Samantha Powers, visited Odesa, viewed the damage, and at a press conference promised $250 million to support developing alternative export routes.[16]

The first attempts to run the blockade were conducted by Israel, Greece and Turkey. The Israeli ship code-named *Ams 1*, the Greek ship *Sahin 2* and the Turkish-Georgian ship *Yilmaz Kaptan* sailed from the Bosphorus Straits and northern Turkey toward Izmail on the Ukrainian arm of the Danube. These cargo ships were not disguised and did not make any attempt at concealment. Each was equipped with an activated radio transponder, revealing their course to anyone with internet access to ship-tracking websites. Four NATO aircraft provided security overhead, a US Navy P-8 patrol plane, a US Army Challenger with surface-scanning radar, a US Air Force RQ-4 drone and an E-3 early-warning plane from NATO. This surveillance flight was supported by Italian Eurofighters and Romanian F-16 jet fighters.

Despite threats from the Russians, the deployed corvette *Sergey Kotov* did not attempt to stop the blockade runners. Instead, on 24 July 2023, the Russians attacked the blockade runners' port of destination, Izmail, and a warehouse in Reni, violating Romanian air space as the drones manoeuvred onto their target.[17] On 2 August, Russian drones attacked the port of Izmail again, destroying grain storage facilities to prevent neutral blockade runners from loading grain. President Zelensky stated that 'In [Moscow's] madness, they need world food markets to collapse.' Moscow claimed that the port and grain infrastructure were housing foreign mercenaries but did not provide any evidence to support their claim. Videos released by Ukraine showed several large buildings in ruins and tons of grain spilled from two wrecked silos. As a result of the attack, wheat prices rose 5 per cent on the international stock market. Between 18 July and 2 August 2023, Russia attacked twenty-six port faculties and five civilian ships and destroyed 180,000 tonnes of grain. The obvious goal of the attacks was to persuade shippers and their insurance companies that Ukrainian ports were unsafe.[18]

Ukraine responded to Russian attacks on its exports and the world's food supply by conducting a series of embarrassing attacks deep inside Russia. By July 2023, Ukrainian drone attacks on the centre of Moscow had become routine. While Ukraine only targeted military-industrial targets, Russian counter-measures often diverted the drones into high-rise civilian buildings.

In response to Russian threats to the world's food supply, NATO conducted several exercises in the NATO-controlled western Black Sea. Defender 23 (22 April–23 June 2023) combined strategic deployment of US forces to prepositioned stocks of equipment with interoperability between allies and partners. The exercise fielded more than 7,000 US troops and 17,000 from twenty nations, including the UK, Estonia, France, Germany, Greece, Italy, Latvia, Poland, Romania and Spain.[19]

NATO's July 2023 summit in Vilnius focused on the Black Sea Region (BSR) fault line between NATO and Russia. The alliance pledged long-term support for Ukraine and recognized its strategic importance to European and worldwide security. Operationally, this decision officially committed NATO to protecting the western Black Sea shipping lane.

On the night of 4 August 2023, a sea drone damaged the *Olenegorsky Gornyak*, a Russian amphibious ship in the port of Novorossiysk.[20] During the night of 5 August 2023, another sea drone damaged the Russian tanker *Sig* in the Azov Sea just north of the Kerch Strait Bridge.[21]

While NATO was flying air cover for the blockade runners, Russia, and its ally Belarus, violated NATO air space on numerous occasions. Two Belarusian helicopters violated Polish air space on 1 August 2023 by flying over the border village of Belovezha. The Mi 24 Hind Gunship and Mi-8MVT-5 helicopter flew under Polish radar. Photos of the incursion taken by Eliza Kowalczyk clearly depicted Belarusian markings on the helicopter. The flight crossed the border and flew 3 km (1.8 miles) into Poland. NATO denied that these incursions had occurred, probably to avoid triggering Article 5, but civilian media reports and photographs documented the violations. Ukraine claimed Russian kamikaze drones had manoeuvred through Romanian air space while attacking port facilities in or near Izmail on 2 August 2023. Despite eyewitness accounts, an investigation by the Romanian Air Force was unable to provide any evidence of the violation. The investigation apparently based its findings on the fact that they did not recover any debris from the drone on Romanian territory.[22] Of course, a kamikaze drone targeting Izmail would not have left debris across the Danube River in Romania. These violations were only the tip of the drone iceberg, and they were not the first violations of NATO air space.

NATO jet fighters scrambled over 570 times in the first year of the war to monitor Russian military flights near NATO members' borders.[23] These combat air patrols continued into 2023. Russian jets attacked US reconnaissance drones over the Black Sea and Syria, while Moscow executed tactical jet fighter training exercises over the Baltic Sea. The exercises were tied to the testing defence of Kaliningrad on the Baltic.[24] Russian fighter jets impeded operations of US aircraft over Syria in July 2023 and increased its harassment of US drones.[25] It is important to note that Russia increased its provocation of NATO and US targets after the successful 17 July 2023 attack on the Kerch Strait Brigade.

After being embarrassed by Ukraine's strategic deep targeting of Moscow, its successful hits on the Kerch Strait Bridge and the Black Sea Fleet throughout July/August 2023, Putin lashed out against Ukraine and NATO, but was careful to avoid triggering Article 5 of the NATO charter. By providing air support for the blockade runners, NATO became a limited active participant in the war, but Putin and his general staff were acutely aware that attacking the blockade runners could be viewed as triggering Article 5. One of the blockade runners belonged to a NATO member (Turkey), the second belonged to a pending NATO member (Sweden) and the third to Israel. Apparently unwilling to take on NATO directly, Putin backed down and resumed targeting cargo ships destined to receive the much-sought-after grain. Russia's actions had political repercussions. The grain was destined for China, Israel, and Africa, and while China and Israel had the money to obtain its requirements from alternative sources, African nations lacked that option.[26]

The cargo ship *Sukru Okan*, flagged from Palau, Philippines, was sailing to Turkey but was intercepted on 13 August 2023 in international waters. The Russians claimed the ship was sailing for Izmail, Ukraine. Its documents clearly indicated that it was sailing to the Romanian port of Sulina, which was near Izmail. The Russians ordered the ship to halt and prepare to be boarded and searched. The *Sukru Okan* refused the order to stand by and continued sailing in an attempt to return to Turkish waters. The Russian patrol ship *Vasily Bykov* then fired automatic weapons across its bow and the ship finally came to a stop. Radio messages were exchanged, and a Russian boarding party was transferred to the *Sukru Okan* by helicopter. The Russian boarding party detained the twelve-person crew and reviewed the ship's documents and the crew's passports. The ship was thoroughly searched, but the Russians did not discover any contraband. The boarding party was surprisingly professional and did not threaten the crew. The captain was forced to sign a document 'in Russian', which he could not read, in which he certified that no injury or damage had been caused by the boarding party. The boarding party disembarked, and the *Sukru Okan* continued on its planned course.[27]

After the graduation of 900 Ukrainian Marine commandos from the UK's six-month training programme, an increase in attacks on Russian military positions, airfields and ports should not have surprised the Russians.[28] The Ukrainians increased drone strikes against Russian installations in Crimea throughout August 2023, and more Commando raids successfully landed on the Peninsula to attack enemy positions.

Despite the Ukrainian Navy being left with nothing more than a 'mosquito fleet' after the first year of the war, it had become active in the western Black Sea by late August 2023. Equipped with small but fast patrol boats, Ukrainian commandos operated between Odesa and Crimea. Staging from abandoned oil rigs, Ukrainian commandos conducted reconnaissance and surveillance operations and assisted in organizing drone attacks in the western Black Sea. Their small patrol boats were not armoured, but the commandos were heavily armed with machine guns, ATGMs, SAMs and Brimstone II anti-ship missiles. A Russian SU-30 jet fighter unsuccessfully targeted a squadron of three commando patrol boats on 23 August 2023. The Ukrainians returned fire with a SAM, damaging the jet and forcing it to withdraw. While this engagement played out, a Ukrainian drone located a S-400 ADA system near Olenivka, just inland from the town of Cape Tarhankut on the western Crimean Peninsula. After discovering the system, the drone relayed the location to an anti-ship missile battery, which destroyed the S-400 ADA system with a Brimstone II anti-ship missile, possibly fired from a commando patrol boat. The Brimstone II has an approximate range of 40–59 km (25–37 miles).[29] The importance of these aggressive contacts manifested itself the next day.

At 0500 on 24 August 2023, four fast boats carrying Ukrainian Marine commandos landed at Cape Tarhankut, Crimea. The mission was to destroy a Russian radar installation. During the attack the commandos raised the Ukrainian flag over the town, then broke contact and returned to their boats, speeding safely away. While reporting the attack, Russian state media claimed that the commandos and their boats had all been destroyed. Russian bloggers reacted to the report with harsh scepticism directed at the state media. The Ukrainian narrative claimed that the commandos destroyed four Russian boats, caused thirty Russian casualties and raised the Ukrainian flag before withdrawing. The raid was symbolic as it occurred in Crimea on Ukrainian Independence Day. The raid was a boost to Ukrainian morale and greatly embarrassed the Russian occupiers of Crimea, but it failed to destroy the radar installation.[30]

Firing missiles and deploying air and sea drones, Ukraine inflicted significant damage on the Black Sea Fleet, Russian naval aviation, C2 and air defence. Successful strikes against a frigate and minesweeper forced the Russians to pull its major surface ships and submarines back to Novorossiysk in the eastern Black Sea. However, the safety of this port was an illusion. On 4 August 2023 a naval drone, carrying 450 kg (992 lbs) of explosive struck a Ropucha-class landing ship at anchor. The drone had travelled undetected 700 km (434 miles). NATO deemed these, and subsequent massed drone attacks, a clear response to Russia's escalation of the war by its attack on Ukrainian grain ports in the Black Sea and Danube region.[31]

Russia illegally laid between 400 and 600 sea mines in international waters between 2022 and 2023 in an attempt to interdict the movement of grain merchant ships. In self-defence, Ukraine legally laid defensive mines in its territorial waters to protect its coastline from external attack. Its mines were legal under Article 51 of the UN Convention, which provides that sea mines are not a violation of international law if used in the defence of a country's territorial waters. However, many of these mines unfortunately drifted into international waters, outside the war zone. Severe storms and rough sea caused more mines to drift, and they ultimately became a threat to all navigation, not just to Russian warships. Some of them washed ashore along the western Black Sea coast. The shifting mines constituted a threat to NATO member countries along the Black Sea and all other shipping moving though the area. Turkey briefly closed the Bosphorus Strait to all sea traffic in order to conduct mine-clearing operations. The Romanian navy destroyed mines that ended up in its territorial waters.[32]

In accordance with the 1936 Montreux Convention, Turkey closed the entrance to the Black Sea (Bosphorus and Dardanelles Straits) to all non-Black Sea riparian state warships.[33] The closure barred Russia from re-enforcing the Black Sea Fleet from the Mediterranean, but also kept NATO ships from entering the nearly landlocked sea. The NATO surface fleet in the Black Sea was limited to the Turkish, Romanian and Bulgarian navies. For the most part, the sky over the Black Sea was considered international airspace, and there were no applicable restrictions or limitations. NATO maintained surveillance flights over the sea and surrounding areas throughout the first and second years of the war.[34]

While NATO flexed its muscles in the region, the Russian Black Sea Fleet was reinforced in October 2023 with two frigates and a submarine, probably from the Caspian Flotilla. Putin announced this redeployment was in response to the US moving an aircraft battlegroup into the eastern Mediterranean in response to the Gaza War, which flared up in October 2023. The movement of the three Russian ships was probably to replace the losses of major surface vessels destroyed during the first two years of the Special Operation.

Ukraine's naval campaign successfully gained control of the western Black Sea in 2023. It established a protected sea lane for the relatively safe resumption of shipping agricultural products to world markets. It drove the majority of the Russian Fleet to naval bases in the eastern Black Sea. NATO established armed combat patrols to provide security to the shipping lane.

Despite setbacks, the Black Sea Fleet remained a dangerous fighting force. Ukraine's success in dominating the western Black Sea was completely dependent on aid from NATO, allied countries and crowdfunded sea drones. An interruption of that aid in 2024 would result in Ukraine losing the battle for dominance of the western Black Sea.

For the first time in history a major naval campaign was dominated by air and sea drones. For the first time in history a world power lost its fleet's flagship to a slow, inexpensive air drone. For the first time in history a country with nothing more than a mosquito navy of sea drones beat back the naval fleet of a major world power. The second year of the Russia-Ukraine war was the beginning of a new chapter in naval warfare – that of the drone.

Chapter 26

The Russian Luhansk-Kharkiv Diversionary Attack

The Russians did not sit idlily by as the Ukrainians commenced their summer counter-offensive. The invaders massed sufficient forces to conduct a diversionary offensive in the Luhansk Oblast in order to divert the Ukrainian general staff's attention away from their main effort in the south. The Russian generals hoped that if the Ukrainians believed the crisis was serious enough they would be forced to shift their strategic reserves from the Zaporizhzhia Oblast to shore up the defences in the Luhansk Oblast.

By July 2023 it was clear that the Ukrainian counter-offensive was unable to quickly penetrate the Russian active defences in the Zaporizhzhia Oblast. The counter-offensive did, however, slowly advance and was able to threaten the Crimea land bridge. Meanwhile, the Russian general staff developed a simple campaign plan to frustrate the Ukrainian counter-offensive.

The Russian strategic objective for 2023 was to capture the large mining and industrial Donbas region, which overlapped both the Donetsk and Luhansk Oblasts. The Donbas is the location of a large coalfield, 23,300 square km (9,000 sq miles), extending from south-eastern Ukraine into the Rostov Oblast in south-western Russia and west to the Don River.

During the summer, the Russian Army needed to exhaust Ukrainian offensive capability in preparation for an autumn offensive to capture the Donesk Oblast generally and the city of Avdiivka specifically. Located in the centre of the Dontesk Oblast, Avdiivka was the location of a large coke and natural gas plant, both used to generate heating. Prior to the invasion in 2022, the population was 31,392, but by 2023 it had dwindled to just 1,600. Avdiivka was strategically important because it was within artillery range of the capital of the Donetsk People's Republic (Donetsk City).

The Russians needed to maintain a sufficient force to protect the militarily important Crimea land bridge, and needed an additional force to prevent the politically important city of Bakhmut from being recaptured. Forces were also allocated for a diversionary offensive (shaping operation) to create a viable threat to the Kharkiv and Luhansk Oblasts. This would force the Ukrainians to reduce their strategic reserve to reinforce the Kharkiv and Luhansk battle groups. As these operations were unfolding, the Russian 8th CAA would reinforce with 40,000 troops for an autumn offensive to capture Avdiivka.

Like the winter 2023 offensive, OK-West's Luhansk summer diversionary offensive would focus on capturing the city of Kupyansk in the Kharkiv Oblast with its important rail junction, and the city of Lyman in the Donetsk Oblast with its key railway hub. If successful in capturing the towns, the Russians would cross the Oskil River in the north and south, pinning the Ukrainians against the Chervono-Oskil Reservoir in the centre; basically, the same plan as the 2023 winter offensive.

The 6th CAA's mission was to capture the city of Kupyansk. Its assault echelon consisted of the 25th Guards Motorized Rifle Brigade, 347th Motorized Rifle Regiment, 1843rd Motorized Rifle Battalion and a Storm-Z detachment. The 138th Separate Guards Motorized Rifle Brigade served as the army's reserve and exploitation force. The 1st Guard Tanks Army was assigned the mission of sweeping south of Kupyansk to capture the four bridges over the Oskil River north of the reservoir. Its first objective was to capture the hard surface PO-7 highway. This would provide it with a high-speed route to attack Kupyansk from the south-west. It would also provide the 1st Tank Army with a supply route that artillery-delivered mines could not effectively interdict, since mines landing on a hard-surface road are easy to see and neutralize. The 2nd Guards Motorized Rifle Division would control the battle on the north side of the sector with two unidentified motorized rifle brigades and the 26th Tank Regiment. The 47th Motorized Rifle Division would control the centre sector with the 7th Motorized Rifle Regiment, 27th Motorized Rifle Brigade and 5th BAR. The 3rd Motorized Rifle Division would control the units south of Svatove and arrayed north to south with the 432nd Guards Motorized Rifle Regiment, 15th, 21st, 20th and UI Motorized Rifle Brigades. All divisions had reserve brigades, but their location and identification are unknown. In addition, the 25th CAA was organizing in Belgorod Oblast.

The 41st CAA was assigned the mission of capturing the strategically important city of Lyman. Massed near the Kreminna salient, the army had been trying to break through to Lyman for ten months. The 144th Motorized Rifle Division and 90th Tank Division were supported by four VDA air assault brigades from the 76th and 98th Airborne Division and three motorized rifle brigades. This force was assigned to the Lyman attack. The 127th Separate Motorized Rifle Brigade and 7th BARs were assigned to protect the main effort's flank by capturing the small village of Bilohorivka (2022 pop. 808) in the Luhansk Oblast. To support the attack, OK-West had organized heavy air support.[1]

Russia deployed a total of 100,000 soldiers, including support services, 900 tanks, 1,500 APCs and 555 artillery systems between Lyman and Kupyansk. It conducted 1,700 artillery missions and 50 air strikes. On 27 August, the 76th Guards Air Assault Division redeployed from Orikhiv in a southern direction.[2]

Contrary to hysterical media reports and bloggers at the time, the Ukrainians were not 'caught totally off guard'. Throughout 2023 they had been preparing three major defence lines to protect the Kharkiv Oblast and to serve as staging areas for the liberation of Luhansk Oblast. The most northern defence line had been established during the Russian 2023 winter offensive. It began at the defences to the approaches to Kupyansk, stretching west 51 km (31 miles) to the Seversk-Donets River, in the vicinity of the hills north of the rural settlement of Pechenihy, with its dam and reservoir.

The second defence line ran along the Zherebets River and protected the approaches to Lyman. This axis had a second echelon line along the Nitrius River. The third defence line ran behind the Oskil Reservoir. The Ukrainians intentionally left a gap between the brigades at Senkove and Kupyansk. There were defensive positions in the gap, but it appeared the Ukrainians were tempting the Russians to try an assault river crossing of the south-flowing Oskil River. The Oskil was an obstacle, but it was significantly smaller and less dangerous to cross than the Dnipro. Russian attempts to cross the meandering Seversk-Donets River near Lyman in 2022 had ended in disaster.

Opposing the 6th CAA and 1st GTA were five mechanized and three Territorial brigades. The 101st and 105th Territorial Defence Brigades defended the city of Kupyansk and the surrounding area. Arrayed south from Kupyansk, along the line of contact to the village of Tabaivka, were the 14th, 88th, 41st, 43rd and 32nd Mechanized Brigades. The 103rd Territorial Brigade defended Tabaivka and the surrounding area. The 10th Tank Brigade deployed north of Kupyansk, and the 95th Air Assault Brigade was held in reserve. Photos of the defenders illustrate that a number of the rank and file were mature soldiers in their thirties.[3] The 14th Mechanized Brigade begun the war as a beefed-up Territorial Defence unit armed with tanks and armoured personnel carriers but had transitioned from light infantry to mechanized infantry.[4]

Opposing the 41st CAA were five mechanized brigades, deployed to defend the projected Russian avenues of attack. Four Territorial brigades held the western and northern edge of the salient. Bilohorivka was defended by a motorized brigade. National Guard battalions defended the gap between Bilohorivka and the mechanized brigades.

Russia launched the diversionary offensive toward the Oskil River in August 2023 and renewed the offensive with the same two attack axes: Kupyansk in the north and Lyman in the south.

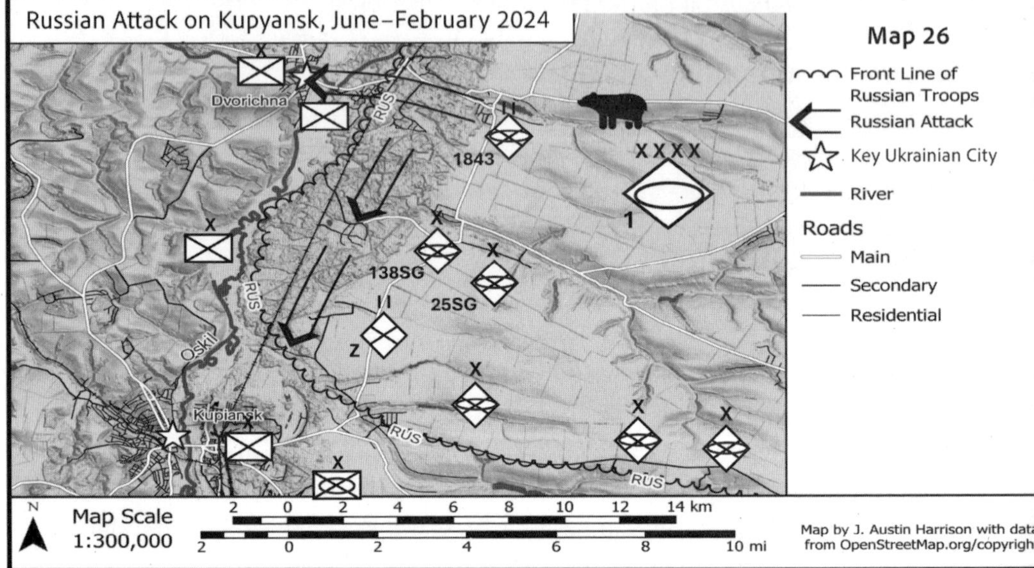

The attack opened with artillery and air bombardment. During the battle, the Russian Air Force flew up to sixty sorties per day, focusing on Ukrainian headquarters and logistic depots, but the glide bombs launched from 50 km (31 miles) away in the Russian rear were not very accurate.

The 6th CAA launched its major attack into the teeth of Kupyansk's defences, but the 6th CAA's attempt to bypass the defences floundered on the Territorial positions in the village of Synkivka, and the Russians were stopped in their tracks.

Following a heavy artillery barrage, the 1st Guards Tank Army brigades launched a mounted assault across an 11 km (6.8 mile) front. The BMP mounted infantry quickly advanced 4 km (2.5 miles) through the Ukrainian security zone. When initially reported in the news, this rapid advance was announced as a breakthrough. It was not. Both sides had protected their security zones with reconnaissance and kamikaze FPB drones instead of foot patrols and observation posts. After the initial 4 km (2.5 mile) rush, the attackers' joyride was over as they ran into the main Ukrainian defences. The Russians quickly captured the rural village of Novoselivske, removing a roadblock on the PO-7 highway. An advance of 13 km (8 miles) north along the highway would threaten to cut off the strong point in the village of Kyslivka.[5]

The situation became so serious that General Syrskyi, Ukraine's Army Commander, visited the front. Intelligence reports indicated that the Russians were creating a strike force to conduct a breakthrough assault on the Kupyansk axis. The force was identified as potentially including eight Storm-Z assault detachments (companies or battalions). These troops employed the 'storm trooper' tactics developed by Wagner Group. They moved forward stealthily under natural cover and relied upon surprise to storm Ukrainian positions. The attackers took advantage of the forest and 2-metre-high grass to close with Ukrainian outposts. After reviewing the situation, General Syrskyi requested that reserves be deployed to the sector and ordered a forced evacuation of thirty-seven villages and the town of Kupyansk. Approximately 11,000 civilians were evacuated, mostly women and children. Unlike the spring evacuation, the men were drafted into the defence force.[6] Based on the pattern of civilian evacuations, the Ukrainians were preparing for a Russian river crossing north of Kupyansk.

The Russians attacked all along the line but made little headway for the remainder of August 2023. When a Russian platoon or company captured a position, a Ukrainian counter-attack threw them back. The Russian Air Force flew over fifty sorties per day. Glide bombs rained down on Ukrainian command posts, supply depots and pontoon bridges over the Oskil River. Russian ground attacks were supported by Ka-52 and Mi-35 gunships.[7]

Casualties were heavy on both sides as August rolled into September. General Syrsky transferred newly formed brigades to the Kupyansk and Lyman sectors. One of the units from the strategic reserve, was the 32nd Mechanized Brigade. A NATO-trained formation, it began the counter-offensive in the strategic reserve. Due to losses of equipment in the south during the counter-offensive, the 32nd Mechanized Brigade was stripped of its M2 Bradleys and Western tanks. When the brigade was transferred it was armed with M-113, T-64BV and 2S1 122mm SP artillery. It deployed in sector as the reserve near the city of Svatove on the Krasna River.[8] When the Russians captured Svatove, the 32nd Mechanized Brigade counter-attacked and regained the lost ground. Platoons and companies fought at close range in a 'see-saw' battle for the remainder of the month. The Russians successfully developed tactics to deploy a 'swarm' of FPV drones on Ukrainian positions, just as their assault closed with the Ukrainian trenches or bunkers. Russian aircraft lobbed glide bombs at Ukrainians, hitting the frontline units and interdicting Ukrainian supply lines. One pilot got lucky and knocked out a bridge over the Oskil. River. The paratroopers were soon pulled out of the fight and redeployed to the south. The newly formed 25th CAA (15,000 men) deployed to the Kreminna sector and replaced the 41st CAA, which rotated out of the line due to heavy losses.[9]

Heavy fighting continued throughout November and December 2023, but the frontline barely moved. Both sides employed similar tactics. Platoons and companies fought for a hill or the ruins of buildings, only to lose them the next day. FPV drones led attacks and conducted reconnaissance. Kamikazi drones hunted tanks and individual soldiers. Glide bombs daily bombarded Ukrainian positions and logistics infrastructure. The end result was that manoeuvre quickly turned into positional warfare. The Russian diversionary offensive eventually forced Ukraine to deploy brigades from its strategic reserve and forced the Ukrainians to expend dwindling ammunition supplies badly needed for the defenders of Avdiivda.

Chapter 27

The Establishment and Defence of the Dnipro Bridgehead

By the end of August 2023, it was clear that the Ukrainians were not going to break through on the Velkyka-Novosilka axis. Late in the month, their Marine Corps rotated out of the line to rest and refit.[1] In September 2023, Russian sources reported that the Marine Corps had redeployed to the Kherson Oblast. By 23 September, the 35th, 36th and 37th Marine Brigades and supporting units, were identified as being in the Kherson Oblast, with 7,000 Marines, 46 tanks, 233 APCs and 7 artillery battalions still in transit. The Corps spent a month resting and refitting. On 18 October, Marine raiders crossed the Dnipro River in small boats and engaged the Russians holding the villages of Poima and Pishchanivaka 16 km (10 miles) east of Kherson.[2]

The Marine deployment presented a viable threat to the 58th CAA's flank and its supply and lines of communications into the Crimean Peninsula. Muddy conditions along the east bank of the Dnipro River and the bed of

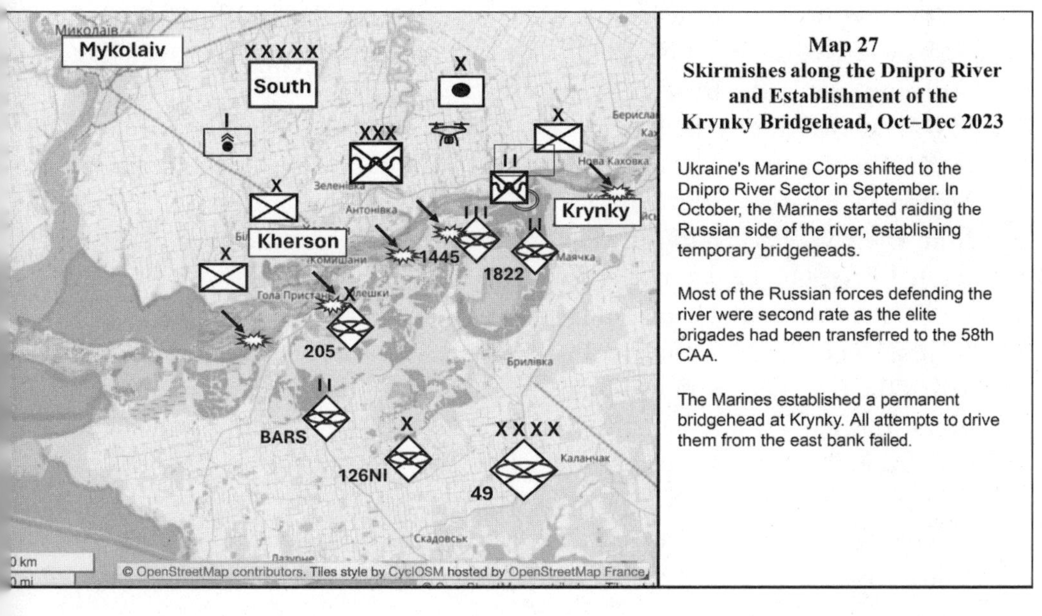

Map 27
Skirmishes along the Dnipro River and Establishment of the Krynky Bridgehead, Oct–Dec 2023

Ukraine's Marine Corps shifted to the Dnipro River Sector in September. In October, the Marines started raiding the Russian side of the river, establishing temporary bridgeheads.

Most of the Russian forces defending the river were second rate as the elite brigades had been transferred to the 58th CAA.

The Marines established a permanent bridgehead at Krynky. All attempts to drive them from the east bank failed.

the drained reservoir made armoured operations impossible. The *Rasputitsa* (autumn season of mud) and subsequent winter freeze did not improve ground conditions. Infantry operations were still viable, but miserable. On the Russian side of the river small armoured platoons could be deployed on the few all-weather roads leading up to the river.

As the Ukrainians started to harass the invaders along the Dnipro River, the Russians deployed five regiments or brigades in their first echelon of defence. Three regiments were in the second echelon, and two brigades were held in reserve. While the Russians had a numerical superiority in troops, except for the 61st Naval Infantry Battalion, 173rd VDV Reconnaissance Brigade, 126th (NI) Coastal Defence Brigade and 25th Spetsnaz Regiment, they were second-rate formations.[3] The 10th Separate Special Purpose Brigade was assigned to monitor the mud flat that had once been the reservoir. The second echelon defence was located 15 km (9.3 miles) south-east off the river, protecting the 58th CAA line of communication. The 439th Guards Rocket Artillery and 227th Artillery Brigades provided fire support.[4] They deployed the equivalent of 10,000–15,000 combat troops to defend the sector and to oppose 8,000 Ukrainian Marine combat troops, probably supported by another 6,000 Territorials.

As Marines, once they became active along the river they were a real nuisance to the Russian defenders. Many had received extensive small boat training by British commandos and Norwegian special forces, and Marine raiders were soon conducting night operations on the Russian side of the river. In apparent reaction to the Marine harassment, the Russian first echelon was reinforced by the end of October with the 127th Separate Intelligence Brigade along with the 'Shoigists' Storm-Z detachment. These reinforcements increased the drone support to the Russian defenders along the river.

By end of October, the Marines established a number of small bridgeheads on the Russian bank of the river. The most important were near the village of Krynky, which is 30 km (18 miles) north-east of Kherson and 2 km (1.2 miles) from the river. Expanding the bridgeheads had been difficult as the river created a serious logistical obstacle. The movement of troops, supplies and vehicles was slow and came under heavy fire from the Russians. Celebrated by pro-Ukrainian bloggers, the first armoured vehicle, a BTR-4, was ferried across the river near Krynky on 7 November.[5] Despite the celebration of this event, the ground between the river and Krynky was swampy and muddy and unsuitable for armoured vehicles; but by 17 November, the Marines had established a battalion strongpoint at Krynky.

The Russian high command observed the Marine activity along the river bank, and it became obvious that second-rate Russian battalions holding

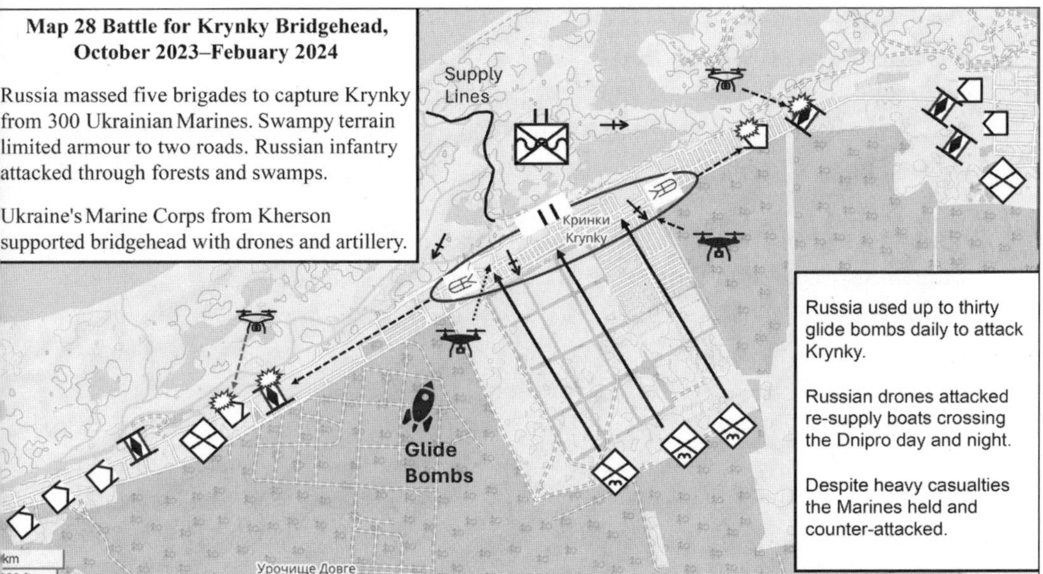

the bank were being outmanoeuvred. The Marines had become a threat, not simply a mere annoyance. If the Ukrainians could expand their bridgeheads to include a hard-surface road from the river to connect with the roads in the Russian rear, the 58th CAA supply lines would be in danger.

With the Ukrainian counter-offensive winding down, the Russians reinforced the Dnipro Sector. During the first half of November 2023, the 70th Motorized Rifle Regiment, the 26th Motorized Rifle Regiment and the 1822nd Rifle Battalion arrived in sector. These units skirmished with the Marines.

When the Marines entered the village of Krynky they had no idea it would become an attrition trap for the Russians. The town was on a road that ran parallel to the river, and on both sides of the road were dense, muddy woods. The only axis capable of supporting heavy armoured vehicles was along the hard-surface road that ran through Krynky, making control of the village extremely important.

Marines moved out on 15 November 2023 to capture the forest area around Krynky, south-east of the village. Once they established a foothold in the forest, the Ukrainians dug in. Russian infantry attacked the Ukrainian positions, and when these attacks failed to dislodge the Marines, a second infantry attack, supported by tanks, was conducted on the eastern edge of the village. Both attacks were successfully repelled. The skirmishing continued with neither side gaining an advantage.

Russian reinforcements continued to pour into the sector. By the end of December, the 104th Airborne Division and the 1445th Motorized Rifle Regiment deployed there. Fully engaged in combat, they suffered heavy casualties. The newly raised 104th Airborne Division became the fifth division in the Russian VDV airborne corps, mustering 6,000 paratroopers at full strength.

By December 2023, Colonel General Mikhail Teplinsky, Commander of the Dnipro Sector, assigned the 18th CAA to manage the battle.[6] Approximately eighteen elite and first-rate battalions were assigned to destroy one Ukrainian Marine battalion in Krynky. By simple battlefield calculations, the Marines stood little chance of success, but they were saved by the terrain. Terrain changes the calculation in every battle.

The Ukrainian-controlled bank of the Dnipro was higher in elevation than the Russian side. Krynky was only 2 km (1.2 miles) from the river. Artillery and FPV drone companies could easily provide defensive fire support to the Marines, and they could also range Russian assembly areas, while the ground around Krynky limited the employment of tanks in any Russian ground assault. The cold and wet weather filled the trenches and foxholes with freezing water. Fighting conditions were worse than could be imagined, but the gallant Marines held on despite Russian determination to take the village.

Finally, the Russians attacked in force on 8 January 2024, supported by artillery drones and aerial glide bombs. Despite the Marine defenders being supported by artillery and literally 'swarms' of FPV drones, the Ukrainian positions in the forest were forced back into the village. Marines repelled nine assaults the first day.[7]

Heavy fighting continued unabated. As the days passed the 300 Marines, supported by drone-operators, artillery gunners and electronic-warfare operators, held out against thousands of Russians. First, soldiers from the 70th Motor Rifle Division attacked and failed to take the town. Next, elite Russian soldiers from the 810th (NI) Brigade and 104th Air Assault Division failed to capture it.

Despite holding on, the Marines were in a desperate situation. They took heavy casualties and the wounded had to be evacuated 2 km (1.2 miles) to the river. They were then loaded onto small boats and transported across the river. The same small boats brought ammunition and supplies that had to be hand-carried to the frontline. The stretcher-bearers and ammunition-carriers slogged through the mud, under constant fire from Russian artillery, FPV drones and glide bombs.

The Ukrainians continued to hold out, despite being badly outnumbered and facing relentless bombardment from the ground and the air. In the weeks before the battle a battalion of the 35th Marine Brigade crossed the Dnipro and re-enforced the Marine Corps with FPV drone detachments and EW drone jammers. The Russians were also fully equipped with FBV drone detachments and jammers. The timing and coordination between drone operators and jammers became an art. Robert Brovi, Commander of the Ukrainian drone battalions, encouraged his operators to post video of their successful attacks, Hundreds of hours of video documenting poor Russian discipline, morale and fieldcraft were posted on social media. A typical video published on 10 January 2024 depicted a $500 FPV drone destroying a $2 million BMP-4 IFV by flying into the open hatch with a grenade. Videos posted on 16 January 2024 showed a host of night attacks destroying Russian IFV, APCs, SP artillery supply trucks and civilian pickup trucks. Several of the vehicles were hit while moving.[8]

During mid-January 2024, Oryx reported that twenty Russian tanks, sixty-five-plus APCs and twenty-five-plus artillery systems were destroyed or disabled around the bridgehead; in other words, a motorized rifle brigade's worth of heavy weapons. The actual numbers were probably much greater, as Oryx only reported loses that were visually confirmed.[9] It seemed that Ukrainian high-tech operators were superior to their Russian counterparts.

Despite these advantages, the fight was not one-sided. A Russian FPV drone operator code-named 'Moses' was very effective in countering Ukrainian drone operators. Operating from a two-storey house in Krynky, Moses expertly flew small FPV drones carrying 2lb payloads. He also hunted small boats and amphibious tractors bringing supplies and reinforcements to the Marines in Krynky. His opponents credited him with hitting thirty-one Ukrainian boats and causing four hundred casualties. He was eventually tracked down and killed by a Ukrainian FPV drone operator, and the Marines captured the house Moses called home.[10] Eliminating Moses shifted the balance of the battle.

Krynky became a free-fire zone for Ukrainian drones. Russian vehicles and infantry were hit by FPV drones within minutes of breaking cover.

'The situation in the Krynky area is only getting worse for us', one Russian observer wrote.[11]

The 17th Tank Regiment of T-90 tanks was probably equipped with individual vehicle jammers and was used to tow damaged vehicles out of the narrow-armoured avenues of approach to Krynky.[12]

The fact that one Marine battalion in Krynky beat off the nine battalions in the 104th Air Assault Division did not result in the Ukrainians breaking out into southern Kherson Oblast and advancing toward Crimea. The Marine Corps had suffered extremely heavy casualties holding Krynky.

In the weeks following the culmination of Kyiv's southern counter-offensive, Ukrainian brigades were rebuilt after having exhausted their offensive combat power or being committed to the Battle for Avdiivka.[13] By early 2024 it became clear that after two months of heavy fighting the Ukrainian General Staff did not expect to attack toward Crimea from the Krynky bridgehead. They planned instead an attritional battle, intending to bleed the Russians dry.[14]

In the repeated assaults to drive the Marines back into the river, the Russians lost approximately 157 armoured vehicles and suffered serious losses. The Russian 810th NI Brigade and the new 104th Air Assault Division suffered extremely heavy casualties. The Ukrainian generals succeeded in their objective, but at a heavy cost, since the Marines' casualty rate was also heavy. While only one battalion held the village, it probably gutted a Marine brigade. By Ukrainian accounts, the Russian drone operator code-named Moses, alone, caused 400 Ukrainian casualties, the equivalent of an entire Marine battalion.

Chapter 28

The Israeli-Hamas War, October 2023 Impact on the Russian-Ukrainian War

While the Russians conducted an offensive to capture Avdiivka before the season of mud prevented offensive operations, Hamas attacked Israel. On the morning of 7 October 2023, Israel awoke to explosions and sirens as Hamas rockets were launched from the Gaza strip, and Hamas militants invaded Israel on motorcycles and ultralights. The attack, codenamed 'Al-Aqsa [Temple Mount] Flood' commenced at approximately 0630 hours local time. In quick succession 3–5,000 rockets were launched at Israeli cities. The 'Iron Dome' regional Anti-Missile Defence System was overloaded, resulting in thousands of missiles reaching their targets. The major cities of Tel Aviv, Ashkelon, Be'er Sheva, Jerusalem, Rehovot and Rishon Lezan were all hit hard, as was the Palmachim Airbase. The rocket attack was coordinated with Hamas ground attacks on Israeli border settlements along the Gaza-Israel border.[1]

Russia does not classify Hamas as a terrorist organization and did not condemn them for their attack on Israel. In fact, one day prior to the attack, Putin hosted a Hamas delegation in Moscow. It can only be presumed that

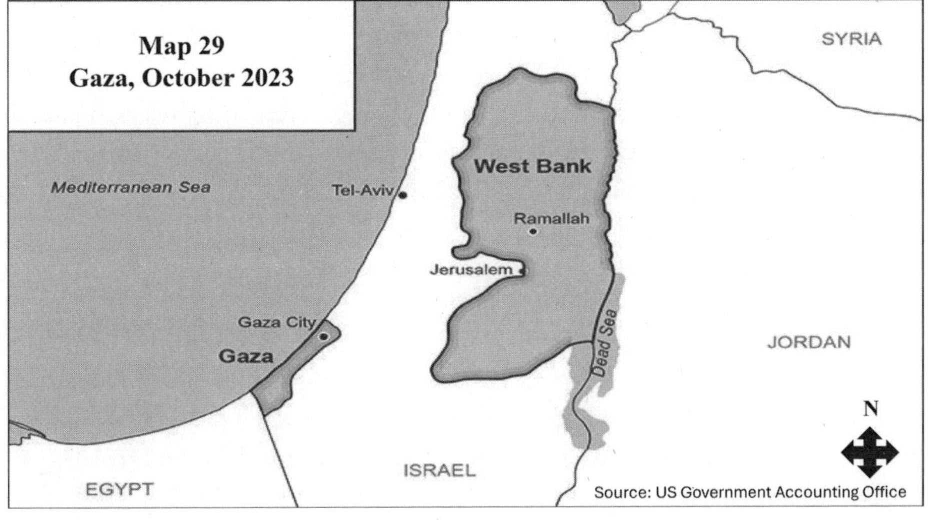

Putin either gave his blessing to the attack or, at the very least, had advance knowledge of Hamas' intentions. On 8 October Ali Baraka, Head of Hamas National Relations Abroad, announced that Russia had granted Hamas a license to produce Kalashnikov assault rifles and ammunition. Ali Baraka claimed that a half hour after the terrorist attack started, Russian officials called and offered verbal support. Russia denied this.[2]

Hamas justified the attack by claiming Jewish occupation of the modern state of Israel was unlawful. They claimed the modern state of Israel should not exist in the land of Palestine, and that it had been created by international Jewish terrorists. In addition, Hamas claimed that Israelis had desecrated the Al-Aqsa Mosque in Jerusalem and murdered unspecified Palestinians. These justifications were disingenuous. After remaining dormant for years, Hamas wanted to shock Israel into overreacting in order to gain international support for its cause, the destruction of the state of Israel. They wanted to remind Israel and the world that they were still a viable threat.[3]

Rockets, weapons and ammunition for the Hamas attack had been shipped from Sudan to Egypt, then trucked into Gaza. Weapons were also smuggled into Gaza from Sinai via tunnels. Iran, the primary weapons supplier to Hamas, was supported either directly or indirectly by militants in Lebanon, Syria, Iraq and Yemen. Russia was also a major supporter of Iran. The supply routes utilized have been referred to as the 'Shi'ite axis' and were protected by Shi'ite paramilitaries in Iraq, Hezbollah in Lebanon, and the Syrian ruling 'Alawite' minority (an offshoot of Shia Islam).[4] Russia was also a major supporter of Hezbollah.

Coinciding with the second year of Russia's Special Operation in Ukraine, US Central Command (Middle East) conducted joint US and Israeli exercises. In June 2023, 'Juniper Oak 23.2', an integrated UAV, aircraft and precision live fire exercise involved 6,400 US troops, 1,500 IDF soldiers and over 140 aircraft. The armoured ground field training exercise 'Iron Bison' was scheduled for October 2023. The US California Army National Guard 40th Infantry Division Forward, commanded by General Michael J. Leeny, was scheduled to participate in Iron Bison. Major Cyrus R. Harrel was part of the 40th Infantry Division Command Post. Major Harrel and First Sergeant David Harpst were preparing to receive 900 soldiers from the 155th Armoured Brigade Combat Team from US Mississippi Army National Guard and the 10th Mountain Division from the US regular army based at Fort Drum, New York. The forces were scheduled to conduct a bilateral land force exercise at Tse Elim (the Israeli version of the US Army National Training Center in the Mojave Desert). Tse Elim is fifteen minutes from the Gaza border. The exercise was cancelled after

Chart 27 Hamas-Iran-Russia Connection

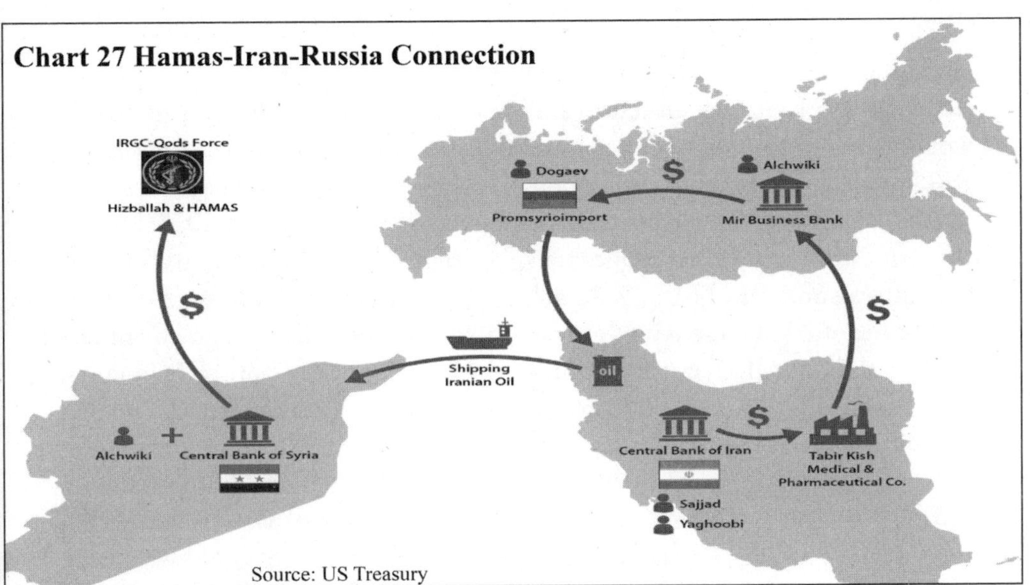

Source: US Treasury

the rocket attack of 7 October. The California National Guard advance party was exfiltrated two days later on a C-17.[5]

Shortly after Hamas' surprise attack the carrier strike group led by the USS *Gerald Ford* entered the eastern Mediterranean. On 15 October 2023 it was announced that the USS *Dwight D. Eisenhower* strike group left Norfolk, Virginia, also bound for the eastern Mediterranean. The combined air groups consisted of 135 F/A-18 fighter jets with additional support fixed wing and rotary wing aircraft.[6] Additional support in the form of F-16s from the New Jersey Air National Guard's 119th Expeditionary Fighter Squadron was rushed to the area.[7]

Between 16 and 26 October Iranian-backed Hezbollah carried out twelve rocket attacks against US bases in Iraq and four in Syria. Russia has strong ties with Iran, Syria and Hezbollah. American military personnel sustained minor wounds. In response, on Friday, 26 October, the US conducted airstrikes against two bases used by militias supported by Iran's Islamic Revolutionary Guard in eastern Syria.[8] On 27 October, US Air Force F-16 fighter jets destroyed weapons and ammunition storage depots near the village of Boukamal. According to US news releases, these strikes were not tied to the violence in Gaza but were in retaliation for Iranian-backed militia attacks against US forces in the region. Also, in response to these attacks, the US deployed additional ADA assists to defend its bases in the Middle East, to include a Terminal High Altitude Area Defence (THAAD) battery, several Patriot batteries and Avenger batteries (Stingers mounted on HUMVEEs).[9]

The instability in the Middle East and previous Hamas attack on Israel and a militant Iran caused Saudi Arabia to seek a military pact with the US to defend the Kingdom, in return for normalizing ties with Israel. The Saudis would agree to this pact even if Israel did not offer major concessions to the Palestinians in their bid for statehood. Crown Prince Mohammed bin Salman met with President Biden during his visit to the Kingdom in July 2023. During the visit the Crown Prince requested an agreement containing mutual defence guarantees similar to NATO's Article 5. He was no doubt aware that at the end of negotiations, the Kingdom would have to settle for an agreement less binding than Article 5, but if concluded the treaty would be a historic moment in the troubled Middle East. It would have been a major step towards creating a coalition to contain Iranian aggression in the region. The normalization of relations between Israel and Saudi Arabia would in time improve the situation of the Palestinians, but the Kingdom's obvious first goal was to ensure US support in providing for its own defence.[10] If the agreement could have been finalized it would have been a major diplomatic victory for President Biden and a boost to his chances in the 2024 presidential election. A US, Israel and Saudi alliance would have also blocked China's and Russia's rising influence in the region. No such alliance was concluded in 2023.

The agreement would have been a major shift in Middle East geopolitics, while reducing the gravity of the Palestinian issue.[11] The Palestinian Authority, and Palestinians in general, were not happy at having their demands downgraded in favour of Saudi security. Palestinian President Mahmoud Abbas asserted that any bargain for peace in the region must recognize the Palestinian right to a state within its 1967 borders, including east Jerusalem. In addition, he demanded that Israel desist from building settlements in what the Palestinian Authority considered to be its territory. If these demands were met, it would have required Israel to abandon Jewish settlements in the West Bank and transfer territory to the Palestinian Authority, land Israel considered strategically important to its defence. Rarely addressed by the media was the fact that the disputed land in question controls the aquifer that drains water from the Israeli highlands to the Jordan River.[12] There is nothing more important than a viable source of water in the desert. Granting these long-standing Palestinian demands would have derailed the terms of the agreement under discussion in 2023 between the US, Israel and Saudi Arabia. Despite this friction, the Biden administration agreed to provide $316 million in assistance to improve the quality of life on the West Bank.[13]

Unfortunately, Netanyahu's government did not quickly develop or publish its political objectives or strategy to end the fighting in Gaza. At the time it was speculated that there were three political options. First, Israel would occupy and administer Gaza while rooting out Hamas operatives and destroying the tunnels they used. Second, Israel would occupy Gaza and eventually pass administration to the Palestinian Authority. Third, Israel would occupy and annex northern Gaza.[14] The uncertainty about Israel's future actions in regard to Gaza greatly contributed to the unrest in the region.

Prior to the Hamas rocket attack on 7 October, the US had worked with Israel to bring stability and security to the region in general and had specifically commited itself to Israel's survival. In the 1990s, the US and Israel established the War Reserve Stock Allies-Israel (aka War Reserve Stockpile Ammunition-Israel) or WRSA-I. It was maintained by US European Command and was one of the biggest ammunition storage depots outside the US. A massive quantity of 155mm munitions and Patriot missiles, along with other ammunition and supplies, was stockpiled in Israel. Thousands of stockpiled artillery rounds were supplied from the Israeli depot. Hundreds of thousands more rounds from South Korea had been stored in Israel but had been provided to Ukraine at the beginning of Putin's Special Operation. It was reported that in total approximately 300,000 155mm shells were transferred from the Israeli depot to Ukraine.[15]

This new war moved the media's attention from the Russian invasion of Ukraine to the humanitarian situation in Gaza and the age-old issue of whether the State of Israel had the right to exist. Russia had cultivated relations with Hamas for decades. Putin did not condemn Hamas' strike on Israel but rather blamed the war on the US.[16] Russia's military bases in Syria supported Hamas and other militant groups in an effort to increase its diplomatic influence in the region.[17]

The Kremlin used the war to sow disinformation and discord among NATO members and western democracies. Hamas' action froze the normalisation process between Israel and Saudi Arabia. The US efforts to de-escalate tensions with Iran were derailed. In a true twist of irony, Hamas and Palestinians blamed Israel for war crimes committed during its retaliatory actions in Gaza. The world took sides: either supporting Israel and its right to defend itself, or with the poor Gazan civilians who had to bear the brunt of their war. This put extreme pressure on Arab governments to oppose the US stabilization plan for the Middle East. On 24 October 2023 US allies Egypt, Jordan and Saudi Arabia condemned Israel and called for an immediate ceasefire. The next day, during a vote of the UN Security Council, the UAE, China and Russia vetoed a US resolution that did not call for a cessation of fighting in Gaza.[18]

On the surface, Russia's alliance of convenience with Iran supported Hamas indirectly. Western-supplied small arms captured on the battlefield in Ukraine had somehow found their way into Hamas' hands.[19] Putin's propaganda machine went into overdrive to support Hamas' version of events.

The fighting continued into 2024 and continued to distract the world's media from the war in Ukraine. The Israeli-Hamas war provided Putin with an opportunity to expand his influence in the region at the expense of regional peace. By not condemning Hamas and clandestinely supporting extremist militants, Putin helped destabilize the region and derailed attempts to create a lasting peace. The US, Saudi and Israeli attempt to normalize relations was put on the back burner, and US support for Israel might possibly reduce the aid available for Ukraine in the future. Whether Putin was a driving force behind the Hamas attack or simply an opportunist taking advantage of the situation, the Hamas-Israel War was a major political victory in Russia's hybrid war against the EU, NATO, US, Ukraine and Israel.

On 25 February 2024, Israeli ambassador to the UN Gilad Erdan delivered a powerful speech to mark the two-year anniversary of the war in Ukraine. He emphasized that Israel stands with Ukraine and warned against deepening ties between Russia, Iran, Syria, Hamas, Hezbollah and North Korea, referring to them as the 'Axis of Evil'.[20] This statement was made a week before the scheduled meeting between Moscow and Palestinian factions, including Hamas. Russia's goal was to create ties between global forces of destabilization. Russia's support of Hamas and Hezbollah resulted in a shift of Israeli policy. Having strong ties with both Russia and Ukraine, Israel had tried to stay neutral at the beginning of Putin's Special Operation, but after the attack of 7 October and Russia's support for Hamas, Israel came out as a strong supporter of Ukraine.[21]

Putin is linked to both Hamas and Hezbollah, and to Iran and Syria.[22] By 'stirring the Middle East pot' and inciting unrest in the region, Russia's hybrid war had several consequences. First, the world's attention was diverted from the Special Operation, and potential economic, humanitarian and military support for Israel would possibly cut into available aid to Ukraine. Perhaps the most critical impact was in delaying US aid to Ukraine during 2023. The US Congress stalled on passing a budget that would have provided enormous amounts of aid to both Ukraine and Israel. The Ukraine aid package was not controversial, but the aid to Israel was debated because of the extreme effects of Israel's retaliatory actions on the Palestinians in Gaza. Biden blamed Congress for the delay in passing the bill and the resulting delay in providing Ukraine weapons and ammunition, suggesting that this was why Ukraine lost the Battle of Avdiivka. The downside for Russia of its political manoeuvring is that Israel, once neutral regarding the Special Operation, has come out as a strong supporter of Ukraine. Ukraine must be happy to know that its new friend has a huge stockpile of tanks and ammunition.

Chapter 29

Friction between President Zelensky and General Zaluzhnyi

In late October 2023, General Zaluzhnyi's interview by *The Economist* revealed a growing friction between the President and his Minister of Defence. More than a personal conflict the interview disclosed a disconnect between political and military strategy. Zelensky's political strategy was focused on world media and allied leaders to garner support and increased aid. Zaluzhnyi's military strategy was more concerned with the combat capabilities of the combatants and the actual battlefield situation on the ground.

General Zaluzhnyi was appointed Commander-in-Chief of Ukrainian Armed forces in July 2022 as tension between Ukraine and Russia escalated, and he began providently working to improve Ukraine's military readiness. A student of NATO's command system, he was not afraid to encourage initiative in junior commanders and soldiers. He altered the rules of engagement in the Donbas, allowing soldiers to return fire without first seeking authorization from senior officers. Zaluzhnyi understood the geopolitical/military process and established contacts with Ukrainian paramilitary and nationalist groups that were distrustful of President Zelensky.[1]

When the invasion began, President Zelensky became the face of Ukrainian defiance and resistance, while General Zaluzhnyi remained in the background, fighting the war. By the summer of 2022, with Kyiv and Kharkiv saved, and the Russians focused on the Donbas, issues began to surface between the President's office and the General Staff. In July the dispute became public. The General Staff issued a directive prohibiting Ukrainians of military age from changing their place of residence without permission from the military. The directive had not been coordinated with the President's office. Zelensky responded by calling the directive 'serfdom' and prohibiting the General Staff from taking such action in the future without Presidential approval.[2]

By October 2023 it was clear that Ukraine's summer offensive had failed to accomplish its objectives, and the friction between the military and civil administrations became more acute. Ukraine had similar problems to Russia with corruption in both departments. The international media soon began to notice, and reported on the friction prior to General Zaluzhnyi's interview with *The Economist* in late October.[3] The General was very candid in his interview. He said that the war was in a 'stalemate phase' and he took ultimate responsibility for the lack of progress during the summer offensive.

President Zelensky was not pleased with General Zaluzhnyi's statement that 'with the culmination of the summer offensive the war was in a stalemate phase'. The General probably should have submitted his interview remarks to a pre-interview review by the President's office, to ensure political acceptability. This was not a problem unique to Ukraine. Other famous generals have historically courted trouble with their political leaders by giving interviews and making statements in the media that expressed opinions and sentiments that were not pre-approved by or aligned with their government's official position; most notably US General Patton's statement that 'we fought the wrong enemy' in referring to Russia after the Second World War, and General MacArthur's public criticism of President Truman's conduct of the Korean War. MacArthur wanted to invade China and end the threat from North Korea, while Truman sought peace through negotiation, fearing that war against China would ultimately involve Russia. The term 'stalemate' had political ramifications that Zaluzhnyi was not attuned to and President Zelensky publicly rebuked him for making an unapproved statement. A spokesman for the President's office explained that the General's statement was inappropriate, because it sowed panic among Ukraine's Western allies. In Zelensky's October 2023 rebuttal he disputed the General's (correct) military assessment of the situation. Zelensky recognized that people were tired of war, but concluded the war was not at a stalemate. The President was afraid that the General's frank statement of the military situation on the ground would undermine support for Ukraine in European capitals, and affect support by the Republican Party in the US. He was also correctly concerned that after the Hamas attack on Israel on 7 October the world's attention, especially in the US, had shifted from the war in Ukraine to the war in the Middle East. Zelensky was also acutely aware of US criticism over the execution and lack of success of the summer counter-offensive.[4]

During February 2024, the Security Service of Ukraine (SBU) had begun to investigate the circumstances by which the Kherson Bridge had not been destroyed during the first days of the invasion. Destroying the bridge was an obvious and crucial part of Ukraine's defence from the very start. Zaluzhnyi's political enemies tried to discredit him by spreading a rumour that he was somehow involved, and seemingly solely to harass the General he was called as a witness to testify before the investigative committee. Rustem Umerov, the newly appointed Defence Minister, began dismissing generals believed to be close to Zaluzhnyi.[5]

Umerov, a Crimean Tatar aged forty-one, born in Samarkand in Uzbekistan, was appointed on 3 September 2023. Stalin had deported his family from Crimea in the 1940s. Elected to the Ukrainian parliament in 2020, he had been part of a task force working on a strategy to recapture Crimea. He also participated in negotiating the Black Sea grain deal and in arranging for PoW exchanges.[6] He fought corruption within the agency since September 2022, and upon taking office, he cleaned house. He removed Hanna Maliar, who was charged with issuing inaccurate public reports and updates.[7] By 18 September 2023, five deputy defence ministers had been fired without providing any explanation. At the time, it was speculated that there were instances of fraud and corruption in purchasing and distributing supplies to the military.[8] After cleaning house, Umerov turned to the military.

On 3 November 2023, President Zelensky announced that Major General Viktor Khorenko, Major General of Special Operations (OSS), was removed without notice, and that he would be replaced by General Serhii Lupanchuk. The removal occurred after Khorenko's first media interview. Umerov did not consult with General Zaluzhnyi before installing Lupanchuk. Afterwards, Zaluzhnyi issued a statement saying that there was no question as to Khorenko's performance or competence.[9] Zaluzhnyi praised Khorenko for the supervision of many daring and successful operations by his commandos, including orchestrating the 2023 fall of the Russian bridgehead on the east bank of the Dnipro River. Ironically, capture and destruction of the bridge over the Dnipro was initially ignored by the media and deemed irrelevant by Russians; however, once a Marine battalion established a combat outpost at the village of Krynky, threatening the supply lines of the 58th CAA, it suddenly became very interesting. Khorenko was ultimately moved into a staff position in Defence Intelligence.[10] Major General Tetiana Ostashchenko from the Medical Forces was also reassigned at this time. The issues may have been the quality of 'tactical medicine' and the rotation of medical personnel.[11]

In September 2023, Umerov reportedly developed a plan to shuffle the generals who he assumed were responsible for the slow progress of the counter-offensive. His actions demonstrated either his lack of knowledge or understanding of military operations, or that he was succumbing to political pressure from hostile opposition leaders.[12]

Maryana Bezhulia, a member of the ruling party in Ukraine's parliament, demanded Zaluzhnyi's resignation. She was supported by many other members of parliament. Zelensky's domestic political opposition seized on the opportunity to exploit the friction between the President and the General, and the President's political opponents attempted to take political advantage of the unsuccessful summer counter-offensive to form a new government.

Unsurprisingly, and despite these political manoeuvres, the Ukrainian public opposed holding elections in wartime, but would have probably rallied around Zelensky. General Zaluzhnyi showed no interest in politically opposing the President. Despite the storm of hysteria roused by civil authorities and his political opponents, General Zaluzhnyi remained focused on providing stable, competent military leadership for the Ukrainian military and the nation.[13]

Employing cyberspace warfare tactics, Moscow planted stories with social media bloggers and created propaganda materials to 'stir the pot' and raise the prospect of civil strife in Ukraine, in order to undermine the foundations of the republic. The Kremlin touted President Zelensky's denial of the failure of the counter-offensive in contradiction of General Zaluzhnyi's statement about the war being at a stalemate to discredit both men. Russian media compared Zelenky's prior statements about defending key cities with the General's stated strategy of developing new fortified defences and falling back from besieged cities like Avdiivda to save lives and to prevent another Russian victory like Bakhmut.[14]

To further promote rivalry and sow discord, Putin's propaganda machine portrayed President Zelensky as an emotional Jew, unstable and out of touch with the realities at the front, and portrayed General Zaluzhnyi as a logical and practical alternative. Even a renowned reporter from *Time* magazine (Simon Schuster) jumped on the Russian propaganda bandwagon as a believer. The propaganda depicted Zelensky as acting independently, unwilling to take advice from anyone and making decisions without input from civilian or military advisers. The anti-Zelensky information in the media had been provided by 'confidential informants', in other words by sources that could not be confirmed or 'fact checked'.[15]

On 12 December 2023, Minister Rustem clarified his position on why he was shuffling the senior military leaders. He indicated that it was his obligation to make changes as required, and defended his actions by confirming that rotation in leadership positions was a normal part of military operations.[16] One only needs to examine the UK shuffle of its generals during the Second World War North African campaign to demonstrate the truth of this. Senior command rotated between Generals Wavell, Auchinleck, Alexander and O'Connor (captured), until Montgomery finally defeated Field Marshal Rommel and the Afrika Korps. Clearly, the requirement to pursue war successfully takes precedent over the career or personal goals of any one individual.

In a democracy, the elected civilian leader has the final decision on the strategy employed to win wars. The prime minster or president selects the senior commander of the armed forces. The responsibility for the outcome of the war falls directly upon the leader's shoulders. The 'buck' for winning or losing stops on his desk.

Chapter 30

Russian 2023 Autumn Offensive, the Battle of Avdiivka

Russia's strategic goal in 2023 was to capture the remaining Donbas region that so far had eluded its control. The majority of Donetsk Oblast, including the city of Avdiivka, had been under Russian control, having been captured with the help of 'separatists' in April 2014, but by 30 July 2014, the Ukrainian army had liberated the city. While Avdiivka was technically a city it was so small and had been bombed so many times the remaining site was more like a small village.

Nevertheless, Avdiivka was considered an important gateway to the nearby provincial capital of Donetsk. Ukrainian control blocked Russia from using the village as part of a potential axis of advance and prevented its use as a supply route and communication hub. It had been fortified since the battles in 2014 with trench systems, protected firing positions, minefields and reinforced concrete bunkers. Capture of the entire region would be a significant political, economic and military victory, ensuring Russia access to its vast coal and untapped gas and oil reserves. After a year of fighting in the area, the Ukrainians held a large section of western Donetsk Oblast, but during the 2023 winter offensive the Russian General Staff turned its attention to the capture of Avdiivka.

The Kremlin decided to resume the Battle for Avdiivka in August or September 2023, to coincide with Putin's visit to China. Avdiivka had only tactical significance. Even if the Russians were able to capture the fortified city, the autumn *Rasputitsa* would prevent any meaningful exploitation. The military factors of terrain and weather argued against renewing the battle late in the campaign season, but the political factors required some kind of victory, any victory, before Putin visited China. For home propaganda consumption, the capture of the fortified city could have been spun into a major victory for the Russian public.

The Russians were expecting to achieve tactical surprise on the transparent battlefield. They took advantage of the heavy traffic going into and out of Donetsk City to mask their troop build-up. They also infiltrated the hills around nearby Novoselivka and occupied towns north-west of Avdiivka to

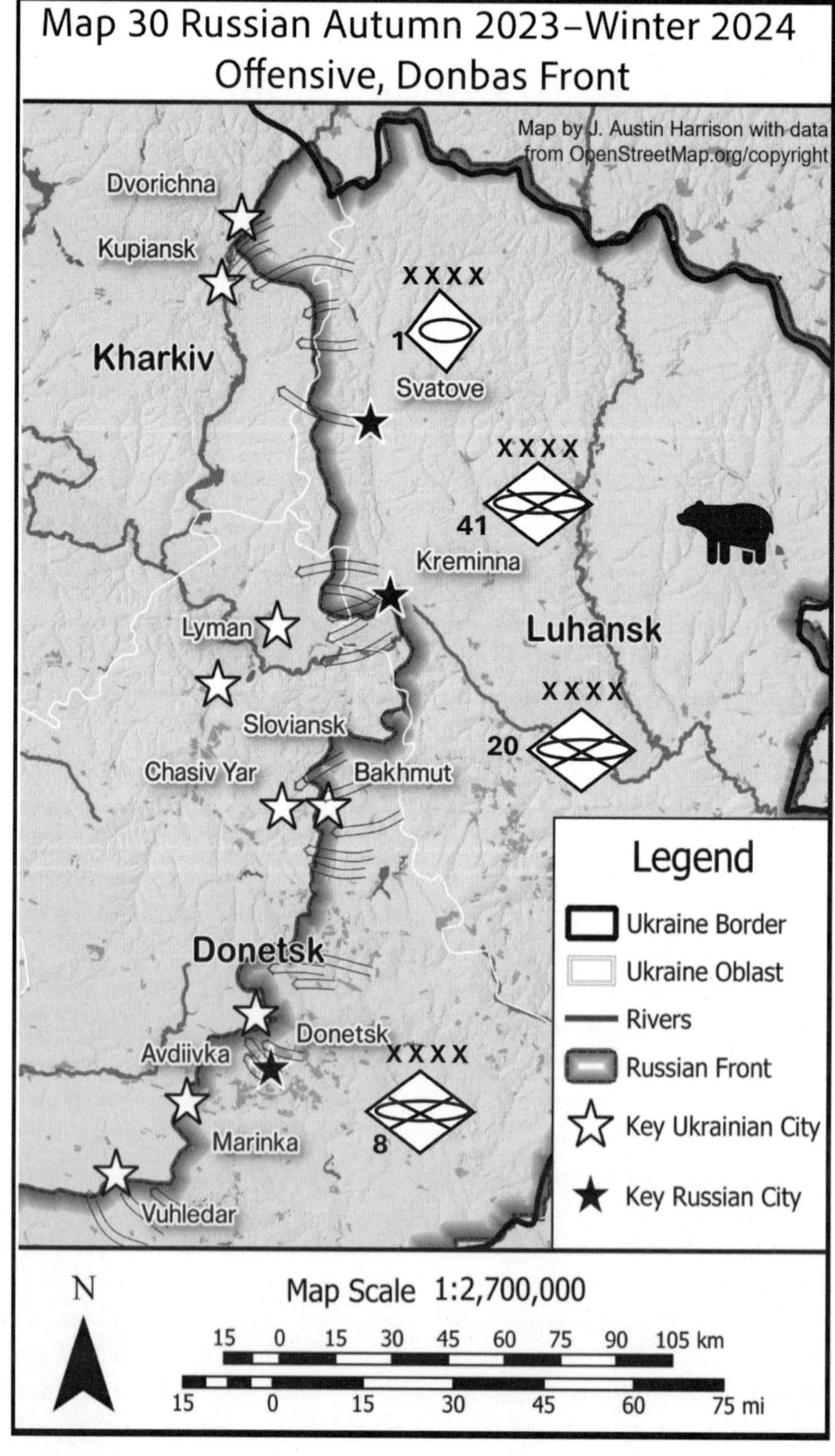
Map 30 Russian Autumn 2023–Winter 2024
Offensive, Donbas Front
Map by J. Austin Harrison with data
from OpenStreetMap.org/copyright
Dvorichna
Kupiansk
Kharkiv
XXXX
1
Svatove
XXXX
41
Kreminna
Lyman
Luhansk
XXXX
20
Sloviansk
Chasiv Yar
Bakhmut
Donetsk
Donetsk
Avdiivka
XXXX
8
Marinka
Vuhledar
Legend
Ukraine Border
Ukraine Oblast
Rivers
Russian Front
Key Ukrainian City
Key Russian City
N
Map Scale 1:2,700,000
15 0 15 30 45 60 75 90 105 km
15 0 15 30 45 60 75 mi

further mask troop movements. This deception operation failed, as Ukrainian reconnaissance teams equipped with FPV drones, NATO satellites and spies on the ground observed the increased activities around Russian government buildings in and around Donetsk City. The increase in the number of civilian cars parked near Russian military buildings clearly indicated that staff officers and commanders were massing in the city. When Russian preliminary air strikes commenced on 9 October 2023, the Ukrainian defenders were ready.[1] The massing of combat vehicles in forward assembly areas had not gone unnoticed by Ukrainian intelligence, and the projected Russian axes of advance were identified, the same avenues of approach used during the winter/spring 2023 Battle for Avdiivka.

The Russian 8th CAA was assigned the mission of capturing Avdiivka. During the 2023 winter offensive, the Russians had captured the towns of Krasnohorivaka, Vesele, Kamianka and Novoselivka Druha. Vesele and Kamianka were only 5 km (3 miles) north-west of the coke plant and the infamous Terrikon Slag Heap in Avdiivka. The Terrikon slag heap, the waste generated from a coke plant, had grown so massive that it acquired a name, and it served not only as a natural barrier but also as a unique observation post from which the surrounding landscape could be viewed for miles around. For the first few months of the battle, the coke plant, the Terrikon Slag Heap and the rail tracks leading into the Avdeyevsky Coke Plant and the village of Stepove constituted key terrain. The area was crisscrossed with tree lines and woods. The Slag Heap was a virtual mountain, 30 metres high, and observers on top were able to detect activities deep into the Russian rear. Capture of the village of Stepove would allow the Russians to interdict supply lines into the city. The rail tracks leading into the coke plant were elevated, having been constructed 2 metres above the surrounding fields, creating a berm 1,000 metres across open fields from the village of Stepove. There were 2,000 metres of open fields from the berm to the first Russian-controlled tree line. This terrain would ultimately mean the fields, tree lines and forests all became kill zones.[2]

The Russians needed to advance 2 km (1.2 miles) to the south-west to capture Sieverne, and 6 km (3.7 miles) to take Orlivka, in order to cut the Ukrainian supply lines. This axis of advance crossed open fields surrounded by tree lines. The axis was dominated by a small ridge running from the town of Umanske to Semenivka. The ridge and Orlivka were protected by a series of lakes and streams.

The 8th CAA intermediate commands included the 1st Army Corps (former DPR) and 20th Motorized Rifle Division. The soldiers manning the assault formations were drawn from the former Donetsk People's Army, which had been incorporated into the Russian Army in February 2023. They were reinforced with regular army regiments and Storm-Z detachments. Prior to this date, the Donetsk soldiers had been seriously under-equipped, but in preparation for the attack the Russians had armed the assault battalions with T-72, 80 and 90 tanks, APCs and IFVs. Because of the proximity of the Russian-occupied city of Donetsk, the assault groups were able to assemble and remain hidden from observation, enabling the Russians to mass several hundred armoured vehicles near the line of contact. The Russians had not, however, come to terms with the transparent battlefield. The attackers deployed fifteen regiments, approximately four divisions, or 45,000 combat troops, against the defending Ukrainian Battle Group. The ground attack would be supported by the Russian Air Force lobbing glide bombs at the defenders.

The city was defended by approximately 6,000 troops in the 110th Territorial Brigade, with the 53rd Mechanized Brigade as the main effort. Another 9,000 troops defended the city's northern and southern flanks.[3] In total, the Ukrainian Battle Group consisted of twenty-one combat battalions, including the 1st Special Purpose Brigade. With the Ukrainian IX and X Corps exhausted after the Ukrainian counter-offensive, the Russians did not expect significant reinforcements to arrive before the city fell.

With a combat ratio of over 3:1 in Russia's favour, a quick victory was expected. Politically, Putin needed a complete victory, or at the very least to successfully encircle the defending Ukrainians, prior to his meeting with the Chinese on 17 October 2023. China would be much more agreeable to supporting a winning combatant than one caught in an operational stalemate. Operationally, capturing Avdiivka would push the front away from Donetsk City. This was critical, as Donetsk City and its international airport were within artillery range of Avdiivka. If Russia could capture Avdiivka, the city would conveniently serve as a springboard to capture the reminder of Ukrainian-controlled Donetsk Oblast. Tactically, if Russia could reduce this salient, it would shorten the frontline by 20 km (12.4 miles), thereby freeing up about ten regiments, or two divisions, for other missions.

As the Ukrainian counter-offensive was winding down, the Russian attack commenced. Probing attacks commenced against Avdiivka on 9 October 2023. Kamikaze tanks were employed to uncover minefields, and fields were set ablaze to uncover mines. Artillery and air strikes increased in intensity around Avdiivka. These attacks, however, were only a diversion to fix Ukrainian attention towards the direction of Donetsk City.

Then, on 10 October 2023, a five-hour preparatory bombardment north of the city, conducted by 200 artillery systems and aircraft, was followed by assault units advancing upon Ukrainian positions. The combat outposts along the line of contact were destroyed or suppressed, as were C2 and supply depots within the city.[4]

The main attack was arrayed in several echelons, consisting of 8,000 combat troops, 40 tanks, and 160 IFVs and APCs of the 114th Separate Motorized Rifle Brigade, the 109th Rifle Regiment and the 277th Rifle Battalion. The Russian attack plan envisioned the main effort as attacking and capturing the railway embankment and the town of Stepove. A supporting attack would bypass the Terrikon Slag Heap and the Avdeyevsky Coke Plant to the north and hit Stepove from the south. The first echelon consistedof the Storm-Z battalions reinforced with IFVs and APCs. These battalions mimicked Second World War Soviet storm companies consisting of infantry armed with only sub-machine guns riding on assaulting tanks and dismounting to assault enemy trenches. In this case they were riding atop their BMP IFVs. Initial reports from the reconnaissance patrols indicated that the plan was working. Russian videos showed Ukrainian defenders retreating from their combat outposts. Russian patrols crossed the railway embankment, reaching the outskirts of Stepove.[5]

The attack commenced at 0500, with Russian battalion-size armoured assault columns moving toward Ukrainian positions, supported by a fire bombardment by 200 artillery systems, 36 air strikes and attack helicopters. The assault battalions moved forward on the limited roads in column. Each column was organized with a breaching team of ten T-90M, T-80VM or T-72B3M tanks followed by three companies of infantry riding 30 IFVs or APCs. The assault motorized rifle battalions had to cross 8–10 km (5–6 miles) of open ground.

During the first hours of the attack, Ukrainian artillery remained silent. FPV reconnaissance drones monitored the advancing Russian columns. In violation of both Soviet and Russian doctrine, the 8th CAA failed to deploy smoke to cover the assaulting battalions' movements, but due to the threat of Ukrainian drones, the Russians were most probably conducting EW jamming operations. The Russian frontline battalion commanders must have believed their movement to contact had been too easy. They were correct. Both Soviet and Russian doctrine dictated that assault battalions and companies should remain in column until within 2,000 metres of an enemy position, unless enemy fire required the column to deploy in combat formation. Ignoring doctrine, the Russians advanced into a kill zone.

The Ukrainian artillery now unmasked itself and rained down a precise bombardment on the Russian ground force. US 155mm cluster and 'scatterable' mine munitions, drones and ATGMs shredded the Russian formations. The Territorial Defence troops positioned at the Avdeyevsky Coke Plant and

Terrikon Slag Heap fired into the flank of at least one column. Russian aircraft sorties lobbed glide bombs onto the Terrikon Slag Heap. The supporting attack on the Avdeyevsky Coke Plant was stopped in its tracks only a few hundred metres north of the Slag Heap. A Russian battalion of twenty armoured vehicles, still arranged in column, was destroyed. The infantry tried to push forward but was targeted by cluster munitions. Russian losses for 10 October 2023 totalled fifteen tanks and thirty-three IFVs, while they took about 500 casualties.[6]

On 11 October, the Ukrainians conducted a limited counter-attack as the Russians retreated to reorganize and assess the situation. Russian regimental and battalion commanders understood that the Avdeyevsky Coke Plant and the Terrikon Slag Heap had successfully guarded the approaches to the village of Stepove. They needed to take Stepove in order to cut the Ukrainian Army supply and communication lines and encircle the defenders of Avdiivka. Any attack on the village of Stepove would be enfiladed by direct fire from the coke plant, since Stepove was only 3 km (1.8 miles) north of the plant, well within ATGM range.

The fixing attacks on 10 October against Avdiivka were conducted by the 1st Separate (Sloviansk) Motorized Rifle Brigade, the Somalia Battalion and an UI battalion. The defenders included Army, Territorial, police and border guards. The soldiers and police had been defending the area since the beginning of the war, they fought from fixed fortified positions, and the Russian attacks were successfully repulsed.

The southern arm was spearheaded by 6,000 combat troops in the 117th Motorized Rifle Regiment, the 87th Rifle Regiment and a Storm-Z Battalion.[7] All the units assigned to the attack were former DPR units. The heavy defensive fire blunted the Russian attack.

On 12 October, the Russians redoubled their attack on the tree line and the railway embankment which was defended by the 116th Territorial Brigade. On 13–15 October, the attacking Russians charged the railway embankment and the Slag Heap.[8] The Russian battalion assaulting this strong position, across open fields, attacked straight into a kill zone which had been mined by the defending Ukrainians. The battalion on the southern flank of the attack received flanking fire from the coke factory and the Slag Heap. They were also repulsed, suffering heavy casualties and great loss of equipment. Russian armoured vehicle losses exceeded 100 in a single day, verified by drone footage.[9] After 96 hours of fighting, the Russians lost 30–40 tanks and 90–100 APCs and IFVs and suffered over 2,000 casualties.[10]

On 13 October, the Russians attacked over the same ground and were again repulsed. Heavy artillery fire and air strikes hammered the Ukrainian positions

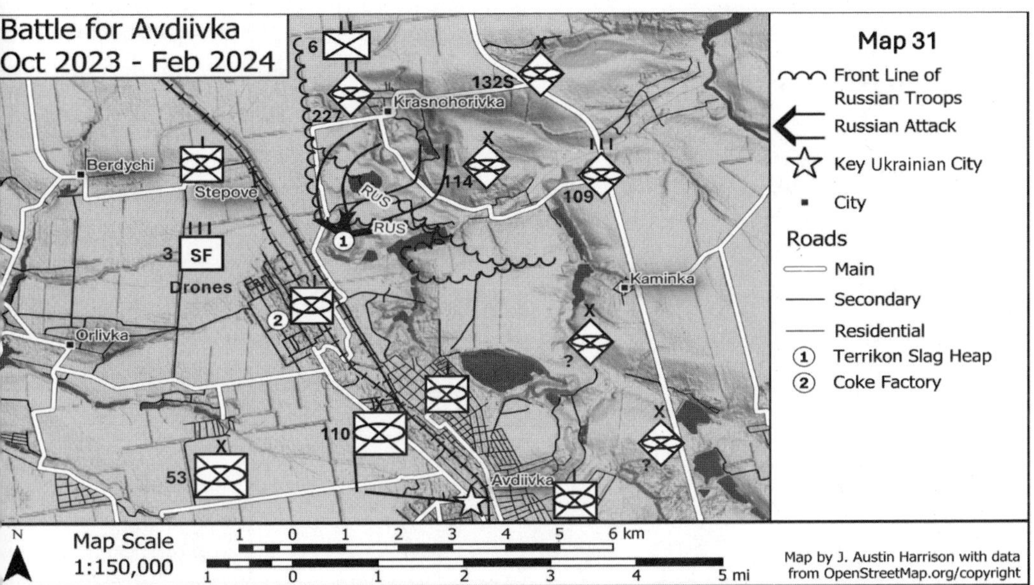

but were unable to suppress the defenders. The Russians fired incendiary munitions to pin defenders in their bunkers, while the Ukrainians targeted the invaders' rear area with artillery. Ukrainian artillery destroyed a key bridge, successfully interdicting the northern arm's main supply line. This slowed down the Russians' ability to reinforce and supply their forward assembly areas. The Russian armoured formation on the southern axis had to cross 8 km (5 miles) of open ground to reach the line of contact. By the end of the day, the Russians had suffered another 1,000 casualties and lost twenty-five tanks and fifty other armoured vehicles, and they had not made any substantial gains.[11]

On 15 October 2023, the Russians finally shifted their main assault toward the Terrikon Slag Heap, held by elements of the 110th Mechanized Brigade, supported by the 55th Artillery Brigade. The Russians massed their assault battalions in tree lines several kilometres from the Slag Heap, in plain view of the defenders' elevated positions and FPV drones.[12]

The Russian tactical battle plan envisioned the Russian tanks establishing support by fire positions, while infantry would be driven by IFVs and APCs across the open field in front of the Terrikon Slag Heap and then dismount. They were expected to climb the heap, which was more like a small cliff, then assault the Ukrainians on top.

FPV drones began to harass the Russian armoured column as it moved from its assembly area. As soon as the Russians broke cover and started to deploy into combat formation, the defenders poured direct and indirect fire onto them. FPV drones dropped grenades on individual vehicles. Under heavy

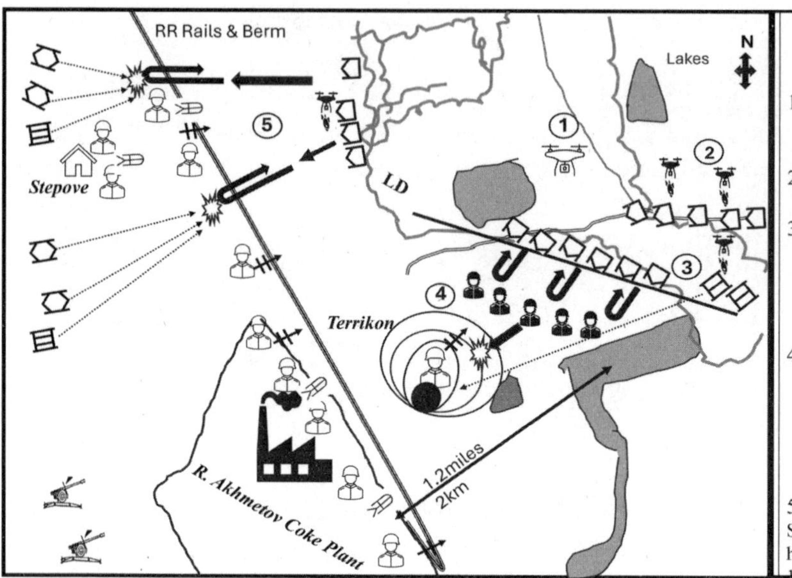

Chart 28 Battle of Terrikon October 2023

1. UA recon drones discover RU massing for attack
2. FPV Kamikaze Drones strike RU battalion.
3. RU M. Rifle Battalion deploys online and crosses LD. Tanks support by fire and are attacked by drones.
4. RU infantry dismount 500m from Terrikon as APCs run for cover. Massed machinegun, artillery destroys RU infantry.
5. RU Supporting Attack

Source: ISW, Deepstate https://deepstatemap.live/en#

fire, the Russian tanks deployed in attack by fire positions, to cover the dash forward of the IFVs. Russian artillery hammering the coke plant and the Slag Heap failed to lay a smoke screen to cover the advancing IFVs. At least a battalion of infantry riding atop their IFVs and APCs attempted to close with the Slag Heap near its steep cliff face. Land mines slowed down the assault formation within the kill zone. Despite continuing heavy losses, Russian infantry dismounted 150 metres from Ukrainian positions, while their IFVs and APCs 'bugged out' and rushed to the rear, seeking cover. Dumped in the open and subjected to heavy machine gun crossfire from the coke plant and the Slag Heap, the dismounted Russian infantry now attempted to climb the 'cliff'. Supporting fire from Russian tanks and ATGMs attempted to suppress the machine guns, but artillery and FPV drones were able to neutralize the support by fire positions.

Ukrainian machine gun positions on the Slag Heap cut down the assaulting Russian infantry. Only one man climbed halfway up before being cut down. The Russian attack was repulsed with heavy losses of both men and equipment.[13]

In response to the costly and bloody repulse of the initial Russian attack, the 114th (DNR), 15th and 21st Motorized Rifle Regiments from the 2nd CAA (Kreminna, Russian-occupied Luhansk Oblast) were committed to the attack on Avdiivka.[14] They repeated the assault on the Terrikon Slag Heap, employing exactly the same methods as before, with exactly the same outcome. The Russians suffered hundreds of casualties, and over a hundred destroyed armoured vehicles were added to the existing pile of 'dead' tanks and IFVs.

The Ukrainians claimed the Russians in one day suffered more than 1,400 casualties and 175 tanks and BMPs destroyed.[15]

The fighting between 10 and 17 October 2023 resulted in the Battle of Avdiivka becoming the worst defeat of 2023 for the 8th CAA and the Kremlin.[16] Fighting continued into November and December, but the victory Putin wanted to save face and garner support from China eluded him. Artur Rehi, an Estonian blogger, translated a Russian blogger's post that provided a detailed after-action report of one the assaults on the city, depicting the horrible loss of life. While the media described these as 'meat grinder' or 'human wave' attacks, any Cold War NATO soldier would recognize them as standard Soviet Cold War tactics. The Russian division-size battle group, like its Soviet predecessor, attacked with two regiments abreast on a narrow front. Unlike the Soviets, however, their successors lacked coordination between the assault regiments to secure the gap between them, or to suppress the defenders. The regiment's armoured battalions in the first echelon moved in column formation to their assigned assault positions. The infantry dismounted while the IFVs and APCs again attempted to return to the rear. As the first echelon columns advanced, they were engaged by ATGMs and defending artillery. Ukrainian artillery, mortars and automatic grenade launchers hammered the first echelon battalions as they dismounted. Once the Russian supporting tanks opened fire, defending kamikaze drones targeted them. Russian artillery fire was not coordinated to provide smoke for the ground assault, and the Ukrainian defensive positions were not suppressed. Defending machine guns

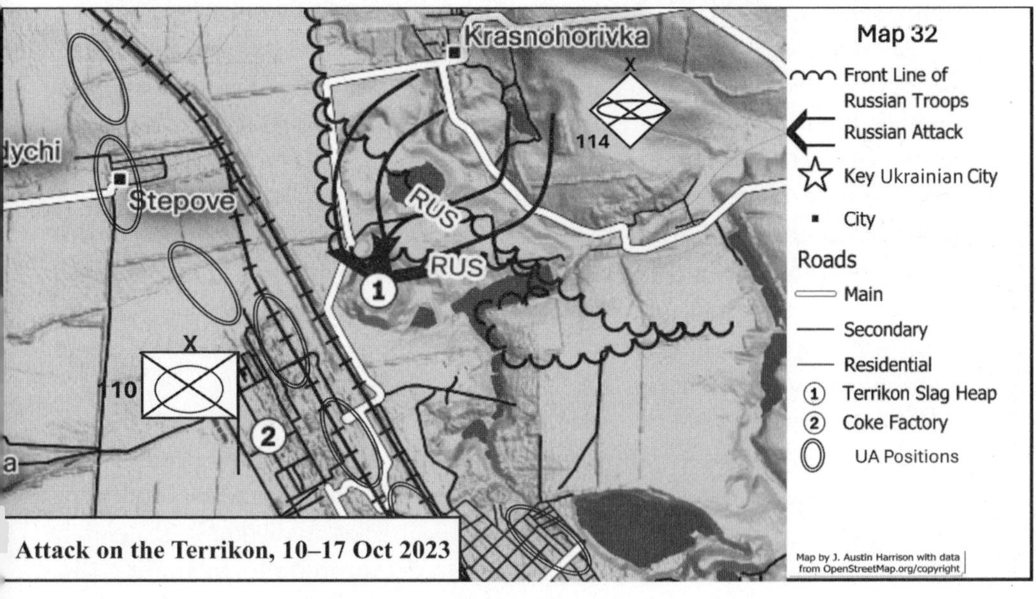

Attack on the Terrikon, 10–17 Oct 2023

rained devastating fire down upon the assaulting Russian infantry. The first echelon's purpose was to fix the Ukrainian defenders, forcing them to expend their ammunition, while the second echelon of Regular troops arrived, atop their APCs like the Soviet '*desideniks*' in the Second World War. They closed with the defenders and overran the Ukrainian positions in the security zone.[17] The lead Russian commanders sent false reports forward to their higher headquarters indicating that the attack was progressing in their favour. As the first battalion stalled, suffering heavy casualties, a second battalion was committed to the same axis and it also suffered needlessly heavy casualties.[18]

From the Ukrainian point of view, the echeloned attacks were difficult to stop. The first and second echelons might have suffered up to 80 per cent casualties, but 20 per cent of the infantry still successfully reached the Ukrainian trenches. The defenders expended their crew-served weapons' ammunition and were physically exhausted. In the resulting 'slugfest', the Ukrainian and Russian infantry engaged each other in close-quarters fighting with assault rifles and grenades.[19]

By 17 October, the Russians had suffered extremely heavy casualties and a huge loss of equipment but had not made any significant gains. As the battle raged, Putin attended the 'Third Belt Forum for International Cooperation' (BRIC), along with other world leaders, in China. The BRIC addressed the potential for major infrastructure projects among its members, including a China-Russia east-west natural gas pipeline. China agreed to work with the Russian-dominated Eurasian Economic Union (EEU) to improve cooperation, economic development and tourism between the countries. Chinese President Xi Jinping expressed his interest in a long-term China-Russia strategic partnership, stating that his goal was to develop a 'multipolar' world.[20] By the end of 2023 and the beginning of 2024, BRIC increased its membership from the five original members (Brazil, Russia, India, China, and South Africa) to include Iran, Saudi Arabia, Egypt, Argentina and the United Arab Emirates. Putin was unable to attend the meeting in Johannesburg due to the International Warrant issued for his arrest for war crimes committed in Ukraine. Nonetheless, the addition of the five new members to BRIC was seen as a political win for both Putin and Xi Jinping, since the group's goal is to develop stronger ties among members and to counterbalance global influence from the EU and the US.

Putin had been negotiating with China and North Korea for months to obtain artillery munitions and other supplies to support his war in Ukraine. It was hardly a coincidence that Putin's meeting with President Xi Jinping was scheduled one week after the renewed Battle of Avdiivka. Putin clearly expected, and needed, a battlefield victory to demonstrate to Xi Jinping that

Russia would ultimately conquer Ukraine. Instead, despite upbeat photo opportunities, Putin arrived 'hat in hand' as a petitioner to the 'Central Kingdom', begging aid from the Chinese Emperor

Xi Jinping knew that China's growing power and global influence was at the expense of a seemingly withdrawing West. The 2023 Presidential Candidate Donald Trump loudly and belligerently espoused policies promoting withdrawal of US support for maintaining world peace and international order. At one point Trump even floated a proposal for the US to withdraw from NATO. The UK's withdrawal from the EU reinforced this perception. Global reaction to Covid, shutting borders and retreating into isolationism, and the short-lived, attempted insurrection by 'Trumpers' in the US: these all reinforced Xi Jinping's perception that 'time and momentum' were on China's side. He decided that it was time to further expand China's interest and participation in a primarily Asian arena to the world at large.[21]

The West however, proved hard to ignore or downplay. Despite China's large and growing economy, Beijing's success was tied to trade with the US. Taking advantage of the Russian-Ukrainian War, China began to apply pressure on Taiwan to test US resolve. The US and Taiwan had historically signed a mutual defence treaty that was effective from 1955 to 1980. However, once the US formally recognized The People's Republic of China in 1980, the treaty was terminated, and the US Congress passed 'The Taiwan Relations Act': 'An Act to help maintain peace, security, and stability in the Western Pacific and to promote the foreign policy of the US by authorizing the continuation of commercial, cultural, and other relations between the people of the United States and the people of Taiwan and for other purposes.' The Act states that 'the US will make available to Taiwan such defence articles and services in such quantity as may be necessary to enable Taiwan to maintain a sufficient self-defence capability.' It is unlike NATO's Article 5 in that the Act does not guarantee mutual defence.

This friction between the US and China was seen as posturing. The war in Ukraine did not impact US military power in the Far East. By this stage in the world order's 'Great Game', the myth of Russian invincibility had been destroyed in 2022. Moscow had fallen in status from a world superpower to a largely unsuccessful pariah nation, its President unable to leave the country due to international arrest warrants and dependent on Chinese foreign aid. The failure to deliver a victory by the time of the forum was a major loss of face for Putin. While the Kremlin prepared to renew the Battle of Avdiivka, the US provided Kyiv with ATACMs.

Between 20 and 31 October 2023, the Russians again attempted to capture Avdiivka. During the fighting of 12–17 October 2023 they managed to gain a foothold in the tree lines a couple of kilometres from the Terrikon Slag Heap. At the closest point, the Russian positions were approximately 2 km (1.2 miles) in front of it. The 8th CAA redoubled its efforts to capture the Slag Heap, and the Ukrainians knew that they were unable to sustain the current defence, and that it was only a matter of time before they would be forced to withdraw. However, the fields were mined, and the Russians had decided to advance on a secondary road that curved in front of the Ukrainian positions and the coke plant.

The Russian assault columns were observed on their approach to the Slag Heap. When they passed through the lines of their forward troops, the assault columns had to traverse over 1,000 metres of open fields, while receiving flanking direct fire, before they could assault the Heap. The Russians massed a reinforced brigade and divided its battalions into assault columns. As the lead battalion broke cover its assault companies were subjected to withering direct and indirect fire. Dozens of tanks and IFVs were knocked out and died amongst the wreckage of earlier attacks. As each assault company was shredded, it was succeeded by follow-on waves. The defending 110th Territorial Brigade, holding the Heap and the industrial complex, burned through ammunition like water. Their drone operators expended crates of grenades in the target-rich environment. Ukrainian artillery fired three times more shells attempting to stop the assault than on a normal day. Russian aircraft supported the attack, hammering the Heap, and in the confusion, the attackers shot down one of their own Mi-8 gunships.

The assaults continued for four days. Among those killed was a Russian battalion commander. Like the charge of the Light Brigade at Balaclava during the Crimean War (1853–56), assaulting armoured vehicles reached the Heap on or about 24 October 2023 and stormed the Ukrainian positions. Like the Light Brigade, a Ukrainian counter-attack retook the positions by killing the surviving attackers. The Russians managed to raise the flag of the 114th Motorized Rifle Brigade atop the mound, but a Ukrainian drone knocked it down. Once the firing positions on the Heap were destroyed, both sides fell back to covered, concealed positions. The hill remained contested but was listed on Deep State and other maps as 'captured'. The Russian bombardment rendered the Heap undefendable. Inability to reoccupy the Heap by either side resulted in losing the tactical advantage of its higher elevation over the surrounding flat terrain. However, ultimately, considering the swarm of drones available for reconnaissance, fire control and strikes, the tactical advantage of occupying the Heap was minor, especially when compared to the lives lost to gain and maintain possession of it.

As the battle for the Terrikon Slag Heap played out in the north, the Ukrainians conducted a spoiling attack on the flank of the southern prong of the Russian pincer. The attack hit the flank of the penetration towards the small settlement of Pisky and the Donetsk airport, the objective of which was to cut the Ukrainian supply line. The 87th Rifle Regiment and the Piatnashka Battalion ('the Vikings'), consisting of Abkhazians, checked the attack, while Storm 'Z' battalions exhausted themselves in the defence of road junctions at the small urban settlement at Sieverne, 4 km (2.49 miles) south-east of the key road junctions in the village of Orlivka. When exhausted they were replaced with the 1st Separate Motorized Rifle (Slovainsk) Brigade and Somalia Battalion. The latter Battalion was not from Somalia, but was given its name because, when formed, they were dressed so shabbily that they were jokingly referred to as Somali pirates. They reportedly later earned the name because they fought so aggressively.[22]

The fighting between October 2023 and February 2024 was inconclusive. Due to the heavy losses of armoured vehicles and other equipment, Russia reverted to Soviet-style tactics – tanks and IFVs supporting advancing infantry platoons or small companies but eventually a wide encirclement – and the 8th CAA focused on turning the battle into a close quarters infantry city fight. The objective was to cut Avdiivka in half and isolate the 2,000–3,000 defenders in the south-eastern part of the city. The Russians also increased the combat strength of the attacking force to a total of 40,000–50,000 combat troops.

In September 2023, the US Congress failed to pass a new Ukrainian aid bill which started a months-long stalemate on funding aid to both Ukraine and Israel. The supply of US artillery and HIMARS rockets dwindled as members of Congress debated. As the months dragged on, Ukrainian ammunition stockpiles shrank dangerously, while the Russians received a million artillery shells from the North Koreans. The Ukrainians realized that their 8,000 defenders could not continue to hold out without artillery support. To make matters worse, the winter weather was reducing the effectiveness of the Ukrainian drones. With these facts in mind, Ukrainian Commander in Chief General Zaluzhnyi ordered the construction of a defensive line on the high ground 10 km (6.2 miles) west of Avdiivka.

While the Ukrainians were slowly being driven back into the city on the east and west flanks, the Russians discovered a way into the Ukrainian rear on the southern perimeter. Surprisingly, Russian soldiers were spotted on the streets of Avdiivka, behind both southern defence lines, in early February 2024. This report confused the local commander, because the Russians had not breached the defences. Suddenly, Ukrainians at the Tsarska Okhota restaurant were attacked from behind. The outnumbered Russian squad was killed, but more squads appeared, and fighting continued throughout the city. Russian reconnaissance troops had discovered a 2,000-metre-long water pipe that serviced a water filtration station and passed under all the Ukrainian fortifications in the southern part of the city. Before the Ukrainians discovered the mystery pipe, an assault group of 150 soldiers breached the Ukrainian rear. The Ukrainians quickly organized a reaction force and pinned the Russians down in a residential area around the exit from the pipe. The Russians could be supplied through the pipe but could not expand their position.[23]

The Russian assault infantry established positions in the residential area south-east of the Terrikon Slag Heap. On 11 February, heavy fighting ensued as the Russians pushed east, threatening to cut the main Ukrainian supply road into the south-eastern part of Avdiivka. The only obstacles between the Russians and the supply road 1,000 metres away were an industrial zone and a truck station.

As the Ukrainian artillery suffered from a shortage of shells due to the delays and debates in the US Congress, repeated counter-attacks could not generate sufficient combat power to dislodge the Russians. Taking advantage of the situation, and supported by swarms of kamikaze drones, the Russian were able to creep forward and established fire control over the supply road and the defenders with mortars, automatic grenade launches and machine guns. The Ukrainians switched to an alternative supply road but the 'writing was on the wall'.[24] Russian aircraft lobbed over fifty glide bombs a day, destroying the factory holding their infantry at bay.

Ukraine's gunline was so short of ammunition that it could not adequately support the defenders as the Russians crept closer and closer to their defensive positions. Rain turned the fields into mud. Severe weather interfered with the drones, and they were unable to make up for the lack of artillery support. The elite 3rd Assault Brigade was taken out of the strategic reserve and committed to counter-attacking the Russians. The gap between the attacking Russians on the right and on the left was only 3 km (1.86 miles) wide when the 3rd Assault Brigade counter-attacked. They held the gap for three days while 2,000–3,000 Ukrainian troops fought their way out of the pocket.

Avdiivka was officially captured on 17 February 2024. Newly appointed General Syrsky, Chief of Staff, did not repeat his mistake as commander on the ground at the Battle of Bakhmut. To preserve lives and essential equipment he ordered the defenders to pull out and withdraw from Avdiivka before they were overrun. The Ukrainians conducted a fighting withdrawal to their new defensive zone, 10 km (6.2 miles) west of the city on an elevated ridge, protected by a small river. Once in open country, the pursuing Russian

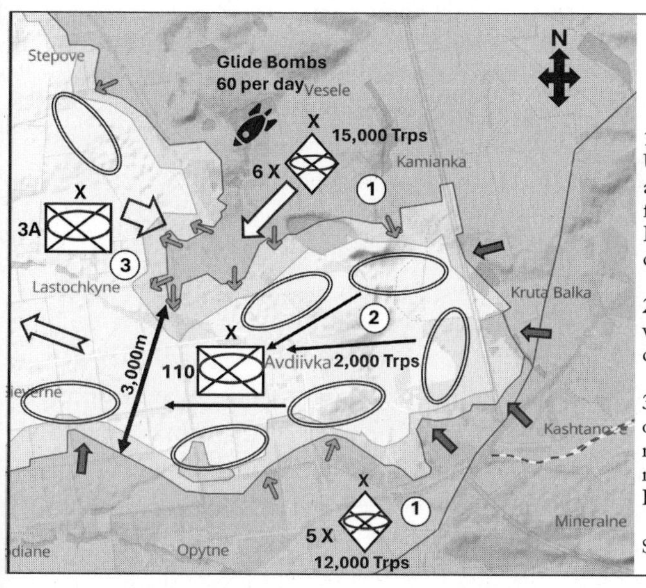

Map 33 Ukrainian Fighting Withdrawal, 10–17 February 2024

1 Russian plan was to encircle the 110th Ukrainian BDE in Avdiivka. Six BDEs attacked on a 1,000m front. Attacks by five BDEs intended to pin the 110th BDE in the city. Glide bombs reduced defences as Russians infantry assaulted.

2 Short of artillery ammo and with bad weather grounding drones, Ukrainians defended from the ruins with small arms.

3 Russians slowly gained ground. Ukraine ordered 110th BDE to conduct a fighting retreat from the city. To keep an escape route open, 3rd Assault BDE attacked Russian penetration.

Source: Deep State Map. © OpenStreetMap

columns suffered heavy casualties as the Ukrainian rearguard hammered them with direct fire and drones.

Upon hearing the news, President Biden declared that the Ukrainian military withdrawal from Avdiivka was clearly the direct result of Congress failing to act promptly and provide the additional funds to support Kyiv's war effort. Adrienne Watson, spokeswoman for the National Security Council, stated, 'The Ukrainians continued to fight bravely, but they are running low on supplies.'[25] President Biden called President Zelensky and acknowledged that Ukrainians were forced to withdraw from Avdiivka because of Congress' inability to approve further aid for Ukraine to fend off Russia's invasion.[26]

Putin scored both a military and a political victory for his home audience in time for his sham election on 15 March 2024. The Russian generals were under tremendous pressure from Putin to capture Avdiivka before the election, and they did so. It was Ivan who paid the price. The seven Russian assault brigades that captured Avdiivka suffered extremely heavy casualties. Russian soldiers tearfully posted videos of their dead comrades. In one video a soldier indicated that only 30 per cent of his battalion remained fit for duty. In their haste to capture the city and please their master, Russians launched glide bombs which hit soldiers on both sides. Ukrainians claimed that after the battle all seven Russian brigades were reduced to 30 per cent strength. They estimated that the Russians suffered 50,000 casualties, and lost 360 tanks, 750 armoured vehicles, 200 artillery systems and five fighter-bombers. The city was reduced to rubble at tremendous human cost – another pyrrhic victory for Putin.[27]

Chapter 31

The Myth of Russian 'Human Wave' or 'Meatgrinder' Tactics

The Russians' successful battle plan for the Battle of Avdiivka was based upon Soviet Cold War tactics but adapted to the new realities of the twenty-first century. The media reported Russian manoeuvres as 'meatgrinder' tactics because of the extremely high number of casualties and the repeated failures of attack formations. Cold War veterans would recognize these tactics as a Soviet 'deliberate attack'. Historians would recall that these were similar to the successful Soviet infantry tactics employed during the Second World War, costly in manpower, but successful in capturing objectives.

In a Soviet-style deliberate attack, heavy artillery and aerial bombardment first suppresses the defenders. A division-size ground manoeuvre force would then execute a high-speed transit from assembly areas in the Soviet rear, in column, and conduct a forward passage of lines. The manoeuvre force deployed into assault formations and struck the defenders on a 2,000–4,000-metre strike zone.

When deploying into combat formation, the tanks normally assumed the lead or took up a support by fire position 3–5km (1.86– 3.11 miles) from the enemy positions, while IFV and APCs rushed forward to dismount their infantry 100 metres from the enemy position.[1] According to Soviet and Russian doctrine, a company's seventy dismounted infantry should advance behind their IFVs and APCs. The realities of the twenty-first century battlefield resulted in the IFVs and APCs delivering the infantry to an attack position (the last covered and concealed position before the enemy defences), then racing to the rear, or to a support by fire position, before they could be destroyed. The deadly battlefield conditions during the Russian-Ukrainian War modified these tactics.

Early in the invasion, when the regiments and brigades had their full complement of vehicles, reinforced motorized rifle units moved forward in pre-battle battalion columns, with companies and platoons also in column. As the battalion column approached the line of contact it deployed into company columns, with combat engineer and tanks leading the IFV and APCs. Terrain, obstacles and the increased drone threat necessitated a 500-metre interval between company columns. It initially appeared that the companies could not

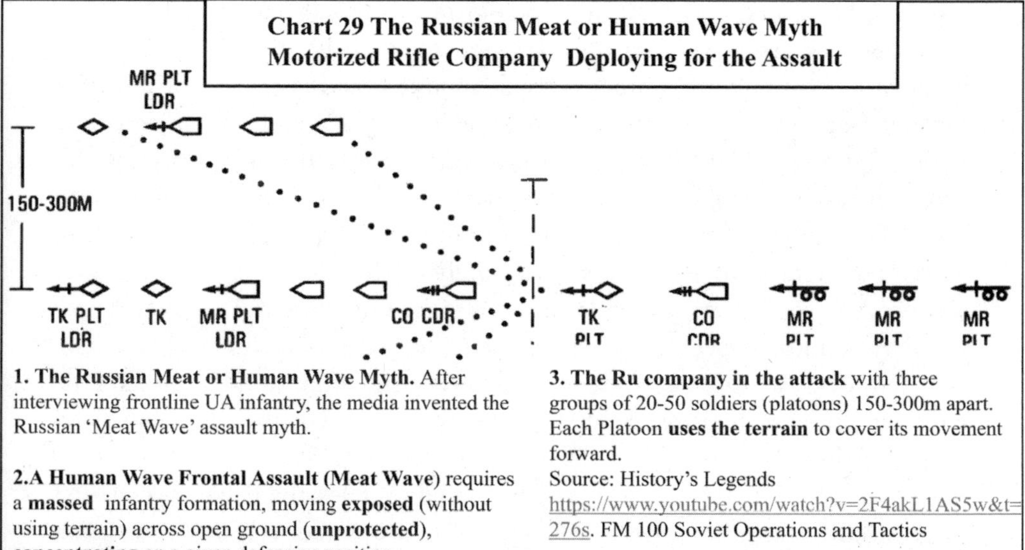

support each other, and the media reported these assaults as 'piecemeal' attacks. This was an illusion. The space between the company columns allowed them to manoeuvre through and around obstacles. When the companies were fully deployed in assault formations, they occupied a front of 500–800 metres, with each platoon occupying a frontage of 100–200 metres. The fully deployed battalion assault formation would be 1,000–1,600 metres wide.

Each motorized rifle battalion contained two echelons of companies, and each regiment and brigade had two echelons of battalions. The battalions and brigades often maintained a reserve and frequently had a Storm-Z battalion attached to the lead regiment or brigade. The Ukrainian defenders had to defeat four to six infantry company assault waves or more daily. Often tanks, IFVs and APCs were interspersed in the assault waves. Depending on the company's strength, each wave consisted of between twenty and seventy soldiers. Soviet doctrine required ADA to be deployed along the route of advance. The doctrine envisioned that the motorized rifle division's ADA battalion would secure the route. This precautionary measure was not employed during the Battle of Avdiivka. Instead, the Russians seemed to rely on jammers to disable Ukrainian ADA.

During the Battle of Avdiivka, reconnaissance and kamikaze drones detected the attack as the lead battalion advance guard left the assembly area. Over each 10 km (6 miles) of the forward edge of the battle area (FEBA) there were between twenty-five and fifty drones from both sides conducting reconnaissance or hunter-killer missions.[2] One major EW system was positioned behind each 10 km (6 miles) of front. Normally larger jammers, like the Shipovnik-Aros, were set up 7 km (4.3 miles) behind the frontline. The Shipovnik-Aros tactical jammer is truck-mounted and is capable of not only jamming an enemy's drones, but also of geo-locating the drone operator for artillery targeting. The downside of using the jammer is that once it is activated, EW direction finding antennas can locate it and pass the location onto Ukrainian artillery. Employment of jamming operations and synchronizing those operations with drone crews was rarely de-conflicted. By 2024, smaller jammers were issued at platoon level and attached to armoured vehicles; larger jammers were deployed to the region, but they were often neutralized. The large jammers radiated a considerable electronic signature, and Ukrainian EW direction finder systems were able to locate them and pass their location on to artillery firing batteries.

In response to their heavy losses of armoured vehicles, the Russians changed their assault waves into pure infantry, with armoured vehicles remaining in support by fire positions. The tactics were similar to those employed by Wagner.[3] Platoon-size groups of fifteen to twenty men would infiltrate and attack positions along the line of contact. Ukrainian drones would direct artillery on these small groups, and any survivors would join their comrades in the attack positions. After Ivans massed in the attack position reached sufficient strength, the assault would commence. Artillery and glide bomb strikes would suppress the Ukrainians as the echeloned assault crossed the line of contact. Once the bombardment lifted, the first wave of disposable infantry entered close combat (assault rifles and hand grenades) with the Ukrainian positions. Close fire support was provided by mortars and automatic grenade launchers, not armoured vehicles.

These assaults were often repelled with heavy casualties, but over days they slowly gained ground. The job of defeating this type of attack fell on the Ukrainian infantry. While these attacks were often reported as 'meatgrinder' or 'human wave', they were conducted with traditional Russian tactics, taking advantage of cover and concealment as they closed with Ukrainian positions. The attacks might very well have appeared to be a 'meatgrinder' or 'human wave' to the defenders as they faced overwhelming numbers of men and equipment that just kept coming and ended with enormous numbers of dead men and destroyed equipment. In reality, the attacks were organized in accordance with doctrine and incorrectly described by Ukrainian propaganda.

Chapter 32

Have Missile, Will Travel

Between summer 2023 and winter 2024, Russia developed glide bombing as an effective tool to suppress and destroy Ukrainian static defences. Releasing bombs from the deep rear, up to 70 km (43 miles) from the line of contact, Russian jet fighter bombers were safe from Ukrainian AD. As the year progressed, Russian glide bomb tactics evolved. During fighting in the Donbas and at the Battles of Avdiivka and Krynky the Russian Air Force flew over sixty sorties per day. The Ukrainians did not have any way to counter the Russian tactics. As 2023 came to a close, Russian pilots became more aggressive in supporting ground operations, edging ever closer to the frontline before lobbing their glide bombs. Reports revealing the US Congress' delay in approving aid and supplying the Ukrainians with weapons and ammunition probably increased Russian pilots' confidence.

On 23 December 2023, the besieged Marines at Krynky received help, seemingly from heaven. Three Sukhoi Su-34 jet bombers began their run 50 km (31 miles) from Krynky and were surprisingly blown from the sky. The Sukhoi Su-34 was a Soviet-era twin-engine supersonic medium-range jet fighter armed with a 30mm gun. It made its first appearance in 1990 in the Soviet Union's Air Force, remained in service with the Russian Air Force and was deployed to Ukraine. Ukrainians reported that at the beginning of the Special Operation Russia was thought to have ten of these aircraft. A few days after the first three Sukhoi Su-34s were amazingly shot from the sky, two more were mysteriously downed.[1] This was not the first time a roving battery was employed.

On 13 May 2023, the Ukrainians moved elements of a battery near the Russian border and ambushed five different jet fighter-bombers. The battery commander admitted in reports that when Russian pilots know there was a Patriot Missile Battery system in the area, they become very cautious and would often decide not to fly there. These incidents were soon forgotten.

The surge in the number of sorties and the increased aggressiveness of the Russian pilots provided Ukrainian air defenders with a unique opportunity. It required them to relocate their limited strategic air defence assets from defending cities and strategic targets to protecting the frontlines. A roving missile battery changed the battlefield dynamics.

Ukraine did not disclose how it destroyed the Russian glide bombers, but based upon the ranges involved, military commentators eventually unravelled the puzzle. Surprisingly, the Ukrainians moved a roving Patriot Missile Battery System up from behind their rear to the frontlines.

The Patriot Missile Battery System is a portable surface-to-air weapon manufactured by US defence contractor Raytheon. The system is designed to target and shoot down enemy missiles, usually deployed to a permanent location to defend a critical target, rather than rove around the battlefield on the back of a truck. Once the Ukrainians loaded the system on to a vehicle and deployed from the rear area into the frontlines, the launchers and trucks became very vulnerable when moving between launch sites, even though they were camouflaged as commercial trucks.[2] A single battery without missiles costs $400 million, while each missile costs $4 million. Each battery is equipped with five to eight launchers and carries two reloads per launcher. Each launcher holds four ready-to-launch missiles. The battery has three sections: missile launchers, C2 vehicles and radars.[3] The phase-array radar system has a range of 150 km (93 miles) and the capacity to track a hundred targets simultaneously, while providing missile guidance data for up to nine missiles. The standard missiles have a range of 70 km (43 miles) with a maximum altitude of 24 km (78,000 ft).[4]

The Patriot Missile System, supplied by the US, has been employed in the following wars: the Gulf War, Iraq War, Israeli Gaza conflict, the Syrian Civil War, the Yemeni Civil War, the border conflict between Saudi Arabia and Yemen, the Ukrainian-Russian War and most recently the Israeli-Hamas War.

The actual number of batteries and launchers sent to Ukraine is classified. Generally, unclassified sources identified the aid provided to Ukraine as a 'Patriot system' rather than a 'Patriot Missile Battery system'. Without all three sections (launcher, radar and C2) of a battery, the 'Patriot system' would not work. The low number of missiles per launcher means the battery could not engage more than nine targets at any one time.[5]

Since its development and deployment, the Patriot Battery Missile System has successfully shot down incoming missiles, most notably in 2003 in the Iraq War. Despite being exported worldwide the System was not recorded as successfully autonomously shooting down an enemy aircraft in combat until the Israeli Defence Force deployed it to destroy two Hamas UAVs during Operation Protective Eagle in 2014; and probably for the first time during the same year, the Israeli Defence Force reported that the system shot down a manned Syrian air force Sukhoi Su-24 that breached Israeli air space over the Golan Heights.

Employing a $4 million missile to shoot down a $250 Iranian drone was not cost effective unless the asset being targeted was of critical importance. Hunting AWACS-type aircraft and jet fighter bombers, however, was a good return on the investment. The Russian A-50 was a Russian reconnaissance plane that served as an Airborne Warning and Control System. It was equipped with a large radar and carried a crew of fifteen. Able to scan several hundred kilometres, it was equivalent to the US AWACS and was often referred to as an 'AWACS'.

The surprise engagements on 23 December 2023 destroyed three Su-34 jet bombers in flight, before they could release their load of eighteen bombs. One crewman survived. The Russians theorized that the Patriot crew had placed a short-range location radar near the frontline. As it detected the jets, the Patriot Missile Battery's extremely powerful long-range multi-phase radar was activated, and the jets were trapped. More surprises awaited the Russians.

The primary target for the Ukrainians became the eight A-50 AWACS command and control aircraft. The A-50 cost $350 million to build and the production line had been closed for decades. Before the Special Operation, Russia had seven of them operational. These irreplaceable aircraft normally operated over the Sea of Azov. The A-50s were able to provide C2 for Russian air operations in southern and eastern Ukraine. This operating area was beyond the range of Ukraine's frontline AD batteries, but a Ukrainian drone targeted and hit one of the jets on the ground.

On 14 January 2024, a Russian A-50 AWACS was destroyed over the Sea of Azov. During the same engagement an IL-22 airborne controlled plane was damaged but made it back to base. On 23 February 2023, a second A-50 AWACS was shot down over the Sea of Azov. The loss of the second aircraft resulted in the Russian Air Force leadership reconsidering the deployment area for the very limited number of these aircraft.[6]

AWACS aircraft were not the only targets of the roving missile battery. On 24 January a II-76 transport was shot down. Jet fighters and bombers were routinely targeted and shot down. Between 17 and 29 February 2024, Russia lost twelve aircraft, including another A-50. A total of three Su-35 and eight Su-34 Russian fighter bombers were lost. The Su-34 was the Russian workhorse for glide bomb delivery.

During Putin's Special Operation, 'necessity had become the mother of innovation'. The roving Patriot Missile Battery System was not ultimately decisive, but it provided a relatively low-cost, effective means to reduce a threat. The loss of the Russian jet bombers was a morale boost to the Ukrainian Marines and soldiers being daily bombarded on the ground. It was also a

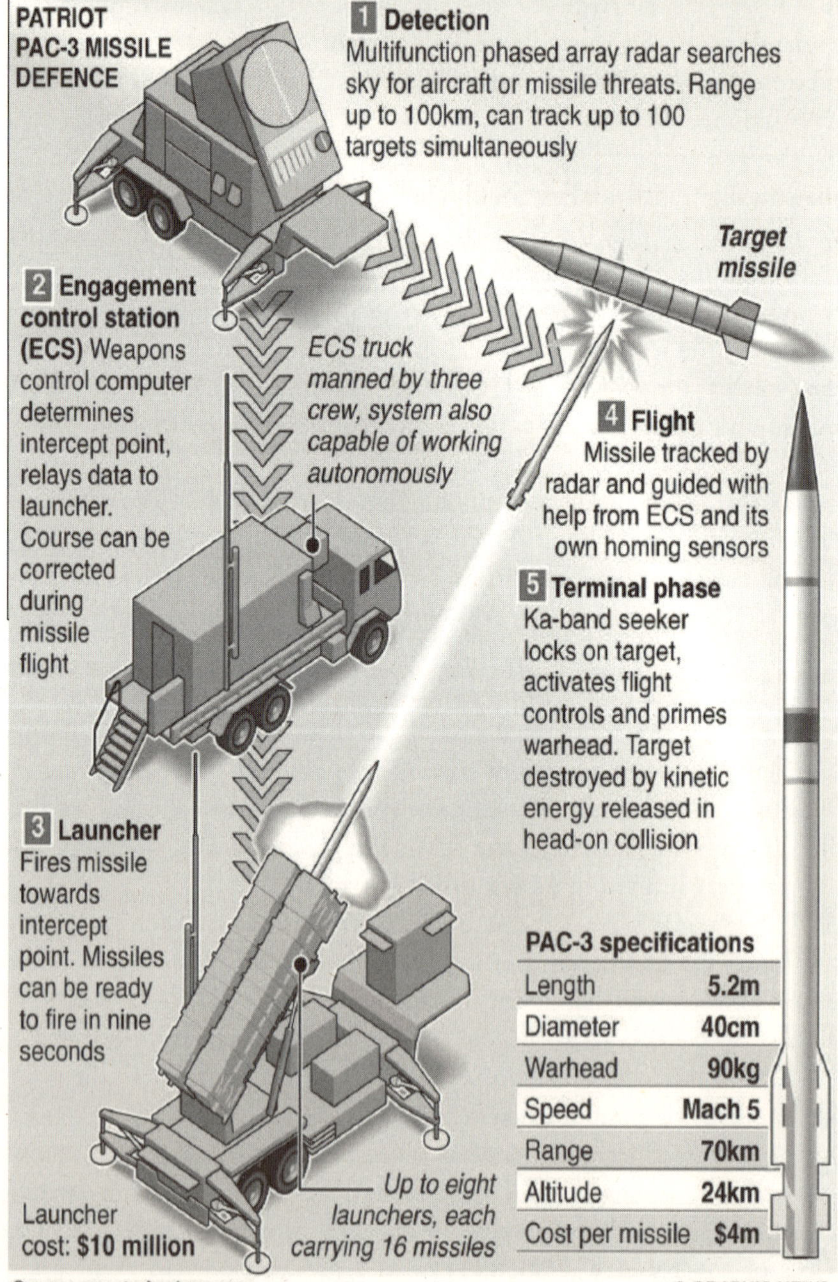
U.S. to supply Patriot missiles to Ukraine
The Patriot missile system would be the most effective long-range defence sent to Ukraine, able to intercept ballistic and cruise missiles – but not cost effective for bringing down cheap Iranian drones
PATRIOT PAC-3 MISSILE DEFENCE
1 Detection
Multifunction phased array radar searches sky for aircraft or missile threats. Range up to 100km, can track up to 100 targets simultaneously
Target missile
2 Engagement control station (ECS) Weapons control computer determines intercept point, relays data to launcher. Course can be corrected during missile flight
ECS truck manned by three crew, system also capable of working autonomously
4 Flight
Missile tracked by radar and guided with help from ECS and its own homing sensors
5 Terminal phase
Ka-band seeker locks on target, activates flight controls and primes warhead. Target destroyed by kinetic energy released in head-on collision
3 Launcher
Fires missile towards intercept point. Missiles can be ready to fire in nine seconds
PAC-3 specifications
Length 5.2m
Diameter 40cm
Warhead 90kg
Speed Mach 5
Range 70km
Altitude 24km
Cost per missile $4m
Launcher cost: $10 million
Up to eight launchers, each carrying 16 missiles
Source: army-technology.com
© GRAPHIC NEWS

message to NATO that Ukraine desperately needed additional strategic and operational air defence systems. This requirement did not go unnoticed.

Pro-Ukrainian Think Tanks urged Ukraine's international partners in 2023 and 2024 to provide Ukraine with a range of air defence systems to counter the Russian aircraft, missile and drone threats. Instead of second line systems and older missiles, NATO encouraged sending the most advanced top of the line systems and missiles. In addition, NATO identified a need to increase the number of missiles delivered to counter the mass of North Korean weapons being shipped to Russia.[7] Before the US Congressional deadlock, the US top priority was to meet Ukraine's air defence requirements, and the US encouraged NATO members to do the same.[8]

Chapter 33

Conclusion

With the fall of Avdiivka, heavy fighting continued along the front, but the tempo of operations was slowed by the winter weather and resulting muddy conditions, rendering the movement of heavy armoured vehicles difficult if not impossible. While men fought and died to take inches of territory, the world focused on the deadlock in the US Congress. In January 2023, the fickle US Congress and public opinion were almost unanimous in their support for Ukraine. During the debates and negotiations to pass the US Fiscal Year (FY) 2024 Budget during a particularly contentious presidential election year, support for Ukraine bcame factionalized. The Republican-controlled Congress linked its domestic agenda of protecting the country's southern border to military aid to Ukraine and Israel. The Biden administration had never clearly stated a strategy to end the Russia-Ukraine War. Biden also failed to publicly identify Ukraine's survival as a vital US interest. The administration and the press failed to adequately convey the message that by ensuring Ukraine's survival, the world could suppress Putin's aggression and the threat he posed to the world order. Support for Ukraine became a political issue during 2023. Biden's political rivals stepped in and took advantage of this gap in his foreign policy. Crafty, self-interested politicians focused the attention of the electorate on domestic issues at the expense of support for Ukraine's liberty. As political debates and negotiations continued, front-running Republican presidential candidates took the position that Ukraine's survival was not in the US's strategic interest. Some candidates even went so far as to suggest that Europe's security was not in the US's strategic interest. The threat to Ukraine's survival and a potential Europe dominated by a resurgent Russia were, they argued, secondary to the crisis of illegal immigration into the US. The reality of the situation was that even the US lacked the funds and resources to address both issues, especially after Israel was attacked by Hamas in October 2023. Israel was a close US ally and had been for decades. Putin's plan to draw off US aid from Ukraine to support Israel seemed to have worked, although support for Israel also became factionalized after photos of its retribution in Gaza were published.

The deadlock in Congress and the negative influence of the leading Republican candidate for president, who opposed aid for Ukraine, cowed

Republican Senators and Congressmen. The former president's potential return to power and the threat to let Russia have Ukraine (and Europe too) energized European leaders with determination to fill projected shortfalls in Ukrainian support.[1] But this would take time. If Ukraine were defeated, it would strike a psychological blow at democratic countries and embolden Putin's drive for further expansion. NATO estimated that it would only take five years for the Russian military to recover from the Special Operation. However, with a large standing army at the end of the war, Putin could try to overrun the Suwalki Gap or invade Baltic NATO members.

US instability caused NATO members to become concerned about a potential Russian attack on its Baltic members, Estonia, Latvia and Lithuania, all three of which border the Baltic Sea just south of St Petersburg. Russian possession of the Baltic states (which, like Ukraine, had been part of the Soviet Union) would greatly increase Putin's buffer zone against democratic influence and would grant him unfettered access through the Baltic, much to the chagrin of Finland and Sweden. The deadlock in Congress encouraged France to step forward with the proposal of sending NATO troops to defend Ukraine's border with Belarus. As a nuclear state and member of NATO and the EU (and with a still fresh memory of being occupied by Nazi Germany), France had an obvious vested interest in the defence of the Baltic states. With the US locked in an internal political struggle, political experts predicted that Russia could launch a pre-emptive ground attack to cut the Suwalki Gap as early as the winter of 2025, after the results of the US presidential election were known. The Baltic states are small, and their armies had provided Ukraine with their Soviet heavy equipment, leaving them primarily with light infantry formations. The Baltic NATO member states have large minorities of Russian speakers, seen as possibly supportive of a potential Russian invasion, much like the separatists in the Donbas region in south-east Ukraine in 2014. NATO had become so concerned with this possibility, prior to Putin's Special Operation, that it stationed small battle groups in each Baltic country. The battle groups were the size of reinforced battalions or understrength regiments and would be at least a speed bump to hinder a potential Russian invasion.

By cutting the Suwalki Gap, Putin could hold the Baltic states hostage and pressure NATO to cut ties with Ukraine. At the end of 2023, 1,000 former Wagnerites were in Belarus training its army. Russian military units were also stationed in Belarus. Russian industry was on a war footing, and Russian available manpower would have supplied Putin with sufficient force to commit one or two CAAs to taking the Suwalki Gap. A future surprise attack across the Gap was entirety possible.

Due to the destabilizing impact of certain statements by a US Presidential candidate, the EU began studying a 'EU Strategic Autonomy' Defence Plan. The plan envisioned Europe pooling resources to defend itself in the absence of US support. Europe has a small nuclear umbrella, since together the UK and France have the nuclear capability to cover all of Europe with the 500 nuclear warheads in their inventory. This number would be more than sufficient to destroy Russia's key cities.[2] This EU's Defence Proposal helps explain why French President Emmanuel Macron proposed sending NATO troops to secure Ukraine's border with Belarus. A secure Ukraine had become part of its plan to defend Europe against Russian aggression. Eventual NATO membership for Ukraine was also part of the plan to deter Russian aggression. The proposal was rejected by most NATO members for fear of escalating the current war, but the fact that Europe proposed plans to defend itself in the absence of US support demonstrated the undercurrent of concern about being abandoned by the US in the future.[3]

By the end of 2023 Russia fully transitioned its economy to a war footing, while the US and NATO countries continued to ramp up production of military equipment and ammunition, but were not expected to be at full capacity until the end of 2024.

Russia's need for additional sources of military supplies resulted in Putin's seeking assistance from the 'Axis of Evil'.[4] This descriptive term is similar to the words used by US President Ronald Reagan in his 'Evil Empire' speech, delivered to the National Association of Evangelicals on 8 March 1983 at the

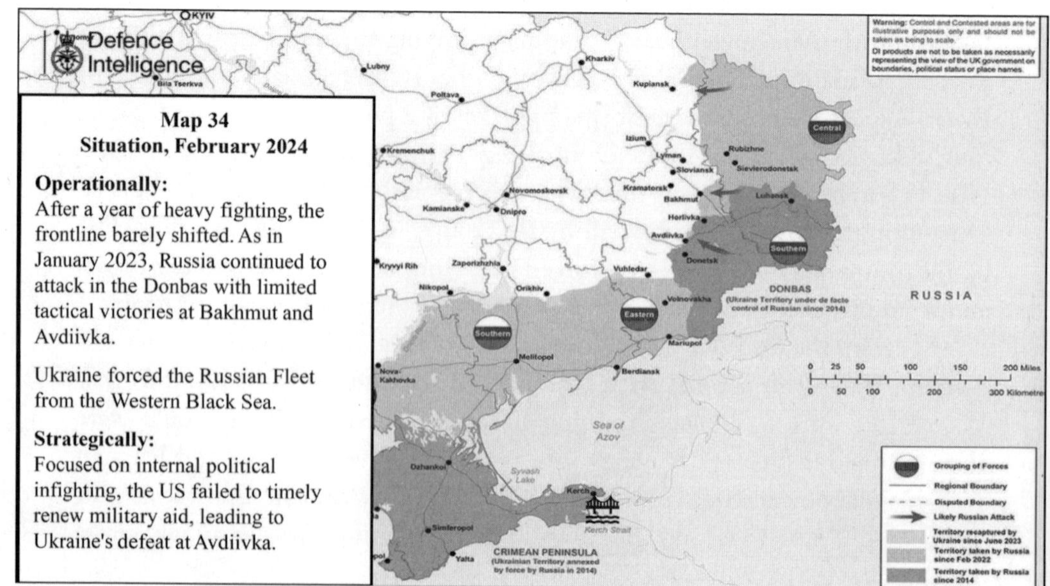

Map 34
Situation, February 2024

Operationally:
After a year of heavy fighting, the frontline barely shifted. As in January 2023, Russia continued to attack in the Donbas with limited tactical victories at Bakhmut and Avdiivka.

Ukraine forced the Russian Fleet from the Western Black Sea.

Strategically:
Focused on internal political infighting, the US failed to timely renew military aid, leading to Ukraine's defeat at Avdiivka.

height of the Cold War and the Soviet-Afghan War. Reagan referred to the Soviet Union as an 'Evil Empire' and as the focus of evil in the modern world. The phrase was later modified to the 'Axis of Evil', first used by US President George W. Bush in his State of the Union Address on 2 January 2002. Bush referred to Iran, Iraq, and North Korea as an 'Axis of Evil' for sponsoring terrorism around the globe and for seeking weapons of mass destruction.

The end of 2023 has seen the development of a new 'Axis of Evil'. The members of the axis are Russia, Iran, North Korea, Hamas and Hezbollah, with China watching from the sidelines. The new Axis of Evil pressured US treaty obligations with Taiwan, South Korea, Japan, Australia, Israel and throughout the Middle East and Asia.

To end the war, Russia must be convinced that its prospects for military success will get worse not better over time. Regardless of how this war ends, it is obvious that with the development and deployment of drone technology on the battlefield the shape of combat in all domains has changed forever; we have witnessed the dawn of drone warfare.[5]

Epilogue

By the end of the second year of Putin's Special Operation Russian war crimes had become so common that they no longer made headlines, but they have not been forgotten, nor forgiven. On 17 March 2023 the International Criminal Court filed an indictment against Putin and Maria Lovova-Belova, the Russian Commissioner for Children's Rights. Lovova-Belova was the motherly face of the Russian abduction of Ukrainian children who surprisingly admitted on the record that more than 700,000 Ukrainian children had been kidnapped from Ukraine and shipped to Russia. She claimed most of the children who came to Russia were accompanied by parents and/or relatives.[1] The official line attempted to justify the kidnapping as a measure to keep the children safe from war. The action violated multiple UN human rights conventions.

The kidnapping of children as a national policy is virtually unknown in Western Europe and the US,[2] but taking the children of ethnic minorities has been a Russian tradition since Tsarist days. Before 1856, it was Russian policy to conscript ethnic minority children at the age of twelve into the Russian army. For six years they were educated at military boarding schools, and upon 'graduation' they began a 25-year term of service in the Imperial Russian Army.[3]

In a resurrection of the Tsarist policy, thousands of Ukrainian children, from infants to 17-year-olds, have been recorded as 'deported' from occupied Ukraine into Russia. The Ukrainian government estimates that between 160,000 and 700,000 children have been abducted. Oddly, while ignoring accusations of other war crimes, Putin, Lovova-Belova and the Russian government have admitted to these abductions, claiming they were 'humanitarian evacuations' to move the children to safety away from the battle front. But instead of giving them safety, the Russians changed the children's citizenship and placed them for adoption in Russian families. Allegations of violence and sexual abuse by their new families was widespread according to Daria Herasymchuk, Ukrainian Children's Rights Commissioner. She alleged the abduction policy constituted acts of genocide.[4]

The Russians used various tactics in implementing the abductions. The occupation authority rounded up children from Ukrainian orphanages, while others from hospitals and schools were 'relocated to safety' inside Russia. The Russian government arranged photo-ops of dazed children being given teddy bears, gift baskets and hugs from strangers. Once in Russia, the children were swiftly put up for adoption. Russian families paid between $300 and $2,000 per child to the state.

Some Ukrainian parents were convinced by their Russian occupiers to send their children to summer camps to avoid the horrors of war. A minimum of 6,000 children were shifted to summer (re-education) camps, some of which were as far away as the Pacific coast. The children never returned, but were held hostage, to ensure their parents' good behaviour. The purpose of the camps was to 're-educate' and erase the children's Ukrainian identity, turning them into good patriotic Russians. Inessa Vertash's 15-year-old son attended a camp at the urging of his Ukrainian headmaster. When she received a rare phone call from her son, he reported that the first two weeks were fine, but he was then transferred to another camp which was more like a prison. Attendees were beaten for not singing the Russian national anthem, some were sexuality abused, all were psychologically manipulated and told that their parents had abandoned them. The kidnappings were part of Putin's attempt to ethnically cleanse the Ukrainian identity, while replenishing the Russian population, which has a very low birth rate.[5] Humanitarian organizations debated the exact number of children transported out of Ukraine into Russia, and the crime was condemned internationally.[6]

Fewer than 500 children have been returned. The Russians have made it difficult for families to reclaim their children. Due to Russian and Ukrainian laws, fathers were banned from travelling to Russia to recover their children, but some mothers who have recovered their children have had to travel to Russia through third countries.

The large-scale movement of children to forty re-education camps violated the 1948 Genocide Convention. There was little prospect of Putin, or Lovova-Belova, being prosecuted for their crimes against children. There was little prospect for bringing any Russian official to trial for participating in the mass deportation or for operating the re-education camps.

During the second year of Putin's Special Operation, Russia continued the indiscriminate bombing of civilian infrastructure, residential areas, hospitals, and schools. Summary executions of civilians, rape, unlawful detention and torture continued unabated in occupied Ukraine. Pro-Ukrainian activists and journalists were especially singled out for abuse by the Russian invaders. The Russian authorities systematically coerced civilian Ukrainians, especially Russian-speakers, to apply for Russian citizenship. Russian occupation authorities pursued a programme of erasing Ukrainian culture and language.

Mass deportations and resettlement was a Tsarist and Soviet practice. It has been estimated that over a million Ukrainians were evacuated or 'detoured' into Russia during the first year of the war. It has not been determined how far this mass migration of people was voluntary or forced.

Ukrainian prosecutors have opened more than 80,000 war crimes cases since the invasion. Only thirty have led to convictions, and all those found guilty were simple soldiers. Estonia, Latvia, Lithuania, Poland, Romania and Slovakia have joined with Ukraine to form a Joint Investigation Team. The EU has created a database for evidence of war crimes. Forensic experts from the US, UK and EU have been periodically sent to assist. Putin and his cronies remain far out of reach of any prosecution, but international indictment and arrest warrants will limit their ability to travel, even after the war.

Notes

Introduction

1. John S Harrel, *The Russian Invasion of Ukraine February–December 2022, Destroying the Myth of Russian Invincibility,* (Yorkshire and Philadelphia: Pen & Sword, 2023).
2. My comrades and I are in our late 60s and early 70s. Too old for frontline service.
3. Staff 'Invasion of Ukraine, D+15, Sitrep, (#200)', *The Five Coat Consulting Group*, https://www.thefivecoatconsultinggroup.com/the-coronavirus-crisis/ukraine-context-d15

Chapter 1

1. Shivan Neftchi, 'Why Ukraine joining NATO would crush Russian Power', *Caspian Report*, 24 September 2023. https://www.youtube.com/watch?v=c1u495VZ4hM
2. CS Staff, 'Understanding the Russian Mindset', *Caspian Report*, 2014 (YouTube Video)
3. Ibid.
4. Diane Donovan, 'Gophers Defeat Russian Invasion', *Grit*, 12 January 2013
5. Fort Ross Interpretive Association, 'Fort Ross Cultural History', https://web.archive.org/web/20100528110415/http://www.fortrossinterpretive.org/FortRossCulturalHistory.php
6. Mary Alice Cook, 'Manifest Opportunity: The Alaska Purchases as a Bridge Between United States Expansion and Imperialism,' *Alaska History*, Vol 26, No.1, Spring 2011, 1–10. http://alaskahistoricalsociety.org/wp-content/uploads/2016/12/Article-on-purchase.pdf
7. CS Staff, 'Understanding the Russian Mindset', *Caspian Report*, 2014 (YouTube Video).
8. Shivan Neftchi, 'Why Ukraine joining NATO would crush Russian power', *Caspian Report*, 24 September 2023. https://www.youtube.com/watch?v=c1u495VZ4hM
9. CS Staff, 'Understanding the Russian Mindset', *Caspian Report*, 2014 (YouTube Video).
10. Ibid.
11. Neftchi, 'Ukraine joining NATO'.
12. Arsalan Bilal, 'Hybrid Warfare – New Threats, Complexity, and "Trust" as the Antidote', *NATO Review*, 30 November 2021 https://www.nato.int/docu/review/articles/2021/11/30/hybrid-warfare-new-threats-complexity-and-trust-as-the-antidote/index.html
13. Harrel (2023).
14. Peter Dickinson, 'Russia's Invasion of Ukraine was never about NATO', *Atlantic Council*, 18 July 2023. https://www.atlanticcouncil.org/blogs/ukrainealert/russias-invasion-of-ukraine-was-never-about-nato/
15. Madeleine Nations, 'Kaliningrad: Russia's Best-Kept Strategic Secret', *Glimpse from the Globe*, 14 October 2020.

https://www.glimpsefromtheglobe.com/regions/russia-and-central-asia/kaliningrad-russias-best-kept-strategic-secret/

Chapter 2

1. Harrel (2023).
2. Sources vary. It was reported that between 200,000 and 300,000 men were mobilized by the Russian Ministry of Defence during the second half of 2022.
3. Jessie Yeung, 'March 25, 2022 Russian-Ukraine news', *CNN*, 26 March 2022. https://www.cnn.com/europe/live-news/ukraine-russia-putin-news-03-25-22/h_c643e508161e80821fff786bbbfbc16e
4. Rob Lee, Michael Kofman, 'How the Battle for the Donbas Shaped Ukraine's Success', *The Foreign Policy Research Institute*, 23 December 2022.
5. Kofman, 'How the Battle for the Donbas Shaped Ukraine's Success'.
6. Ibid.
7. Ibid.
8. Ibid.
9. Filipp Lebedey & Felix Light, 'Wagner's Convicts tell of horrors of Ukraine war and loyalty to their leaders', *Reuters*, 16 March 2023, White House Press Briefing, 17 February 2023, by Press Secretary Karine Jean-Pierre and NSC Coordinator for Strategic Communications John Kirby. Assumes a ratio of 1 KIA for 3 total casualties.
10. Samuel Charap & Miranda Piebe, 'Avoiding a Long War, US Policy and the Trajectory of the Russian-Ukraine Conflict', *Rand Corporation*, Santa Monica, CA 2023. https://www.rand.org/pubs/perspectives/PEA2510-1.html, David Von Drehle, 'Opinion, Why a negotiated peace with Putin is the safest way out', *The Washington Post,* 30 September 2022, AP Staff, 'Chinese President Xi calls for Ukraine peace talks,' AP, 6 April 2023
11. Josh Christenson, 'Critical threat to US interests: poll', *AP*, 15 March 2023.
12. Miles J Herszenhorn, 'Where do 2024 candidates stand on Ukraine? Trump, DeSantis, Ramaswamy, JFK Jr. want less US Involvement', *USA Today*, 11 July 2023.
13. Richard Iron CMG OBE, 'A Strategic Analysis of the Russo-Ukraine War', *Australian Institute of International Affairs.*' https://www.youtube.com/watch?v=pqZFi0jNZdI
14. CIA, Foreign Threats to the 2020 US Federal Elections, March 10, 2021. https://www.dni.gov/files/ODNI/documents/assessments/ICA-declass-16MAR21.pdf
15. Ibid.
16. Justice News, 'Russian National Charged in Conspiracy to Act as an Agent of the Russian Federation Within the United States', *US Department of Justice*, 16 July 2018. https://www.justice.gov/opa/pr/russian-national-charged-conspiracy-act-agent-russian-federation-within-united-states.
17. Justice News,'Russian National Sentenced to 18 Months in Prison for Conspiring to Act as an Agent of the Russian Federation Within the United States', *US Department of Justice*, 26 April 2019. https://www.justice.gov/usao-dc/pr/russian-national-sentenced-18-months-prison-conspiring-act-agent-russian-federation.
18. Mikhail Japaridze, 'Butina says being in US prison was "torture",' *TASS*, 3 November 2019. https://tass.com/society/1086781.
19. FBI Most Wanted, Russian Interference in the 2016 US Elections, July 13, 2018. https://www.fbi.gov/wanted/cyber/russian-interference-in-2016-u-s-elections

Chapter 3

1. Staff, 'Invasion of Ukraine, D+15, Sitrep, (#200)', *The Five Coat Consulting Group*, https://www.thefivecoatconsultinggroup.com/the-coronavirus-crisis/ukraine-

context-d15. The Member-States of the Eurasian Economic Union are the Republic of Armenia, the Republic of Belarus, the Republic of Kazakhstan, the Kyrgyz Republic and the Russian Federation.http://www.eaeunion.org/?lang=en#about.

2. Mick Ryan, 'An update on Ukraine's Campaigns, Measuring Success in Ukraine's Multidomain Efforts', *Futura Doctrina*, 23 August 2023. https://mickryan.substack.com/p/an-update-on-ukraines-campaigns?utm_source=substack&utm_medium=email
3. Mick Ryan, 'The Ukrainian Offensives are coming (part 2)', *Futura Doctrina*, 29 April, 2023. https://mickryan.substack.com/p/the-ukrainian-offensives-are-coming-34c
4. Andrew S. Harvey, PhD, 'The Levels of War as Levels of Analysis', *Military Review*, November-December 2021, 75–81. https://www.armyupress.army.mil/Portals/7/military-review/Archives/English/ND-21/Harvey-Levels-of-War-1.pdf
5. Scott Nicholas Romaniuck, 'Military Strategy and the Three Levels of Warfare', *Defence Report,* 2017. https://defencereport.com/wp-content/uploads/2017/11/Romaniuk-Military-Strategy-and-the-Three-Levels-of-Warfare.pdf
6. *FM 3-0 Operations,* (Department of the US Army: Washington D.C., October 2022), 1–10 to 1–13. https://irp.fas.org/doddir/army/fm3-0.pdf
7. The domains were simplified and modified from the US Army's definitions.
8. Mick Ryan, 'The Ukrainian Offensives are coming (part 1)', *Futura Doctrina*, 29 April, 2023. https://mickryan.substack.com/p/the-ukrainian-offensives-are-coming
9. Illia Ponomarenko, 'Russia's new guided bombs pose increasing serious threat to Ukraine', *The Kyiv Independent*, 10 April 2023.
10. ADP 3-0 Operations, US Army Publication, 31 July 2019, 4–3 to 4–6.
11. Ibid., 3–12.

Chapter 4

1. Colonel Markus Reisner (Austrian Army), 'War for Ukraine – First Conclusions from 2022 and New Challenges 2023', *Osterreichs Bundesheer*, 13 January 2023. https://www.youtube.com/watch?v=54daqNraMxE
2. The Telegraph, 'Wagner's mutiny is the tip of the iceberg of Russia's rebellion', *Defense in Depth*, 1 July 2023. https://www.youtube.com/watch?v=ofe_w2dVENM
3. William Spaniel, 'Why Putin Fragmented His Military: A Tale of Internal Rivalries and Intentional Mismanagement', 13 May 2023. https://www.youtube.com/watch?v=KxxywKsDBHA
4. Ibid.
5. Dr. Lester W. Grau & Charles K Bartles, *The Russian Way of War, Force Structure, Tactics, and Modernization of the Russian Ground Forces*, (USA Foreign Military Studies: 2016), 28–30. https://www.armyupress.army.mil/portals/7/hot%20spots/documents/russia/2017-07-the-russian-way-of-war-grau-bartles.pdf
6. Riley Bailey, Grace Mappes, Niclole Wolkov, Angelica Evans and Mason Clark, Russian Offensive Campaign Assessment, 1 September 2023, *Critical Threats*, 1 September 2023. https://www.criticalthreats.org/analysis/russian-offensive-campaign-assessment-september-1-2023-64f27969624c3,
DE Staff, 'What is the 25th Army (25CAA), and How Can the Battles for Bakhmut Hinder Russia, *Defense Express*, 21 September 2023

https://en.defence-ua.com/news/what_is_this_25th_army_25_caa_and_how_can_the_battles_for_bakhmut_hinder_russia_from_deploying_a_new_airborne_division-8006.html

7. Ibid.
8. Dr. Lester W. Grau & Charles K Bartles, *The Russian Way of War, Force Structure, Tactics, and Modernization of the Russian Ground Forces*, (USA Foreign Military Studies: 2016), 30–1.
   https://www.armyupress.army.mil/portals/7/hot%20spots/documents/russia/2017-07-the-russian-way-of-war-grau-bartles.pdf
9. Sebastien Roblin, 'Ukraine Is Forming Three New Army Corps – Should Bring Back Divisions Too?', *1945*, 31 March 2023.
   https://www.19fortyfive.com/2023/03/ukraine-is-forming-three-new-army-corps-should-it-bring-back-divisions-too/
10. Mason Clark & Karolina Hird, *Russian Regular Ground Forces Order of Battle*, (ISW: October 2023), 10–13.
    https://www.understandingwar.org/sites/default/files/October%2012%2C%20 2023%20Russian%20Orbat_Final.pdf
11. Harrel (2023), 49–56.
12. Estimates varied as to the actual Russian and Ukrainian casualties during the first year of the war.
13. Olga Ivshina, 'Counting the dead: confirmed Russian losses in Ukraine now exceed 20,000',*BBC,* 21 April 2023.
    https://bbcrussian.substack.com/p/ukraine-war-russia-casualties-by-april-2023, Jan. Kallberg,'The War in Ukraine – Russian officer losses reach strategic impact', *Cyberdefense*, 5 January 2023.
    https://cyberdefense.com/flipside-of-russian-war-of-attrition-strategy-officer-losses/
14. Alia Shoaib, 'How the Russian elite was decimated in Ukraine – 29 generals and commanders who were killed in action', *Insider*, 31 December 2022.
    https://www.businessinsider.com/ukraine-russian-officer-elite-decimated-9-who-were-killed-in-combat-2022-3
15. Bill Entart, 'Reflections from the River, Charm School',*Buzzsprout*, 25 July 2020.
    https://www.buzzsprout.com/1089968/4644785
16. The author attended Charm School in 2006. I was promoted to brigadier in 2005 while commanding NATO Multinational Brigade East Kosovo Force and US Army Forces Commander Kosovo, Northern Macedon and Albania. Most attendees were promotable colonels.
17. Jan Kallberg, 'The War in Ukraine-Russian – officer losses reach strategic impact', *cyberdefense*, 5 January 2023. https://cyberdefense.com/flipside-of-russian-war-of-attrition-strategy-officer-losses/
18. Olga Ivshina, 'Lost battalions: calculating Russia's casualties in six months of war in Ukraine', *BBC,* 22 August 2022.
    https://bbcrussian.substack.com/p/lost-battalions-calculating-russias
19. Mark Urban, 'The Cost of the Ukraine war for one Russian regiment', *BBC,* 6 April 2023.https://www.bbc.com/news/world-europe-65179074
20. Ukrainian Ministry of Defence, January 2023.
    https://www.ukrinform.net/rubric-ato/3647444-ukraines-armed-forces-destroy-another-530-russian-invaders-23-tanks-1-aircraft.html
21. Simon Ellery, Tucker Reals, 'Russia pulls mothballed Cold War-era tanks out of deep storage as Ukraine War grinds on', *CBS*, April 18, 2023.
    https://www.cbsnews.com/news/russia-ukraine-war-cold-war-era-soviet-tanks-t54-t55-out-of-storage/

22. David Axe, 'The Russians Are Pulling 70-Year Old T-55 Tanks Out of Storage', *Forbes*, March 22, 2023. https://www.forbes.com/sites/davidaxe/2023/03/22/the-russians-are-pulling-70-year-old-t-55-tanks-out-of-storage/?sh=deb26a465939, Ryan Pickrell, 'Russia is pulling old, obsolete tanks out of storage because it is losing so many in its war with Ukraine, intelligence suggests', *Business Inside*, 27 May 2022. https://www.businessinsider.com/russia-old-tanks-storage-ukraine-war-losses-intel-2022-5
23. Jan Kallberg,'Leader Loss: Russian Junior Officer Casualties', *CEPA*, 23 December 2022. https://cepa.org/article/leader-loss-russian-junior-officer-casualties-in-ukraine/

Chapter 5

1. Michael Bohnert, 'The Uncounted Losses to Russia's Air Force', *Rand*, 14 August 2023. https://www.rand.org/pubs/commentary/2023/08/the-uncounted-losses-to-russias-air-force.html
2. Jack Watling & Nick Reynolds, 'Meatgrinder: Russian Tactics in the Second Year of its Invasion of Ukraine', *RUSI*, 19 May 2023, 22–5.
3. David Axe, 'After Losing An Eighth of Their Helicopters, Russian Attack Regiments Are Switching Their Tactics', *Forbes*, 14 February 2023 https://www.forbes.com/sites/davidaxe/2023/02/14/after-losing-an-eighth-of-their-helicopters-russian-attack-regiments-are-switching-up-their-tactics/?sh=135208ed4de9
4. Oryx, Documenting Russian and Ukrainian Destroyed Equipment. https://www.oryxspioenkop.com/2022/02/attack-on-europe-documenting-equipment.html
5. Jack Watling & Nick Reynolds, 'Meatgrinder: Russian Tactics in the Second Year of its Invasion of Ukraine', *RUSI*, 19 May 2023. 20–2.
6. 'Russian Black Sea Fleet's Warships Return to Naval Bases after massive drills', *TASS*, 31 January 2022. https://tass.com/defense/1395149
7. https://warontherocks.com/2022/04/the-russo-ukrainian-war-at-sea-retrospect-and-prospect/
8. https://www.navalnews.com/naval-news/2022/01/analysis-russia-to-dominate-the-black-sea-in-case-of-ukraine-conflict/
9. Milan Vego, 'Littoral Warfare', *On Naval War College Review*, Vol. 68: No. 2 Article 4, 1–67, 2–5.
10. Staff Russian Air Force (2023), *WDMMA*, 17 December 2022. https://military-history.fandom.com/wiki/Russian_Navy#The_Black_Sea_Fleet
11. Harrel (2023) 86–90
12. Raul Pedrozo, 'The Russian-Ukrainian Conflict: Blocking Access to the Black Sea', *Naval War College Review*, No. 4, Article 5, Autumn 2022
13. Benoit Gorgemans, 'The Caspian Flotilla: Russia's Offensive Reinvention', *US Naval Institute*, August 2021. https://www.usni.org/magazines/proceedings/2021/august/caspian-flotilla-russias-offensive-reinvention
14. H.I. Sutton, 'Russian Navy's Way Around Turkey Closing The Bosphorus to Its Warships, Literally', *Covert Shores*, May 2022 http://www.hisutton.com/Russian-Navys-Secret-Internal-Waterways.html
15. https://www.navylookout.com/assessing-russias-first-major-naval-loss-of-the-war-in-ukraine/
16. https://babel.ua/en/news/80586-the-ukrainian-armed-forces-launched-more-than-10-accurate-strikes-on-the-snake-island-the-russian-pantsir-c1-system-was-destroyed?utm_source=page&utm_medium=read_more

17. David Brennan, 'Russian Black Sea Fleet's Losses Since Ukraine War Began: Full List', *Newsweek*, 8 November 2023.
https://www.newsweek.com/russian-black-sea-fleet-losses-ukraine-war-full-list-warships-sunk-damaged-1841828
18. Note, Ukrainian anti-aircraft missiles have damaged smaller Russian vessels. The anti-aircraft missiles locked on to the vessels' heat signatures.
19. https://www.navalnews.com/naval-news/2022/05/russian-navys-5-significant-losses-in-the-ukraine-war-so-far/

Chapter 6

1. Artem Starosiek, 'Catalog of Kremlin's PMCs: 37 Private Military Companies of the Russian Federation', *Kyiv Post*, 29 April 2023
https://www.kyivpost.com/post/16412
2. Sebastien Roblin, 'Captured Manual Reveals Russia's New "Assault Detachment" Doctrine', *Forbes*, 28 February 2023.
https://www.forbes.com/sites/sebastienroblin/2023/02/28/captured-manual-reveals-russias-new-assault-detachment-doctrine/?sh=5c2417df4bb3
3. Ibid.
4. Volodymyr Decenko, 'Evolution of Russian Tactics in Ukraine From Failed Blitzkrieg to Assault Infantry', *Euromaidan Press*, January 31, 2023.
https://euromaidanpress.com/2023/01/31/evolution-of-russian-tactics-in-ukraine-from-failed-blitzkrieg-to-assault-infantry/
5. Alex Horton, 'Russia's commando units gutted by Ukraine War, US leak shows', *The Washington Post*, 14 April 2023
https://www.washingtonpost.com/national-security/2023/04/14/leaked-documents-russian-spetsnaz/

Chapter 7

1. Harrel (2023), 5–8.
2. William Shotyk &Andrii Oleksandrenko, Opinion: Russia Will Get Bogged Down in the Pripet Marshes if it Attacks from Belarus, *Kyiv Post*, 26 February 2023.
https://www.kyivpost.com/opinion/13527
3. ML Tactical Map, *Miltaryland,* 25 September 2023.
https://militaryland.net/maps/operational-sectors/
4. ML Tactical Map, *Miltaryland*, 25 September 2023.
https://militaryland.net/maps/operational-sectors/
5. HL,'Ukraine Should Cancel its Counter-offensive', *History Legends*, June 2023.
https://www.youtube.com/watch?v=v4tzu9FzuxY
6. ML UA Marine Corps, *Miltaryland,* 25 September 2023
https://militaryland.net/maps/operational-sectors/
7. David Axe, 'Ukraine Has Four Marine Brigades. It has Packed All of Them into a 10 Mile Sector', *Forbes*, 4 August 2023.
https://www.forbes.com/sites/davidaxe/2023/08/04/ukraine-has-four-marine-brigades-it-has-packed-all-four-into-a-10-mile-sector/?sh=798814222068
8. ML Tactical Map, *Miltaryland*, 25 September 2023
https://militaryland.net/maps/operational-sectors/
9. ML Ukrainian Units, *Miltaryland*, 25 September 2023
https://militaryland.net/maps/operational-sectors/
10. What Russia Faces: Primer to Ukraine's Ground Forces https://www.youtube.com/watch?v=U26SNwTH8p0&t=301s

11. Mykola Bielieskov, 'Ukraine's Territorial Defence Forces: The War So Far and Future Prospects', *RUSI,* 11 May 2023. https://rusi.org/explore-our-research/publications/commentary/ukraines-territorial-defence-forces-war-so-far-and-future-prospects, Stefan Korshak, 'Ukraine Combat Unit Replaced, Circumstances Currently, Murky', *KP*, 19 September 2023. https://www.kyivpost.com/post/21777
12. Mykola Bielieskov, 'Ukraine's Territorial Defence Forces: The War So Far and Future Prospects', *RUSI,* 11 May 2023. https://rusi.org/explore-our-research/publications/commentary/ukraines-territorial-defence-forces-war-so-far-and-future-prospects
13. ML Staff, Offensive Guard, *Military Land*, 12 September 2023. https://militaryland.net/ukraine/offensive-guard/#google_vignette
14. Author's interview with General (retd) David Baldwin, March 2023.
15. ML Staff, Offensive Guard, *Militaryland*, 12 September 2023. https://militaryland.net/ukraine/offensive-guard/#google_vignette
16. Jim Garamone, 'Ukraine-California Ties Show Worth of National Guard Program', *US DoD*, 18 March 2022. https://www.defense.gov/News/News-Stories/Article/Article/2971781/ukraine-california-ties-show-worth-of-national-guard-program/
17. F Staff, 'Offensive Guard: what are the brigades, requirements, training, salaries and benefits?' *Fakty*, 4 February 2023. https://fakty.com.ua/en/ukraine/suspilstvo/20230204-gvardiya-nastupu-yaki-ye-brygady-vymogy-pidgotovka-zarplata-ta-pilgy/
18. UP Staff, 'Eight Offensive Guard brigades being prepared, new ones will be formed-Ukraine's Interior', *Ukrainska Pravda*, 2 May 2023 https://www.pravda.com.ua/eng/news/2023/05/2/7400270/
19. Daryna Kolomiiets, 'Ukraine's New Offensive Guard: What it is and how to Join', *Kyiv Post*, 13 February 2023. https://www.kyivpost.com/post/12095
20. Sergiy Karazy, 'Ukraine trains 40,000 storm brigade troops for counter-offenive', *Reuters*, 21 April 2023. https://www.reuters.com/world/europe/ukraine-trains-40000-storm-brigade-troops-counter-offensive-2023-04-05/
21. UI Staff, 'Ukraine's Offensive Guard soldiers already fighting on the southern and eastern fronts-National Guard', *Ukrinform*, 12 September 2023. https://www.ukrinform.net/rubric-ato/3743930-ukraines-offensive-guard-soldiers-already-fighting-on-southern-and-eastern-fronts-national-guard.html
22. ML Staff, 'Ukrainian Order of Battle', *Militaryland*, 22 September 2023. https://militaryland.net/ukraine/armed-forces/
23. 3rd Assault Brigade Home Page. https://ab3.army/en/about-the-brigade/
24. Sergio Miller, 'Portrait of Ukrainian Advances', *WavellRoom,* 15 August 2023. https://wavellroom.com/2023/08/15/portrait-of-a-ukrainian-offensive-oshbr/
25. ML Staff, 'Ukrainian Order of Battle, 3rd Assault Brigade', *Militaryland*, 22 September 2023. https://militaryland.net/ukraine/armed-forces/3rd-assault-brigade/
26. Ibid.
27. Helene Cooper and Erics Schmitt, 'Ukraine's Western-Trained Brigades Begin to Enter the Fight', *New York Times,* 23 June 2023. https://www.nytimes.com/2023/06/23/us/politics/ukraine-military-training.html

28. DW Staff, 'Ukraine, updates: US trains Ukrainian forces in Germany', *DW*, January 16, 2023.
https://www.dw.com/en/ukraine-updates-us-trains-ukrainian-forces-in-germany/a-64401767, C. Todd Lopez, DOD Official Says Training for Ukrainians Is Ongoing. *US Department of Defence*, 30 March 2023.
https://www.defense.gov/News/News-Stories/Article/Article/3347269/dod-official-says-training-for-ukrainians-is-ongoing/
29. Eric Schmitt, 'Ukrainian Soldiers Speed through US Training on Patriot Missiles', *New York Times*, 21 March 2023.
https://www.nytimes.com/2023/03/21/world/europe/ukrainian-soldiers-us-patriot-missiles.html
30. EN Staff, 'US to begin training Ukrainian troops on Abrams tanks', *Euronews,* 21 April 2023.
https://www.euronews.com/2023/04/21/us-to-begin-training-ukrainian-troops-on-abrams-tanks
31. Jonathan Holmes & Lee Madan, 'King Charles watches Ukrainian troops training in Wiltshire', *BBC,* 20 February 2023.
https://www.bbc.com/news/uk-england-wiltshire-64709125#
32. Chris Fletcher, Senior Army Medical Officer, UK Armed Forces on track to train 37,000 Ukrainian recruits, *UK Army*, 26 June 2023.
https://www.army.mod.uk/news-and-events/news/2023/06/uk-armed-forces-on-track-to-train-37-000-ukrainian-recruits/
33. Spc. Danielle Rayon, 'Oklahoma's Task Force Tomahawk prepares for Africa deployment', *Oklahoma National Guard*, 12 April 2023
https://ok.ng.mil/News/Article/3359892/oklahomas-task-force-tomahawk-prepares-for-africa-deployment/. In 2004 when my brigade deployed for peacekeeping in Kosovo, it was required to complete four months of post-mobilization training before a 12-month deployment.
34. UK Govt Press Release: British Commandos train hundreds of Ukrainian Marines in UK programme. 11 August 2023.
https://www.gov.uk/government/news/british-commandos-train-hundreds-of-ukrainian-marines-in-uk-programme
35. Arthur Rehi, Ukrainians just annihilated an entire Wagner unit in Bakhmut/ Moscow Parade failure/Ukraine Update, 10 May 10 2023, https://www.youtube.com/watch?v=1yYmUrInOWs,
Interfax-Ukraine Staff, 'Eight new UAV strike companies formed in Ukraine,' Interfax-Ukraine, May 8, 2023. https://en.interfax.com.ua/news/general/908782.html
36. Vikram Mittal, 'The Challenges of Counter-Drone Technology as Seen in Recent Conflicts', *Forbes*, 18 October 2023.
https://www.forbes.com/sites/vikrammittal/2023/10/18/the-challenges-of-counter-drone-technology-as-seen-in-recent-conflicts/?sh=70ab5b507013

Chapter 8

1. BBC Staff, 'Russia-supporting Wagner Group mercenary numbers soar', *BBC,* 22 December 2022.
2. Reuters staff, 'White House: Wagner Group has suffered over 30,000 casulties in Ukraine', *Reuters*, 17 February 2023.
3. Mac Santora, Josh Holder, Marc Hernandez & Andrew E, Kramer, 'The War's Violent Next Stage', *New York Times*, 10 February 10, 2023.
4. Ibid.
5. UAF, Russia's Losses as of January 15, 2023, *Kyiv Independent*, 15 January 2023.

6. Dr Nathan Provost, 'Continuous Contact: Grant's Tactical Doctrine in the Eastern Theater', *Emerging Civil War,* 4 August 2020. Archer Jones, *Civil War Command & Control, The Process of Victory and Defeat* (The Free Press: New York, 1992), 181–218. Herman Hattaway &Archer Jones, *How The North Won, A Military History of the Civil War* (University of Illinois Press: Chicago, 1991), 629–77.
7. James Feigenbaum, James Lee, & Filippo Mezzanotti, 'Capital Destruction and Economic Growth: The Effects of Sherman's March, 1850–1920', *American Economic Journal: Applied Economics,* Vol. 14, No. 4, October 2022, 301–42.
8. John S Harrel, *Soviet Cavalry Operations during the Second World War & The Genesis of the Operational Manoeuvre Group,* (Yorkshire-Philadelphia: Pen & Sword, 2019), 26–33, 56–61.
9. Henri Bidou, 'Battle of Verdun, World War I [1916]', *Britannica,* 14 February 2023.
10. Deep State Ukraine Map. https://deepstatemap.live/en#12/47.9199/37.5952
11. Riley Bailey, 'Russian Offensive Campaign Assessment, April 1, 2023', *Critical Threat,* 1 April 2023 https://www.criticalthreats.org/analysis/russian-offensive-campaign-assessment-april-1-2023
12. FM 100-2-1 The Soviet Army Operations and Tactics, 13-1– 13-4. Grau & Bartles, *The Russian Way of War,* 41, 49, 100, 141, 232
13. FM 3-50 *Smoke Operations, US Army,* 4 December 2023.
14. Modern Tank Cloaking Devices? How Thermal Smoke Works, King Military, 2021. https://www.youtube.com/watch?v=des5fjUnbIc
15. In the time the author was a California Army National Guard tank commander, and a battalion commander, for M60A3 Patton and M1IP Abram tanks, he never fired the vehicles' smoke grenades.
16. Harrel (2023), 188.
17. The quote has slight variations depending on the source.
18. Marc Santora, 'The War's Violent Next Stage', *New York Times,* 10 February 2023. https://www.nytimes.com/interactive/2023/02/10/world/europe/russia-ukraine-offensives-maps.html, New York Post, Snejana Farberov, 'Russia massing 500k soldiers and 1.8k tanks to launch offensive in 10 days,' *New York Post,* 9 February 2023, https://nypost.com/2023/02/09/russia-readying-500k-troops-to-launch-assault-in-10-days/

Chapter 9

1. This estimate is the author's and is based upon US, UA and RU sources and Oryx vehicles' loss data for the period. It reflects the estimate of combat troops and does not reflect the number of logistics soldiers.
2. Deep State Map Ukraine January–June 2023. https://deepstatemap.live/en#10/49.0990/37.5719
3. Chris York, 'Kupyansk: Why This Small Ukrainian Town is now the Focus of Brutal Russian Assaults', *Kyiv Post,* 11 August 2023. https://www.kyivpost.com/post/20455
4. Ibid.
5. Yevlash, 'Russian 25th Army fully staff, takes up positions near Kreminna, *Ukrinform,* 1 October 2023. https://www.ukrinform.net/rubric-ato/3768429-russian-25th-army-fully-staffed-take-up-positions-near-kreminna-yevlash.html
6. Harrel (2023), 138.
7. 13 March: Ukrainians Ruin a Major Russian Attack/War In Ukraine Explained, https://www.youtube.com/watch?v=oOoozPh4Nhk&t=160s

8. 18 Feb 23: Not Very Clever. Russians Lose Thousands for 2 Useless Villages/War in Ukraine Explained.
   https://www.youtube.com/watch?v=zQ9FrbYuZPQ
9. 13 March: Ukrainians Ruin A Major Russian Attack/War In Ukraine Explained, https://www.youtube.com/watch?v=oOoozPh4Nhk&t=160s
10. VOA Staff, Ukraine Evacuating Kupyansk Residents amid Russian Attacks, *VOA*, 12 March 2023
    https://www.voanews.com/a/zelenskyy-russia-has-become-a-synonym-for-terror-/7001158.html
11. Oliver Slow, 'Ukraine war: Kyiv orders partial evacuation of liberated city', *BBC*, 3 March 2023.
    https://www.bbc.com/news/world-europe-64833750, Chris York, 'Kupyansk: Why This Small Ukrainian Town is now the Focus of Brutal Russian Assaults', *Kyiv Post*, 11 August 2023.
    https://www.kyivpost.com/post/20455
12. Matthew Mpoke, 'Ukraine Steps up Calls for Evacuation of Kupyansk under Relentless Russian Shelling', *New York Times*,
    https://www.nytimes.com/2023/03/12/world/europe/ukraine-russia-Kupyansk.html
13. 13 March: Ukrainians Ruin A Major Russian Attack/War In Ukraine Explained, https://www.youtube.com/watch?v=oOoozPh4Nhk&t=160s
14. Ibid.

Chapter 10

1. Deep State, 27 May 2023. https://deepstatemap.live/en#11/48.0609/37.8040
2. 15 Mar: Danger! Russians Breach Ukrainian Defense near Avdiivka/War in Ukraine Explained.
   https://www.youtube.com/watch?v=ONtxtkvWpdU
3. DE Staff, 'Ukraine's White Wolves Destroy 72 Units of Russian Military Equipment with Attack Drones' (Video), *Defense Express*, 28 October 2023
   https://en.defence-ua.com/news/ukraines_white_wolves_destroy_72_units_of_russian_military_equipment_with_attack_drones_video-8384.html
4. Brendan Cole, 'Ukraine Says SBU "White Wolves" Destroyed 10 Russian Tanks in One Night,' *Newsweek*, 18 March 2023.
   https://www.newsweek.com/ukraine-sbu-white-wolves-destroyed-10-russian-tanks-one-night-1788708
5. Francis Farrell, 'Surviving Avdiivka: Russia intensifies assault on city deemed a second Bakhmut', *Kyiv Independent*, 23 March 2023
6. 20 Mar: Russian Tanks Attack Avdiivka From All Sides/War in Ukraine Explained.
   https://www.youtube.com/watch?v=vV039qbcC8k&t=57s
7. Jeffery Gettleman & Finbarr O'Reilly, 'Every Block is Another Battle: Ukraine's Latest Eastern Stand', *The New York Times*, 13 June 2023.
   https://www.nytimes.com/2023/06/13/world/europe/ukraine-russia-war-marinka.html

Chapter 11

1. Chris Cappy, 'Vuhledar, Why Russian Repeats the Same Mistakes, Task and Purpose', March 2023.
   https://www.youtube.com/watch?v=hwuRpYw7vyw&t=1063s
2. Luke Mogelson, 'Trapped in the Trenches in Ukraine', *New Yorker*, 2–9 January 2023 issue.

3. David Axe, 'Russian Marines are Getting Killed and Wounded by the Hundreds in Ukraine', *Forbes*, 7 November 2022.
4. Deep State Map of Vuhedar, 26 January 2023. https://deepstatemap.live/en#14/47.7667/37.2585
5. Kastus Kalinouski was a Belarusian and Polish national hero who led the January 1863 uprising against the Russian Empire in Belarus and Lithuania.
6. The Kastus Kalinouski Regiment website, 14 January 2023 https://bel.army/en/about/
7. David Axe, 'The Ukrainian Army's Jaeger Brigades are Middleweight Forces Troops', *Forbes*, December 2022. https://www.forbes.com/sites/davidaxe/2022/12/26/the-ukrainian-armys-jaeger-brigades-are-its-middleweight-forest-fighters/?sh=5a15f3bb6c5b
8. ML Staff, '55th Artillery Brigade', *Militaryland,* 14 January 2024 https://militaryland.net/ukraine/armed-forces/55th-artillery-brigade/
9. Deep State Map, January–February 2023. https://deepstatemap.live/en#10/47.7523/37.3940
10. Charles K. Bartles, 'The Russian Naval Infantry: Increasing Amphibious Warfare Capabilities', *US Army TRADOC*, 2018.
11. Alex Horton, 'Russia's commando units gutted by Ukraine war, US leak shows', *Washington Post*, 14 April 2023 https://www.washingtonpost.com/national-security/2023/04/14/leaked-documents-russian-spetsnaz/
12. Mark Galeotti, 'Spetsnaz: Operational Intelligence, Political Warfare, and Battlefield Role', *Marshall Center*, February 2020. http://www.marshallcenter.org/en/publications/security-insights/spetsnaz-operational-intelligence-political-warfare-and-battlefield-role-0
13. Deep State Map of Vuhedar, 26 January 2023. https://deepstatemap.live/en#14/47.7667/37.2585
14. Paul Mutter, 'The Chechen Wars Cast a Long Shadow', *Medium*, 28 March 2015 https://medium.com/war-is-boring/the-chechen-wars-cast-a-long-shadow-7b058a84ffe9, 'Led by an Armored Bulldozer, Shia Militia Fought to Restore their Credibility', *Medium*, 25 November 2014. https://medium.com/war-is-boring/led-by-an-armored-bulldozer-shia-militia-fought-to-restore-their-credibility-8a6467a29174
15. Deep State Map of Vuhedar, 26–29 January 2023. https://deepstatemap.live/en#14/47.7667/37.2585
16. Twitter video showing thermobaric rockets hitting Vuhledar, Donetsk Oblast, 27 January 2023 at 1455 local time. https://twitter.com/Osinttechnical/status/1619106760136216577?lang=en
17. Without going into the mathematics and trajectories of high velocity tank rounds, the tank would need to be positioned on a very steep ramp to get the angle needed to drop an HE round behind a small hill 5 km to its front. It would then need an artillery officer and howitzer ballistic computer to determine the correct angles.
18. War in Ukraine, 7 March 2023. https://www.youtube.com/watch?v=5cmnaxoEq5c
19. War In Ukraine, 14 April 2023, https://www.youtube.com/watch?v=CCUzPBdct4A
20. Marc Santora, 'Moscow's Military Capabilities are in Question after Failed Battle for Ukrainian City', *New York Times*, 16 February 2023
21. MT Staff, 'Top Russian General Dismissed After Vuhledar Defeat', *Moscow Times,* 3 April 2033 https://www.themoscowtimes.com/2023/04/03/top-russian-general-dismissed-after-vuhledar-defeat-a80690

Chapter 12

1. Staff, 'Why Russia is Obsessed with Capturing this one Town', *The Infographic Show*, downloaded 3 January 2023. https://www.youtube.com/watch?app=desktop&v=BBJUrJffXYw
2. Olga Kyrylenko, 'Invincibility Centre Bakhmut. What is happening at the most difficult axis of the front', *Ukrainska Pravda*, 8 December 2022. https://www.pravda.com.ua/eng/articles/2022/12/8/7379743/
3. MISSING
4. Alia Shoaib, 'Take a look inside the incredible underground city carved from salt that Russia and Ukraine are battling over', *Business Insider*, 14 January 2023 https://www.businessinsider.com/inside-salt-mines-soledar-wagner-russia-claims-seized-2023-1
5. Jean-Philippe Lefief, 'War in Ukraine: Understanding the battle of Soledar', *Le Monde*, 16 January 2023 https://www.lemonde.fr/en/international/article/2023/01/16/war-in-ukraine-understanding-the-battle-of-soledar_6011752_4.html
6. Veronika Melkozerova, 'This is what madness looks like: Russians unleash massive assault on Soledar in eastern Ukraine', *Politico*, 22 January 2022 https://www.politico.eu/article/madness-russia-ukraine-war-assault-soldier-soledar-bakhmut/
7. *Kyiv Independent* Staff, 'Russia controls administrative territory of Soledar', *Kyiv Independent*, 15 January 15, 2023.
8. War in Ukraine, 31 March: Genius. Ukrainians Deliver Ammo Underground, https://www.youtube.com/watch?v=9EF4JU2-sNY
9. KP Staff, 'Wagner Chief Threatens to Pull Out of Bakhmut to Avoid 'Senseless Death,' The Kyiv Post, May 5, 2023
10. Artur Rehi, 'Wagner is leaving Bakhmut, Ukrainian drone strike Kermlin?', Ukraine Update, 5 May2023, https://www.youtube.com/watch?v=1Zff3PqD7dg
11. War in Ukraine, March 29: Ukrainians Unleash Elite Snipers in Bakhmut, https://www.youtube.com/watch?v=wDIy7pkJtHI
12. War in Ukraine, March 29, 2023, https://www.youtube.com/watch?v=wDIy7pkJtHI
13. Artur Rehi, 'Wagner is leaving Bakhmut, Ukrainian drone strike Kermlin?', Ukraine Update, 5 May 2023, https://www.youtube.com/watch?v=1Zff3PqD7dg
14. War in Ukraine, 1 April: Unexpected. Ukrainians Forced to Cancel Bakhmut Counter Offensive, https://www.youtube.com/watch?v=VkmL0bncJ3k
15. K&G Staff, Russia slow down, Ukraine prepares for counter-offensive, Kings & Generals, 15 April 2023, https://www.youtube.com/watch?v=-i_qpQI29Io&t=4s
16. War in Ukraine, 3 April: Last Resort. Russian Go All-In to crush Ukrainian Defense, https://www.youtube.com/watch?v=VpIOZPXAmL8
17. War In Ukraine, 4 April: Ukrainians Unleash Western Artillery in Bakhmut, https://www.youtube.com/watch?v=dLTWzCVzXkI
18. War in Ukraine, 5 May 2023, https://www.youtube.com/watch?v=rBw1KIWWeyw&t=104s
19. Siobhan O'Grady, Kamila Hrabchuk & Kostiantyn Khudov, 'How Ukrainian Forces denied Russia victory in Bakhmut by Victory Day', *Washington Post*, 12 May 2023
20. War in Ukraine, 8–10 May2023. https://www.youtube.com/watch?v=V2xK5CuhCJI, https://www.youtube.com/watch?v=NdnQRCiPtVM, Arthur Rehi, 'Ukrainians just annihilated an entire Wagner unit in Bakhmut/ Moscow parade failure', Ukraine Update, 10 May 2023. https://www.youtube.com/watch?v=1yYmUrInOWshttps://www.youtube.com/watch?v=TtSf_APspX8

21. War in Ukraine, 11 May 2023. https://www.youtube.com/watch?v=PD-ODf5vkSY&list=RDCMUCcNB1tZYpeDetqCadElv9Ow&start_radio=1
22. Ibid.
23. Arthur Rehi, 'Ukrainian breakthroughs in Bakhmut area/ Russian soldiers are panicking', Ukrainian Update. https://www.youtube.com/watch?v=UkZf42xnm0c
24. Arthur Rehi, 'Ukrainians just annihilated an entire Wagner unit in Bakhmut', 10 May 2023. https://www.youtube.com/watch?v=1yYmUrInOWs, Marc Santora &Andrew E Kramer, 'Ukraine's Advances Near Bakhmut Exposes Rifts in Russian Forces,' *New York, Times*, 12 May 2023. https://www.nytimes.com/2023/05/12/world/europe/ukraine-bakhmut-russia.html
25. Marc Santora & Andrew E Kramer, 'Ukraine's Advances Near Bakhmut Exposes Rifts in Russian Forces', *New York, Times*, 12 May 2023. https://www.nytimes.com/2023/05/12/world/europe/ukraine-bakhmut-russia.html
26. Siobhan O'Grady, Kamila Hrabchuk & Kostiantyn Khudov, 'How Ukraine forces denied Russia victory in Bakhmut by Victory Day', *Washington Post*, 12 May 2023. https://www.washingtonpost.com/world/2023/05/12/bakhmut-ukraine-russia-prigozhin/
27. Adam Taylor, 'Ukrainians fighting outside Bakhmut see Russian mercenaries withdrawing', *Washington Post*, 28 May 2023. https://www.washingtonpost.com/world/2023/05/28/bakhmut-wagner-mercenaries-ukraine-withdrawal/
28. War in Ukraine, 26 May 2023: 'Wagner Chief's Confession: 95% of Wagner Killed or Mutilated in Bakhmut'. https://www.youtube.com/watch?v=ECSxkpIVDV0&list=RDCMUCcNB1tZYpeDetqCadElv9Ow, DW Staff, Ukraine Updates: 'Wagner Group reports 10,000 prisoner deaths.' Ukraine Updates: *DW*, 24 May 2023. https://www.dw.com/en/ukraine-updates-wagner-group-reports-10000-prisoner-deaths/a-65714776
29. War in Ukraine, 26 May 2023: 'Wagner Chief's Confession: 95% of Wagner Killed or Mutilated in Bakhmut.' https://www.youtube.com/watch?v=ECSxkpIVDV0&list=RDCMUCcNB1tZYpeDetqCadElv9Ow, EM Staff, 'Frontline report: Prigozhin's video exposes high losses and failures of Wagner Group in battle for Bakhmut', *Euromaidan Press*, 26 May 2023. https://euromaidanpress.com/2023/05/27/frontline-report-prigozhins-video-exposes-high-losses-and-failure-of-wagner-group-in-battle-for-bakhmut/
30. Brad Dress, 'Why the Wagner boss is saying Russia could lose the war" *The Hill*, 25 May 2023. War in Ukraine, 26 May 22023: 'Wagner Chief's Confession: 95% of Wagner Killed or Mutilated in Bakhmut.' https://www.youtube.com/watch?v=ECSxkpIVDV0&list=RDCMUCcNB1tZYpeDetqCadElv9Ow, Valerie Hopkins, 'The Wagner group forecasts disaster if Russia does not move into total war footing', *New York Times*, 24 May 2023. https://www.nytimes.com/2023/05/24/world/europe/wagner-group-prigozhin-russia.html, War In Ukraine, Wagner Chiefs Confession: 95% of Wagner Killed and Mutilated in Bakhmut, May 26, 2023. https://www.youtube.com/watch?v=ECSxkpIVDV0&t=127s
31. Deep State, 27 May 2023. https://deepstatemap.live/en#13/48.5861/37.9547

Chapter 13

1. Perun, 'Russia's Winter Offensive in Ukraine-From Bakhmut to Vuhledar, outcomes, lessons and costs.' https://www.youtube.com/watch?v=qPhycuLAtaw
2. WO2 Blair Battersby, 'Russia's Approach to War in its So-Called "Special Operation" in Ukraine Has Evolved over the Past 21 Months, Suggesting Ways in which US Army OPFOR Training Can Evolve to Match', *US Army TRADOC*, 2023.

https://oe.tradoc.army.mil/2023/12/15/tradoc-russian-assault-groups-evolution-in-ukraine/
3. Jack Watling & Nick Reynolds, 'Meatgrinder: Russian Tactics in the Second Year of its Invasion of Ukraine', *RUSI*, 19 May 2023.
4. Ibid.
5. Illia Ponomarenko, 'Russia's New Guided Bombs Pose Increasingly Serious Threat to Ukraine', *Kyiv Independent*, 10 April 2023.

Chapter 14

1. Janice Gross Stein, 'Escalation Management In Ukraine: Assessing the US Response to Russia's Manipulation of Risk', *Henry A. Kissinger Center for Global Affairs*, August 2023 https://sais.jhu.edu/kissinger/programs-and-projects/kissinger-center-papers/escalation-management-ukraine-response-russias-manipulation-risk
2. Ibid.
3. The US Fiscal Year runs from 1 October of one calendar year to 30 September of the next.
4. Mike Stone, 'Exclusive: Pentagon accounting error overvalued Ukraine weapons aid by $3billion', *Reuters*, 19 May 2023.
https://www.reuters.com/world/europe/pentagon-accounting-error-overvalued-ukraine-aid-by-3-billion-sources-2023-05-18/, R Staff, 'Pentagon's Ukrainian accounting error revised up to $6.2 billion', *Reuters*, 20 June 2023.
https://www.reuters.com/world/us/pentagons-ukraine-accounting-error-revised-up-62-billion-2023-06-20/
5. Jonathan Masters & Will Merrow, 'How Much Aid Has the US Sent to Ukraine', *Council on Foreign Relations*, 8 December 2023
https://www.cfr.org/article/how-much-aid-has-us-sent-ukraine-here-are-six-charts#:~:text=Since%20the%20war%20began%2C%20the,Economy%2C%20a%20German%20research%20institute.
6. Claire Mills, 'Military assistance to Ukraine since the Russian invasion', UK Parliament, 10 May 2023. https://commonslibrary.parliament.uk/research-briefings/cbp-9477/#:~:text=As%20the%20second%20largest%20donor,match%20that%20funding%20in%202023).
7. K Staff, 'One Year of Support to Ukraine: US leads, EU Follows', *Keil Institute for the World Economy*, 21 February 2023. https://www.ifw-kiel.de/publications/media-information/2023/one-year-of-support-to-ukraine-us-leads-eu-follows/
8. French Government, 'France's Assistance to Ukraine – February 2023.' https://franceintheus.org/IMG/pdf/france_s_assistance_to_ukraine_-_february_2023.pdf
9. Christoph Tresbesch, 'Foreign support to Ukraine: Evidence from a database of military, financial and humanitarian aid,' *Vox Ukraine*, 14 June 2023
https://voxukraine.org/en/zovnishnya-pidtrymka-ukrayiny-pro-shho-svidchat-dani-stosovno-vijskovoyi-finansovoyi-ta-gumanitarnoyidopomogy
10. Christoph Tresbesch, 'Foreign support to Ukraine: Evidence from a database of military, financial and humanitarian aid,' *Vox Ukraine*, 14 June 2023
https://voxukraine.org/en/zovnishnya-pidtrymka-ukrayiny-pro-shho-svidchat-dani-stosovno-vijskovoyi-finansovoyi-ta-gumanitarnoyi-dopomogy
Dr. Christoph Trebesch, 'Ukraine Support Tracker: A Database for Military, Financial and Humanitarian Aid to Ukraine', *Keil Institute*, 31 July 2023.
https://www.ifw-kiel.de/topics/war-against-ukraine/ukraine-support-tracker/
Ruby Mellen & Arthur Galocha, 'A look at the amount of US spending powering Ukraine's defence', *Washington Post*, 10 August 2023.
https://www.washingtonpost.com/world/2023/08/04/ukraine-war-us-spending/

11. Christoph Tresbesch, 'Foreign support to Ukraine: Evidence from a database of military, financial and humanitarian aid,' *Vox Ukraine*, 14 June 2023 https://voxukraine.org/en/zovnishnya-pidtrymka-ukrayiny-pro-shho-svidchat-dani-stosovno-vijskovoyi-finansovoyi-ta-gumanitarnoyidopomogy
12. Ibid.
13. Ibid.
14. Hyunjoo Jin & Chibuike Oguh, 'Explainer: How Musk funded the $44 billion Twitter deal', *Reuters*, 28 October 2022 https://www.reuters.com/markets/us/how-will-elon-musk-pay-twitter-2022-10-07/
15. US DoE Press Release, 'US Department of Education Estimate: Biden-Harris Student Debt Relief of Cost and Average of $30 Billion Annually Over Next Decade', US Department of Education, 29 September 2022. https://www.ed.gov/news/press-releases/us-department-education-estimate-biden-harris-student-debt-relief-cost-average-30-billion-annually-over-next-decade
16. Jonathan Masters & Will Merrow, 'How Much Aid Has the US Sent Ukraine? Here are Six Charts', *Council on Foreign Relations,* 22 February 2023. https://www.cfr.org/article/how-much-aid-has-us-sent-ukraine-here-are-six-charts
17. Napoleon himself. https://www.napoleon-series.org/research/napoleon/c_quotes.html
18. In unclassified discussions with US Army and Army National Guard generals, the author and his peers identified Ukraine's requirements for HIMARS early in February 2022. We all received the same military education and were aware of the training and equipment required for breaching a fortified zone.
19. https://www.whitehouse.gov/briefing-room/statements-releases/2022/03/16/fact-sheet-on-u-s-security-assistance-for-ukraine/
20. Staff, 'Germany to send Ukraine weapons in historic shift on military aid'. *Politico*, 26 February 2022. https://www.politico.eu/article/ukraine-war-russia-germany-still-blocking-arms-supplies/
21. 'Fact Sheet On German Military Aid to Ukraine', *Oryx,* September 1, 2022, https://www.oryxspioenkop.com/2022/09/fact-sheet-on-german-military-aid-to.html
22. Stetson Payne, 'Soviet-Era T-72 Tanks to Be Transferred to Ukraine From NATO Countries: Reports', The War Zone, 3 April 2022. https://www.thedrive.com/the-war-zone/45050/soviet-era-t-72-tanks-to-be-transferred-from-nato-states-to-ukraine
23. MGM-140 Army Tactical Missile System (ATACAMS) have a range of 185 miles/300 km, and Precision strike Missile, 310 miles/500 km. Both the towed M777 and M109 Paladin series Self Propelled Howitzers have a maximum range of 30,000 metres and fire the Copperhead laser-guided anti-tank munition.
Sebastien Roblin, 'US HIMARS Rocket Artillery Going to Ukraine Would Be A Game Changer', *1945*, 30 April 2022. https://www.19fortyfive.com/2022/04/u-s-himars-rocket-artillery-going-to-ukraine-would-be-a-game-changer/.
24. FASCAM rounds scatter anti-tank mines that remain active for a fixed duration and then self-detonate.
25. Gustav Gressel, Rafael Loss, Jana Puglien, 'The Leopard plan: How European tanks can help Ukraine take back its territory', *European Council on Foreign Relations*, 9 September 2022.
26. 'One battalion of SP 155mm and four battalions of towed 155mm howitzers. France agrees to deliver French-made Caesar 15mm wheeled howitzers to Ukraine.' 22 April 2022. www.armyrecognition.com. The Dutch are sending a battalion of SP 155mm. Autoevolution.com

27. Sabine Siebold et al., 'Germany okays sale of former GDR infantry fighting vehicles to Ukraine', *Reuters*, 1 April 2022. https://www.reuters.com/world/europe/germany-okays-sale-former-gdr-infantry-fighting-vehicles-ukraine-2022-04-01/,
28. Robert Muller et al.,'Czech Republic sends tanks, infantry fighting vehicles to Ukraine', *Reuters*, 5 April 2022. https://www.reuters.com/world/europe/czech-republic-sends-tanks-ukraine-czech-tv-reports-2022-04-05/, 1
29. Gressel, (9 September 2022). https://ecfr.eu/article/the-leopard-plan-how-european-tanks-can-help-ukraine-take-back-its-territory/
30. Miranda Murrey, 'Rheinmeatall wants to deliver 20 new Leopard 2 tanks to Ukraine-Handelsblatt', *Zawya*, 25 April 2022, *Reuter News*. https://www.zawya.com/en/special-coverage/russia-ukraine-crisis/rheinmetall-wants-to-deliver-20-new-leopard-2-tanks-to-ukraine-handelsblatt-fp0op3a1
31. Anne Applebaum, 'Germany is Arguing with itself over Ukraine', *The Atlantic*, 20 October 2022.
32. Both M1A1 and Leopard II are armed with the same 120mm main gun.
33. Reid Standish, Interview: 'How Can Ukraine Prepare For a New Fight against Russia In The Donbas?'*Radio Free Europe*, 10 April 2022. https://www.rferl.org/a/russia-eastern-ukraine-offensive-donbas-next-phase/31795550.html, Frank Hoffman, 'Who repairs Ukraine's Western Weapons?' *DW*, 26 September 2022. https://www.dw.com/en/ukraine-war-how-to-repair-the-ukrainian-armys-modern-weapons/a-63215373
34. Gramer, 'German Tanks in Ukraine'.
35. Applebaum (20 October 2022).
36. David MacDougall, '"Free the Leopards!" Campaign aims to "embarrass" Germany into sending tanks to Ukraine', *Euronews,* 1 January 2023. https://www.euronews.com/2023/01/05/free-the-leopards-campaign-aims-to-embarrass-germany-into-sending-tanks-to-ukraine
37. Staff, 'Zelensky: Ukraine needs 300–500 tanks,' *Kyiv Independent* , 27 January 2023. https://kyivindependent.com/news-feed/zelensky-ukraine-needs-300-500-tanks, David E Sanger, Eric Schmitt & Helene Cooper, 'How Biden Reluctantly Agreed to Send Tanks to Ukrine', *New York Times*, 25 January 2023. https://www.nytimes.com/2023/01/25/us/politics/biden-abrams-tanks-ukraine-russia.html
38. Dan Sabbagh & Phillip Olterman, 'US and Germany agree to send infantry fighting vehicles to Ukraine', *Guardian*, 5 January 2023. https://www.theguardian.com/world/2023/jan/05/germany-tanks-ukraine-russia-war
39. Clea Caulcutt, 'At Last, Ukraine gets Western Tanks', *Politico*, 5 January 2023 https://www.politico.eu/article/emmanuel-macron-sending-western-tanks-to-ukraine-amx-10-rc-volodymyr-zelenskyy/
40. Staff, 'Military Support for Ukraine', German Federal Government. https://www.bundesregierung.de/breg-en/news/military-support-ukraine-2054992
41. Staff, 'M2 and M3 Bradley Fighting,' *Vehicles Global Security*, 2022. https://www.globalsecurity.org/military/systems/ground/m2.htm
42. Siobhan O'Grady & staff, 'Russian missiles rain down on Ukrainian cities; Britain to send battle tanks', *Washington Post*, 14 January 2023. https://www.washingtonpost.com/world/2023/01/14/challenger-2-tanks-ukraine/
43. C. Todd Lopez, 'Ukrainians to Get US Tanks by Fall', US DoD, 21 March 2023. https://www.defense.gov/News/News-Stories/Article/Article/3336826/ukrainians-to-get-us-tanks-by-fall/#:~:text=The%20Defense%20Department%20announced%20in,year%20to%20make%20that%20happen.

44. Adam Taylor, Willian Neff & Danel Wolfe, 'For Ukraine, what's so special about Germany's Leopard 2 tanks?' *Washington Post*, 25 January 2023. https://www.washingtonpost.com/world/2023/01/24/leopard-2-ukraine-germany-m1-abrams/
45. EU Staff, 'Russia's war on Ukraine: Western-made tanks for Ukraine', European Parliament, April 2023. https://www.europarl.europa.eu/RegData/etudes/ATAG/2023/739316/EPRS_ATA (2023)739316_EN.pdf.
46. Tec Staff, 'Isn't Leopard 1 too old to make a difference in Ukraine? Not at all – especially after upgrades', Technology.Org, 25 March 2023. https://www.technology.org/2023/03/25/isnt-leopard-1-too-old-to-make-a-difference-in-ukraine-not-at-all-especially-after-some-upgrades/
47. Tec Staff, 'Leopard 1 can be effective in Ukraine with the right ammo', Technology.org, April 2023. https://www.technology.org/2023/04/25/leopard-1-can-be-effective-in-ukraine-with-the-right-ammo/
48. RCAC Staff, 'Modern Anti-Tank Ammunition', The Ontario Regiment RCAC Museum. https://www.ontrmuseum.ca/tankmuseum/blog-post/modern-anti-tank-ammunition/
49. Fact Sheet on US Security Assistance to Ukraine, 10 November 2022.
50. Lara Seligman & Paul McLeary, 'US speeds up delivers of Abrams tanks, Patriots to Ukraine', *Politico*, 21 March 2023. https://www.politico.com/news/2023/03/21/us-delivery-tanks-missiles-ukraine-00088098
51. Lolita C Baldor, 'US to begin training Ukrainian troops on Abrams tank', *AP*, 21 April 2023. https://apnews.com/article/abrams-tanks-ukraine-training-war-russia-aid-6de94897aad37e6d30e744df0dad07bd
52. David Axe, 'Some of Ukraine's Heavy Brigades Don't Have Real Tanks Yet. Here's How They Might Fight', *Forbes*, 26 March 2023. https://www.forbes.com/sites/davidaxe/2023/03/06/some-of-ukraines-heavy-brigades-dont-have-real-tanks-yet heres-how-they-might-fight/?sh=455590ff774e
53. War in Ukraine, 11 May 2023. https://www.youtube.com/watch?v=PD-ODf5vkSY&list=RDCMUCcNB1tZYpeDetqCadElv9Ow&start_radio=1
54. Peter Dickinson, 'Britain becomes first country to supply Ukraine with long-range missiles', Atlantic Council, 11 May 2023. https://www.atlanticcouncil.org/blogs/ukrainealert/britain-becomes-first-country-to-supply-ukraine-with-long-range-missiles/
55. Boyko Nikolov, 'Su-24 and Su-27 can carry a Storm Shadow missile, but not program it', *BulgraianMilitary.com*, 12 May 2023. https://bulgarianmilitary.com/2023/05/12/su-24-and-su-27-can-carry-a-storm-shadow-missile-but-not-program-it/
56. Todd Lopez, 'US Open to Training Ukrainian F-16 Pilots if Needed,' US DoD Press Release, 21 August 2023.
57. Gerry Doyle & Mariano Zafra, 'The Air War over Ukraine', *Reuters*, 14 December 2023
58. Lara Seligman, 'How Biden got to yes on F-16s and Ukraine', *Politico*, 22 May 2023. https://www.politico.com/news/2023/05/22/biden-f-16s-ukraine-g7-00098243
59. Justin Hayward, 'How Much Does An F-16 Cost?' *Simple Flying,* 3 December 2023 https://simpleflying.com/how-much-does-an-f-16-cost/#:~:text=Coming%20to%20more%20recent%20variants,to%20%2460%20to%20%2470%20million.&text=Of%20course%2C%20military%20sale%20prices,this%20type%20can%20be%20difficult.
60. Eric Schmitt & Lara Jakes, 'Pentagon Plans To Begin Training Ukrainian Pilots on F-16s in US', *New York Times*, 24 August 2023. https://www.nytimes.com/2023/08/24/world/europe/us-ukraine-f16-jets-training.html

61. Gerry Doyle & Mariano Zafra, 'The Air War over Ukraine', *Reuters*, 14 December 2023.
62. Lara Jakes, Eric Schmitt & Thomas Gibbons-Neff, 'What's Stopping Ukraine Flying F-16s', *New York Times*, 31 August 2023. https://www.nytimes.com/2023/08/30/us/politics/ukraine-plane-f16.html
63. Gerry Doyle & Mariano Zafra, 'The Air War Over Ukraine', *Reuters*, 14 December 2023. Lara Jakes, Eric Schmitt & Thomas Gibbons-Neff, 'What's Stopping Ukraine Flying F-16s', *New York Times*, 31 August 2023. https://www.nytimes.com/2023/08/30/us/politics/ukraine-plane-f16.html
64. Gerry Doyle &Mariano Zafra, 'The Air War over Ukraine', *Reuters*, 14 December 2023.
65. Ibid.
66. Ibid.

Chapter 15

1. Staff, 'How crowdfunding is shaping the war in Ukraine', *Economist*, 27 July 2022.
2. GoFundMe, downloaded 22 January 2023. https://www.gofundme.com/c/crowdfunding#:~:text=Crowdfunding%20harnesses%20the%20power%20of,or%20help%20an%20entire%20community.
3. European Commission, https://single-market-economy.ec.europa.eu/access-finance/guide-crowdfunding/what-crowdfunding/crowdfunding-explained_en https://single-market-economy.ec.europa.eu/access-finance/guide-crowdfunding/what-crowdfunding/crowdfunding-explained_en
4. Fundable, downloaded 22 January 2023. https://www.fundable.com/crowdfunding101/history-of-crowdfunding
5. IC Staff, 'Internal Market, Industry, Entrepreneurship and SMEs,' European Commission, retrieved 23 January 2023. https://single-market-economy.ec.europa.eu/access-finance/guide-crowdfunding/what-crowdfunding/crowdfunding-explained_en
6. EC Staff, 'What Are The Risks?', European Commission, Downloaded 23 January 2023. https://single-market-economy.ec.europa.eu/access-finance/guide-crowdfunding/what-crowdfunding/what-are-risks_en
7. Arnold Schwarzenegger Russian Speech in Full: Star urges Putin to end Ukraine invasion. 17 March 2022. https://www.youtube.com/watch?v=ShVXeiro7eI
8. Dominique Soguel, 'From citizens' pockets to soldiers' hands: Ukraine crowdfunded war', *Christian Science Monitor*, 23 April 2023 https://www.csmonitor.com/World/Europe/2023/0403/From-citizens-pockets-to-soldiers-hands-Ukraine-s-crowdfunded-war
9. TE Staff, 'How crowdfunding is shaping the war in Ukraine', *Economist*, 27 July 2022 https://www.economist.com/the-economist-explains/2022/07/27/how-crowdfunding-is-shaping-the-war-in-ukraine
10. Jane Arraf, 'Crowdfunding a War: How Online Appeals Are Bringing Weapons to Ukraine', *New York Times*, 10 May 2022. https://www.nytimes.com/2022/05/10/world/middleeast/ukraine-crowdsourcing-online-donations.html
11. Arthur Rehi Collects Kamikaze Drones to Destroy 50 Russian Tanks, October 2023. https://www.youtube.com/watch?v=8njltcSoFDA. Note: the author contributes to this fund.
12. EP Staff, 'Fundraising Campaign for 500 Drones for Ukraine Launched in Lithuania', *European Pravda*, 19 July 2023. https://www.eurointegration.com.ua/eng/news/2023/07/19/7166089/

13. Elsia Court, 'Minister: Drone fundraising campaign raises $1 million within hours', *Kyiv Independent*, 7 January 2023 https://kyivindependent.com/minister-fundraising-campaign-for-10-000-drones-launched-1-million-already-raised/
14. M Staff, 'All 10,000 FPV drones from Operation Unity are already in the army', *Militarnyi*, 22 December 2023 https://mil.in.ua/en/news/all-10-000-fpv-drones-from-operation-unity-are-already-in-the-army/
15. Sam Lagrone, 'Ukraine Launches Crowd Funding Driver for $250k Naval Drones', *USNI News*, 11 November 2023 https://news.usni.org/2022/11/11/ukraine-launches-crowd-funding-drive-for-250k-naval-drones
16. Stefan Korshah, 'Ukraine's War-Critical Hobby Drones vs. Russian Swarms-Pilots Say Crowdfunding Won't Cut it', *Kyiv Post*, 20 December 2023. https://www.kyivpost.com/post/25710
17. Ibid.
18. James Beardsworth, 'Russian Military's Supply Problems in Ukraine', *Moscow Times*, 5 October 2022 https://www.themoscowtimes.com/2022/10/05/crowdfunding-spotlights-russian-militarys-supply-problems-in-ukraine-a78969
19. Edmund Burke, Psalm 94:1–3
20. Sam LaGrone, 'Naval Drones', *USNI News*, 11 November 2023. https://news.usni.org/2022/11/11/ukraine-launches-crowd-funding-drive-for-250k-naval-drones
21. Victoria Kim, 'Elon Musk Acknowledges Withholding Satellite Service to Thwart Ukrainian Attack', *New York Times*, 8 September 2023 https://www.nytimes.com/2023/09/08/world/europe/elon-musk-starlink-ukraine.html#:~:text=Within%20days%20of%20Russia%27s%20full,drone%20strikes%20and%20gather%20intelligence.
22. Ibid.
23. Ibid.
24. Alex Marquardt, 'Exclusive: Musk's SpaceX says it can no longer pay for critical satellite services in Ukraine, asks Pentagon to pick up the tab', *CNN*, 14 October 2022. https://www.cnn.com/2022/10/13/politics/elon-musk-spacex-starlink-ukraine/index.html
25. Mike Stone & Joey Roulette, 'SpaceX's Starlink wins Pentagon contract for satellite services to Ukraine', *Reuters*, 1 June 2023. https://www.reuters.com/business/aerospace-defense/pentagon-buys-starlink-ukraine-statement-2023-06-01/#:~:text=SpaceX%27s%20Starlink%20wins%20Pentagon%20contract%20for%20satellite%20services%20to%20Ukraine,-By%20Mike%20Stone&text=WASHINGTON%2C%20June%201%20(Reuters),the%20Pentagon%20said%20on%20Thursday.
26. Britney Nguyen, 'Ukraine claims Russia is buying Starlink terminals in Arab countries after Elon Musk denied selling to Russian forces', *Quartz*, 13 February 2024 Verified reliable by *Ground News*

Chapter 16

1. US Staff, 'Russian State-Sponsored Cyber Actors Target Cleared Defense Contractor Networks to Obtain Sensitive US Defense Information and Technology', *US Cybersecurity & Infrastructure Security Agency*,' 16 February 2022. https://www.cisa.gov/news-events/cybersecurity-advisories/aa22-047a

2. Grace B. Mueller, 'Cyber Operations during the Russo-Ukrainian War', *CISI,* 13 July 2023
3. Ibid.
4. Juan Andres Guerrero, 'Acid Rain/A Modem Wiper Rains Down on Europe', *Sentinel LABS*, 31 March 2022. https://www.sentinelone.com/labs/acidrain-a-modem-wiper-rains-down-on-europe/
5. Maria Sheahan, 'Satellite outages knocks out thousands of Enercon's wind turbines', *Reuters*, 28 February 2022. https://www.reuters.com/business/energy/satellite-outage-knocks-out-control-enercon-wind-turbines-2022-02-28/
6. Cynthia Brumfield, 'Incident response lessons learned from the Russian attack on Viasat', *CSO*, 16 August 2023. https://www.csoonline.com/article/649714/incident-response-lessons-learned-from-the-russian-attack-on-viasat.html
7. Sean Lyngaas,'Russian hackers targeted NATO forces and diplomats to aid Ukraine war effort', *CNN*, 7 December 2023. https://www.cnn.com/2023/12/07/politics/russian-hackers-nato-forces-diplomats/index.html#
8. US Staff, 'CISA and Partners Release Advisory on Russian SVR-affiliated Cyber Actors Exploiting CVE-2023-1793', *US Cybersecurity & Infrastructure Security Agency*, 13 December 2023 https://www.cisa.gov/news-events/alerts/2023/12/13/cisa-and-partners-release-advisory-russian-svr-affiliated-cyber-actors-exploiting-cve-2023-42793#:~:text=Since%20September%202023%2C%20Russian%20Foreign,them%20to%20bypass%20authorization%20and
9. US Staff, 'The Power of Resilience,' *US Cybersecurity & Infrastructure Security Agency*,' 9 August 2023. https://www.cisa.gov/news-events/news/power-resilience
10. CEDF Staff, 'CRDF Global Becomes Platform for Cyber Defense Assistance Collaborative (CDAC) for Ukraine, Receives Grant from Craig Newmark Philanthropies,' *CRDFGL BAL*, 14 November 2022. https://www.crdfglobal.org/news/crdf-global-becomes-platform-for-cyber-defense-assistance-collaborative-cdac-for-ukraine-receives-grant-from-craig-newmark-philanthropies/
11. 'Cyber Operation of Russian Intelligence Services as a Component of Confrontation on the Battlefield', *Ukrainian Security Service*, Downloaded 25 February 2024. https://ssu.gov.ua/uploads/files/DKIB/technical-report.pdf
12. TG Staff, 'Ukraine remains Russia's biggest cyber focus in 2023', *Google's Threat Analysis Group*, 19 April 2023. https://blog.google/threat-analysis-group/ukraine-remains-russias-biggest-cyber-focus-in-2023/
13. Ibid.
14. TG Staff, 'Ukraine remains Russia's biggest cyber focus in 2023', *Google's Threat Analysis Group*, 19 April 2023. https://blog.google/threat-analysis-group/ukraine-remains-russias-biggest-cyber-focus-in-2023/
15. Greg Austin & Natallia Khaniejo, 'Impact of the Russian-Ukraine War on National Cyber Planning: A Survey of Ten Countries', *IISS*, December 2023

Chapter 17

1. Deep State Map, 20 November 2023. https://deepstatemap.live/en#11/47.4267/35.9068
2. The first-rate Nazi divisions were fighting the Soviets on the Eastern Front.
3. Rick Atkinson, 'Operation Cobra and the Breakout at Normandy', US Army, 22 July 2010. https://www.army.mil/article/42658/operation_cobra_and_the_breakout_at_normandy
4. Alan Clark, *Barbarossa: The Russian-German Conflict 1941–1945*, (New York, 1966), 327.
5. Lloyd Clark, *Kursk: The Greatest Battle: Eastern Front 1941,* (London: Headline Publishing Group, 2012),
6. Peter Dickinson,' Ukraine's counter-offensive is a marathon not a blitzkrieg,' Atlantic Council, 22 June 2023.
7. Artur Rehi, 'Huge Russian losses in Kherson front/Wagner PMC will be Eliminated by Putin! Estonian Soldier Reacts', 27 June 2023. https://www.youtube.com/watch?v=9JZK5pS_qmU
8. R Staff, 'Who are the Freedom of Russian Legion and Russian Volunteer Corps?' *Reuters*, 5 June 2023. https://www.reuters.com/world/europe/who-are-armed-fighters-russias-belgorod-region-2023-06-05/
9. ISW, Russian Offensive Campaign Assessment, 22 May 2023 https://understandingwar.org/backgrounder/russian-offensive-campaign-assessment-may-22-2023
10. Rob Picheta, Sebastian Shukla & Anna Chernova, 'Pro-war Putin critic Igir Girkin sentenced to four years in Russian prison on extremism charges', *CNN*, 25 January 2024. https://www.cnn.com/2024/01/25/europe/igor-girkin-russia-trial-verdict-intl/index.html
11. MT Staff, 'Officials Disclose Russian Troop Deaths 1 Month After Cross-Border Incursion', *Moscow Times*, 28 June 2023 https://www.themoscowtimes.com/2023/06/28/officials-disclose-russian-troop-deaths-1-month-after-cross-border-incursion-a81679

Chapter 18

1. Mykola Bielleskoy, 'Ukraine's drone army is bringing Putin's invasion to Russia', *Atlantic Council*, 26 September 2023.
2. Tom Balmforth, 'Ukraine to produce thousands of long-range drones in 2024, minister says', *Reuters*, 12 February 2023. https://www.reuters.com/business/aerospace-defense/ukraine-produce-thousands-long-range-drones-2024-minister-says-2024-02-12/#:~:text=KYIV%2C%20Feb%2012%20(Reuters),Petersburg%2C%20Ukraine%27s%20digital%20minister%20said.
3. E Staff, 'Can Ukrainian drone attacks hurt Russia?', *Economist*, 5 January 2024
4. 15 May: No Antidote. Strorm Shadow Missile Destroys Another Russian Base/War In Ukraine Explained. https://www.youtube.com/watch?v=VpOIeA-Ez0Q
5. 24 May: Multiple Russian Convoys Caught in the Move and Destroyed/War In Ukraine Explained. https://www.youtube.com/watch?v=3VxMqN9XFeE
6. 30 May: Mission Retribution. No One Expected Such Results/War In Ukraine Explained. https://www.youtube.com/watch?v=gS0873Lxsi8

7. Mykola Bielleskoy, 'Ukraine opens new front with drone strikes on Russia's energy sector', *Atlantic Council*, 6 February 2024,
8. Sarah Rainsford, 'Ukraine drones hit St Petersburg gas terminal in Russia', *BBC,* 21 January 2023 https://www.bbc.com/news/world-europe-68046347#
9. 1 December: Huge Success! Russian Bases Decimated. Logistics Crippled/War in Ukraine Explained.
10. CNBC Staff, 'Ukraine's SBU hits Russia's Volgograd oil refinery in drone attack, source says', *CNBC*, 3 February 2023 https://www.cnbc.com/2024/02/03/ukraines-sbu-hits-russias-volgograd-oil-refinery-in-drone-attack-source-says.html

Chapter 19

1. James Waterhouse, 'Ukraine war: Russian attack on Ukraine cities hits deadly new level', *BBC*, 29 December 2023, https://www.bbc.com/news/world-europe-67843312#
2. Suriya Evans-Pritchard Jayanti, 'Russia resumes bombing campaign of Ukraine's civilian energy infrastructure', Atlantic Council, 22 September 2023 https://www.atlanticcouncil.org/blogs/ukrainealert/russia-resumes-bombing-campaign-of-ukraines-civilian-energy-infrastructure/#:~:text=Russia%20resumes%20bombing%20campaign%20of%20Ukraine%27s%20civilian%20energy%20infrastructure,-By%20Suriya%20Evans&text=In%20the%20early%20hours%20of,by%20Ukrainian%20air%20defense%20forces.
3. ISW Campaign Assessment, 28 December 2023. https://understandingwar.org/backgrounder/russian-offensive-campaign-assessment-december-28-2023
4. E Staff, 'Can Russia repeat its winter bombing of Ukraine's electricity grid?' *Economist*, 4 October 2023. https://www.economist.com/the-economist-explains/2023/10/04/can-russia-repeat-its-winter-bombing-of-ukraines-electricity-grid
5. TMT Staff, 'In Photos: The Aftermath of Russia's Massive Drone and Missile Attack on Ukraine', *Moscow Times*, 29 December 2023. https://www.themoscowtimes.com/2023/12/29/navalny-ally-fadeyeva-jailed-9-years-for-extremism-a83603
6. Peter Dickinson, 'Ukraine needs urgent air defense aid as Putin launches bombing campaign', Atlantic Council, 2 January 2024 https://www.atlanticcouncil.org/blogs/ukrainealert/ukraine-needs-urgent-air-defense-aid-as-putin-launches-bombing-campaign/
7. 'A look at Russian missile attacks on Ukrainian targets since the war began in February 2022', *AP*, 29 December 2023. https://apnews.com/article/russia-ukraine-invasion-war-military-0fd6866d7ee2aec12e51daa1e7c5c881
8. TG Staff, 'Poland reports airspace incursion as Russia launched huge strikes on Ukraine', *Guardian*, 29 December 2023. https://www.theguardian.com/world/2023/dec/29/russia-launches-huge-wave-missile-strikes-ukraine

Chapter 20

1. Ilya Tsukanov, 'What is the "Surovikin Defensive Line" which Ukrainian Forces Can't Crack?', *Sputnik International*, 22 June 2023. https://sputnikglobe.com/20230622/what-is-surovikin-defensive-line-which-ukrainian-forces-cant-crack-1111393818.html

2. Major General Ivan Ivanovich Popov is being investigated for war crimes committed by the 58th CAA during the invasion of Ukraine. https://russian-torturers.com/en/profile/1632
3. Seth G Jones, Alexander Palmer & Joseph S Bermuder Jr, 'Ukraine's Offensive Operations: Shifting the Offense-Defense Balance', *CSIS*, 9 June 2023.
4. Jack Watling & Nick Reynolds, 'Special Repost, Stormbreak: Fighting Through Russian Defences in Ukraine's 2023 Offenive', *RUSI*, September 2023, 15.
5. Rochan Staff, 'Ukraine Conflict Monitor: The aftermath of the Nova Kakhovka Dam Collapse', *Rochan Consulting*, 9 June 2023. https://rochan-consulting.com/ukraine-conflict-monitor-the-aftermath-of-the-nova-kakhovka-dam-collapse/
6. Rochan Staff, 'Conflict Monitor: The Operational-Strategic situation in Southern Ukraine', *Rochan Consulting*, 14 June 2023 https://rochan-consulting.com/ukraine-conflict-monitor-the-operational-strategic-situation-in-southern-ukraine/
7. Jack Watling & Nick Reynolds, 'Special Report, Stormbreak: Fighting Through Russian Defences in Ukraine's 2023 Offensive', *RUSI*, September 2023,15–16.
8. Marco Hernandez & Josh Holder, 'Defenses Carved into the Earth', *New York Times*, 14 December 2022. https://www.nytimes.com/interactive/2022/12/14/world/europe/russian-trench-fortifications-in-ukraine.html
9. The *bocage* in Normandy dated to the Middle Ages and was too thick to be crossed by tanks without special field-expedient hedge cutters.
10. David Axe, 'At the Bleeding Edge of Ukraine's Counter-offensive, the Ukrainian Marine Corps Switches up its Tactics', *Forbes*, 6 June 2023. https://www.forbes.com/sites/davidaxe/2023/06/06/at-the-bleeding-edge-of-ukraines-counter-offensive-the-ukrainian-marine-corps-has-worked-out-new-infantry-tactics/?sh=28b5824316ef
11. ORYX Ukrainian Equipment Losses, 25, July 2023. https://www.oryxspioenkop.com/2022/02/attack-on-europe-documenting-ukrainian.html
12. Jack Watling & Nick Reynolds, 'Special Report, Stormbreak: Fighting Through Russian Defences in Ukraine's 2023 Offensive', *RUSI*, September 2023, 5.
13. Ibid. 5–6.
14. Ibid.
15. Ibid. 13–14.
16. Issue 315, Weekly Update, Rochan Consulting, 5–11 June 2023. https://rochan-consulting.com/issue-315-5-june-11-june-2023-weekly-update/
17. Lara Jakes, Andrew E. Kramer & Eric Schmitt, 'After Suffering Heavy Losses, Ukrainian Pause to Rethink Strategy" *New York Times*, 15 July 2023. https://www.nytimes.com/2023/07/15/us/politics/ukraine-leopards-bradleys-counter-offensive.html
18. David Axe, '25 Tanks and Armored Fighting Vehicles Gone In a Blink: The Ukrainian Defeat Near Mala Tokmachka Was Worse Than We Thought', *Forbes*, 27 June 2023 https://www.forbes.com/sites/davidaxe/2023/06/27/25-tanks-and-fighting-vehicles-gone-in-a-blink-the-ukrainian-defeat-near-mala-tokmachka-was-worst-than-we-thought/?sh=6b7771897918
19. Lara Jakes, Andrew E. Kramer & Eric Schmitt, 'After Suffering Heavy Losses. Ukrainian Pause to Rethink Strategy', *New York Times*, 15 July 2023. https://www.nytimes.com/2023/07/15/us/politics/ukraine-leopards-bradleys-counter-offensive.html

20. Martin Fornusek, 'Germany says it reached agreement with Poland on Leopard II repair center', *Kyiv Independent*, 24 July 2023. https://kyivindependent.com/germany-says-it-reached-agreement-with-poland-on-leopard-2-repair/
21. Isabelle Khurshudyan, Alex Horton & Kamila Harbchuk, 'Ukraine's new Bradley Fighting Vehicles face damage and quick repairs', *Washington Post*, 20 July 2023. https://www.washingtonpost.com/world/2023/07/20/bradley-ukraine-war-vehicles/
22. Oryx, 'Attack on Europe: Documenting Ukrainian Equipment Losses during the Russian Invasion of Ukraine', 24 July 2023. https://www.oryxspioenkop.com/2022/02/attack-on-europe-documenting-ukrainian.html
23. FM 6-27 Commander's Handbook Law of Land Warfare (US Army 2019) par 2–118
24. Ibid.
25. 'Russian troops flee their own flood on stolen blue-and-yellow paddleboard-video', *The New Voice of Ukraine*, 8 June 2023. Rochan Staff, 'Ukraine Conflict Monitor: The aftermath of the Nova Kakhovka Dam Collapse', 9 June 2023. https://rochan-consulting.com/ukraine-conflict-monitor-the-aftermath-of-the-nova-kakhovka-dam-collapse/ https://english.nv.ua/russian-troops-flee-their-own-flood-on-stolen-blue-and-yellow-paddleboards-video-50330426.html

Chapter 21

1. Deep State Map Ukraine, July 2023 https://deepstatemap.live/en#12/48.4934/37.9492
2. Konrad Muzyka, 'Ukraine Conflict Monitor 12–18 August 2023 *Rochan,* 2023. https://rochanconsulting.substack.com/p/ukraine-conflict-monitor-12-august
3. War in Ukraine Explained, 14 May 2023, A Huge Group of Russian Get Taken into a Pocket and Destroyed/ https://www.youtube.com/watch?v=SbAl-2laYV0
4. Nick Starkov, 'Ukraine recaptures village near Bakhmut, Zelenskiy says', *Reuters*, 17 September 2023 https://www.reuters.com/world/europe/ukraine-general-says-klishchiivka-village-near-bakhmut-recaptured-2023-09-17/
5. Lara Jakes, 'After Suffering Heavy Losses Ukrainians Paused to Rethink Strategy', *New York Times*, 15 July 2023. https://www.nytimes.com/2023/07/15/us/politics/ukraine-leopards-bradleys-counter-offensive.html
6. Colonel Markus Reisner (Austria), 'The Ukraine offensive failed –what's next?' 15 December 2023. https://www.youtube.com/watch?v=EWjMr3RZ8Ss&t=939s
7. History Legends, 'How Russia Stopped Ukraine's Counter-offensive', July 2023. https://www.youtube.com/watch?v=UAcl0PTqql8&t=745s
8. Colonel Markus Reisner (Austria), 'The Ukraine offensive failed –what's next?' 15 December 2023. https://www.youtube.com/watch?v=EWjMr3RZ8Ss&t=939s
9. ATP 3021, Forms of Manoeuvre, 2–14. https://www.moore.army.mil/Infantry/DoctrineSupplement/ATP3-21.8/chapter_04/section_02/page_0040/index.html#:~:text=A%20turning%20movementis%20a%20form,forces%20to%20meet%20the%20threat.
10. Deep State Map Ukraine, 31 July 2023. https://deepstatemap.live/en#11/47.4121/35.7983

11. War In Ukraine Explained, 31 July 2023: 'Breached! Ukrainians Advanced by 5km on Multipipe Axes.'
https://www.youtube.com/watch?v=STwXO5k0_3k
12. War In Ukraine Explained, 22 August: 'Ukrainian Bradleys Demolish Russian Tanks'
https://www.youtube.com/watch?v=ZcgIpBs41qw
13. War In Ukraine, 23 August: 'Insane Marine Operation. Wagner Chief Dead. Russian Helicopter Stolen.'
https://www.youtube.com/watch?v=4bC51Lo0PRE
14. War in Ukraine Explained, 24 August: 'Night Ambush: Half-Asleep Naked Russians Run in.' Panic.https://www.youtube.com/watch?v=c9klvscOSqs
15. Susie Blann, 'Ukraine targets a key Crimean city a day after striking Russia's Black Sea Fleet Headquarters', *AP*, 23 September 2023
https://apnews.com/article/russia-ukraine-war-crimea-9c287d5bad840beedbd68eb32c4c76a3
16. Lockheed Martin MGM-168 ATAMCS Block IVA.
https://www.designation-systems.net/dusrm/m-168.html
17. Mike Stone, 'US-supplied ATACMS enter the Ukraine War', *Reuters*, 19 October 2023
https://www.reuters.com/world/atacms-us-may-send-ukraine-their-cluster-bomb-payloads-2023-10-19/
18. History Legends, 'Ukraine's Summer Offensive Has Failed, October 2023.'
https://www.youtube.com/watch?v=OsYtZCLBO9k&list=PLLyrWXxpwLyXqTJqExB4w4whnDm-GIDL6&index=3
19. E Staff, 'Ukraine's commander-in-chief on the breakthrough he needs to beat Russia', *Economist*, 1 November 2023
https://www.economist.com/europe/2023/11/01/ukraines-commander-in-chief-on-the-breakthrough-he-needs-to-beat-russia
20. Ibid.
21. Ibid.

Chapter 22

1. Deep State Maps, 22–25 June 2023.
2. Euro Staff, 'Russia to supply Wagner Group more weapons and ammunition after threat to withdraw', *Euronews*, 7 May 2023
https://www.euronews.com/2023/05/07/russia-to-supply-wagner-group-more-weapons-and-ammunition-after-threat-to-withdraw
3. Brad Lendon, 'Wagner chief says his forces are dying as Russia's military leaders "sit like fat cats"', *CNN*, 5 May 2023. https://www.cnn.com/2023/05/05/europe/wagner-military-group-prigozhin-ammunition-tirade-intl-hnk-ml/index.html
4. Euro Staff, 'Russia to supply Wagner Group more weapons and ammunition after threat to withdraw', *Euronews*, 7 May 2023
https://www.euronews.com/2023/05/07/russia-to-supply-wagner-group-more-weapons-and-ammunition-after-threat-to-withdraw
5. George Wright, 'Ukraine war: Wagner chief vows to hand Bakhmut to Russian army by June', *BBC News*, 22 May 2023.
https://www.bbc.com/news/world-europe-65670534
6. Ben Tobias, 'Ukraine war: Wagner detains Russian officer over 'dunk' attack', *BBC News*, 5 June 2023.
https://www.bbc.com/news/world-europe-65809844
7. Allison Quinn, 'Hijacked Russian Radio Station Air What Sounds Like Prigozhin Campaign A.', *Daily Beast*, 7 Jun 2023

https://www.thedailybeast.com/hijacked-russian-radio-stations-air-what-sounds-like-prigozhin-campaign-ad

8. Oleksiy Sorokin, 'Prigozhin accuses Russian army of attacking Wagner, threatens respond', *Kyiv Independent*, 24 June 2023.
https://kyivindependent.com/prigozhin-accuses-russian-army-of-attacking-wagner-threatens-to-respond/
9. Andrew Roth, 'Who is Vikto Medvedchuk and why does his arrest matter to the Kremlin?', *Guardian*, 13 April 2023.
https://www.theguardian.com/world/2022/apr/13/viktor-medvedchuk-arrest-matter-to-kremlin
10. WSJ Staff, 'Russia Issues Arrest Warrant for Wagner Chief Yevgeny Prigozhin', *WSJ*, 23 June 2023.
https://www.youtube.com/watch?v=oIMEcT9HgAw&t=7s
11. At the time, some experts thought the air strike on the Wagner camp was staged.
12. 'Russia's Prosecutor General reports on armed mutiny case to Putin',*TASS*, 24 June 2023. https://tass.com/russia/1637473
13. Mikes Ives & Eric Nagouney, 'What's happening in Russia? Here's what we know', *New York Times*, 24 June 2023.
https://www.nytimes.com/2023/06/24/world/europe/russia-prigozhin-wagner-chief-rostov.html
14. Charles Maynes, 'Wagner Group chief says his mercenaries will halt their march on Moscow', *NPR*, 24 June 2023.
https://www.npr.org/2023/06/24/1184166949/wagner-group-moscow-halting-march-russia.
15. ISW, Russian Offensive Campaign Assessment, 25 June 2023.
https://understandingwar.org/backgrounder/russian-offensive-campaign-assessment-june-25-2023
16. Miquel Ros, 'Wagner forces shoot down Russian aircraft: a summary', *Aerotime*, 6 June 2023
https://www.aerotime.aero/articles/wagner-forces-shoot-down-russian-aircraft, War In Ukraine Explained: 'Russians Kill Each Other in Sudden Violent Coup', 23 June 2023.
https://www.youtube.com/watch?app=desktop&v=fmITp1Kz1yU
17. The Mi-8, Mi-35M and Ka-52 gunships would have been from different companies.
18. EM Staff, 'Frontline report: Russia suffers record aircraft losses during Wagner mutiny', *Euromaidan Press*, 25 June 2023.
https://euromaidanpress.com/2023/06/25/frontline-report-russia-suffers-record-aircraft-losses-due-to-wagner-coup/
19. Max Seddon, 'Prigozhin to move to Belarus as part of deal to end Wagner uprising', *FT Live*, 24 June 2023. https://www.ft.com/content/9cd09366-25db-4057-a41d-0ea04b659d97
20. Debora Patta & Sarah Carter, 'How Russia's Wagner Group funds its role in Putin's Ukraine war by plundering Africa's resources', *CBS News*, 16 May 2023.
https://www.cbsnews.com/news/russia-wagner-group-ukraine-war-putin-prigozhin-africa-plundering-resources/
21. Mark Tubridy, Pyotr Kozlov & Samantha Berkhead, 'Prigozhin Charged With "Inciting Armed Revolt" After Vowing to stop "Evil" Military Leadership', *Moscow Times*, 23 June 2023.
https://www.themoscowtimes.com/2023/06/23/prigozhin-charged-with-inciting-armed-revolt-after-vowing-to-stop-evil-military-leadership-a81615

22. The number of Wagnerites present for duty may have been greatly exaggerated by Prigozhin. Wagner Group probably only had 5,000 combatants (infantry and tank crews) when Bakhmut was captured on 21 May 2023.
23. Elland Peltier, 'Russia tells Central African Republic Leaders, who rely on Wagner mercenaries not to worry', *New York Times*, 29 June 2023. https://www.nytimes.com/live/2023/06/29/world/russia-ukraine-news, NYT Staff, 'Russia-Ukraine War, Kremlin Makes Show of Putin's Support and Deflects Questions About Missing General,' 29 June 2023
https://www.nytimes.com/live/2023/06/29/world/russia-ukraine-news
24. GS Staff, '58th Combined Arms Army, Global Security',
https://www.globalsecurity.org/military/world/russia/58-army.htm
25. AP Staff, 'A Russian general says he was fired for pointing out challenges his troops are facing', *NPR*, 14 July 2023
https://www.npr.org/2023/07/14/1187644890/russian-general-fired-for-being-critical
26. GDC Staff, 'Fearing Coup: Putin Removes Major General Vladimir Seliverstov From His Position', Global Defense Corp, 17 July 2023
https://www.globaldefensecorp.com/2023/07/17/fearing-coup-putin-removes-major-general-vladimir-seliverstov-from-his-position/
27. WSJ Staff, 'Dozens of Senior Russian Officers Detained, Fired After Wagner Mutiny,' *Moscow Times*, 13 July 2023.
https://www.themoscowtimes.com/2023/07/13/dozens-of-senior-russian-officers-detained-fired-after-wagner-mutiny-wsj-a81830
28. Mary Ilyushina & Natalia Abbakumova, 'Kremlin, shifting blame for war failures, axes military commanders', *Washington Post*, 8 October 2022.
https://www.washingtonpost.com/world/2022/10/07/russia-military-commanders-dismissed-war/
29. Max Seddon, 'Yevgeny Prigozhin in fatal plane crash, Russian officials say', *Financial Times*, 23 August 2023.
https://www.ft.com/content/812c9da3-80f2-4fe1-8fad-0b4441d1977a
30. AP Press, 'Russian officials say Wagner boss Prigozhin was on passenger list of jet that crashed', *NPR*, 23 August 2023.
https://www.npr.org/2023/08/23/1195466126/russia-wagner-prigozhin-crash#:~:text=Hourly%20News-,Yevgeny%20Prigozhin%2C%20Wagner%20boss%2C%20said%20to%20be%20passenger%20on%20deadly,people%20on%20board%2C%20officials%20said.
31. 'Prigozhin plane crash: Wagner mercenaries left wondering what's next', *Times Radio*, 23 June 2023.
https://www.youtube.com/watch?v=ZSJs0AjEzQo
32. War In Ukraine Explained, 24 August 2023: 'Night Ambush: Half Asleep Russian Run in Panic.' https://www.youtube.com/watch?v=c9klvscOSqs
33. Isabel Van Brugen, 'Wagner Group Vows 'Revenge After Prigozhin's Death', *Newsweek*, 24 August 2023.
https://www.newsweek.com/wagner-group-vows-revenge-prigozhin-death-plane-jet-crash-russia-1822138
34. Jeremy Wilson, 'These are the prominent critics and enemies Putin is suspected of having killed', *Insider*, 23 August 2023.
https://www.businessinsider.com/list-of-people-putin-is-suspected-of-assassinating-2016-3
35. WP Staff, 'List of Soviet and Russian assassinations', Wikipedia, 23 August 2023.
https://en.wikipedia.org/wiki/List_of_Soviet_and_Russian_assassinations

36. CBS Staff, 'Navalny Sentenced to 19 more years in prison', *CBS News*, 4 August 2023. https://www.cbsnews.com/news/alexey-navalny-russia-putin-critic-extremism-verdict-prison-sentence/

Chapter 23

1. Nadine El-Bawab, 'Finland begins construction of barrier wall along border with Russia', *ABC News,* 1 March 2023. https://abcnews.go.com/International/finland-begins-construction-barrier-wall-border-russia/story?id=97548905
2. NATO Staff, Vilnus Summit Communique, Par 11–13. https://www.nato.int/cps/en/natohq/official_texts_217320.htm?selectedLocale=en
3. US Army Europe and Africa, Public Affairs, 17 June 2023. https://www.europeafrica.army.mil/DefenderEurope/
4. C. Todd Lopez, 'Multinational Exercise Defender 23 Kicks off This Month in Europe', US *Department of Defense*, 5 April 2023. https://www.defense.gov/News/News-Stories/Article/Article/3353612/multinational-exercise-defender-23-kicks-off-this-month-in-europe/
5. PAO, 'Minnesota Red Bulls participate in European exercise Immediate Response 23', Minnesota National Guard PAO, 26 May, 2023. Brigade size task forces. https://ngmnpublic.azurewebsites.us/minnesota-red-bulls-participate-in-european-exercise-immediate-response-23/
6. NATO Staff, 'Germany host biggest every air exercise of NATO forces', NATO, 12 June 2023. https://www.nato.int/cps/en/natohq/news_215611.htm
7. Thomas Gibbons-Neff & Eric Schmitt, 'Miscommunication Nearly Led to Russian Jet Shooting Down British Spy Plane, US Officials Say', *New York Times*, 12 April 2023. https://www.nytimes.com/2023/04/12/world/europe/russian-jet-british-spy-plane.html
8. Eric Schmitt, 'Russian Warplane Hit American Drone over Black Sea, US Says', *New York Times*, 14 March 2023. https://www.nytimes.com/2023/03/14/us/politics/russia-us-drone-black-sea.html
9. Marc Santora, 'Danube Ports, a Lifeline for Ukraine, Come Under Russian Threat', *New York Times*, 1 August 2023 https://www.nytimes.com/2023/08/01/world/europe/ukraine-grain-danube-ports-russia.html
10. Martin Goillandeau, Sharon Braithwaite & Oleg Racz, 'Wagner troops moving toward Polish border and could try sneaking across, PM says', *CNN*, 29 July 2023. https://www.cnn.com/2023/07/29/europe/wagner-poland-suwalki-intl/index.html
11. LTG (Ret) Ben Hodges & Janusz Bugajski, 'Securing the Suwalki Corridor', *CEPA*, July 2018. https://web.archive.org/web/20220410162602/https://cepa.org/cepa_files/2018-CEPA-report-Securing_The_Suwałki_Corridor.pdf
12. Ibid.
13. 'Wagner forces in Belarus have moved toward Suwalki Gap for hybrid attack on Poland, says PM', Notes from Poland, 29 July 2023. https://notesfrompoland.com/2023/07/29/wagner-forces-in-belarus-have-moved-towards-suwalki-gap-for-hybrid-attack-on-poland-says-pm/#:~:text=Yesterday%2C%20Ukraine%27s%20National%20Resistance%20Centre, smuggling%20and%20transporting%20illegal%20migrants".
14. DE Staff, 'British Cavalry Protects Polish Border with Belarus: Not a Joke But Real NATO Reconnaissance Unit', *Defense Express*, 25 July 2023

https://en.defence-ua.com/news/british_cavalry_protects_polish_border_with_belarus_not_a_joke_but_a_real_nato_reconnaissance_unit-7428.html. M Staff, 'British Cavalry Soldiers switch to horses in Poland', *Militarnyi*, 25 July, 2023 https://mil.in.ua/en/news/british-cavalry-soldiers-switch-to-horses-in-poland/

15. Sebastian Robin, 'In a Russia-NATO War, the Suwalki Gap Could Decide World War III', *The National Interest*, 26 June 2023. https://nationalinterest.org/blog/reboot/russia-nato-war-suwalki-gap-could-decide-world-war-iii-188690

Chapter 24

1. USDA Staff, 'Ukrainian Grain Transportation', *USDA*, June 2023 https://www.ams.usda.gov/sites/default/files/media/UkraineJune2023.pdf
2. P Staff, 'The Black Sea & Naval War in Ukraine – Drones, Grain Blockades & Bridge to Crimea', *Peron*, 31 July 2023 https://www.youtube.com/watch?v=H8D7ioiW0JA&t=2054s
3. EU Staff, 'Infographic – How the Russian Invasion of Ukraine has further aggravated the global food crisis', *European Council*, 28 February 2024. https://www.consilium.europa.eu/en/infographics/how-the-russian-invasion-of-ukraine-has-further-aggravated-the-global-food-crisis/
4. Lord (Mark) Lancaster (UK), *NATO (Draft) Defense and Security Committee (DSC) Sub-Committee On Future Security and Defense Capabilities (DSCFC)*, (NATO: 18 August 2023), 9–10. https://www.nato-pa.int/download-file?filename=/sites/default/files/2023-09/020%20DSCFC%2023%20E%20rev.1%20-%20BLACK%20SEA%20-%20LANCASTER%20REPORT.pdf
5. Alexandra Prokopenko, 'What's in the Ukrainian Grain Deal for Russia', *Carnegie*, 26 July 2023. https://carnegieendowment.org/politika/87576
6. Tass Staff, 'Russia to find way to help countries in need of food, senior Russian diplomat promises', *Tass*, 22 July 2023. https://tass.com/politics/1650421
7. Ibid.
8. Lord (Mark) Lancaster (UK), *NATO (Draft) Defense and Security Committee (DSC) Sub-Committee On Future Security and Defense Capabilities (DSCFC)*, (NATO: 18 August 2023), 9-10. https://www.nato-pa.int/download-file?filename=/sites/default/files/2023-09/020%20DSCFC%2023%20E%20rev.1%20-%20BLACK%20SEA%20-%20LANCASTER%20REPORT.pdf
9. P Staff, 'The Black Sea & Naval War in Ukraine – Drones, Grain Blockades & Bridge to Crimea', *Peron*, 31 July 2023 https://www.youtube.com/watch?v=H8D7ioiW0JA&t=2054s
10. Daniel Wallis, 'Explainer: What is Russia's Problem with the Black Sea grain deal', *Reuters*, 16 June 2023. https://www.reuters.com/world/europe/what-is-russias-problem-with-black-sea-grain-deal-2023-06-16/
11. Sam LaGrone & Heather Mongilio, 'Russia Lays Mines in Black Sea to Block Ukrainian Ports, NSC Says', *USNI News*, 19 July 2023 https://news.usni.org/2023/07/19/russia-says-all-ships-in-the-black-sea-heading-to-ukraine-are-potential-carriers-of-military-cargo
12. iC Staff, 'Friday Fun Fact #2: The largest ships can cost over $200 million to construct', i*Containers*, 28 February 2024.

https://www.icontainers.com/us/2016/11/04/friday-fun-fact-2-the-largest-ships-can-cost-over-200-million-to-construct/

13. Carolyn Cohn & Jonathan Saul, 'March, Lloyd's Ukraine launched war risk ship insurance to cut grain costs', *Reuters*, 15 November 2023. https://www.reuters.com/business/marsh-lloyds-launch-ukraine-war-risk-ship-insurance-cut-grain-costs-2023-11-15/#:~:text=The%20programme%20will%20provide%20cover,lead%20insurer%20on%20that%20programme.
14. Deep State Map, 2 August 2023 https://deepstatemap.live/en#8/45.723/31.231

Chapter 25

1. Oryx Staff, 'List of Naval Losses During the Russian Invasion of Ukraine', *Oryx*, 20 November 2023. https://www.oryxspioenkop.com/2022/03/list-of-naval-losses-during-2022.html
2. Heather Mongillio, 'A Brief Summary of the Battle of the Black Sea', *USNI News*, 15 November 2023.
3. Milan Vego, *On Littoral Warfare*, (US Naval War College Digital Commons) 2015.
4. Heather Mongillio, 'A Brief Summary of the Battle of the Black Sea', *USNI News*, 15 November 2023.
5. UK Press release: 'British Commandos train hundreds of Ukrainian Marines in UK Programme', GOV.UK, 11 August 2023. https://www.gov.uk/government/news/british-commandos-train-hundreds-of-ukrainian-marines-in-uk-programme
6. Victoria Kim, Richard Perez-Pena & Andrew E. Kramer, 'Elon Musk Refused to Enable Ukraine Drone Attack on Russian Fleet', *New York Times*, 8 September 2023. https://www.nytimes.com/2023/09/08/world/europe/elon-musk-ukraine-starlink-drones.html#:~:text=Elon%20Musk%20foiled%20an%20attack, wielded%20by%20a%20multibillionaire%20businessman.
7. Carrington Malin,'Has Russia destroyed Ukraine's naval drone capability', *Armada International*, 17 August 2023. https://www.armadainternational.com/2023/08/has-russia-destroyed-ukraines-naval-drone-capability/
8. Sebastien Poblin, 'Robot Kamikaze Boats Blew up Russia's Bridge to Crimea. Again', *Popular Mechanics*, 17 July 2023. https://www.popularmechanics.com/military/navy-ships/a44566646/robot-kamikaze-boats-blow-up-russia-bridge-to-crimea-again/
9. Kelly McLaughlin, 'Ukraine attacked Russia's main naval base in Crimea with sea drones, the city's Russian governor said', *Insider,* 24 April 2023. https://www.businessinsider.com/ukraine-attacked-crimea-naval-base-sea-drones-russian-governor-says-2023-4
10. NN Staff, 'New Ukrainian naval drone attack on port of Sevastopol', *Naval News*, 17 July 2023. https://navyrecognition.com/index.php/naval-news/naval-news-archive/2023/july/13355-new-ukrainian-naval-drone-attack-on-port-of-sevastopol-crimea.html
11. SOF Staff, 'Kerch Bridge Connecting Crimea to Russia Damaged', *SOF News*, 8 October 2022. https://sof.news/conflicts/kerch-bridge/
12. Fredrick Kunkle, David L. Stern &Mary Ilyushina, 'Ukraine Hits Crimean Bridge, but railway undamaged: Russia halts grain deal', *Washington Post*, 17 July 2023. https://www.washingtonpost.com/world/2023/07/17/kerch-bridge-crimea-grain-ukraine-russia/

13. WIU Staff, '17 Jul: Nice! Ukrainians INCAPACITATED THE RUSSIAN ARMY IN 1 MOVE, *War in Ukraine*, 17 July 2023. https://www.youtube.com/watch?v=pnlXOJ33S94
14. FN Staff, 'Why Kerch Bridge is so important: Six reasons it is still standing despite attacks', *Forces Net*, 19 July 2023. https://www.forces.net/ukraine/six-reasons-why-crimea-bridge-still-standing-despite-attacks
15. Andrew Jeong, Victoria Bisset & Miriam Berger, *Washington Post*, 2 August 2023. https://www.washingtonpost.com/world/2023/08/02/russia-ukraine-war-news/
16. G Staff, 'Odesa suffers "hellish night" as Russia attacks Ukraine grain faculties', *Guardian*, 19 July 2023. https://www.theguardian.com/world/2023/jul/19/odesa-suffers-hellish-night-as-russia-attacks-ukraines-grain-facilities
17. David Axe, 'NATO Planes Watched as Three Civilian Ships Ran Russia's Naval Blockade of Ukraine', *Forbes*, 31 July 2023 https://www.forbes.com/sites/davidaxe/2023/07/31/nato-planes-watched-as-three-civilian-ships-ran-russias-naval-blockade-of-ukraine/?sh=1279d3bd1b72
18. Pavel Polityuk, 'Russia strikes Ukraine's Danube port, driving up global grain prices', *Reuters*, 2 August 2023. https://www.reuters.com/world/europe/russia-hits-port-grain-silo-ukraines-odesa-region-official-2023-08-02/
19. Sgt. Alexander Chatoff, 'NATO rockets fly from the Black Sea Coast in Support of Exercise Sabre Guardian', *US Army*, 7 June 2023. https://www.army.mil/article/267359/nato_rockets_fly_from_the_black_sea_coast_in_support_of_exercise_saber_guardian_23
20. Yuliya Talmazan AND Matthew Mulligan, 'Russian warship appears damaged in Ukrainian sea drone attack on key naval base,' NBC, 4 August 2023.
21. Tim Lister, Victoria Buteenko & Kostan Nechyporenko,'Ukraine hits Russian Oil tanker with sea drones hours after attacking naval base', *CNN,* 5 August 2023.
22. EP Staff, 'Romania Has Not Found Any Debris from Russian Shahed Drone on its Territory near Izmail', *European Pravda*, 3 August 2023
23. RFE Staff, 'NATO Jets Scrambled 570 Times Last Year to Check Military Flights', *Radio Free Europe*, 9 February 2023
24. A Staff, 'Russian fighter aircraft hold combat drills over Baltic Sea', *Al Jazeera*, 27 June 2023.
25. AP Staff, 'Russian jets harass US Drones aircraft over Syria for the second time in 24 hours', *AP*, 5 July 2023. Tara Copp & Lolita C. Baldor, 'Russian fighter jet flies dangerously close to US warplane over Syria', *AP*, 17 July 2023.
26. Pavel Polityuk, 'Russia strikes Ukraine's Danube port, driving up global grains prices', *Reuters,* 2 August 2023.
27. Darya Tarasova, Gul Tuysuz & Lauren Kent, 'Russia fires warning shots and boards cargo ship in Black Sea', *CNN*, 13 August 2023 https://www.cnn.com/2023/08/13/europe/russia-warning-shots-black-sea-intl/index.html
28. UK MoD Press Release, 'British Commandos train hundreds of Ukrainian Marines in UK programme', 11 August 2023. https://www.gov.uk/government/news/british-commandos-train-hundreds-of-ukrainian-marines-in-uk-programme
29. Michael Peck, 'The UK is sending Ukraine a newer, longer-range missile that lets humans guide it all the way to the target', *Insider,* 23 December 2022.

https://www.businessinsider.com/uk-sending-ukraine-brimstone-anti-armor-ground-attack-missile-2022-12
30. War in Ukraine Explained, 24 August: Night Ambush: Half-Asleep Naked Russians Run in Panic https://www.youtube.com/watch?v=c9klvscOSqs
31. Lord (Mark) Lancaster (UK), *NATO (Draft) Defense and Security Committee (DSC) Sub-Committee on Future Security and Defense Capabilities (DSCFC)*, (NATO, 18 August 2023), 8.
https://www.nato-pa.int/download-file?filename=/sites/default/files/2023-09/020%20DSCFC%2023%20E%20rev.1%20-%20BLACK%20SEA%20-%20LANCASTER%20REPORT.pdf
32. Ibid. 10–11.
https://www.nato-pa.int/download-file?filename=/sites/default/files/2023-09/020%20DSCFC%2023%20E%20rev.1%20-%20BLACK%20SEA%20-%20LANCASTER%20REPORT.pdf
33. Heather Mongilio, 'Turkey Closes Bosphorus, Dardanelles Straits to War Ships', *USNI News*, 28 February 2023. https://news.usni.org/2022/02/28/turkey-closes-bosphorus-dardanelles-straits-to-warships
34. Ben Hubbard & Gulsin Harman, 'Why the Black Sea is a Flashpoint between Russia and the West', 21 March 2023
https://www.nytimes.com/2023/03/15/world/middleeast/black-sea-ukraine-war.html

Chapter 26

1. The Russian order of battle and command relationship was based upon his experience as a tactical intelligence officer and understanding of Soviet/Russian doctrine.
2. Konrad Muzyka, 'Ukraine Conflict Monitor 24 August–1 September 2023', *Rochan,* 2023.
3. Ukrainians were generally not conscripted until their mid-twenties. The rank and files soldiers were more mature then their opponents or NATO soldiers.
4. HL ,'Major Russian Offensive on Strategic Kupyansk', *History Legends*, 15 August 2023. https://www.youtube.com/watch?v=C_U6iyIpeyY
5. Ibid.
6. Ibid. 'Kings and Generals. Ukraine Breaks through the Surovikin Lines', Russian Invasion Documentary.
https://www.youtube.com/watch?v=ONum4RbudQ0
7. Konrad Muzyka, 'Ukraine Conflict Monitor 12–18 August', *Rochan,* 2023. Konrad Muzyka, 'Ukraine Conflict Monitor 19–27August, *Rochan,* 2023.
https://rochanconsulting.substack.com/p/ukraine-conflict-monitor-12-august
8. David Axe, 'The Ukrainian Army Apparently Downgrades its New 32nd Briagde and Deployed it Somewhere Quiet', *Forbes*, 5 July 2023.
https://www.forbes.com/sites/davidaxe/2023/07/05/the-ukrainian-army-apparently-downgraded-its-new-32nd-brigade-and-deployed-it-somewhere-quiet/?sh=e777343185f0
9. Konrad Muzyka, 'Ukraine Conflict Monitor 23–29 September 2023', *Rochan,* 2023, Konrad Muzyka, 'Ukraine Conflict Monitor 28 September–3 October 2023', *Rochan,* 2023.

Chapter 27

1. Konrad Muzyka, 'Ukraine Conflict Monitor 23–29 September 2023, *Rochan,* 2023. https://rochanconsulting.substack.com/p/ukraine-conflict-monitor-23-september
2. Konrad Muzyka, Rochan's Report: 'Ukrainian Options in the Kherson Direction', 18 October 2023.

https://rochanconsulting.substack.com/p/rochans-report-ukrainian-options?utm_source=substack&publication_id=1229756&post_id=138069356&utm_medium=email&utm_content=share&utm_campaign=email-share&triggerShare=true&isFreemail=false&r=1pm3vy

3. Ibid.
4. Deep State Map, 18 October 2023.
   https://deepstatemap.live/en#10/46.4965/33.1870
5. Artur Rehi, 'Ukrainian Armor Crossed the Dnipro River', Ukrainian War Update, 7 November 2023.
   https://www.youtube.com/watch?v=eCudiw1RGJM
   Denys Davydov, 'Update from Ukraine/Ukraine Moves to the South/ Russians can't hold the ground', 07 November 2023.
   https://www.youtube.com/watch?v=c-WdcmxQXYk
6. The higher command structure was not clear at time of writing.
7. M Staff, 'Ukrainian Marines Repel Russian Assault on Krynky', *Militarnyi*, 8 January 2024
   https://mil.in.ua/en/news/ukrainian-marines-repel-russian-assault-on-krynky/
8. Alex Kokcharow, 'Russian Combat Units Suffer Brutal Losses in Dnipro Bridgehead Battles', *Kyiv Post*, 17 January 2024
   https://www.kyivpost.com/post/26857
9. Ibid.
10. David Axe, 'Ukrainian Troops Killed the Most Dangerous Man In Krynky, A Russian Drone Operator', *Forbes*, 2 February 2024.
    https://www.forbes.com/sites/davidaxe/2024/02/02/ukrainian-troops-killed-the-most-dangerous-man-in-krynky-a-russian-drone-commander-it-was-their-cue-to-go-on-the-attack/?sh=1f877d9c6928
11. David Axe, 'Exceptionally Heavy Losses as Russia's Newest Airborne Division Attacks Ukraine's Dnipro Bridgehead', *Forbes*, 15 December 2023
    https://www.forbes.com/sites/davidaxe/2023/12/15/exceptionally-heavy-losses-as-russias-newest-airborne-division-attacks-ukraines-dnipro-bridgehead/?sh=3c62c04911c6
12. Stefan Korshak, 'Russian Combat Units Suffer Brutal Losses in Dnipro Bridgehead Battles', *Kyiv Post*, 17 January 2024.
    https://www.kyivpost.com/post/26857
13. David Axe, 'Exceptionally Heavy Losses as Russia's Newest Airborne Division Attacks Ukraine's Dnipro Bridgehead', *Forbes*, 15 December 2023
    https://www.forbes.com/sites/davidaxe/2023/12/15/exceptionally-heavy-losses-as-russias-newest-airborne-division-attacks-ukraines-dnipro-bridgehead/?sh=3c62c04911c6
14. David Axe, 'It's Not Suicide – It's Attrition Warfare', *Forbes*, 21 December 2023.
    https://www.forbes.com/sites/davidaxe/2023/12/21/the-battle-for-krynky-is-a-nightmare-for-both-sides-but-its-not-suicide-its-attritional-warfare/?sh=22f52e2c33f8

Chapter 28

1. David Gritten, 'Strikes on Gaza after Palestinian militants entered Israel', *BBC*, 7 October 2023.
2. Till Schmidt, 'An Axis of Evil against the Western World', *Zentrum Liberale Moderne*, 27 October 2023.
   https://libmod.de/en/an-axis-of-evil-against-the-western-world/

3. 'The Israel-Hamas War – What We Know So Far', *Kings & Generals*, October 2023 https://www.youtube.com/watch?v=9UTckJi7hQ4
4. Samia Nakhoul, 'How Hamas secretly built a "mini-army" to fight Israel', Reuters, 16 October 2023. https://www.reuters.com/world/middle-east/how-hamas-secretly-built-mini-army-fight-israel-2023-10-13/#:~:text=After%20Israel%20withdrew%20from%20Gaza,the%20Sinai%20Peninsula%2C%20they%20added.
5. On 7 October 2023, my son, Major Cyrus Harrel, and his team were in Tel Aviv packing up to drive south when the rockets started to fall. Interview with Major Cyrus R. Harrel, USA.
6. Oren Liebermann, Natasha Bertrand & Brad Lendon, 'US sending second carrier strike group, fighter jets to region as Israel prepares to expand Gaza Operations', *CNN*, 15 October 2023 https://www.cnn.com/2023/10/14/middleeast/us-aircraft-carrier-eisenhower-israel-gaza-intl-hnk-ml/index.html
7. C. Todd Lopez, 'F-16s Head to Middle East to Help Protect US Troops', *US DoD*, 24 October 2023 https://www.defense.gov/News/News-Stories/Article/Article/3567672/f-16s-head-to-middle-east-to-help-protect-us-troops/
8. Chris Gordon, 'Response to Iran Militia Attacks', *Air & Space Forces Magazine*, 26 October 2023. https://www.airandspaceforces.com/warnings-military-response-attacks-us-bases-middle-east/
9. Lolita Baldor, 'US fighter jets strike Iran-linked sites in Syria in retaliation for attacks on US troops', *AP*, 27 October 2023 https://apnews.com/article/syria-airstrikes-iran-revolutionary-guard-af3c7a0f069b8c8b08f6feaa0e165d6a. Lolita C Baldor, 'US fighter jets strike Iran-linked sites in Syria in retiation for attacks on US Troops, *Los Angeles Times*, 27 October 2023. https://www.latimes.com/world-nation/story/2023-10-27/u-s-fighter-jets-strike-iran-linked-sites-in-syria-in-retaliation-for-attacks-on-us-troops,
   Jim Garamone, 'DoD Continues Efforts to Support Israel, Limit Spread of War', *US DoD*, 30 October 2023 https://www.defense.gov/News/News-Stories/Article/Article/3573065/dod-continues-efforts-to-support-israel-limit-spread-of-war/
10. Samia Nakhoul, James MacKenzie, Matt Spetanlnich & Aziz El Yaakoubi, 'Exclusive: US-Saudi defense pact tied to Israel deal, Palestinian demands put aside', *Reuters*, 29 September 2023. https://www.reuters.com/world/us-saudi-defence-pact-tied-israel-deal-palestinian-demands-put-aside-2023-09-29/
11. Adam Gallagher, 'Is a Saudi-Israel Normalization Agreement on the Horizon?' United States Institute of Peace, 28 September 2023. https://www.usip.org/publications/2023/09/saudi-israel-normalization-agreement-horizon
12. I attended a seminar on the Israeli water issue while serving as US War College Fellow at the Mershon Center for International Security and Peace Keeping at Ohio State University in 1979.
13. Jonathon B. Lincoln, 'Middle East Peace: The Biden Administration's Approach', *Rand*, 31 August 2022. https://www.rand.org/blog/2022/08/middle-east-peace-the-biden-administrations-approach.html

14. KG Staff, 'Israel-Hamas: Before the Ground Assault', *Kings and Generals Modern Affairs*, 30 October 2023.
https://www.youtube.com/watch?v=gn8T2fDSpMk
15. Eric Schmitt, 'Pentagon Sends US Arms Stores in Israel to Ukraine', *New York Times*, 17 January 2023.
https://www.nytimes.com/2023/01/17/us/politics/ukraine-israel-weapons.html
16. Francesca Ebel, 'Russian cites "concern" but does not condemn Hamas attack on Israel', *Washington Post*, 9 October 2023.
https://www.washingtonpost.com/world/2023/10/09/russia-hamas-israel-iran-ukraine/
17. Holl Ellyatt, 'Russia can gain from Middle East turmoil – but it could backfire if the war spirals out of control', *CNBC*, 13 October 2023.
https://www.cnbc.com/2023/10/13/russia-benefits-from-the-war-between-israel-and-hamas-in-3-ways.html
18. Marwan Kabalan, 'Hamas' attack on Israel has changed the Middle East', *Al Jazeera*, 28 October 2023.
19. Alisa Orlova, 'Russian Transfers Captured Ukrainian Weapons to Hamas in Bid to Discredit Kyiv', *Kyiv Post*, 9 October 2023
https://www.kyivpost.com/post/22522
20 Ambassador to UN Gilad Erdan, Twitter, 29 February 2024
https://twitter.com/giladerdan1?lang=en
21. Tovah Lazaroff, 'Russia deepening ties with global axis of evil', *Jerusalem Post*, 27 February 2024
https://www.jpost.com/international/article-789156
22. Aurora Ortega, 'Hizbullah and Russia's Nascent Alliance', *RUSI*, 23 May 2023

Chapter 29

1. Konstantin Skorkin, 'Are Ukraine's President and Chief Commander Really at War?' *Carnegie Politika*, 6 December 2023
https://carnegieendowment.org/politika/91182
2. Ibid.
3. TE Staff, 'An interview with General Valery Zaluzhnu, head of Ukraine's Armed Forces', *Economist*, 15 December 2023,
https://www.economist.com/Zaluzhnyi-transcript?utm_medium=cpc.adword.pd&utm_source=google&ppccampaignID=17210591673&ppcadID=&utm_campaign=a.22brand_pmax&utm_content=conversion.direct-response.anonymous&gad_source=1&gclid=Cj0KCQiAwbitBhDIARIsABfFYIIsroJ7YsLh-QJtqH6YA-Or2wiLYpdD0E-eSn6RXlxEMS9Wu-ypuDsaAgVcEALw_wcB&gclsrc=aw.ds
4. Andrew E. Kramer, 'Zelensky Rebuke of Top General Signals Rift in Ukrainian Leadership', *New York Times*, 4 November 2023.
https://www.nytimes.com/2023/11/04/world/europe/zelensky-rebuke-general-Zaluzhnyi.html. General Zaluzhnyi's full essay is linked to this article.
5. Konstantin Skorkin, 'Are Ukraine's President and Chief Commander Really at War?' *Carnegie Politika*, 6 December 2023
https://carnegieendowment.org/politika/91182
6. R Staff, 'Who is Rustem Umerov, Ukraine's likely new defense minister?' *Reuters*, 4 September 2023
https://www.reuters.com/world/europe/who-is-rustem-umerov-ukraines-likely-new-defence-minister-2023-09-04/

7. US News Staff, 'Ukraine Removes Deputy Defense Minister After New Minister's Appointment', *US News*, 18 September 2023 https://www.usnews.com/news/world/articles/2023-09-18/ukraine-dismisses-six-deputy-defence-ministers-in-reshuffle-at-ministry
8. Illia Novikov, 'Ukraine fires 6 deputy defense ministers as heavy fighting continues', *AP*, 18 September 2023. https://apnews.com/article/ukraine-russia-deputy-defense-ministers-fired-ab8f88ff31f26ae29b35bd14406e62f3
9. Valenyna Romanenko, 'Former Special Operations Forces Commander learns of his dismissal from news', *Ukrainian Pravda*, 3 November 2023, https://www.pravda.com.ua/eng/news/2023/11/3/7427118/
10. YN Staff, 'Zelensky explains what former Commander Khorenko of Special Operations will do', *Yahoo News* (from Ukraine *Pravda*), 3 November 2023 https://news.yahoo.com/zelenskyy-explains-former-commander-khorenko-172317765.html
11. VOA Staff, 'Zelensky Calls for Rapid Operations Changes for Soldiers, Sacks Commander', *VOA Ukraine*, 19 November 2023 https://www.voanews.com/a/zelenskyy-calls-for-rapid-operations-changes-for-soldiers-sacks-commander/7361684.html
12. Alisa Orlova, 'He is needed in Another Directions – Defense Ministry on Dismissal of Special Operations Commander', *Kyiv Post*, 5 November 2023. https://www.kyivpost.com/post/23686
13. Konstantin Skorkin, 'Are Ukraine's President and Chief Commander Really at War?' *Carnegie Politika*, 6 December 2023 https://carnegieendowment.org/politika/91182
14. RT Staff, 'They will cling to Avdiivka to the bitter end. Why does Zelensky need a second]d Bakhmut', *RTVI* (Russian Federation News Agency), November 2023. Retrieved from Ground News, 22 January 2023. https://ground.news/article/will-the-battle-of-avdiivka-become-bakhmut-20_32e490
15. Ibid.
16. Zachary Goelman, 'Ukrainian commanders not about to be dismissed, defense minister says', *Reuters*, 12 December 2023. https://www.reuters.com/world/europe/ukrainian-commanders-not-about-be-dismissed-defence-minister-says-2023-12-12/

Chapter 30

1. Carlotta Gall, 'Both Sides Pay a Bloody Price for Coveted Ukrainian City', *New York Times*, 30 October 2023. https://www.nytimes.com/2023/10/30/world/europe/ukraine-avdiivka.html#:~:text=Ukrainian%20reconnaissance%20teams%20saw%20signs,were%20gathering%2C"%20he%20said.
2. Konrad Muzya, 'Russian Options in the Donetsk Direction – The Avdiivka Axis', *Rochan Consulting*, 24 October, 2023. https://rochanconsulting.substack.com/p/russian-options-in-the-donetsk-direction
3. Ibid.
4. History Legends, 'Costly Russian Storm-Z Assault on Fortress Avdiivka', 23 October 2023. https://www.youtube.com/watch?v=eREr43Xl7ck
5. Ibid.

6. War in Ukraine 10 Oct: Suicide Operation. Russian Set Record Losses in 1 Day. https://www.youtube.com/watch?v=nZxku2U_SxE
7. Deep State Map, 10–16 October 2023. https://deepstatemap.live/en#11/48.1276/37.8726
8. History Legends, 'Costly Russian Storm-Z Assault on Fortress Avdiivka', 23 October 2023. https://www.youtube.com/watch?v=eREr43Xl7ck
9. War in Ukraine 11 Oct: 'Reality Hits in the Face. Russians Had No Tanks on 2nd Day of Offensive.' https://www.youtube.com/watch?v=LMoPXxT3Eqk&t=17s
10. Stefan Korshak, 'Worst Russian Land Battle Defeat in Nine Months – Kremlin Forces Hit a Wall at Avdiivka', *Kyiv Post*, 13 October 2023. https://www.kyivpost.com/post/22706
11. War in Ukraine 13 Oct: 'Massacre! Russian Lose 1,030 Troops, 75 Tanks & Armored Vehicles in 1 Day.' https://www.youtube.com/watch?v=rjqmUZaF5JU
12. David E. Sanger, Lara Jakes, Marc Santor, Constant Meheut & John Ismay, 'Ukraine Uses Powerful American-Supplied Missiles for First Time', *New York Times*, 17 October 2023. https://www.nytimes.com/2023/10/17/world/europe/ukraine-atacms-attacks-russia.html
13. War in Ukraine Explained, 15 Oct: 'Storming Terrikon: Insane Russian 0% Survival Rate Attack.' https://www.youtube.com/watch?v=p_CNhVFeQdk
14. ISW, Russian Offensive Campaign Assessment, 16 October 2023.
15. War in Ukraine Explained, 20 Oct: 'Record Russian Losses 1,400 men,175 Tanks & BMPs in 1 Day.' https://www.youtube.com/watch?v=NwUYDJbFzQY&t=1s
16. Stefan Korshak, 'Worst Russian Land Battle Defeat in Nine Months –Kremlin Forces Hit a Wall at Avdiivka,' Kyiv Post, 13 October 2023. https://www.kyivpost.com/post/22706
17. Artur Rehi, 'Russian Meat Assults Got Worse!' *Ukraine Update*, 30 October 2023. https://www.youtube.com/watch?v=7FY4EolmKBA

18 Artur Rehi, 'Russian Army Suffers Hugh Losses', *Ukrainian War Update*. 31 October 2023. https://www.youtube.com/watch?v=HEDpmjobu14

19. Arthur Rehi, 'Russia Lost Entire Fuel Train in Donetsk', *Ukraine War Update*, 1 November 2023. https://www.youtube.com/watch?v=I5znJvLvkGg&t=608s
20. PRC Press Release, 'Xi Jinping Holds Talks with Russian President Vladimar Putin', *Ministry of Foreign Affairs of the People Republic of China*, 18 October 2023 https://www.fmprc.gov.cn/mfa_eng/zxxx_662805/202310/t20231018_11163382.html
21. Rush Doshi, 'The Long Game, China's Grand Strategy to Displace American Order', *Brookings*, 2 August 2021, https://www.brookings.edu/articles/the-long-game-chinas-grand-strategy-to-displace-american-order/
22. War In Ukraine Explained, 22 Oct: 'Brace for it! Ukrainians Conduct a Massive Counter-attack,' https://www.youtube.com/watch?v=5tJRSYjql70&t=169s, Deep State Map, 20–31 October 2023

https://deepstatemap.live/en#12/48.1085/37.6450. History Legends, 'Russian Armored Columns Steamroll North of Aviivka', 6 November 2023 https://www.youtube.com/watch?v=-_3Joe31u_Q
23. War In Ukraine Explained, 4 Feb 2024: 'Nice. A Huge Group of Russians Gets Taken into a Pocket.' https://www.youtube.com/watch?v=9EZsO1MXIqM
24. War In Ukraine Explained. 11 Feb 2024: Russians Panic! Ukrainian Reinforcements Arrived To Storm Northern Flank. https://www.youtube.com/watch?v=XUvotmRGo54&t=55s
25. Julian E Barnes, 'Biden Administration Blames Congress for Fall of Ukrainian City', New York Times, 17 February 2024.
26. Sam Fossum, 'Biden blames "congressional inaction" for Ukrainian withdrawal from town in call with Zelensky', *CNN*, 17 February 2024.
27. War In Ukraine Explained, 18 Feb 2024: 'Shocking Footage Reveals The Real Cost Russians Paid for Avdiivka.' https://www.youtube.com/watch?v=VNTC0H1zWwI

Chapter 31

1. FM100-2-1 Soviet Tactics and Operations, US Army,
2. Watling & Reynolds, Meat Grinder (May 2023),
3. See chapter in above on Wagner tactics.

Chapter 32

1. EM, 'Frontline report: Ukraine moves Patriot system closer to the frontline, resulting in three Russian aircraft downed', *Euromaidan*, 23 December 2023. https://euromaidanpress.com/2023/12/23/frontline-report-ukraine-moves-patriot-system-closer-to-frontline-resulting-in-three-russian-aircraft-downed/?swcfpc=1
2. Julian E. Barnes, 'Ukraine's Creative Use of Weapons Carries Promises and Risks', *New York Times*, 8 February 2024
3. Alex Horton, 'These are the Western air defense systems protecting Ukraine', *Washington Post*, 19 May 2023.
4. Staff, 'Patriot Air and Missile Defense System for Ukraine', *CRS,* 18 January 2023
5. Mark F. Cancian, 'Patriot to Ukraine: What Does it Mean?' *CSIS,* 16 December 2022.
6. Yuri Zoria, 'UK intel: Two A-50 AWACS aircraft downed in two months show Russia's difficultly securing air assists', *Euromaidan*, 27 February 2024. https://euromaidanpress.com/2024/02/27/uk-intel-two-a-50-awacs-aircraft-downed-in-two-months-show-russias-difficulty-securing-air-assets/?swcfpc=1
7. Olivia Yanchik, 'Ukraine needs enhanced air defenses as Russia expands missiles arsenal', *Atlantic Council*, 2 March 2024. https://www.atlanticcouncil.org/blogs/ukrainealert/ukraine-needs-enhanced-air-defenses-as-russia-expands-missile-arsenal/#:~:text=Ukraine%27s%20international%20partners%20need%20to,arsenal%2C%20as%20have%20gun%20trucks.
8. C. Todd Lopez, 'Air Defense Remains Top Priority at Meeting on Ukraine Defense', *US DoD*, 19 September 2023. https://www.defense.gov/News/News-Stories/Article/Article/3531013/air-defense-remains-top-priority-at-meeting-on-ukraine-defense/

Chapter 33

1. Kate Sullivan, 'Trump says he would encourage Russia to 'do whatever the hell they want' to any NATO country that doesn't pay enough,' *CNN,* 11 February 2024.

https://www.cnn.com/2024/02/10/politics/trump-russia-nato/index.html

2. E Staff, 'Can Europe defended itself without America?' *Economist*, 18 February, 2023. https://www.economist.com/briefing/2024/02/18/can-europe-defend-itself-without-america#
3. Clea Caulcutt, 'Macron stands by remarks about sending troops to Ukraine', *Politico*, 29 February 2024.
   https://www.politico.eu/article/emmanuel-macron-ukraine-western-troops-remarks/
4. Statement of Israeli Prime Minister Netanyahu on 30 October 2023.
5. Justin Bronk, 'Europe Must Urgently Prepare to Deter Russia without Large-Scale US Support', *RUSI*, 7 December 2023.
   https://rusi.org/explore-our-research/publications/commentary/europe-must-urgently-prepare-deter-russia-without-large-scale-us-support

Epilogue

1. RFE Staff, 'More than 700,000 Ukrainian Childern Taken to Russia Since Full-Scale War Started, Offical Says', *Radio Free Europe*, 31 July 2023.
   https://www.rferl.org/a/russia-children-taken-ukraine/32527298.html
2. The US did force Native American children to attend boarding schools. Upon graduation they were intended to return home. Most schools were run by religious institutions and the children were often mistreated.
3. David B. Green, '1856: Russia Stops Conscripting Jewish Children', *Haaretz*, 26 August 2012.
   https://www.haaretz.com/jewish/2012-08-26/ty-article/1856-russia-stops-drafting-jewish-kids/0000017f-db8b-db5a-a57f-dbeb5fe90000
4. W Staff, 'Stealing Ukraine's Children', *The Week*, 7 April, 2023, 11.
5. Ibid.
   Vladyslav Havrylov, 'Russia's mass abduction of Ukrainian children may qualify as genocide', *Atlantic Council*, 27 July 2023,
6. Ievgenia Gidulianova, 'Ukrainian Children in Search of a Way Home from Russia', *HRWF*, 15 December 2023.

Select Bibliography

Books and Articles

A Staff, 'Russian fighter aircraft hold combat drills over Baltic Sea', Aljazeera, 27 June 2023.

Applebaum, Anne, 'Germany is Arguing with itself over Ukraine', *The Atlantic*, 20 October 2022.

AP Staff, 'Russian jets harass US Drones aircraft over Syria for the second time in 24 hours,' *AP*, 5 July 2023.

Axe, David, 'The Ukrainian Army's Jaeger Brigades Are Middleweight Forces Troops', *Forbes*, 26 December 2022 .

——, 'Russian Marines Are Getting Killed and Wounded By The Hundreds in Ukraine', *Forbes*, 7 November 2022.

——, 'After Losing an Eighth of their Helicopters, Russian Attack Regiments are Switching their Tactics', *Forbes*, 14 February 2023.

——, 'At the Bleeding Edge of Ukraine's Counteroffensive: the Ukrainian Marine Corps Switches up its Tactics, *Forbes*, 6 June 2023.

——, '25 Tanks and Armoured Fighting Vehicles, Gone in a Blink: the Ukrainian Defeat near Mala Tokmachka was Worse than we Thought', *Forbes*, 27 June 2023.

——, 'NATO Planes Watched as Three Civilian Ships Ran Russia's Naval Blockade of Ukraine, *Forbes*, 31 July 2023.

——, 'Exceptionally Heavy Losses as Russia's Newest Airborne Division Attacks Ukraine's Dnipro Bridgehead', *Forbes*, 15 December 2023

——, It's not Suicide – it's Attrition Warfare', *Forbes*, 21 December 2023.

——, 'Ukrainian Troops Killed the Most Dangerous Main in Krynky, a Russian Drone Operator, *Forbes*, 2 February 2024.

——, 'The Russians are Pulling 70-year-old T-55 Tanks out of Storage', *Forbes*, 22 March 2023.

——, 'The Ukrainian Army Apparently Downgrades its New 32nd Brigade and Deployed somewhere Quiet', *Forbes*, 5 July 2023.

——, 'Ukraine Has Four Marine Brigades. It has Packed All Of Them Into A 10 Mile Sector,' *Forbes*, 4 August 2023.

——, 'Some Of Ukraine's Heavy Brigades Don't Have Real Tanks Yet. Here's How They Might Fight,' Forbes, March 6, 2023.

Arraf, Jane, 'Crowdfunding a War: How Online Appeals are Bringing Weapons to Ukraine', *New York Times*, 10 May 2022.

Austin, Greg and Khaniejo, Natallia, Impact of the Russian-Ukraine War on National Cyber Planning: A Survey of Ten Countries, *IISS*, December 2023.

Atkinson, Rick, 'Operation Cobra and the Breakout at Normandy', US Army, 22 July 2010.

Bailey, Riley, 'Russian Offensive Campaign Assessment, April 1, 2023', *Critical Threat*, 1 April 2023.

Baldor, Lolita, 'US to begin training Ukrainian troops on Abrams tank', *AP*, 21 April 2023.

Baldor, Lotita' 'US fighter jets strike Iran-linked sites in Syria in retaliation for attacks on US Troops', *Los Angeles Times*, 27 October 2023.

Balmforth, Tom, 'Ukraine to produce thousands of long-range drones in 2024, minister says', *Reuters*, 12 February 2023.

Barnes, James E, 'Ukraine's Creative Use of Weapons Carries Promises and Risks, *New York Times*, 8 February 2024.

Barnes, Julian E, 'Biden Administration Blames Congress for Fall of Ukrainian City', *New York Times*, 17 February 2024.

Bartles, Charles K, 'The Russian Naval Infantry: Increasing Amphibious Warfare Capabilities', *US Army TRADOC*, 2018.

Battersby, WO2 Blair, 'Russia's Approach to War in its So-Called 'Special Operation' in Ukraine Has Evolved over the Past 21 Months, Suggesting Ways In Which US Army OPFOR Training Can Evolve Match, *US Army TRADOC*, 2023.

Beardsworth, James, 'Russian Military's Supply Problems in Ukraine', *The Moscow Times*, 5 October 2022

Bielieskov, Mykola, 'Ukraine's Territorial Defence Forces: The War So Far and Future Prospects,' *RUSI*, 11 May 2023.

——, 'Ukraine's drone army is bringing Putin's Invasion to Russia,' *Atlantic Council*, 26 September 2023.

——, 'Ukraine opens new front with drone strikes on Russia's energy sector,' *Atlantic Council*, 6 February 2024,

Bilal, Arsalan, 'Hybrid Warfare – New Threats, Complexity, and "Trust" as the Antidote', *NATO Review*, 30 November 2021.

Bohnert, Michael, 'The Uncounted Losses to Russia's Air Force', *Rand*, 14 August 2023.

Brumfield, Cynthia, 'Incident response lessons learned from the Russian attack on Viasat', *CSO*, 16 August 2023.

Bronk, Justin, 'Europe Must Urgently Prepare to Deter Russia without Large-Scale US Support" *RUSI*, 7 December 2023.

Cappy, Chris, 'Vuhledar, Why Russian Repeats the Same Mistakes',*Task and Purpose*, March 2023.

Caulcutt, Clea, 'At Last, Ukraine Gets Western Tanks', *Politico*, 5 January 2023.

——, 'Macron stands by remarks about sending troops to Ukraine,' *Politico*, 29 February 2024.

CEDF Staff, 'CRDF Global Becomes Platform for Cyber Defense Assistance Collaborative (CDAC) for Ukraine, Receives Grant from Craig Newmark Philanthropies', *CRDFGL BAL*, 14 November 2022.

Charap, Samuel &Piebe,Miranda,'Avoiding a Long War, US Policy and the Trajectory of the Russian-Ukraine Conflict,'*Rand Corporation*. 2022.

Chatoff, Sgt. Alexander, 'NATO rockets fly from the Black Sea Coast in Support of Exercise Sabre Guardian', *US Army*, 7 June 2023.

Christenson, Josh, 'Critical threat to US interests: poll, *AP*, 15 March 2023.

CIA, Foreign Threats to the 2020 US Federal Elections, March 10, 2021.

Clark, Alan, *Barbarossa: The Russian-German Conflict 1941*, (London: Headline Publishing Group, 1966).

Clark, Lloyd, *Kusk: The Greatest Tank Battle: Eastern Front 1943*, (London: Headline Publishing Group, 2012)

Clark, Mason and Hird, Karolina, *Russian Ground Forces Order of Battle*, (ISW: October 2023)

Cohn, Carolyn and Saul, Jonathan, 'March, Lloyd's Ukraine launched war risk ship insurance to cut grain costs', *Reuters*, 15 November 2023.

Cook, Mary Alice, 'Manifest Opportunity: the Alaska Purchases as a Bridge between United States Expansion and Imperialism', *Alaska History*, Vol 26, No.1, Spring 2011.

Cooper, Helene and Schmitt, Eric, 'Ukraine's Western-Trained Brigades Begin to Enter the Fight', *New York Times*, 23 June 2023.

Copp, Tara, and Baldor, Lolita C., 'Russian fighter jet flies dangerously close to US warplane over Syria', *AP*, 17 July 2023.

Court, Elsia, 'Minister: Drone fundraising campaign raises $1 million within hours', *Kyiv Independent*, 7 January 2023

DE Staff, 'Ukraine's White Wolves Destroy 72 units of Russian Military Equipment with Attack Drones (Video)', *Defense Express*, 28 October 2023.

Dickinson, Peter, 'Britain becomes first country to supply Ukraine with long-range missiles', *Atlantic Council*, 11 May, 2023.

——, 'Russia's Invasion of Ukraine was never about NATO', *Atlantic Council*, 18 July 2023.

——, 'Ukraine needs urgent air defense aid as Putin launches bombing campaign', *Atlantic Council*, 2 January 2024

Donovan, Diane, 'Gophers Defeat Russian Invasion', *Grit*, 12 January 2013.

Doshi, Rush, 'The Long Game: China's Grand Strategy to Displace American Order', *Brookings*, 2 August 2021,

Doyle, Gerry and Zafra, Mariano, 'The Air War over Ukraine', *Reuters*, 14 December 2023.

Dress, Brad, 'Why the Wagner boss is saying Russia could lose the war', *The Hill*, 25 May 2023.

DW Staff, 'Ukraine, updates: US trains Ukrainian forces in Germany', *DW*, 16 January 2023.

E Staff, 'Can Europe defended itself without America?', *The Economist*, 18 February, 2023.

E Staff, 'Can Russia repeat its winter bombing of Ukraine's electricity grid?', *The Economist*, 4 October 2023.

Ebel, Francesca, 'Russian cites "concern" but does not condemn Hamas attack on Israel', *Washington Post*, 9 October 2023.

EC Staff, 'Internal Market, Industry, Entrepreneurship and SMEs', *European Commission*, retrieved 23 January 2023.

Ellyatt, Holl, 'Russia can gain from Middle East turmoil – but it could backfire if the war spirals out of control', *CNBC*, 13 October 2023.

——, 'Romania Has not Found any Debris from Russian Shahed Drone on its Territory near Izmail', *European Pravda*, 3 August 2023

——, 'What Are The Risks?, *European Commission*, downloaded 23 January 2023.

EM Staff, 'Frontline report: Ukraine moves Patriot system closer to the frontline, resulting in three Russian aircraft downed', *Euromaidan*, 23 December 2023.

EN Staff, 'US to begin training Ukrainian troops on Abrams tanks', *Euronews*, 21 April 2023.

EP Staff, 'Fundraising Campaign for 500 Drones for Ukraine Launched in Lithuania', *European Pravda*, 19 July 2023.

EU Staff, Infographic – 'How the Russian invasion of Ukraine has further aggravated the global food crisis', *European Council*, 28 February 2024.

EU Staff, 'Russia's war on Ukraine: Western-made tanks for Ukraine', *European Parliament*, April 2023.

F Staff, 'Offensive Guard: what are the brigades, requirements, training, salaries and benefits?', *Fakty*, 4 February 2023.

Farberov, Snejana, 'Russia massing 500k soldiers and 1.8k tanks to launch offensive in 10 days', *New York Post*, 9 February 2023.

Farrell, Francis, 'Surviving Avdiivka: Russia intensifies assault on city deemed a second Bakhmut', *Kyiv Independent*, March 23, 2023

Feigenbaum, James, Lee, James and Mezzanotti, Fillippo, 'Capital Destruction and Economic Growth: the Effects of Sherman's March, 1860–1920', *American Economic Journal: Applied Economics,* Vol. 14, No. 4, October 2022

Fletcher, Chris, 'Senior Army Medical Officer: UK Armed Forces on track to train 37,000 Ukrainian recruits', *British Army*, 26 June 2023.

FM 100-2-1 *Soviet Army Operations and Tactics* (US Army, 1984) (available online)

FM 3-50, *Smoke Operations,* (US Army, 2023) (available online)

FN Staff, 'Why Kerch Bridge is so important: six reasons it is still standing despite attacks', *Forces Net*, 19 July 2023.

Fornusek, Martin, 'Germany says it reached agreement with Poland on Leopard II repair center', *Kyiv Independent*, 24 July 2023.

Fossum, Sam, 'Biden blames "congressional inaction" for Ukrainian withdrawal from town in call with Zelensky', *CNN*, 17 February 2024.

G Staff, 'Odesa suffers "hellish night" as Russia attacks Ukraine grain facilities', *Guardian*, 19 July 2023.

Galeotti, Mark, 'Spetsnaz: Operational Intelligence, Political Warfare, and Battlefield Role', *Marshall Center*, February 2020.

Gall, Carlotta 'Both Sides Pay a Bloody Price for Coveted Ukrainian City', *New York Times*, 30 October 2023.

Gallagher, Adam, 'Is a Saudi-Israel Normalization Agreement on the Horizon?', *United States Institute of Peace*, 28 September 2023.

Garamone, Jim, 'DOD Continues Efforts to Support Israel, Limit Spread of War', *US DoD*, 30 October 2023

Gettleman, Jeffery and O'Reilly, Finbarr, 'Every Block is another Battle: Ukraine's Latest Eastern Stand', *New York Times*, 13 June 2023.

Gidulianova, Ievgenia, 'Ukrainian Children in Search of a Way Home from Russia', *HRWF*, 15 December 2023.

Goelman, Zachary, 'Ukrainian commanders not about to be dismissed, defense minister says', *Reuters*, 12 December 2023.

Gordon, Chris, 'Response to Iran Militia Attacks', *Air & Space Forces Magazine*, 26 October 2023.

Gorgemans, Benoit, 'The Caspian Flotilla: Russia's Offensive Reinvention', *US Naval Institute*, August 2021

Grau, Dr Lester and Bartles, Charles K, *The Russian Way of War, Force Structure, Tactics, and Modernization of the Russian Ground Forces,* (USA Foreign Military Studies: 2016).

Green, David B, '1856: Russia Stops Conscripting Jewish Children', *Haaretz*, 26 August 2012.

Gressel, Gustav, Loss, Rafael and Puglien, Jana, 'The Leopard plan: How European tanks can help Ukraine take back its territory', *European Council on Foreign Relations*, 9 September 2022.

Gritten, David, 'Strikes on Gaza after Palestinian militants entered Israel', BBC, 7 October 2023.

Harrel, John S, *The Russian Invasion of Ukraine February–December 2022: Destroying the Myth of Russian Invincibilit,* (Yorkshire and Philadelphia: Pen & Sword, 2023)

——, *Soviet Cavalry Operations During the Second World War & The Genesis of the Operational Manoeuvre Group,* (Yorkshire and Philadelphia: Pen & Sword, 2019).

Harvey, Andrew S., 'The Levels of War as Levels of Analysis', *Military Review*, November/December 2021.

Hattaway, Herman and Jones, Archer, *How The North Won, A Military History of the Civil War*, (Univ. of Illinois Press: Chicago, 1991).

Hayward, Justin, 'How Much Does an F-16 Cost?', *Simple Flying*, 3 December 2023.

Hernandez, Marco and Holder, Josh, 'Defences Carved into the Earth,' *New York Times*, 14 December 2022.

Herszenhorn, Miles J, 'Where do 2024 candidates stand on Ukraine? Trump, DeSantis, Ramaswamy, JFK Jr. want less US Involvement', *USA Today*, 11 July 2023.

HL Staff, 'Major Russian Offensive on Strategic Kupyansk', *History Legends*, 15 August 2023.

Hoffman, Frank, 'Who repairs Ukraine's Western Weapons?', *DW*, 26 September 2022.

Holmes, Jonathan and Madan, Lee, 'King Charles watches Ukrainian troops training in Wiltshire', *BBC*, 20 February 2023.

Hopkins, Valerie, 'The Wagner group forecasts disaster if Russia does not move into total war footing', *New York Times*, 24 May 2023.

Horton, Alex, 'Russia's commando units gutted by Ukraine war, US leak shows', *Washington Post*, 14 April 2023.

——, 'These are the Western air defense systems protecting Ukraine', *Washington Post*, 19 May 2023.

Hubbard, Ben and Harman, Gulsin, 'Why the Black Sea is a Flashpoint between Russia and the West', *New York Times*, 21 March 2023.

IC Staff, 'Internal Market, Industry, Entrepreneurship and SMEs', *European Commission*, retrieved 23 January 2023.

Ivshina, Olga, 'Lost battalions: calculating Russia's casualties in six months of war in Ukraine', *BBC*, 22 August 2022.

Jakes, Lara, Kramer, Andrew E and Schmitt, Eric, 'After Suffering Heavy Losses, Ukrainian Pause to Rethink Strategy', *New York Times*, 15 July 2023.

——, 'What's Stopping Ukraine Flying F-16s', *New York Times*, 31 August 2023.

Japaridze, Mikhail, 'Butina says being in US prison was "torture"', *TASS*, 3 November 2019.

Jayanti, Suriya Evans-Pritchard, 'Russia resumes bombing campaign of Ukraine's civilian energy infrastructure', *Atlantic Council*, 22 September 2023.

Jin, Hyunjoo and Oguh,Chibuike, 'Explainer: How Musk funded the $44 billion Twitter deal,' *Reuters*, 28 October 2022.

Jones, Seth G, Palmer, Alexander and Bermuder Jr, Joseph S, 'Ukraine's Offensive Operations: Shifting the Offense-Defense Balance', *CSIS*, 9 June 2023.

Justice News, 'Russian National Charged in Conspiracy to Act as an Agent of the Russian Federation within the United States', *US Department of Justice*, 16 July 2018.

Kabalan, Marwan, 'Hamas' attack on Israel has changed the Middle East', *Aljazeera*, 28 October 2023.

Kallberg, Jan, 'Leader Loss: Russian Junior Officer Casualties', *CEPA*, 23 December 2022.

Karazy, Sergiy, 'Ukraine trains 40,000 storm brigade troops for counter-offensive', *Reuters*, 21 April 2023.

KG Staff, 'Israel-Hamas: before the Ground Assault', *Kings and Generals Modern Affairs*, 30 October 2023.

KI Staff, 'Zelensky: Ukraine needs 300–500 tanks', *Kyiv Independent*, 27 January 2023.

Kim, Victoria, 'Elon Musk Acknowledges Withholding Satellite Service to Thwart Ukrainian Attack', *New York Times*, 8 September 2023.

Kofman, Rob Lee, 'How the Battle of Donbas Shaped Ukraine's Success', *The Foreign Policy Research Institute,* 23 December 2022.
Kokcharow, Alex, 'Russian Combat Units Suffer Brutal Losses in Dnipro Bridgehead Battles', *Kyiv Post*, 17 January 2024
Kolomiiets, Daryna 'Ukraine's New Offensive Guard: What It is and How to Join, '*Kyiv Post*, 13 February 2023.
Korshak,Stefan, 'Worst Russian Land Battle Defeat in Nine Months –Kremlin Forces Hit a Wall at Avdiivka', *Kyiv Post*, 13 October 2023.
——, 'Ukraine's War-Critical Hobby Drones vs. Russian Swarms – Pilots Say Crowdfunding Won't Cut it', *Kyiv Post*, 20 December 2023.
Kunkle, Fredrick, Stern, David L and Ilyushina, Mary, 'Ukraine hits Crimean bridge, but railway undamaged: Russia halts grain deal', *Washington Post*, 17 July 2023.
Kyrylenko, Olga, 'Invincibility centre Bakhmut. What is happening at the most difficult axis of the front', *Ukrainska Pravda*, 8 December 2022
K&G Staff, 'Russia slow down, Ukraine prepares for counteroffensive, *Kings & Generals*, 15April 2023
KP Staff, 'Wagner Chief Threatens to Pull out of Bakhmut to Avoid "Senseless Death"', *Kyiv Post*, 5 May 2023.
LaGrone, Sam and Mongilio, Heather, 'Russia Lays Mines in Black Sea to Block Ukrainian Ports, NSC Says', *USNI News*, 19 July 2023
——, 'Ukraine Launches Crowd Funding Driver for $250k Naval Drones', *USNI News*, 11 November 2023.
Lancaster, Lord Mark, *NATO (Draft) Defence and Security Committee (DSC) Sub-Committee on Future Security and Defense Capabilities (DSCFC)*, (NATO: 18 August 2023), pp. 10–11.
Lazaroff, Tovah, 'Russia deepening ties with global axis of evil', *Jerusalem Post*, 27 February 2024.
Lebedey, Filipp and Light, Felix, 'Wagner's convicts tell of horrors of Ukraine war and loyalty to their leaders', *Reuters*, 16 March 2023
Lee, Rob, andKofman, Michael, 'How the Battle for the Donbas Shaped Ukraine's Success', *The Foreign Policy Research Institute,* 23 December 2022.
Lefief, Jean-Philippe, 'War in Ukraine: understanding the Battle of Soledar', *Le Monde*, 16 January 2023.
Liebermann, Oren, 'US sending second carrier strike group, fighter jets to region as Israel prepares to expand Gaza Operations', *CNN*, 15 October 2023.
Lister, Tim, Buteenko, Victoria and Nechyporenko, Kostan 'Ukraine hits Russian oil tanker with sea drones hours after attacking naval base', *CNN,* 5 August 2023.
Lincoln, Jonathon B, 'Middle East Peace: the Biden Administration's Approach', *Rand*, 31 August 2022.
Lopez, C. Todd, 'Ukrainians to Get US Tanks by Fall', *US DoD*, 21 March 2023.
—— 'F-16s Head to Middle East to Help Protect US Troops', *US DoD*, 24 October 2023
——, 'Air Defense Remains Top Priority at Meeting on Ukraine Defense', *US DoD*, 19 September 2023.
Lyngas, Sean, 'Russian hackers targeted NATO forces and diplomats to aid Ukraine war effort', *CNN*, 7 December 2023.
M Staff, ' All 10,000 FPV drones from Operation Unity are already in the army,' *Militarnyi*, 22 December 2023.

M Staff, 'Ukrainian Marines Repel Russian Assault on Krynky', *Militarnyi*, 8 January 2024.

MacDougall, David, 'Free the Leopards! Campaign aims to "embarrass" Germany into sending tanks to Ukraine', *Euronews*, 1 January 2023.

McLaughlin, Kelly, 'Ukraine attacked Russia's main naval base in Crimea with sea drones, the city's Russian governor said,' *Insider*, 24 April 2023.

Marquardt, Alex, 'Exclusive: Musk's SpaceX says it can no longer pay for critical satellite services in Ukraine, asks Pentagon to pick up the tab', *CNN*, 14 October 2022.

Malin, Carrington, 'Has Russia destroyed Ukraine's naval drone capability', *Armada International*, 17 August 2023.

Masters, Jonathan and Merrow, Will, 'How Much Aid Has the US Sent Ukraine? Here are Six Charts, *Council on Foreign Relations,* February 22, 2023.

——,'How Much Aid Has the US Sent to Ukraine', *Council on Foreign Relations*, 8 December 2023.

Melkozerova, Veronika, 'This is what madness looks like: Russians unleash massive assault on Soledar in eastern Ukraine', *Politico*, 22 January 2022.

Miller, Sergio, 'Portrait of Ukrainian Advances', *WavellRoom,* 15 August 2023.

Mills, Claire, 'Military assistance to Ukraine since the Russian invasion', *UK Parliament*, 10 May 2023.

ML Staff, 'Ukrainian Order of Battle', *MilitaryLand*, 22 September 2023.

Mongilio, Heather, 'Turkey Closes Bosporus, Dardanelles Straits to War Ships', *USNI News*, 28 February 2023.

——, 'A Brief Summary of the Battle of the Black Sea', *USNI News,* 15 November 2023.

Murrey, Miranda, 'Rheinmetall wants to deliver 20 new Leopard 2 tanks to Ukraine – *Handelsblatt*', *Zawya*, 25 April 2022

Mittal, Vikram, 'The Challenges of Counter-Drone Technology as Seen in Recent Conflicts',*Forbes*, 18 October 2023.

Mpoke, Matthew, 'Ukraine Steps up Calls for Evacuation of Kupiansk under Relentless Russian Shelling', *New York Times*, 12 March 2023.

Mueller, Grace B, 'Cyber Operations during the Russo-Ukrainian War', *CISI,* 13 July 2023

Muller, Robert, 'Czech Republic sends tanks, infantry fighting vehicles to Ukraine', *Reuters*, 5 April 2022.

Mutter, Paul, 'The Chechen Wars Cast a Long Shadow', *Medium*, 28 March 2015.

Muzya, Konrad, 'Russian Options in the Donetsk Direction – The Avdiivka Axis', *Rochan Consulting*, 24 October, 2023.

MT Staff, 'Top Russian General Dismissed after Vuhledar Defeat', *Moscow Times,* 3 April 2033.

——, 'Official Discloses Russian Troop Deaths 1 Month after Cross-Border Incursion', *Moscow Times*, 28 June 2023.

——, 'In Photos: The Aftermath of Russia's Massive Drone and Missile Attack on Ukraine', *Moscow Times*, 29 December 2023.

Nakhoul, Samia, 'Exclusive: US-Saudi defense pact tied to Israel deal, Palestinian demands put aside,' Reuters, 29 September 2023.

——, 'How Hamas secretly built a "mini-army" to fight Israel', *Reuters*, 16 October 2023.

Nations, Madeleine, 'Kaliningrad: Russia's Best-Kept Strategic Secret', *Glimpse from the Globe*, 14 October 2020.

Neftchi, Shivan, 'Why Ukraine joining NATO would crush Russian Power', *Caspian Report*, 24 September 2023.

Nikolov, Boyko, 'Su-24 and Su-27 can carry a Storm Shadow missile, but not program it', *BulgarianMilitary.com*, 12 May 2023.

Nguyen, Britney, 'Ukraine claims Russia is buying Starlink terminals in Arab countries after Elon Musk denied selling to Russian forces', *Quartz,* 13 February 2024. Verified reliable by Ground News.

NN Staff, 'New Ukrainian naval drone attack on port of Sevastopol', *Naval News*, 17 July 2023.

Novikov, Illia, 'Ukraine fires 6 deputy defense ministers as heavy fighting continues', *AP*, 18 September 2023.

US News Staff, 'Ukraine Removes Deputy Defense Minister after New Minister's Appointment', *US News*, 18 September 2023

Ortega, Aurora, 'Hizbullah and Russia's Nascent Alliance', *RUSI*, 23 May 2023

O'Grady, Slobhan, Hrabchuk, Kamila and Khudov, Kostiantyn, 'Russian missiles rain down on Ukrainian cities; Britain to send battle tanks', *Washington Post*, 14 January 2023.

——, 'How Ukrainian Forces denied Russia victory in Bakhmut by Victory Day', *Washington Post*, 12 May 2023.

Orlova, Alisa, 'Russian Transfers Captured Ukrainian Weapons to Hamas in Bid to Discredit Kyiv', *Kyiv Post*, 9 October 2023.

Orlova, Alisa, 'He is needed in another Direction – Defense Ministry on Dismissal of Special Operations Commander', *Kyiv Post*, 5 November 2023.

Oryx Staff, Fact Sheet On German Military Aid to Ukraine, *Oryx,* 1 September 2022.

——, 'List of Naval Losses during the Russian Invasion of Ukraine', *Oryx*, 20 November 2023.

P Staff, 'The Black Sea & Naval War in Ukraine – Drones, Grain Blockades & Bridge to Crimea', *Perun*, 31 July 2023

Payne, Stetson, 'Soviet-Era T-72 Tanks to be Transferred to Ukraine from NATO Countries: Reports', *The War Zone*, 3 April 2022.

Peck, Michael, 'The UK is sending Ukraine a newer, longer-range missile that lets humans guide it all the way to the target', *Insider,* 23 December 2022.

Pedrozo, Raul, 'The Russian-Ukrainian Conflict: blocking Access to the Black Sea', *Naval War College Review*, No. 4, Article 5, Autumn 2022.

Picheta, Rob, Shukla, Sebastian and Chernova, Anna, 'Pro-war Putin critic Igir Girkin sentenced to four years in Russian prison on extremism charges', *CNN*, 25 January 2024.

Poblin, Sebastien, 'Robot Kamikaze Boats Blew up Russia's Bridge to Crimea. Again', *Popular Mechanics*, 17 July 2023.

Polityuk, Pavel, 'Russia strikes Ukraine's Danube port, driving up global grain prices', *Reuters*, 2 August 2023.

Ponomarenko, Illia, 'Russia's new guided bombs pose increasing serious threat to Ukraine', *Kyiv Independent*, 10 April 2023.

PRC Press Release, 'Xi Jinping Holds Talks with Russian President Vladimar Putin,' *Ministry of Foreign Affairs of the People Republic of Chins*, 18 October 2023.

Prokopenko, Alexandra, 'What's in the Ukrainian Grain Deal for Russia', *Carnegie*, 26 July 2023.

Provost, Dr Nathan, 'Continuous Contact: Grant's Tactical Doctrine in the Eastern Theatre', *Emerging Civil War*, 4 August 2020, Archer Jones, *Civil War Command & Control, The Process of Victory and Defeat*, (The Free Press: New York, 1992).

R Staff, 'Who are the Freedom of Russian Legion and Russian Volunteer Corps?', *Reuters*, 5 June 2023.

R Staff, 'Pentagon's Ukrainian accounting error revised up to $6.2 billion', *Reuters*, 20 June 2023.
Rainsford, Sarah, 'Ukraine drones hit St Petersburg gas terminal', *BBC*, 21 January 2024.
Rehi, Artur, 'Wagner is leaving Bakhmut, Ukrainian drone strikes Kermlin?', Ukraine Update, 5 May2023,
Rayon, Spc. Danielle, 'Oklahoma's Task Force Tomahawk prepares for Africa deployment', *Oklahoma National Guard*, 12 April 2023.
Rehi, Arthur, 'Ukrainians just annihilated an entire Wagner unit in Bakhmut/Moscow Parade failure/Ukraine Update',*YouTube* 10 May 2023.
Reisner, Colonel Markus (Austrian Army), 'War for Ukraine – First Conclusions from 2022 and New Challenges 2023',*Osterreichs Bundesheer*, 13 January 2023.
RFE Staff, 'NATO Jets Scrambled 570 Times Last Year to Check Military Flights', *Radio Free Europe*, 9 February 2023.
——, 'More than 700,000 Ukrainian Children Taken to Russia Since Full-Scale War Started, Offical Says', *Radio Free Europe*, 31 July 2023.
Roblin, Sebastien, 'US HIMARS Rocket Artillery Going to Ukraine Would be a Game Changer', *1945*, 30 April 2022.
Rochan Staff, 'Ukraine Conflict Monitor: The aftermath of the Nova Kakhovka Dam collapse', *Rochan Consulting*, 9 June 2023.
——, 'Conflict Monitor: The Operational-Strategic situation in Southern Ukraine', *Rochan Consulting*, 14 June 2023.
Romanenko, Valenyna, 'Former Special Operations Forces Commander learns of his dismissal from news', *Ukrainian Pravda*, 3 November 2023.
Romaniuck, Scott Nicholas, 'Military Strategy and the Three Levels of Warfare', *Defence Report*, 2017.
Ryan, Mick 'The Ukrainian Offensives are coming (Part 1)', *Futura Doctrina*, 29 April, 2023
——, 'The Ukrainian Offensives are coming (Part 2)', *Futura Doctrina*, 29 April, 2023.
——, 'An update on Ukraine's Campaigns, Measuring Success in Ukraine's Multidomain Efforts', *Futura Doctrina*, 23 August 2023.
RT Staff, 'They will cling to Avdiivka to the bitter end. Why does Zelensky need a second Bakhmut?', *Russian Federation News Agency*, November 2023.
Sabbagh, Dan and Olterman, Phillip, 'US and Germany agree to send infantry fighting vehicles to Ukraine', *Guardian*, 5 January 2023.
Sanger, David E, Schmitt, Eric and Cooper, Helene, 'How Biden Reluctantly Agreed to Send Tanks to Ukraine', *New York Times*, 25 January 2023
——, 'Ukraine Uses Powerful American-Supplied Missiles for First Time', *New York Times*, 17 October 2023.
Santora, Marc, 'The War's Violent Next Stage', *New York Times*, 10 February 2023.
——, 'Moscow's Military Capabilities are in Question after Failed Battle for Ukrainian City', *New York Times*, 16 February 2023.
Schmitt, Eric, 'Pentagon Sends US Arms Stores in Israel to Ukraine', *New York Times*, 17 January 2023.
——, 'Ukrainian Soldiers Speed through US Training on Patriot Missiles', *New York Times*, 21 March 2023.
——, 'Pentagon Plans to Begin Training Ukrainian Pilots on F-16s in US', *New York Times*, 24 August 2023.
Schmidt, Till, 'An Axis of Evil Against the Western World', *Zentrum Liberale Moderne*, 27 October 2023.

Schwarzenegger, Arnold, Russia Speech in Full: 'Star urges Putin to end Ukraine invasion', *YouTube*, 17 March 2022.

Seligman, Lara and McLeary, Paul, 'US speeds up deliveries of Abrams tanks, Patriots to Ukraine', *Politico*, 21 March 2023.

Sheahan, Maria, 'Satellite outages knocks out thousands of Enercon's wind turbines', *Reuters*, 28 February 2022.

——, 'How Biden got to yes on F-16s and Ukraine', *Politico*, 22 May 2023.

Shoaib, Alia, 'Take a look inside the incredible underground city carved from salt that Russia and Ukraine are battling over', *Business Insider*, 14 January 2023

Siebold, Sabine, 'Germany okays sale of former GDR infantry fighting vehicles to Ukraine', *Reuters*, 1 April 2022.

Skorkin, Konstantin, 'Are Ukraine's President and Chief Commander really at War?' *Carnegie Politika*, 6 December 2023

SOF Staff, 'Kerch Bridge Connecting Crimea to Russia Damaged', *SOF News*, 8 October 2022.

Soguel, Dominique, 'From citizens' pockets to soldiers' hands: Ukraine crowdfunded war', *Christian Science Monitor*, 23 April 2023.

Spaniel, William, 'Why Putin Fragmented his Military: a Tale of Internal Rivalries and Intentional Mismanagement', *YouTube*, 13 May 2023.

Standish, Reid, (Interview), 'How Can Ukraine Prepare for a New Fight against Russia in the Donbas?', *Radio Free Europe*, 10 April 2022.

Stein, Janice Gross, 'Escalation Management in Ukraine: Assessing the US Response to Russia's Manipulation of Risk', *Henry A. Kissinger Center for Global Affairs*, August 2023.

Stone, Mike, 'Exclusive: Pentagon accounting error overvalued Ukraine weapons aid by $3 billion', *Reuters*, 19 May 2023.

——, 'SpaceX's Starlink wins Pentagon contract for satellite services to Ukraine', *Reuters*, 1 June 2023.

Sutton, H.I, 'Russian Navy's Way around Turkey Closing The Bosporus to Its Warships, Literally', *Covert Shores*, May 2022.

Talmazan, Yuliya, and Mulligan, Matthew, 'Russian warship appears damaged in Ukrainian sea drone attack on key naval base', *NBC*, 4 August 2023.

Tarasova, Darya, Tuysuz, Gul and Kent, Laruen, 'Russia fires warning shots and boards cargo ship in Black Sea', *CNN*, 13 August 2023

TASS staff, 'Russian Black Sea Fleet's Warships Return to Naval Bases after Massive Drills', *TASS*, 31 January 2022.

——, 'Russia to find way to help countries in need of food, senior Russian diplomat promises', *TASS*, 22 July 2023.

Taylor, Adam, Neff, Willian and Wolfe, Daniel, 'For Ukraine, what's so special about Germany's Leopard 2 tanks?', *Washington Post*, 25 January 2023.

TE Staff, 'How crowdfunding is shaping the war in Ukraine', *The Economist*, 27 July 2022.

TEC Staff, 'Isn't Leopard 1 too old to make a difference in Ukraine? Not at all – especially after upgrades', *Technology.Org*, 25 March 2023.

TG Staff, 'Ukraine remains Russia's biggest cyber focus in 2023, *Google's Threat Analysis Group*, 19 April 2023.

——, 'Poland reports airspace incursion as Russia launched huge strikes on Ukraine', *Guardian*, 29 December 2023.

Tresbesch, Dr Christoph, 'Foreign support to Ukraine: evidence from a database of military, financial and humanitarian aid', *Vox Ukraine*, 14 June 2023.

——, 'Ukraine Support Tracker: a Database for Military, Financial and Humanitarian Aid to Ukraine', *Keil Institute*, 31 July 2023.

Tsukanov, Ilya, 'What is the "Surovikin Defensive Line" which Ukrainian Forces Can't Crack?', *Sputnik International*, 22 June 2023.

UI Staff, 'Ukraine's Offensive Guard soldiers already fighting on the southern and eastern fronts – National Guard', *Ukrinform*, 12 September 2023.

UK MoD Press Release, 'British Commandos train hundreds of Ukrainian Marines in UK programme, 11 August 2023.

UP Staff, 'Eight Offensive Guard brigades being prepared, new ones will be formed- Ukraine's Interior, *Ukrainska Pravda*, 2 May 2023.

Urban, Mark, 'The cost of the Ukraine war for one Russian regiment', *BBC*, 6 April 2023.

USDA Staff, 'Ukrainian Grain Transportation', June 2023.

US DoE Press Relief, 'US Department of Education Estimate: Biden-Harris Student Debt Relief Cost an Average of $30 Billion Annually over Next Decade', *US Department of Education*, 29 September 2022.

US Staff, 'The Power of Resilience', *US Cybersecurity & Infrastructure Security Agency*, 9 August 2023.

——, 'CISA and Partners Release Advisory on Russian SVR-affiliated Cyber Actors Exploiting CVE-2023-1793', *US Cybersecurity & Infrastructure Security Agency*, 13 December 2023

——, 'United States and Ukraine Expand Cooperation on Cybersecurity', *US Cybersecurity & Infrastructure Security Agency*, 27 July 2022.

——, 'Russian State-Sponsored Cyber Actors Target Cleared Defense Contractor Networks to Obtain Sensitive US Defense Information and Technology', *US Cybersecurity & Infrastructure Security Agency*, 16 February 2022.

——, Fact Sheet on US Security Assistance to Ukraine, 10 November 2022.

——, 'United States and Ukraine Expand Cooperation on Cybersecurity', *US Cybersecurity & Infrastructure Security Agency*, 27 July 2022.

Vego, Milan, 'Littoral Warfare', *On Naval War College Review*, Vol. 68: No. 2 Article 4, 1–67.

VOA Staff, 'Ukraine Evacuating Kupiansk Residents amid Russian Attacks', *VOA*, 12 March 2023.

——, 'Zelensky Calls for Rapid Operations Changes for Soldiers, Sacks Commander', *VOA Ukraine*, 19 November 2023

W Staff, 'Stealing Ukraine's Children', *The Week*, 7 April, 2023, 11. Vladyslav Havrylov, 'Russia's mass abduction of Ukrainian children may qualify as genocide', *Atlantic Council*, 27 July 2023.

Waterhouse, James, 'Ukraine war: Russian attack on Ukraine cities hits deadly new level', *BBC*, 29 December 2023.

Watling, Jack and Reynolds, Nick, 'Meatgrinder: Russian Tactics in the Second Year of its Invasion of Ukraine, *RUSI*, 19 May 2023.

——, 'Special Report, Storm break: Fighting through Russian Defences in Ukraine's 2023 Offensive', *RUSI*, September 2023.

Yanchik, Olivia, 'Ukraine needs enhanced air defenses as Russia expands missiles arsenal', *Atlantic Council*, 2 March 2024.

Yeung, Jessie, 'March 25, 2022 Russian-Ukraine news', *CNN*, 26 March 2022

YN Staff, 'Zelensky explains what former Commander Khorenko of Special Operations will do', *Yahoo News* (from *Ukraine Pravda*), 3 November 2023.

York, Chris, 'Kupyansk: Why this Small Ukrainian Town is now the Focus of Brutal Russian Assaults', *Kyiv Post*, 11 August 2023.

Zafra, Doyle and Zafra, Mariano, 'The Air War over Ukraine', *Reuters*, 14 December 2023.

Zoria, Yuri, 'UK intel: Two A-50 AWACS aircraft downed in two months show Russia's difficulty securing air assists', *Euromaidan*, 27 February 2024.

Online News and Article Annalist Services

Atlantic, Online, New Magazine, The
BBC, Online News Service
Economists, The, Online, New Magazine
Forbes, Online News Magazine
Graphic News, Online Illustrated Newspaper
Ground News, Online News Article Annalist Service
Guardian, The, Online, New Magazine
Kyiv Independent, The, Online Newspaper
Kyiv Post, The, Online Newspaper
Moscow Times, The, Online Newspaper
New York Time, The, Online Newspaper
Oryx, Online News Service
Reuters, Online New Magazine
TASS Russian Online News Service
Washington Post, Them Online Newspaper

Online Blogs Covering the Russian-Ukrainian War, Government Information Websites

Australian Institute of International Affairs
Austrian Army
Atlantic Council, The
Davydov, Deny, News from Ukraine
Deep State Ukraine
European Council on Foreign Relations
Five Coat Consulting
Foreign Policy Research Institute, The
Futura Doctrina
History Legends
Institute for the Study of War
Keil Institute for World Economy
Kings and Generals
Konrad Muzya, Rochan Consulting
Lensandowski, Paul, US Army Combat Veteran Reacts
Militaryland,
NATO Homepage
Perun
Rand Corporation
Rhi, Arthur, Lithuanian Soldier
Royal United Services Institute (RUSI)
UK Ministry of Defence
UK Foreign Office
Ukrainian Ministry of Defence

Ukrainian Security Service
US Central Intelligence Agency
US Cybersecurity & Infrastructure Security Agency
US Department of Defense
US Department of Justice
War In Ukraine Explained

Index